The Pope in Poland

RUSSIAN AND EAST EUROPEAN STUDIES

JONATHAN HARRIS, EDITOR

The POPE *in*
POLAND

The PILGRIMAGES *of* JOHN PAUL II, 1979–1991

JAMES RAMON FELAK

UNIVERSITY *of* PITTSBURGH PRESS

Published by the University of Pittsburgh Press, Pittsburgh, Pa., 15260

Copyright © 2020, University of Pittsburgh Press

All rights reserved

Manufactured in the United States of America

Printed on acid-free paper

10 9 8 7 6 5 4 3 2 1

Cataloging-in-Publication data is available from the Library of Congress

ISBN 13: 978-0-8229-4598-7

ISBN 10: 0-8229-4598-3

Cover photograph: Warsaw, 1979. King's Castle, Pope John Paul II's first Pilgrimage to Poland. Photo by Chris Niedenthal / agencja FORUM / Alamy Stock Photo

Cover design: Alex Wolfe

To my godfather, John P. Zawicki

In memory of my godmother, Jessie Z. Balogh (1921–2005)

CONTENTS

The Pope in Poland

INTRODUCTION

OCTOBER 16, 1978, MARKED AN EXTRAORDINARY EVENT IN THE
modern history of the Roman Catholic Church, and of Europe. After
a succession of Italian-born popes dating back to 1523, the College of
Cardinals, meeting in conclave at the Vatican, chose Karol Wojtyła,
archbishop of Kraków, as the 264th pope of the Catholic Church,
filling the seat vacated by the recently deceased John Paul I. As astonishing as it was that the first ethnic Pole was ascending to the Chair
of Saint Peter in Rome, this was not the biggest surprise. Even more
extraordinary was the fact that Wojtyła came from the communist
side of the Iron Curtain. A citizen of an atheistic Marxist regime
situated within the Soviet bloc was now the head of the world's largest
and most significant religious organization.

Taking the name John Paul II, Wojtyła conducted his early pontificate during the period of late communism, the years leading up
to the collapse of the communist regime in the Soviet Union and its
"inner" empire of non-Russian Soviet republics and "outer" empire of
satellite states in East-Central Europe. John Paul became a leading
player in the drama that climaxed with the revolutions of 1989, not
only responding to but also helping to shape developments in his

native Poland, which in turn helped shake the communist world at its foundation. This book examines this Polish pope as his pontifical career intersected with the critical final decade of Communist Party rule in Poland and the immediate aftermath of communism's collapse.

WHY POLAND?

Poland is arguably one of the key countries of modern history, especially twentieth-century history. After being occupied for more than a century by its neighbors—Russia, Prussia (later Germany), and Austria—it emerged from World War I as a newly independent state. Plagued by social, economic, ethnic, and political problems and situated dangerously between Hitler's Germany and Stalin's Soviet Union, with both empires coveting territory that Poland acquired after World War I, the Poles experienced a joint occupation by the Nazis and their Soviet partners in September 1939. Less than two years later, they saw their former country become a major battleground as Nazi Germany and the Soviet Union engaged in their "sweaty tug-of-war."[1] Poland, in fact, constituted a notable part of what Timothy Snyder calls the "Bloodlands," that area between central Poland and western Russia where fourteen million people were killed in cold blood between 1933 and 1945 by the regimes of Hitler and Stalin (not counting deaths on the battlefield, or directly caused by the war, or killings perpetrated by regimes or groups other than the Nazis or Soviets). Massive deportation of Poles to the Soviet east, the execution of twenty-two thousand Polish military officers and other professionals at Katyń Forest and other killing sites in April 1940 by the Soviet NKVD, the Nazi Holocaust that exterminated the vast majority of Poland's former Jewish citizens, and the brutal suppression of the Warsaw Uprising in August 1944 by Nazi forces while the Soviet Red Army watched from the other side of the Vistula River are all part of the story of wartime horrors experienced by those with the misfortune to be living in this part of the world during these fateful years.

The war culminated with the Soviet occupation of Poland and the imposition of a communist regime under the command of Poland's Communist Party, officially entitled the Polish United Workers'

Party (Polska Zjednoczona Partia Robotnicza, or PZPR). There also ensued the shifting of Poland's borders westward, giving what had been eastern Poland to Stalin, while Poland acquired portions of eastern Germany. These "recovered territories" were crucial for the communist regime—they constituted compensation for Poland's loss of its eastern territories to the Soviet Union, they put Poland at odds with the Federal Republic of Germany (West Germany), which refused to reconcile itself to these losses, and they represented one of the chief patriotic accomplishments of the communists. Now under a communist regime and part of the Soviet bloc, Poland retained its poignancy. Of all the communist states on earth, none experienced such upheaval and on such a scale as Poland.[2] While a few other communist countries had intermittent unrest, and Hungary even went so far as to launch a veritable revolution against communism in 1956, only Poland saw a succession of uprisings spanning four decades and involving large and important segments of society. Workers played a major role in these developments, which erupted in 1956 in Poznań, in 1970 in the ports on the Baltic coast, and in 1976 in various cities across Poland. Worker unrest was driven primarily by economic grievances—wages, working conditions, food prices and shortages—and was calmed by a combination of violent repression and concessions. At times the unrest was strong enough to bring a change in leadership, as in 1970, when the reformist Edward Gierek replaced Władysław Gomułka as head of the Communist Party after Baltic shipyard workers rose up in protest against a rise in food prices. Gierek's expectation was to take advantage of Western credits, which had become readily available thanks to a relaxing of Soviet-American tensions, and infuse them into the Polish economy in hopes of developing industries whose products could then be sold back to the West at a profit. As it turned out, Gierek's plan did not live up to its promise, as mismanagement, corruption, unwise investment, and bad timing all conspired to foil his hopes. By the mid-1970s Poland was heavily in debt to the West and compelled to export food in order to pay back what it had borrowed. This move led to meat shortages and to worker unrest in July 1976, when the government again abruptly raised food prices. After employing the police to crush worker demonstrations, Gierek's honeymoon was over and his popularity slumping.

Students and intellectuals also engaged the regime via protests and other illegal activities. In 1956, they played an important role in pushing for a reformist type of Marxism against the Stalinist regime. In 1957 and 1968, they demonstrated against government censorship of Polish thought and culture. Completely disillusioned with the regime and its ideology by the early 1970s, several thousand Polish intellectuals engaged in oppositional activity in the second half of the decade, especially in the aftermath of the government crackdown on worker unrest in 1976. By the late 1970s, a variety of oppositional groups had emerged, spanning the ideological spectrum from the social democratic Left to the nationalist Right and including not only intellectuals but also students and some workers and farmers. These oppositionists organized the signing of protest letters, unofficial commemorative events, and lectures on taboo topics. They published underground books, periodicals, and leaflets, creating a "second circulation of culture" as an alternative and rival to the regime's official one. One group of intellectuals formed an illegal organization in support of the workers in September 1976. Calling itself KOR (Komitet Obrony Robotników, or Committee of Defense of the Workers), it provided legal support to persecuted workers, material aid to their families, and publicity for their plight through contacts with the Western media. By 1978, Polish labor activists had developed a free trade union in nascent form. These unprecedented bonds between intellectuals and workers added a unique dimension to Poland's sociopolitical landscape and laid the foundation for trouble the regime would have to face in the near future.

Another characteristic of Poland's unique situation was the strong role of the Catholic Church.[3] No organization in Poland came close to its capacity to mobilize the population. For example, during the turbulent year of 1956, large numbers of Polish Catholics turned out for events commemorating the three-hundredth anniversary of King Jan Kazimierz designating the Blessed Virgin Mary as Queen of Poland and professing an oath of loyalty to her. This honor bestowed on

Mary followed from the belief that it was her intercession that enabled a Polish victory over the invading Swedes at Jasna Góra monastery in Częstochowa, the site of the famous Black Madonna icon, in late 1655, an event immortalized by Henryk Sienkiewicz in his 1886 novel *Potop (The Deluge)*. Beginning in 1957 and continuing for the next nine years, the Church carried out its Great Novena, a series of pastoral initiatives in preparation for the one-thousandth anniversary of Poland's "baptism," the acceptance of Christianity by the early medieval chieftain Mieszko in 966. The Great Novena included catechesis on an annual theme (such as marriage, family, social justice, youth, Mary, etc.) and the visit to each parish of a replica of the Black Madonna icon.[4] The Church's commemoration challenged the one organized by the regime, which remembered 966 largely as the origin of the Polish state, with the government expressing appreciation over the fact that the borders of the early medieval state resembled those of post–World War II Poland, that is, without the eastern territories annexed by the Soviet Union and including lands Poland acquired from Germany after World War II.

Several important features of the Church in Poland are of particular significance here. First, though the Church clearly represented an alternative view of the world compared to that of the communists, faced persecution and harassment from the government, defended its interests forcefully, and pressed the regime to accommodate societal demands for reform, it was also instrumental in keeping the population calm during times of crisis and even in encouraging Poles to cooperate with the government at key junctures. For example, during the turbulence of 1956, Cardinal Stefan Wyszyński, the Church's primate in Poland, addressed the nation.[5] He stated, "We are witness to a difficult and extraordinary period in our national life, a period in which our duty commands us to speak less of our rights and more about our obligations. We turn to the heart of our nation, so well known for its preparedness to sacrifice for the homeland. But today, the willingness to toil for the homeland is even more important than the readiness to make supreme sacrifices. The Poles know how to die courageously, but they must learn how to work courageously."[6]

Such behavior by the Church created a situation in which the regime grudgingly felt that it must maintain decent working relations with the Church in order to keep the peace. In practice, this meant that Polish Catholics were able to operate their own independent periodicals, including the weekly *Tygodnik Powszechny* (Universal Weekly) and the monthly *Znak* (Sign); their own autonomous university, the Catholic University of Lublin (Katolicki Uniwersytet Lubelski, or KUL); and hold several seats in Parliament (the Sejm) as part of a small Catholic circle of parliamentarians. Beginning in 1980, the regime also engaged in dialogue with Church leaders through the so-called Joint Commission of Representatives of the Government and Episcopate, which met periodically to discuss issues involving relations between Church and state.[7] There was nothing in the entire communist world even remotely resembling the autonomy and influence enjoyed by the Church in Poland. Still, this should not be seen as too rosy a picture. Not only did the Church continually face various kinds of harassment but Catholic intellectuals unwilling to engage positively with the regime were excluded from the public sphere; some were imprisoned or even killed.

Another important feature of the Church under communism was its capacity to establish links with the other two groups in Poland that were giving the communists headaches—the working class and the intellectuals. Poland's industrial working class manifested higher degrees of religious belief and commitment than workers in most other European countries. For example, sociological studies from the 1970s found extremely high levels of belief in God among workers in some areas—84 percent in Nowa Huta, for example.[8] Worker protest came to draw heavily on Catholic symbolism and included Catholic social teaching among its inspirations and religious issues among its demands. Moreover, Poland had a sizable Catholic intelligentsia, some of whom belonged to the so-called Club of the Catholic Intelligentsia (Klub Inteligencji Katolickiej) in several major cities. Catholic intellectuals maintained links with non-Catholic intellectuals, some of which were facilitated by priests and even bishops themselves. These relationships would grow in the 1980s, when some clergy made their premises, mimeograph machines, paper, and message boards available to the "second culture" and some parishes organized aid to families of political prisoners.[9] Moreover, the leading Catholic periodicals were of a high intellectual caliber, published Catholic as well as non-Catholic contributors, and earned the respect of both Catholic and non-Catholic intellectuals.

Another asset the Church enjoyed during this period was being well led, with Primate Wyszyński at the top. Cardinal Wyszyński, who had suffered three years of internment in the mid-1950s for standing up to the regime, had an enormous amount of prestige to match his courage, intelligence, and capacity for leadership. Wyszyński had a knack for dealing with the communists, knew which battles to fight and which to avoid, and insisted on unity among his bishops and clergy. Under his tutelage the Church in Poland was able to maintain and enhance its independence and defend its rights, increase its prestige in society, and intervene in support of societal pressure for change. Perhaps most important, the Church served as a calming influence because it placed a priority on maintaining workable relations with the authorities while not compromising on what it regarded as essential.

Entering the second half of the 1970s, Poland's leaders were in an especially unenviable situation. As communists, they had inherited the stigma of representing a regime imposed on Poland by Russia, widely regarded by Poles as a major historic enemy, with grievances against it dating back centuries and including occupations (1772–1918, 1939–1941), wars (1920–1921), uprisings (1794, 1830, 1863), massacres (1940), and betrayals (1939, 1944). Moreover, Gierek had to manage a nation with a tradition of resistance to foreign oppression and a recent, formidable wartime resistance under its belt. The economy was a mess, with an astronomic foreign debt and the lines for food getting longer and longer. Attempts to alleviate financial strain on the system by raising the price of meat brought vigorous resistance from the working class. Engaged intellectuals had formed an underground opposition and even a "second culture" as an alternative to the official one. The Church, under highly competent leadership, far surpassed the Communist Party in prestige, possessed a degree of independence unimaginable anywhere else in the communist world, and had to be accommodated by the party in order to preserve social peace. Workers, intellectuals, and Church leaders had established links with each other. This was by any measure a nightmare scenario for Gierek. It could not have gotten worse. And then it did. The archbishop of Kraków, Karol Wojtyła, in an astonishing turn of events, was elected pope.

WHY JOHN PAUL II?

Karol Wojtyła was not just any bishop. Since 1964 he had held one of the most important and prestigious positions in the Church in Poland, as archbishop of Kraków, and since 1967 he had been one of Poland's two cardinals. Moreover, he was a charismatic figure with the intelligence, experience, temperament, and skill set to make him a formidable foil to Poland's communist leadership. He would become one of the major figures of twentieth-century history, not least because of the impact he had on events that helped undermine communism in Poland, with implications for other parts of the Soviet bloc. Born on May 18, 1920, Wojtyła grew up in the town of Wadowice in southern Poland, the son of a lieutenant in the former Austro-Hungarian and current Polish army and his wife.[10] The family of four was cut in half when Karol's mother died when he was five years old and his older brother when he was thirteen. Young Karol's interests revolved around sports and religion, though as he got older theater became his passion. He went off to study Polish language and literature at Kraków's Jagiellonian University at age eighteen, but before his sophomore year began, Nazi Germany invaded Poland and closed the university. A year and a half later, his father died, leaving Wojtyła without immediate family. He spent the rest of the war working in a quarry and a chemical plant, performing plays forbidden by the Nazis in the local underground theater, and, beginning in autumn 1942, studying clandestinely for the priesthood in a secret seminary eventually housed in the archbishop's residence in Kraków. Shortly after the end of the war, in November 1946, Wojtyła was ordained a priest. He then spent the next year and a half in Rome, where he earned a doctorate in philosophy from the Angelicum, before returning to Poland in summer 1948. His early pastoral assignments involved a few months assisting at a rural parish, followed by an assignment to Saint Florian's Church in Kraków, where he largely ministered to students from Jagiellonian University. Wojtyła had notable success at this assignment, incorporating outdoor activities into his ministry (hiking, skiing, kayaking) and bonding through this experience with a network of young adults eventually numbering around two hundred. In 1951, he returned to Jagiellonian to attain a doctorate in philosophy and began teaching ethics at the Catholic University of Lublin in 1954. In 1956, he was appointed to the chair of ethics in KUL's Faculty of Philosophy, and shortly thereafter he wrote a series on ethics for *Tygodnik Powszechny*. In 1958, he was named an auxiliary bishop in Kraków. In 1964, he became archbishop of that important diocese, once the seat of Poland's great medieval saint and martyr, Stanisław of Szczepanów. Interestingly, the communists seemed to have had little objection, and in fact even a preference for Wojtyła, seeing his inexperience, his seeming disinterest in politics, and his passion for the intellectual life and culture as indications that he would be more amenable to the government than a more traditional churchman. In fact, his interest in dialoguing with non-Catholics, nontraditional approaches to ministry, and modern taste in the arts set him apart from many Polish bishops, including Cardinal Wyszyński.

As archbishop, however, Wojtyła became a thorn in the side of the regime in a number of ways. He had good rapport with the working class. Along with his manual labor experience during the war, Wojtyła was interested in Church outreach to workers and had an affinity for the worker-priest movement that had developed in Belgium and France in the late 1940s and early 1950s. He made it one of his goals as bishop to achieve the construction of new churches in Kraków's working-class districts, including the city's huge industrial-residential suburb of Nowa Huta, intentionally built without churches by the communist regime after the war. The joint effort by workers, their local priests, and their bishop on behalf of church construction demonstrated the affinity that many workers had for their faith and strengthened the bond between the clergy and the working class. Wojtyła also maintained strong relations with intellectuals, both Catholic and non-Catholic, keeping in close contact with the circle around *Znak*, the editorial board of *Tygodnik Powszechny*, and the Club of the Catholic Intelligentsia in Kraków, as well as developing relations with members of KOR after it emerged in 1976. Wojtyła had the rare ability to feel at home among intellectuals, of which he was one himself; workers, with whom he spent several years during the war; and the rural population, whose piety he treated with respect and admiration.

Wojtyła was also someone to whom his flock could relate, and vice versa. For one thing, he had suffered—losing his entire immediate family before he was twenty-one. For another, he had a normal Polish upbringing, unlike many clergy who were spirited off to seminary at a young age. He grew up playing soccer, being an altar server at the local church, hanging out with his theater friends, attending high school in Wadowice and his first year of college at Jagiellonian. He also shared with fellow Poles the sociopolitical experiences that shaped their collective life—living under Nazi German occupation, serving in the cultural resistance, and then experiencing the communist regime in its Stalinist and post-Stalinist manifestations. Moreover, Wojtyła had the enormous advantage that comes with the priestly profession—that of hearing thousands of confessions, thereby surely giving him a sensitivity to the particular pressures, temptations, compromises, and challenges that his fellow Catholics faced while living under a Marxist-Leninist regime inimical to their faith. He also got a sense for the lives of ordinary Poles by maintaining his contacts with the network of students he had gathered while ministering at Saint Florian's. Finally, Wojtyła also had an exceptional grasp of Polish history and culture and was able to speak to Poles in their own patriotic idiom, using the saints and heroes, thinkers and creators, triumphs, tragedies, and momentous events of Polish history to inspire, warn, and guide his listeners. Add to this a charismatic personality, a sense of humor, and an actor's sense of timing, and it becomes clear that in Wojtyła the communists had an exceptionally daunting adversary. It did not take long for the regime to realize that the archbishop was not the harmless character they had expected and hoped for.

In step with Wojtyła's enhanced influence and prestige in Poland went a growing reputation in the Catholic Church internationally. He was an active participant in the Second Vatican Council (1962–1965), first as an auxiliary bishop and then as archbishop of Kraków. He played an important role in the composition of one of the council's flagship documents, *Gaudium et spes*, and enthusiastically disseminated the teachings of the council, especially among youth, back in his diocese in Poland.[11] His growing reputation at the council made him one of the persons under consideration when the College of Cardinals assembled to choose a new pope in October 1978.

WHY PILGRIMAGES?

This study of John Paul's engagement with his native land focuses on the first four visits he made to Poland as pope—in 1979, 1983, 1987, and 1991. Each visit took place in the month of June, and all were four years apart. Although the four pilgrimages took place over a relatively brief twelve-year period, each proceeded in a markedly different context from the others, a testimony to the dynamism of the evolving situation in late communist Poland. They also bookend nicely the last days of communism. Each visit, or what the pope called "pilgrimages," was dramatic in its own way. The first three were to a communist country and involved much preparation, negotiation, political sensitivity, and potential for trouble; the fourth was to a Poland that had freshly replaced its communist leadership and exited the Soviet bloc, which itself was dissolving along with the Union that had created it.

My contention is that a pilgrimage can provide unique insights for several reasons. First off, it was during the pilgrimages that John Paul could concentrate his attention on developments in Poland. Unlike the occasional addresses and statements from Rome that alluded to the Polish situation, a pilgrimage gave him several dozen consecutive events, spread out over more than a week, at which to address what was on his mind in connection with his native land. These were occasions for which the pope was sure to be well prepared, thinking strategically, putting much thought into carefully chosen words. A pilgrimage also involved the pope being present in a personal way, in many cases speaking at a site connected with the points he was trying to make, be it the tomb of Saint Stanisław at Wawel Cathedral in Kraków, the death cell of Maximilian Kolbe at Auschwitz, the tomb of the unknown soldier in Warsaw, or the military base at Westerplatte outside Gdańsk, where Polish soldiers held off the Nazis at the start of the war. This presence was magnified by the enormous crowds of Poles being themselves present to the pope. The visits also brought to the surface issues that were absent or less salient in other contexts. For instance, John Paul could allude to historic taboos or contemporary injustices in a highly visible way, with the attention not just of hundreds of thousands of Poles but of the world media as well. The pilgrimages also brought with them high stakes. They could have huge consequences for Poland's relations with the Soviet Union, for its relations with the West, for domestic peace, for the position of the opposition in the country, for Church-state relations, and for relations within the Communist Party.

The first pilgrimage (1979) was the pope's homecoming—triumphant and momentous. John Paul upstaged Poland's communist leaders, drawing enormous crowds night after night, alluding to past events and present realities that had been more or less off limits since the communists took charge of the country after World War II. After nine days of this, Poland was never the same again. This transformation helped make possible the Solidarity revolution that erupted in summer 1980, as Polish workers, with broad support across the nation, rose up, demanded, and received the right to form independent and self-governing labor unions and to strike when necessary. Although this springtime for Polish labor would soon be aborted when the new party leader, General Wojciech Jaruzelski, declared martial law in December 1981, it had ramifications over the next decade in Poland and even the entire Soviet bloc. In this sense, John Paul could be seen as an important catalyst.

The second pilgrimage (1983) came at a time of gloom and doom. Bitterness and despondency characterized the popular mood in the wake of martial law. In this fraught context, the pope brought comfort and hope. He also weighed in on one of the biggest questions of the time—where the Church in Poland would position itself in terms of its relation to the government and to the Solidarity opposition. John Paul's answer had implications for Poland's stability, its potential for political reform and social reconciliation, and its expectations for the future. But above all, the pope came as comforter to his people in their distress.

The third pilgrimage (1987) is generally considered the least significant of the four and has received the least attention.[12] However, it gives insight into John Paul and his relation to his native land no less than the 1979 and 1983 pilgrimages. Greatly influenced by the growing reformist spirit in the Soviet Union under Mikhail Gorbachev and the desire of the Polish government to reconcile with society, Poles now had greater freedom than during earlier visits. This meant that the pope could speak much more bluntly about Poland's present problems, past events, and future prospects and concerns than he had previously. Here his role as critic was most pronounced.

The fourth pilgrimage (1991) was to a postcommunist Poland. Tellingly, John Paul decided not to celebrate the fall of communism but instead spent much of the pilgrimage admonishing Poles about the ways they might abuse, and were already abusing, their newfound freedom. He structured the visit around the Ten Commandments and devoted considerable attention to Poland's relations with its neighbors to the east, especially Eastern Christians. Above all, John Paul used this visit to challenge his compatriots to find their own road to a free and democratic future, one informed by Catholic teaching, instead of uncritically imitating models from the West.

It should be noted that John Paul made a second visit to Poland in summer 1991, in August. Although he treated it as stage two of a single visit 1991 visit, it is not included in this study for several reasons. First, the chief purpose of the visit was to attend World Youth Day (WYD), held in Częstochowa.[13] This meant that the concerns of the visit were not developments in Poland but rather those that were broadly European, as well as global and universal, and oriented specifically toward youth.[14] Although there were plenty of Polish youth in attendance at WYD, and even though the pope did not ignore them in his various addresses, the main thrust of his engagement transcended the Polish context and thus represents a visit quite unlike the four earlier pilgrimages in content.[15] Second, it also differed in form from earlier visits in that it was relatively brief and narrowly focused. The pope spent barely more than a day at places outside Częstochowa, limiting himself to a brief stop in Kraków, where he visited a pediatric hospital, dedicated a new seminary, and met with members of a female religious order, as well as a visit to his hometown of Wadowice, where he blessed a new church and visited a nearby religious shrine. The only event at which he addressed a broader Polish audience during the entire visit was a beatification mass in Kraków for Aniela Salawa, a maid and lay Franciscan from the early twentieth century who had lived a life of tragedy and heroic virtue in Kraków. Finally, John Paul did not raise any significant new issues or express any teachings or insights that he had not already covered during his June 1991 visit or earlier pilgrimages.

This book is structured around these four visits as introduced above, with a chapter devoted to each. A number of questions are addressed in these various contexts: What was the pope's modus operandi? Where did he go? What sorts of audiences did he address? What kinds of issues did he raise? What did he have to say (or not say) about the social, economic, political, cultural, and international situation of Poland? About communist policies? About Marxist ideology? What did he do or say that annoyed, frightened, or mollified the regime? How did he respond to pressure from the government? How did he employ Catholic notions of sacred time and sacred space during his pilgrimages? How did he draw from Polish history, as well as Church history, to address the current situations? Which saints and other personalities from Poland's past did he point to and to what ends were they utilized? How did he relate to the West, to Europe, to the Soviet bloc? How did he talk about Christianity in Poland, past and present? What did he say about (or sometimes to) those peoples with whom Poles had a problematic past, such as Germans, Russians, Jews, or Ukrainians?

Structurally, the chapters on the communist-era pilgrimages are organized chronologically, while the chapter on the postcommunist visit is organized thematically. I have done this for several reasons. Given the unique tension connected with a papal visit to a communist country, particularly one in which the visitor himself can potentially leverage his enormous public prestige into considerable trouble for the government, the communist-era pilgrimages could not but follow a dramatic course played out day by day. If the government was upset with something the pope did or said, it generally intervened with Church authorities. The authorities also closely monitored the coverage of the visit as it unfolded in the Western media. At times we see John Paul provoking a response from the regime and then deciding what sort of adjustments to make, if any, in the face of governmental pushback. This ebb-and-flow of tension is best discussed in chronological order. The communist-era pilgrimages were also especially carefully choreographed to fit the pope's overall intent for each visit. The 1979 pilgrimage, for example, was designed to feature Saint Stanisław and culminate in a visit to his tomb, preceded by visits to shrines connected with Saint Wojciech and the Blessed Virgin Mary. The government also had an interest in the sequencing of the papal itinerary. His 1987 visit, for instance, had to begin in Warsaw on the insistence of the government, though the pope had hoped to launch it in Kraków. Such issues were less pressing during the 1991 pilgrimage and did not involve such delicate negotiations with the state. Furthermore, the 1991 visit entailed the pope giving his views on a vast array of issues facing Poles in the present and future, and he scattered them across the entire nine days, visiting and revisiting particular issues as they connected with one of the Ten Commandments. For example, he discussed abortion on four different days, the problematic aspects of Poland's socioeconomic transformation on four different occasions, and relations with Eastern Christians on five. Therefore, a thematic approach lends itself best to this visit. It not only helps to avoid repetition, but by clustering the various components of John Paul's assessment of the Polish situation, it makes it easier to discern his preferred vision for Poland's future.

Depending on how one counts them, John Paul made between

eight and nine pilgrimages total to his native Poland.[16] I elected to focus on the first four. I chose not to limit the study to the visits during communist rule, largely because ending in 1987 would minimize an important feature of John Paul—he was not just an opponent of communism but also very uneasy with the sort of society that had developed in the West. The 1991 pilgrimage presents an opportunity to explore this issue in more depth. Thus, this study follows the papal pilgrimages through communism's final decade in Poland and into the early postcommunist future.

METHODS AND SOURCES

At the heart of this study are the pope's own words. There are transcripts for all of John Paul's public and semipublic speeches and homilies from each of the four pilgrimages, assembled in a collection by the Znak publishing house.[17] I was also able to acquire audio recordings of each of the pope's addresses, which often makes it possible to verify the accuracy of the transcript as well as note the frequency and the length of interruptions by the audience with applause, chanting, and singing.

Another important source for this study are the reports by the government, the Communist Party, and the state security services pertaining to the papal visits. These are available only for the first three pilgrimages, while Poland was under communist rule. The government office in charge of relations with the Church, the Urząd do Spraw Wyznań (USW, or Office of Confessional Affairs) produced summaries and analyses of each visit. Because the government itself had approved the papal visits, USW analysts were often tasked with putting the visit in a positive light, so alongside concerns about the pope's words and deeds are plentiful references to ways in which the pope was allegedly furthering the interests of the regime. This was the case particularly for the first pilgrimage. Another office that monitored and analyzed the pilgrimages was the Wydział Administracyjny, Komitet Centralny Polskiej Zjednoczonej Partii Robotniczej (Administrative Section, Central Committee of the Polish United Workers' Party). Alongside these governmental and party assessments, mainly found at the Archiwum Akt Nowych (AAN) in Warsaw, are the reports by the security services, held at the Instytut Pamięci Narodowej (IPN, or Institute of National Remembrance), also in Warsaw. These Interior Ministry reports deal chiefly with security-related issues but also contain descriptions and sometimes analyses of the visits as well.

A number of other primary sources help to provide context along with some analysis. These include the Western press (especially the *New York Times* and *Washington Post*, which devoted extensive coverage to the pilgrimages), the Polish Communist Party daily (*Trybuna Ludu*), the Polish Catholic weekly newspaper (*Tygodnik Powszechny*), the Polish political journal *Polityka*, and some pertinent memoirs by major figures of the time in Poland, including Solidarity's leader, Lech Wałęsa. Politburo member Mieczysław Rakowski has published his diaries from his political career, though because of various additions, deletions, and revisions before publication, they serve better as memoir here than as a day-to-day account of Rakowski's political past.[18]

PURPOSE OF THE STUDY

The intention of this study is to focus on John Paul II himself—above all on his words and actions during his visits to Poland. This is not a study of late communist Poland and the collapse of communism or of Church-state relations in the Polish People's Republic, though my intention is to make some contribution to our understanding of each of these issues. Rather, the book is about how a Polish pope dealt with and tried to influence a rapidly evolving situation in a homeland that lay very close to his heart. My hope is that it deepens our appreciation of John Paul II, especially as he intersects with some of the central developments pertinent to the greatest political revolution of the late twentieth century, and thereby enhances our understanding of both the man and the situation.

1

CATALYST

The 1979 Pilgrimage

Not long after the election of Karol Wojtyła as pope in October 1978, the prospects of a visit to his homeland became manifest. The day after his election, the leadership of the Polish Conference of Catholic Bishops expressed the hope that John Paul would visit Poland during 1979 for the nine-hundredth anniversary of the martyrdom of Saint Stanisław and in 1982 for the six-hundredth anniversary of the arrival in Częstochowa of the celebrated icon of the Black Madonna.[1] John Paul expressed a similar wish when speaking to Poles who attended his inauguration in Rome.[2] It was now up to Poland's regime to accommodate, deny, or alter these hopes.

There were good reasons to disallow a papal visit. As noted earlier, Poland was a country in which communism already had a rocky road, particularly because Poles viewed it as a foreign system imposed by an external enemy. The economic situation was worsening, most obviously in a huge debt crisis and incessant food shortages. Major labor unrest had broken out in 1970–1971 and 1976, large numbers of critically engaged intellectuals and activists had established a widespread unofficial culture replete with dissident groups of various stripes, and a powerful Catholic Church claimed the primary allegiance of vast numbers of Poland's citizens. Perhaps most ominously, links had become established over the previous decades among the workers, the dissident intelligentsia, and the Church. In such a context, hosting a series of large-scale events that would involve a mix of religion and patriotism in an atmosphere with all the energy and euphoria of a major athletic competition could spell disaster. It would also provide an opportunity that the regime's opponents could exploit, and, given the great international interest in such a visit, any unpleasant developments would get maximum publicity in the Western media. Moreover, the Soviet Union looked askance at their Polish communist allies taking such a potentially dangerous step. In his memoirs, Communist Party chief Edward Gierek notes that the prospect of a papal visit to Poland distressed the Soviet leadership. Soviet leader Leonid Brezhnev even telephoned Gierek to sound him out on the matter, and he tried to persuade Gierek to oppose the visit, arguing that the visit could bring Poland's communists "great troubles."[3] As Soviet foreign minister Andrei Gromyko later informed Gierek, the Soviets regarded John Paul as a "dangerous ideological and political enemy," for both Poland and the Soviet Union, one who was clever, knowledgeable, and impressively physically fit.[4]

On the other hand, some of the same factors that argued against permitting a visit also argued for it. Poland's population badly wanted the visit, and Gierek, having been unable to deliver on his promises to give Poles a better life economically in the 1970s, could at least give them the pope. Furthermore, refusing a visit by John Paul would damage Poland's prestige in the West at a time when Poland needed the indulgence of Western governments and financial institutions as it tried to manage its heavy foreign debt. Perhaps the visit was a risk worth taking. In justifying the idea to the Soviets, Gierek told Brezhnev when they met in March 1979 that John Paul was a Polish citizen and had the right to visit his homeland and that to deny him a visit would provoke social tensions. However, the Polish government did insist that the pope not come in May, lest the feast day of Saint

Stanisław be an occasion to make Church-state conflict a theme of the visit, and that the pilgrimage promote Polish patriotism and focus on issues of peace, détente, and disarmament.[5]

Church and state soon began to negotiate the possibility, and then the particulars, of a papal visit. The government's expressed position that John Paul, as a citizen of Poland, had a right to visit his homeland came with the understanding that the authorities would have to agree to the timing and conditions of his visit. The sticking point was the desire of pope and Church that the visit correspond with the commemoration of the nine-hundredth anniversary of the martyrdom of Saint Stanisław in early May.[6] This was an extremely important event for John Paul and the Church in Poland. Stanisław was his saintly predecessor as bishop of Kraków and one of Poland's greatest saints and patrons. The Church had been involved in a years-long series of preparatory events in advance of the anniversary, with Cardinal Wojtyła playing a major role in them. He in no way wanted to miss their culmination. However, bestowing the prominence and prestige of a papal visit on the Stanisław celebrations did not sit well with the regime. As understood in Polish Catholic martyrology, Stanisław had confronted the Polish king, Bolesław II the Bold (Bolesław II Śmiały), about certain immoral policies of the monarch and ended up slain by the king's command. Thus, Stanisław was a symbol of ecclesial resistance to state power.[7] This issue was further complicated by the fact that the communists, in their accounts of the conflict, sided with Bolesław, calling him a "hero and patriot."[8] Nor did it help that both Cardinal Wyszyński and John Paul had recently presented Stanisław as a champion of human rights, an identification that would make any communist regime uneasy.[9]

Talks over this issue continued, at times reaching a very high level, as when Gierek himself met with Wyszyński for four hours on January 24.[10] The communists refused to budge on the matter of timing, and the Church eventually agreed that the visit would be in June rather than May. It also agreed that Saint Stanisław would be treated as a figure of national reconciliation rather than church-state division.[11]

Moreover, both sides agreed that the visit was to have a predominantly religious character, a point the pope himself was to stress on a number of occasions throughout the pilgrimage. The continuing talks treated other matters as well, such as media coverage, transportation, security, and venues, with agreement finally reached that John Paul would visit Poland June 2–10, with stops in Warsaw, Gniezno, Częstochowa, and Kraków and its vicinity. Absent from the itinerary, among other things, were visits to Silesia (Gierek's home political base) and Lublin, site of Poland's (and the entire communist world's) only independent Catholic university, where Wojtyła had taught for nearly a quarter of a century before his election as pope. The Church was able to work around these restrictions—if John Paul could not go to Silesia or Lublin, then pilgrims from Silesia and students and faculty from Lublin would hear him address them in special events at Częstochowa. Even more significantly, if he could not be in Poland for Stanisław's feast and commemoration, the Church would extend the celebration to coincide with the final days of the pope's visit in early June. The June date also meant that John Paul would be in the country for the celebration of the great feast of Pentecost, which he would use in spiritually, culturally, and politically powerful ways, as we shall see.[12]

As the papal visit drew near, Komitet Obrony Robotników (KOR, Committee of Defense of the Workers), Poland's leading dissident organization, took several important steps. First, on May 19 it addressed a letter to John Paul praising him as "a spokesman for the best values of Polish culture, a culture that is free from narrow nationalism, a culture that is based on tolerance and pluralism, a culture that is associated with the Christian world of values. We find this sense in your sermons and messages, and especially in the encyclical *Redemptoris hominis*, which is so important to us."[13] The letter then cited those parts of the encyclical in which the pope condemned violations of inalienable human rights by the state (or by a party that identifies itself with the state) and emphasized the need for the moral participation of society in the exercise of authority. Also in advance of John Paul's arrival, KOR issued a call for prison reform and for a widespread amnesty in conjunction with the pope's visit, an issue not popular with Poles but one in line with John Paul's own thinking.[14] Finally, KOR and the rest of Poland's opposition, as KOR co-founder Jan Józef Lipski puts it, "discreetly stepped aside" during the papal visit, "so as not to complicate the situation."[15]

WARSAW

Upon arrival at what was then Warsaw's Okęcie Airport, the first thing John Paul did was to greet his native land by kissing the tarmac, a practice he made customary during his many travels worldwide. He was cordially greeted by a high-level delegation of state and Church officials, and he then listened to welcoming speeches by Poland's chief of state, Henryk Jabłoński, and the head (or primate) of the Catholic Church in Poland, Cardinal Stefan Wyszyński. He followed with some brief remarks in which he thanked the government for "taking a benevolent position toward my visit" and laid out his goals. He stated, "My visit is dictated by strictly religious motives" and indicated that his intentions were to serve the cause of peace, dialogue, reconciliation and cooperation between nations, and social justice; to bring internal unity to Poles; and to further the development of good relations between state and Church.[16]

The initial formalities taken care of, John Paul then went to meet, in succession, representatives of the Church, the state, and the nation. As his motorcade traversed the approximately eight miles from the airport to Warsaw's Old Town, hundreds of thousands of people lined the route, many of them cheering, singing, and laying down flowers, with Polish and papal flags and welcome banners hanging from adjacent residences.[17] First, he attended a gathering of clergy and faithful at the Cathedral of Saint John the Baptist in Warsaw's Old Town, where he praised Cardinal Wyszyński as the "keystone" of the Church in Poland, asserted that the fact of the cathedral being built anew after its destruction during the Warsaw Uprising in 1944 was a symbol of the resilience of the Church, and quoted one of his own favorite Polish poets, Cyprian Norwid, about Poles' "great common duty" to the fatherland. John Paul also connected his pilgrimage with the nine-hundredth anniversary of the martyrdom of Saint Stanisław, something the government was hoping he would downplay.

Next the pope went to Belvedere Palace, the seat of Poland's president of the Council of State, for a high-level meeting with communist leaders, in particular Communist Party chief Edward Gierek. Gierek greeted the pope warmly and spoke favorably of recent international developments such as détente and arms limitation, though in an anti-NATO reference he mentioned the threat posed by the neutron bomb. He saluted Polish heroism and sacrifice during World War II and spoke of the "just borders, and lasting guarantee of independence, sovereignty, and security based on reliable allies," especially the Soviet Union, that Poland enjoyed after the war.[18] He went on to praise the many accomplishments of the past thirty-five years of communism in Poland, including fundamental social transformation, industrialization, urbanization, and cultural development, and he expressed hope that the papal visit would contribute to Church-state cooperation, the unity of the Polish nation, and the success of the Polish People's Republic (Polska Rzeczpospolita Ludowa, or PRL).

How would John Paul respond to these remarks combining cordial welcome with communist self-congratulation? Not with diplomatic formalities but rather a well-crafted, substantial speech that included a number of seemingly ambiguous formulations that could be regarded as affirming while in fact challenging Gierek and the regime. The pope thanked Gierek for his "very kind" words, as well as the authorities for supporting and helping to organize his visit.[19] Like Gierek, he recalled Poland's tragic past, especially during World War II. He praised the reconstruction of the Royal Castle (Zamek) in Warsaw as a symbol of Poland's statehood and sovereignty and noted that "the sovereignty of society, of the nation, of the Fatherland, is the raison d'être of the state." He went on to stress that national independence was especially meaningful for Poles given how much they had suffered and sacrificed for it, including enduring a lengthy period without their own state from the late eighteenth to the early twentieth century (the so-called era of the Partition). He condemned "all forms of political, economic, and cultural colonialism" as being counter to international harmony, and he esteemed alliances based on mutual respect and co-operation for the welfare of all partners. In speaking out for peace and disarmament, the pope asserted that genuine peace can be built only on the foundation of respect for "the objective rights of the nation, such as the right to existence, to freedom, to sociopolitical subjectivity, and to the creation of their own culture and civilization." John Paul also stressed the important and positive role the Catholic Church played and was continuing to play in the history of the Polish nation, and he mentioned the Church's ongoing efforts in Poland to secure conditions for this activity.

The communists, publicly at least, preferred to see the pope's words as affirming their self-image—Poland enjoying the "objective rights of nations" under their rule, which honored human rights and defended Polish sovereignty in an alliance system founded on mutual respect. But a more accurate reading, one that takes the Polish context into account, would see John Paul as reminding his audience that Poland was in fact part of a bloc based more on colonialism than mutual respect, with the objective rights of the nation, as well as the human rights of individuals, far from honored. Thus, any talk of national sovereignty, rights of the nation, or human rights could be taken as an implicit challenge to the regime. Moreover, references to Poland's past could also be problematic—not only the implicit reference to the Partitions (of which Russia was a central participant) but especially the remarks about World War II and its aftermath. While citing the suffering, sacrifices, and heroism of the wartime experience, John Paul added that "with bitterness we think about the disappointments that we were not spared." This remark could implicate the Soviet Union for a number of injustices that it inflicted upon Poles—its occupation of their country from 1939 to 1941 in cooperation with Nazi Germany; its mass killings at Katyń and elsewhere; its brutal and often deadly deportation of hundreds of thousands to exile deep in the Soviet Union; its reluctance to come to the assistance of the Warsaw Uprising in 1944—as well as implicate all the Allies for concluding the Yalta agreement that handed Poland over to the communists. Although the pope made none of these linkages explicit, a listener aware of Poland's history could certainly draw such intimations from the reference to "bitter disappointments." John Paul concluded his address by expressing his "gratitude and esteem" to Gierek for all his efforts toward "the general good of Poles and proper importance of Poland in international life," along with his respect for each government official on whom weighed heavily "the responsibility . . . toward history and their own conscience." Thus, what could superficially be taken as papal praise was in fact a challenge, admonishing Poland's leaders that they would have to answer to their consciences and to history for their stewardship of his and their common native land.

If the meeting with Gierek was not enough drama for one day, the pope then went on to Warsaw's enormous Victory Square, where he celebrated mass late that afternoon for a crowd numbering in the hundreds of thousands, perhaps more than a million.[20] The focus of the event was on the altar erected on the square, the thirty-six-foot plywood cross standing behind it, and the pope himself, whose greeting of the crowd with outstretched arms became iconic.[21] People wept openly. During the mass, the pope gave one of his most significant homilies ever, one that communists found unsettling in a number of ways.[22] First, John Paul directly connected his pilgrimage to the anniversary of Saint Stanisław's martyrdom, despite party efforts to obstruct such a link. Speaking on the eve of the feast of Pentecost, traditionally understood as the birthday of the Church, the pope tied that feast to the baptism of Poland's ruler in 966, Prince Mieszko, and then to Stanisław himself, who as bishop was a successor to the apostles who had gathered at the first Pentecost and "who purchased his mission at the see of Kraków with his blood nine hundred years ago." Second, John Paul made reference to some historic events the regime would have preferred remain unmentioned. The pope noted the unfulfilled desire of Pope Paul VI to visit Poland, especially for the celebration of the one-thousandth anniversary of the "baptism of Poland" in 1966, a visit that did not materialize due to opposition from the communist authorities. Moreover, John Paul got more specific with respect to the "bitter disappointments" he had vaguely mentioned at Belvedere, noting that Poles were abandoned by the Allied powers in their fight against the Nazis in the Warsaw Uprising of 1944, clearly an indictment of the Soviet Union for its failure to assist Poles at that time. However, the most serious challenge to the regime at Victory Square was the pope's elaboration of his view that Jesus Christ stands at the center of any understanding of human history, an approach that ran totally contrary to the communist interpretation of the past.[23]

Reiterating one of his favorite teachings from the Second Vatican Council, John Paul affirmed that "it is impossible to understand the human person fully without Christ."[24] His dignity, his mission, his final destiny, who he in fact is, are all connected with Jesus Christ. Moreover, John Paul continued, because a nation is understood through the lives of each of its persons, it is impossible to understand the history of Poland, of what the Polish nation brought to the development of humanity, without Christ. This holds even for Poland's nonbelievers, according to the pope. Rooted in Christ as an old oak is rooted in the soil, the nation was able to withstand the strong winds that history inflicted upon it.[25] Jesus Christ, according to the pope, is an open book of teaching about humanity, the dignity and rights of humans, and also about the dignity and rights of nations. John Paul's high regard for the concept of nation also came through when he stated that "there is no way to understand the human person other than in that community which is his nation." He then made this connection between person, nation, and Jesus Christ concrete by alluding to the Gospel seed that dies before it brings forth new life.[26] He thus linked Jesus Christ's death on the cross with the many sacrifices made by Poles in past and present, as well as with the fruits that these sacrifices ultimately bore. This fit extremely well with the overall tenor of John Paul's pilgrimage and its repeated references to the lives, deaths, and fruits of such great figures as Saint Stanisław, Saint Wojciech, and Saint Maximilian Kolbe and visits to places connected with them.[27] It also resonated well with the Victory Square venue, which was the site of the Tomb of the Unknown Soldier, at which the pope had knelt earlier that evening with Cardinal Wyszyński. In so doing, as John Paul noted in his homily, he gave honor to each seed that, falling in the ground and dying in it, bears fruit. Whether this be the seed of the soldier's blood spilled on the field of battle or the martyr's sacrifice in camps and prisons. Whether this be the seed of heavy, daily work in the sweat of one's brow in the fields, in workshops, in mines, in foundries and factories. Whether this be the seed of family love, which does not shrink before the gift of life of a new person and takes up the whole labor of upbringing. Whether this be the seed of creative work in the schools, institutes, libraries, in the workshops of national culture. Whether this be the seed of prayer and service to the sick, suffering, abandoned. Whether this be the seed of suffering itself in hospital beds, in clinics, in sanatoria, in homes; . . . everything that constitutes Poland.

John Paul thus linked Jesus Christ not only with Poland's great martyrs and heroic warriors fighting "for your freedom and ours" but also to the sacrifices made in the ordinary daily lives of countless contemporary Poles—workers, farmers, teachers, parents, and many others.[28] In a dramatic culmination to his homily, and in a manner appropriate to the eve of Pentecost, John Paul concluded by calling down the Holy Spirit upon Poland, combining words from Scripture with references to his native land:

> Let your Spirit come down!
> Let your Spirit come down!
> And renew the face of the earth.
> Of this Land.
> Amen.

These words, a refrain recited in conjunction with Psalm 104, are a standard part of the Catholic liturgy for Pentecost Sunday. They had particular resonance among Poles, however, because in Polish, the word for "earth" and "land" is the same, *zem*, so the pope was calling down the Holy Spirit to renew not only the face of the earth (*zem*) but also the face of Poland, that is, of "this Land" (*zem*).[29]

John Paul's homily sparked more than a dozen bursts of applause, notably at his reference to the abandonment of Poles during the Warsaw Uprising, his talk of the centrality of Jesus Christ for understanding the human person and the nation, his litany of "everything that constitutes Poland," and his calling down of the Holy Spirit. At times, the crowd sang and chanted "We want God."[30] John Paul also drew sustained applause when, referring to the sacrifices over the ages by the Polish "Unknown Soldier" near whose grave he stood, he asked whether "there can be a just Europe without an independent Poland on the map." Poland's communist authorities were extremely displeased with this speech, more so than with any other he would give that week in Poland. In their internal reports on the event, government and party analysts accused him of turning a religious celebration into a political rally.[31] They were annoyed by his allusions to Paul VI's inability to visit Poland in 1966 and to the Warsaw Uprising. One report noted the divergence in tone and content between the Victory Square homily and John Paul's more cordial and positive speeches at the airport and at Belvedere Palace, calling it "an attempt at creating a psychosis of struggle and threats" that evinced a crusading mentality.[32] By introducing an "exclusivist Christology," the Victory Square speech compromised the possibility of dialogue and cut against the strengthening of national unity that John Paul had claimed as one of his goals for the visit during his speech at the airport earlier that day.[33] John Paul was accused of understanding unity in his own sense as the domination of the "stereotype Pole-Catholic" and presenting a view of the history of the nation and its culture and development as integrally and exclusively connected with the Catholic Church.[34] One analyst claimed that John Paul was denying to nonbelievers the right to understand the history of Poland and its culture and that he strongly tied the national to the religious, returning to the "old formula of equating Polishness with Catholicism."[35] Another report quoted some of the pope's "inappropriate" words from Victory Square: "Those without Christ cannot understand their own nation; they do not know how to draw the correct conclusions from history; they do not understand dignity and morality."[36] Although not a precise rendering of what the pope said, these comments were accurate enough and make it clear that John Paul had touched a nerve among Poland's rulers.

Later that evening, John Paul met with representatives of Warsaw's "creative intelligentsia" at Cardinal Wyszyński's residence and, according to a police report, told his audience that "everything that lies on my heart I said at Victory Square. We said it together—me and you; the people of Warsaw said it. What I didn't say, the people said, not with spoken words, because you know. . . ." Then he added, "Perhaps I said a little too much, or said it too sharply, but one must stand up for what one believes."[37] If accurate, these papal comments show John Paul as acknowledging those very elements of his style that so troubled the regime and that underscored the dangers inherent in inviting him to his native land, where such opportunities would present themselves. The next day brought another such opportunity, as the pope once more raised communist hackles with an address they regarded as provocative.

GNIEZNO

On June 3, after a morning speech to university students in front of the Church of Saint Anna, near the University of Warsaw, during which John Paul continued the themes of Pentecost and the Holy Spirit of the evening before, the pope departed for the next stop on his pilgrimage—Gniezno. This western Polish city had enormous historical and religious significance for Poles. It was the center of the nascent Polish state and Church in the tenth century, as well as the site of the tomb of Wojciech, the great saint and missionary, one of the featured figures on John Paul's pilgrimage. Wojciech was a Bohemian (ethnically Czech) bishop who, among other things in his illustrious ecclesiastical career, went on an expedition to evangelize the pagan Baltic tribes in Poland's northeast, among whom he was ultimately martyred in 997.[38] In preparation for this mission voyage, Wojciech spent some time at the princely Polish court in Gniezno, and his body was brought there for interment after his martyrdom. It was in the year 1000, in the presence of Wojciech's relics, that the Polish ruler Bolesław I the Brave (Bolesław I Chrobry), the German emperor

Otto III, and a papal envoy of Pope Sylvester II met to establish the first metropolitanate of the Church in Poland, thereby laying the foundation for Church hierarchy in that new country in the so-called Act of Gniezno. This event also came to be regarded by Poles as an important step in the establishment of an independent Polish state, a step fostering its development and stability.[39]

John Paul spoke of these historic events during the high point of his visit to Gniezno, a mass celebrated that afternoon on the hill of Wzgórze Lecha, on the feast of Pentecost.[40] In his homily, he connected the first Pentecost, at which the Holy Spirit unleashed the evangelizing energies of the apostles, with the evangelical fruits of Wojciech's mission and martyrdom. While speaking of the Bohemian Czech Wojciech, John Paul noted a Czech-language banner in the crowd reading "Father, Remember Your Czech Children." To this cri de coeur from one of the most oppressed churches in Europe, the pope forcefully replied that they would not be forgotten—and not just the Czechs but all the peoples of the Slavic world, whose languages would be heard by history's first Slavic pope. John Paul stated that it was providential that there was now a Slavic pope, one able "to reveal the spiritual unity of Christian Europe"—the pope was shouting these words—then continued, "constituted by two great traditions—West and East." He called on Eastern Christians, in a spirit of ecumenism, to cooperate in the great evangelizing work of the Holy Spirit.[41] He went on to speak of the history of the evangelization of the various Slavic peoples of Europe, listing the approximate conversion dates of at least a dozen Slavic groups, beginning with the Croats and Slovenes in the seventh century. A crucial part of this papal mission, according to him, was to speak out to the Church, to Europe, and to the world about these "often forgotten nations and peoples." By implication, this homily was challenging Soviet cultural hegemony over the Slavic and East European sphere and, by bringing attention to those silenced Christians in the communist world, was raising issues of human rights as well. It is no surprise that it irked Poland's communist leaders, as we shall see.

John Paul's words at Gniezno were indicative of the new direction in which he was taking the Vatican's so-called Eastern policy (or Ostpolitik). Under Popes John XXIII and Paul VI, the Vatican had sought to improve relations with the communist world, which had been mutually hostile under the pontificate of Pius XII.[42] John XXIII, believing that communist regimes were here to stay, thought that improved relations with the communist world were necessary in order to protect the Church behind the Iron Curtain. This policy of "saving what could be saved" entailed the Vatican toning down its anticommunist rhetoric, distancing itself from the West in international politics, and limiting and even discouraging the underground churches operating in some communist states so as not to impede the desired smoother relations at the summit. Pope John, and his successor Paul VI, put emphasis on developing diplomatic relations between the Apostolic See and various communist states, with the goal of securing a modicum of protection for churches in Eastern Europe, obtaining release of incarcerated bishops and priests, filling vacant episcopal appointments, and, not least, helping to preserve peace in a world marked by tense moments such as the U-2 incident, the construction of the Berlin Wall, and the Cuban Missile Crisis. This Ostpolitik focused on diplomacy and aimed at state-to-state agreements between the Holy See and particular communist governments. The figure most associated with this policy was Agostino Casaroli, an accomplished Vatican diplomat under John XXIII and Paul VI and elevated to secretary of state by John Paul II in 1979. Nevertheless, despite this advancement of Casaroli to the top diplomatic position in the Vatican, John Paul in fact started moving away from the accommodationist position associated with Casaroli and previous popes. While John XXIII and Paul VI engaged in a delicate diplomatic dance with the Soviet Union and its allies, John Paul II was not afraid to step on toes if need be. We see this in his pan-Slavic appeal across the Catholic-Orthodox divide, his expression of solidarity with the repressed churches in places like Czechoslovakia, and his broaching of human rights questions.[43]

John Paul's mass at Gniezno was sandwiched between two other high points of his visit there. First, upon arrival he addressed a vast crowd, perhaps half a million, in a meadow a few miles outside town, at Gebarzewo.[44] The audience was overwhelmingly working people and farmers. At this venue, the pope, quoting Jesus Christ's words "Let the little children come to me" (Matthew 19:14) and noting that it was the United Nations International Year of the Child, put a big stress on the importance of catechizing children. In so doing, he was indirectly admonishing not only a regime that did not always make that easy for Polish parents but also those parents themselves, lest they shirk this crucial religious responsibility. During his speech, John Paul spoke of all Poles together as a "royal Piast tribe," an expression from the celebrated Polish patriotic song "Rota."[45] Then, surveying the crowd, he went on to say, "I greet everyone and leave no one out. Including the representatives of the local authorities, the representatives of the crowd control service and the police. Everyone! A royal Piast tribe!" Although the regime's analysts would regard this as papal praise for the police, heard in context it sounds as though the pope was affirming that even those "lost sheep" who served the regime remained a part of the nation.[46]

The pope concluded his visit to Gniezno later that day with a speech on Polish culture to an assembly of youth.[47] He focused on the "Bogurodzica," a late medieval Polish hymn to Mary that exemplified the crucial role that the Christian faith had played in Polish culture over the centuries. The pope noted how culture helped the Polish nation retain its spiritual independence during its nearly 125-year-long loss of political independence during the Partitions. He spoke of Christianity's rich resonance in Polish culture and observed that from the beginning it bore a very expressly Christian stamp, as the "Bogurodzica" itself exemplifies. In making these points, he quoted the great nineteenth-century Polish writer Adam Mickiewicz, saying that "a civilization, genuinely worthy of man, must be Christian."[48]

Both the Western media and the communist regime were paying close attention to the papal pilgrimage, now two days old, with the communists greatly concerned with what the Western media were saying. The American press was playing up the confrontational dimensions of the visit, with headlines such as "Pope Gets Big Welcome in Poland, Offers Challenge to the Authorities" and "Pope Urges Rights for Fellow Slavs, Addresses Fate of Christians in Eastern Europe."[49] The communists did see some things they liked about the visit so far. For example, the crowds were peaceful and orderly, something noticed by the Western press as well. Moreover, communist analysts noted that John Paul's meeting with General Secretary Gierek took place in a more cordial atmosphere than diplomatic protocol required.[50] However, though Poles were behaving and the pope was gracious, the regime found much that was disconcerting in the pope's words and deeds during the first two days. Besides the concerns noted above about the homily on Victory Square, papal remarks in Gniezno deepened communist anxieties. They did not appreciate his talk of a personal papal mission to the Slavic world, nor of the centrality of Christianity for Polish culture. Government analysts referred to his outreach to the entire Slavic world as a "Christian pan-Slavism" that was taking Vatican Ostpolitik in a new direction.[51] One report said that the pope's words on Slavs and Slavdom had the flavor of a Crusade, characteristic of the "imperialism" of the Church.[52]

These issues and those raised on Victory Square were serious enough that Poland's leaders undertook several interventions in hopes that they could preempt further uncomfortable comments from John Paul. Stanisław Kania, the Politburo member responsible for overseeing the state security services, wrote to Franciszek Macharski, John Paul's successor as archbishop of Kraków, with his concerns. In what was overall a cordial letter, Kania expressed the party's anxiety over John Paul's deviation at Victory Square and Gniezno from the positive tone of his speeches at the airport and at Belvedere. He singled out several transgressions by the pope—his reference to Poland being "abandoned" during the Warsaw Uprising; his violation of "the spirit of tolerance" by his talk about the centrality of Jesus Christ in Poland's history; his reminder that Paul VI was not allowed to visit Poland in 1966; and his stress on "evangelization of the Slavs," with its implications for "contemporary political realities." He also expressed consternation that in none of John Paul's speeches were "the Hitlerite invaders and occupiers . . . called by name."[53] Simultaneously, Kania sent Kazimierz Kąkol, head of the Office of Confessional Affairs, to meet with Archbishop Macharski in the hope that he would convey the regime's concerns to the pope himself. Macharski tried to calm communist anxieties in his responses. He noted the disciplined and orderly conduct of the Polish crowds and their cooperation with the organs of public order. He pointed to the lack of manifestations of "primitive religious fanaticism." He argued that the pope's heavy stress on the role of the Church in Poland's history was a counterweight to official minimization of that role and was a position taken by all of Poland's bishops. He contended that John Paul's outreach to Slavdom was not a call to crusade but a way of treating the East as an equal partner in dialogue and not as "barbarians" in need of Western culture. Finally, Macharski assured Kąkol that he had read the texts of the papal speeches for the upcoming events and that "they are not bad." He asserted that John Paul had no intention of doing in Poland anything like what France's President Charles de Gaulle had done during his 1967 visit to Quebec, when the latter provocatively shouted "Long live free Quebec!" to a large crowd in Montreal.[54] The concerns raised by Kąkol and tempered by Macharski, coming from the highest echelons of the party, were a far cry from the positive face of the visit presented in the communist press, revealing those anxieties the party wanted to keep out of the public eye.

The interventions by Kania and Kąkol with Macharski were not the only ones the party was making at this time. Casaroli was also a prime recipient of regime complaints about the course of the pilgrimage. As Vatican secretary of state and architect of improved relations between the Vatican and the Soviet bloc, he was the go-to guy for Poland's communists. They perceived that he too would like the pope to express himself more circumspectly at the large papal events and not rock the diplomatic boat with statements offending his hosts. Kazimierz Szablewski, the head of the team responsible for working contacts with the Holy See at the Polish embassy in Rome, had the task of conveying the government's concerns to Casaroli.[55] On June 3, at the foot of the helicopter set to whisk John Paul off to Gniezno, Szablewski informed Casaroli of the regime's dissatisfaction with the pope's words at Victory Square. Casaroli shared his concern and added that he was unable to vet the pope's words because the text was available only in Polish. According to Szablewski's notes on the meeting, Casaroli pledged to exert greater control over subsequent papal speeches (and insist on receiving copies of the texts in Italian) and hold subsequent meetings with Szablewski as the pilgrimage proceeded. Although Casaroli passed these concerns on to the pope, the papal homily at Gniezno troubled the regime as much as the one at Victory Square had. This led to a further meeting of Szablewski with Casaroli at Częstochowa on June 5. The regime was especially concerned with where John Paul might take things during his upcoming visit to Auschwitz, and Szablewski implied that if John Paul did not alter his course, progress in mutual relations would be jeopardized. The authorities were especially afraid that John Paul might endorse German-Polish reconciliation at Auschwitz, and they had similar fears about what he might say in his farewell speech at the Kraków airport. Casaroli assured them that he would do everything possible to see that the papal speeches were kept within the tone of the address at Belvedere and that the pope was not intending to raise the issue of reconciliation at Auschwitz. Casaroli also promised to get Szablewski a copy of the pope's farewell address.

CZĘSTOCHOWA

While Church and government officials worked behind the scenes to influence the course of the visit, John Paul proceeded with his pilgrimage. From Gniezno he moved on to the next stop on his route—the city of Częstochowa, particularly its great monastery on the nearby hill of Jasna Góra. While Gniezno was associated with Saint Wojciech, Częstochowa was intimately linked with Mary, Mother of God and Queen of Poland.[56] Jasna Góra was the site of Poland's greatest religious object, the icon of the Black Madonna of Częstochowa, also known as Our Lady of Częstochowa or Our Lady of Jasna Góra. This painting of Mary with Jesus originated mysteriously in the fourteenth century and came to symbolize the Polish nation and its suffering over the centuries, making Jasna Góra the national shrine, the most significant site for religious pilgrimage in Poland. John Paul planned a relatively lengthy stay there, covering nearly three full days and involving more than twenty events at which he spoke.

His first significant address at Częstochowa was his homily at the mass held at Jasna Góra upon his arrival, before a crowd numbering probably half a million.[57] Polish Catholic pageantry was on full display, and the pope was as charming as ever. The town was festooned with red-and-white Polish flags, yellow-and-white Vatican ones, and blue Marian ones. Flowers were strewn everywhere, and many children wore colorful regional costumes. Under a red-and-gold canopy, John Paul presided over a religious service that contained much spontaneous singing. Certain comments elicited thunderous and sustained applause. The pope halted his homily repeatedly to joke and lead hymns and folksongs. The massive crowd broke into the popular Polish song of congratulation and good wishes, "Sto Lat!" Despite the festive, even raucous atmosphere, the throngs of people, in typical Catholic fashion, knelt at once "like instantly scythed wheat" when the pope directed them to pray.[58] After the mass, John Paul plunged into the crowd, "giving blessings, shaking hands, and touching outstretched babies as people cheered 'Niech Żyje'—'Long live the Pope.'"[59]

John Paul's homily placed great emphasis on the place of Mary in Poland's history, as well as on the renewal and deepening of devotion to her among his compatriots. He spoke of her "maternal concern" for every person in Poland and her "maternal presence in the life of the Church and Fatherland." John Paul noted the tradition of Poles coming to Jasna Góra to bring their concerns to Mary, something he had done on a number of occasions, including during the Nazi occupation. At Jasna Góra, "we were always free." There, one could "feel how the heart of the nation beats in the heart of the Mother. . . . How many times it beat with the groans of the historical Polish suffering! But also with the shouts of joy and victory!" The pope went on to note more recent times when Poles had recourse to Jesus Christ's mother—the dedication of Poland to the Immaculate Heart of Mary by its leading bishops in 1946; the celebration at Jasna Góra in 1956 on the three-hundredth anniversary of the proclamation by King Jan Kazimierz of Mary as Queen of Poland, in the wake of the successful breaking of the Swedish siege of Częstochowa of 1656; the Act of Dedication to Mary by Cardinal Wyszyński in 1966 on the occasion of the one-thousandth anniversary of the baptism of Poland, in which Poles pledged their servitude (*niewola*) to Mary. This last reference prompted the pope to elaborate on the meaning of servitude and freedom. Among other things, John Paul affirmed that servitude done in love is not felt as servitude, as, for example, when a mother is obliged to care for a sick child. In fact, it is the greatest freedom, he said, and Poles, in servitude to Mary, would always be free at Jasna Góra.

Although political themes were muted in the June 4 homily, John Paul did manage to hit on a couple of issues sensitive to the regime. Once again, he noted the absence of Paul VI at the 1966 millennial commemorations in Poland and went off-text to share a memory of saying mass at the time beneath a portrait of the absent pontiff. He also made another reference to the Church's aspiration for freedom to proclaim its saving mission. If there was anything for the communists to like in the speech, it was the pope's positive reference to the incorporation of the northern and western lands into the Polish state after World War II, as well as his kind words for Agostino Casaroli, John Paul's new secretary of state, given his reputation for having improved relations with communist regimes under Paul VI. However, as the papal speech in Gniezno the day before made clear, Vatican Eastern policy was headed in a new direction, making this gesture little more than an offer of thin gruel.

The next day's highlight was John Paul's address to the plenary session of the Conference of the Episcopate of Poland.[60] Here the focus was on relations between the Church and the state, and the pope drew from the two featured saints of his pilgrimage, Wojciech and Stanisław, to make a number of important points that challenged the regime in several ways. First, he used both saints to underscore the importance of the Church hierarchy in Poland, past and present. The pope once again noted that Poland's hierarchy was established through the Act of Gniezno, taking place at the tomb of the martyred Wojciech in 1000. Stanisław later became, as bishop of Kraków, "one of the pillars of that hierarchical order." John Paul went on to note that, in various periods of Poland's history and especially in the most difficult periods, when Poles lacked their own state, the Church hierarchy played a crucial role, providing structure and assistance to Poles and helping them to maintain and even deepen their national identity, adding that Poles continue to seek this support in the hierarchy of the Church.

Stanisław was important, however, not only as an example of hierarchy. For one thing, John Paul used him to highlight Poland's historical connections to the West. He pointed out that Stanisław's conflict with the state was similar to developments elsewhere in Europe in the same historical period—the martyrdom of Archbishop of Canterbury Thomas Becket in England due to a conflict with his king, and Pope Gregory VII's involvement in the famous Investiture Controversy with Holy Roman Emperor Henry IV. John Paul also held up Stanisław as "the patron of the moral order," the latter having met his death at the hands of a king to whom he proclaimed "the truth of the faith and the principles of Christian morality." In meeting martyrdom for this reason, Stanisław demonstrated that the moral law was binding on everyone, kings (and, implicitly, party secretaries) included. The martyred bishop of Kraków also served as a model for Poland's modern bishops as they carried out their responsibility to speak out against the threats to morality of their own time, such as family breakdown, abortion, and insobriety.

By encouraging the hierarchy to continue to play an important role in Polish society and to speak up for Christian moral principles even at the risk of offending the state, John Paul was presenting yet another challenge to the communist authorities. This was buffered somewhat by his call for Church-state dialogue and cooperation. However, this too marked a departure from the Eastern policy of his predecessors, for John Paul stressed that the Church in Poland, not the Vatican, should be the regime's direct negotiating partner. Moreover, this papal call for dialogue and cooperation was conditioned upon the "full respect for the convictions of people of faith, full guarantee of their civil rights and of the normal conditions of activity of the Church." This was probably asking more of a communist regime than it could deliver without fundamentally changing its character, even in Poland, where religious believers had more freedoms than in most communist countries. John Paul went on to raise another issue uncomfortable for the regime—that the state was not only ruler but was supposed to help and support the people: "it is supposed to be an expression of the full sovereignty of the nation, and not the sovereignty of its own structure in relation to the nation." Finally, John Paul spoke of the connection between Europe and Christianity, both in its past (Christianity "is found at the root of the history of Europe. It forms its spiritual genealogy") and its future ("Christianity must assume anew its part in the formation of the spiritual unity of Europe" and "Europe must return to Christianity"). Thus, while the pope's homily from the day before may not have been as hard-hitting as his words at Victory Square or in Gniezno, his address to the Conference of Bishops made it clear that his pressure on the regime had not eased up.[61]

Later that day, the pope celebrated a mass for pilgrims from one of the regions that the regime would not let him visit—Lower Silesia. His homily focused on the themes of national reconciliation and national unity and highlighted one of Silesia's most celebrated saints, Hedwig of Silesia.[62] From a prominent Bavarian family, she married a Polish duke of the Piast dynasty and was the mother of his successor, Henry the Pious, who died at Legnica while defending Europe from Mongol invasion in 1241. John Paul credited Hedwig with giving her son the courage to fight the Mongols and for commending the Battle of Legnica to Christ crucified. He drew an analogy between Hedwig and Jesus's mother Mary, both of whom lost a son who gave his life for our salvation—Jesus to save us from sin and open for us the prospect of eternal life, Henry to halt the Mongol advance into central Europe.[63] This event for Poles was an early example of the concept of *antemurale Christianitatis* (bulwark of Christendom), the idea that as an eastern bastion of Western Christianity, the Poles were on the front lines in holding off invasions of religious enemies from the East, a tradition that included not just the Mongols but later the Ottoman Turks, the Russians, and in recent times the Soviet communists.[64] The pope spoke of the special place Hedwig had in his heart, in part because he was elected pope on what was her feast day in Poland (October 16). Her shrine at Silesia's Trzebnica monastery, an abbey she founded and where she resided during the final years of her life, was one of the places that John Paul wanted to visit during his trip.[65] Greeting pilgrims from the region, the pope presented them with an Easter candle and a chalice for her shrine. John Paul noted in his homily that Hedwig, given her German ancestry and great contribution to Poland, was an exemplar of national reconciliation between Poles and Germans. He also spoke of another kind of reconciliation—the internal unity of Poles. Pointing to a cause of national disunity, he mentioned that some of the country's citizens were privileged while others faced discrimination. Whether he was speaking of socioeconomic equality or the privileged position of communists, either way the pope's statement was yet another pointed, if subtle, indictment of the regime. John Paul went on to note Saint Stanisław's role as patron of Polish national unity, and he reiterated those rights of the nation that he had listed during his speech at Belvedere a few days earlier. Notably, the pope evoked warm, sustained applause when he greeted Catholic pilgrims visiting from Berlin. After mass, John Paul joked with the crowd as they celebrated his presence with the singing of "Sto Lat."

On June 6, his final day in Częstochowa, John Paul once again addressed pilgrims from places in Poland that the regime did not want him to visit. The first of these speeches was to visiting faculty and students from the Catholic University of Lublin (KUL), where he had taught from 1954 to 1978. In greeting the audience, the pope made reference to the fact that they had to meet at Jasna Góra rather than in Lublin, lamented the difficulties the regime presented to access to the event, and expressed his deep solidarity with a student protest about which he had recently learned.[66] This, and a number of the pope's other comments, drew boisterous and sustained applause from the enthusiastic crowd. Noting that Jesus Christ did not promise his disciples an easy life, John Paul affirmed that being a follower of Christ entailed risks, and he encouraged the students to take those risks. He noted that in Mexico, which he had visited that spring, the Church became unusually strong despite persecution because people there accepted the risk the Gospels say that Jesus called on his followers to take. Then John Paul applied the notion of risk-taking to the Polish context in a surprising way. After stating that one can weaken or even harm the cause of Christ by choosing a worldview or ideology diametrically opposed to Christianity, he affirmed that "every person who chooses a worldview honestly, according to his own conviction, deserves respect." The dangerous person, in the pope's estimation, was the one "who does not take a risk, who does not choose according to his deepest convictions" but rather seeks material prosperity, a person guided by conformism, "moving first to the left, then to the right, according to how the wind is blowing." John Paul added that "for both the cause of Christianity and the cause of Marxism in Poland, it is best when people are able to accept this risk, the Gospel risk of life, confessing to its truth with all of the consequences." Although the crowd listened to these words of the pope in silence, it erupted with nearly a minute of applause when he said that Poland's future depended on how many people would be mature in this manner.

Later that day, the pope addressed pilgrims from another area he was not permitted to visit—Upper Silesia and the Dąbrowski Basin. The regime made it clear during negotiations with Poland's Catholic hierarchy about the papal visit that John Paul would have to stay out of Silesia.[67] The pope was hoping to visit Piekary, a favorite pilgrimage site because of its famed Marian shrine, as well as Trzebnica and Wrocław. However, it is not surprising that the regime forcefully dashed such hopes. The prospect of jubilant and adoring crowds of blue-collar workers in that heartland of Polish industry celebrating the pope was a nightmare the communists hoped to avoid. Such a visit would also force the regime into the unenviable choice of either allowing large numbers of laborers to miss work or dealing with their wrath if forced to miss the pope. Allowing John Paul into Silesia also ran the risk (or better said, would bring the certainty) that Communist Party leader Gierek would be upstaged in his home base. Furthermore, the authorities were especially perturbed that Bishop Herbert Bednorz of Katowice had been urging Silesians to agitate on behalf of a papal visit.[68]

To this audience containing prominent groups of miners and industrial workers from a heavily industrial region, John Paul spoke about the importance, nature, and dignity of labor.[69] He stressed its ethical dimension, its close connection to prayer, and the fact that it cannot satisfy all the needs of the human heart. A burst of sustained applause followed the pope's admonition not to exclude God and prayer from one's life, and the audience also responded positively to his praise of motherhood as a labor in and of itself and crucial for the moral health of society, as well as his assertion that a man should be paid enough to support his family.[70] The pope praised Poland's industrial accomplishments, noting that "this enormous Polish industrial complex, its fruits, its reality, its reputation throughout the world, lies enormously on my heart." Such words would have been music to communist ears, except that John Paul also devoted much attention to stressing the close relationship of Polish workers to Catholicism, incarnate in the many factory chimneys and church towers of Silesia, where "an enormous development of industry . . . went hand in hand with the building of churches," unlike many other regions of Europe, where industrialization was accompanied by de-Christianization. While communists may have appreciated the pope's affirmation of Poland's industrial accomplishments, they surely did not want to be reminded of the Polish working class's atypical allegiance to Catholicism.

In attempting to put a positive face on the Częstochowa stage of the papal sojourn, communist analysts in their internal reports noted favorably John Paul's praise for Casaroli and appreciation of Poland's accomplishments since 1945, be it the acquisition of stable borders encompassing the so-called Recovered Territories (Ziemie Odzyskane) of the north and west, which Poland received after Germany's defeat in 1945, or the massive industrialization during the postwar period.[71] At least one report expressed appreciation for the pope's condemnation of opportunism and careerism and his valuing of sincere Marxists in his address to the pilgrims from KUL. The author went on to state that in Poland a loss of religiosity led not to Marxism but to ideological indifferentism and that it was better for the construction of socialism to have individuals with religious motivations than ideologically indifferent opportunists, the latter being more susceptible to the "influence of bourgeois ideology."[72]

However, agreement that Poland had too many opportunists and careerists in elite positions was hardly the kind of convergence the party wanted to have with the pope. Moreover, the papal appearances in Częstochowa contained plenty to irritate the regime. John Paul twice noted the absence of Paul VI at the country's millennial celebrations in 1966, and he made indirect references to his own difficulties in visiting Lublin and Silesia.[73] In a speech to women religious, he made an oblique reference to repression of religious orders in the Soviet bloc, telling his audience that "it suffices to look to the south, to the east," to appreciate the better situation of religious orders in Poland.[74] His calls on youth to take risks, as well as on bishops to emulate Saint Stanisław in speaking out for morality, could spur behavior unwelcome by the regime. His exuberant affirmation of the connection between Catholicism and the Polish working class trampled on the conventional Marxist view of class and history, and he cut against the regime's take on Polish history with his affirmation of Mary's crucial role therein, complementing his stress two days earlier at Victory Square on Jesus Christ's role.

Częstochowa was also the point on the papal tour where Western media began to notice public disaffection with the regime's handling of the events. Pilgrims complained of roadblocks and other obstacles keeping them from getting to papal events, industrial workers complained of not being allowed time off work to see the pope, and Poles in general criticized the meager television coverage of the events in Jasna Góra (ten minutes per day) and radio coverage that did not convey the pope's actual words.[75] In fact, domestic media coverage was an ongoing problem during the pilgrimage. Cameras focused on the pope himself, generally keeping the enormous crowds and their lively responses out of sight and earshot. When they did show the crowd, it was generally groups of nuns, women, and pensioners. The portions of papal speeches broadcast on radio and television tended to be those in which the pope was addressing themes congenial to the regime—peace, patriotism, national unity—while sensitive topics were left out.[76] Jan Kubik describes his own experiences attending a papal event for youth at Skałka, where media coverage omitted memorable incidents such as the pope being showered with flowers or the crowd angrily shouting and gesturing at a police helicopter.[77]

KRAKÓW AND VICINITY

After completing the "Marian" phase of his pilgrimage at Jasna Góra, John Paul moved on to the final leg of his journey, to Kraków and its environs. There the pope was returning to the region of his birth, the site of his university studies and much of his seminary education and priestly career, and his residence as bishop and archbishop from 1958 until his election as pope. This was also the see of Saint Stanisław, one of John Paul's early predecessors as bishop of Kraków, and the pope took advantage of the opportunity to discuss the saint and his significance. John Paul also planned side trips to his hometown of Wadowice, to one of his favorite devotional sites, at Kalwaria Zebrzydowska, and, most dramatically, to the concentration-and–death camp complex, Auschwitz-Birkenau. That was one of the major highlights of this visit, along with his celebration of mass before an enormous crowd in Kraków's spacious Commons (Błonia) and his visit to a monastery on the edge of the great working-class industrial suburb of Nowa Huta, where he celebrated mass with a homily tailored to his predominantly working-class audience.

The pope's arrival in Kraków on June 6 marked the first time during the visit that the regime made a blatant show of force, with a convoy of approximately seventy-five vehicles filled with militia members driving down the city's main boulevard as crowds proceeded to the site where John Paul's helicopter would land.[78] The militia were jeered and booed as they drove past Kraków's complex of student dormitories. Despite this reminder of their presence, police generally stayed out of the way during the pope's sojourn in Kraków; most of them were stationed on the city's outskirts, controlling entry into the city and remaining on hand should they be needed to quell unrest.

After a short greeting upon arrival, the pope addressed clergy at Wawel Cathedral, where he announced that Saint Stanisław's feast day was being elevated to an obligatory memorial on the calendar of the universal Church. The next day, John Paul visited two places of great significance to his early life—the shrine of Kalwaria Zebrzydowska and his hometown of Wadowice. The high point and culmination of the day, however, was his visit to Auschwitz-Birkenau, where the pope gave what was one of his most significant homilies of his entire career.

John Paul's visit consisted of two parts—a stop at the concentration camp, Auschwitz I, and a mass at Auschwitz II, or Birkenau, the notorious Nazi death camp.[79] The former event was not open to the public, though large crowds lined the road that the pope traveled from his helicopter landing to the gates of the camp. John Paul walked right through the infamous wrought iron gate bearing the words "Arbeit Macht Frei" to pay a visit to block 11, and in particular to cell 18, where Maximilian Kolbe, a Polish Franciscan friar, voluntarily offered to take the place of a fellow inmate who, upon being selected by the Nazis for death by starvation, lamented that he had a wife and children. After kneeling and praying in the cell, kissing the floor, and leaving a bouquet of red and white flowers and an Easter candle brought from Rome, the pope proceeded to the adjacent courtyard, where he laid flowers and knelt in prayer at yet another infamous site, the "Wall of Death," against which as many as twenty thousand prisoners had been shot. Attendance at this visit was limited to dignitaries of Church and state, some of whose presence was highly symbolic. For example, West Germany's Cardinal Hermann Volk accompanied the pope to the Wall of Death. In addition, John Paul embraced seventy-eight-year-old Franciszek Gajowniczek, who was alive because it was his place

Kolbe had taken in the starvation cell back in 1941. Finally, high-level representatives of the communist regime were also on hand, including Kąkol and Poland's foreign minister, Emil Wojtaszek.

Next the pope took the short two-mile trip to Birkenau by helicopter. The event, a mass before a vast audience, was of a substantially different nature than the one at Auschwitz I, and the venue was rife with symbolism. The altar was built over the former terminus of the railroad tracks, and it was topped with barbed wire. Above the altar was a large, rough-hewn cross, with a ring of barbed wire at its center reminiscent of the crown of thorns worn by Jesus Christ at his execution. Hanging from the cross was a piece of cloth made to resemble a prisoner uniform from Auschwitz, with the red triangle that identified Polish inmates inscribed with Kolbe's number—16670. Television cables were strung through barbed wire, and papal flags flew from the rotting wooden watchtowers. Camp survivors, wearing camp uniforms, were given a place of honor and received Holy Communion directly from the pope. The two hundred of them who were clergy concelebrated the mass with John Paul. The liturgical color was red, representing martyrdom, and the pope changed into his vestments in a former women's barracks. The site also featured a row of memorial tablets written in the languages of the victims at the camp, a monument to the "martyrdom of nations." Significantly, John Paul stopped to reflect at three of the nineteen tablets—the ones in Hebrew, in Russian, and in Polish.

The crowd gathered for the mass was estimated at anywhere between hundreds of thousands and a million.[80] John Paul opened his homily by speaking of Maximilian Kolbe's heroic act of self-sacrifice, which, according to the pope, brought the victory of faith and love to a place "built for hatred and for the contempt for man . . . a place built for cruelty."[81] He likened Kolbe's "spiritual victory" to that of Jesus Christ himself on the cross. Such acts of love by Kolbe and others in the camps represented a manifestation of humanity in the face of a system that horribly trampled human dignity. As with the deaths of Saints Wojciech and Stanisław, Kolbe's martyrdom too brought fruits, a witness to the power of love even in the grimmest of circumstances.

Alongside his emphasis on the fruits that come from suffering, a motif of the papal pilgrimage overall, John Paul also reiterated another major theme of his tour—human dignity and the human rights that flow from it. Referring to his first and recent encyclical *Redemptoris hominis*, of which human rights was a central feature, the pope spoke of the United Nations Declaration of Human Rights and the words of fifteenth-century Polish political thinker Paweł Włodkowic to affirm the rights both of individuals and of nations.[82] This emphasis also held a central place in John Paul's assessment of the horrors witnessed at this site. As Jonathan Huener points out, John Paul situated Poland's wartime losses within the broader context of Poles' struggle for national independence, thereby implying a parallel with the contemporary situation.[83] We see this in the pope's words before the memorial tablet in the Polish language, when he said, after mentioning the millions of Poles who died during the war, "Once again a stage of the age-old struggle of this nation, my nation, for its fundamental rights among the nations of Europe. Once again a loud shout for the right to its own place on the map of Europe."[84]

Woven through the papal homily at Birkenau were reasons for the horrors. John Paul spoke of an "insane ideology" in which "the rights of man were subordinated to the requirements of the system . . . subordinated so absolutely that they in fact do not exist." Along with ideology and violation of human rights, the pope also associated the mass murder at Auschwitz with war itself, with its "calculated technology of annihilation." Pointing to an antidote to these problems, he cited the two predecessors from whom he took his double name, John XXIII and Paul VI—Pope John's confirmation of the dignity of the human person and inviolable and inalienable human rights, in his encyclical *Pacem in terris*, and Pope Paul's appeal "never again war, never again war!" from his 1965 address to the United Nations.[85] This call for peace, along with several references to human rights, and their violation, elicited strong applause from the multitude present.

The homily at Birkenau is particularly important in terms of how John Paul dealt with three groups with whom Poles have traditionally had problematic relationships—Germans, Jews, and Russians. The pope made it clear that God's commandment of love of neighbor meant "respect for the other," dialogue with the other, "the capacity of seeking and recognizing what can be good and positive also in someone who confesses ideas differing from ours, and even in someone who to a certain degree errs." Citing the teaching of Pope John XXIII, John Paul asserted that "never can one nation be developed at the cost of another . . . at the price of dependence, conquest, rape, of its exploitation, of its death." However, John Paul clearly did not want to use the occasion at Auschwitz to incite Polish animosity toward the Germans. In keeping with a practice he carried through his entire pilgrimage, with very little exception, he deliberately did not refer to them by name. He stated, "We are standing at a place where we want to think about every nation and every person as a brother," adding that he had come to remember, not to accuse.[86] These conciliatory comments were well received, as evidenced by several surges of lengthy applause from the crowd.

Regarding Jews, the pope made a point of pausing before the Hebrew-language tablet, noting in his homily that the sons and daughters of this nation were destined for total extermination. This demonstrative show of respect was especially significant given that the Polish communist regime had long either underemphasized wartime Jewish suffering or subsumed it under a more broadly conceived suffering of Poles.[87] In other ways, however, John Paul's approach to the Jewish legacy at Auschwitz was problematic and ambiguous to some degree. First, when seeking to explain the reasons for the mass killing, he made no mention of antisemitism. His assignment of causes for the horror were ideology, war, and the violation of national rights, and in the case of the Jews, the right to exist. Second, when referring to the traditional (and now revised) number of "four million people of various nations" killed at Auschwitz, the pope did not mention that the overwhelming majority of those killed were Jews.[88] Third, while in his homage to the Jews at the Hebrew tablet he referred to them as a nation, when he spoke of the impact of the six million lives lost by the Polish nation during the war, he clearly counted Jews as part of the Polish nation.[89] This reflects a long-standing (and still-standing) ambiguity as to whether Jews in Poland are also Poles or members of a separate nation living in Poland as Polish citizens. It becomes particularly problematic when it seems to mask Jewish losses and/or inflate Polish losses. Fourth, at one point in his homily John Paul referred to Auschwitz as "this Golgotha of our times." This phrase epitomized one of the thrusts of the pope's address, which was in effect to reclaim the memory of Auschwitz from the communists and bring it into line with popular Polish Catholic understanding, with its stress on meaningful sacrifice and heroic resistance for faith and fatherland.[90] However, though in no way intended as antisemitic, such an analogy associating Jesus's death at Calvary (which Christians traditionally blamed on Jews) with the site where nearly one million Jews were killed could hardly be welcomed by Jews. Finally, despite the heroism of Maximilian Kolbe, he was a controversial figure in Polish-Jewish relations, given his association with antisemitic media in Poland in the 1920s and 1930s.[91]

It was John Paul's approach to the Russians, however, that carried the most political weight at the moment of his pilgrimage. After pausing before the Hebrew tablet and before pausing at the Polish one, the pope stopped at the Russian one. In his homily he stated, "The tablet with an inscription in the Russian language, I add no commentary. We know about what sort of nation this tablet speaks. We know what was the share of this nation in the final terrible war for the freedom of peoples. Also before this tablet we are not permitted to pass indifferently." This acknowledgment of Russia's role in the defeat of Nazi Germany, even if understated, greatly pleased the communists.[92] These words did not appear in the pope's written text for the occasion but were inserted by the pope extemporaneously, surely in an effort to ease the government's anxiety that the Soviet role in the defeat of the Nazis in Poland would not be given its due.[93] At the same time, a number of references in the papal address, particularly those connected with human rights and their violation and with suppression of national independence, could apply to both the Nazi and communist regimes. While the government could regard these simply as condemnations of the Nazis, the crowd no doubt also saw them as applying to past and present Soviet and communist abuses against Poles, as evidenced by the strong applause such references sparked.[94]

The communists expressed, both publicly and in their internal documents, pleasure at the pope's comments at Auschwitz about Polish heroism and suffering, Nazi atrocities, peace, and the Soviet contribution to the defeat of Nazi Germany.[95] Moreover, though the pope stated explicitly that he did not come to Auschwitz to accuse, he at least did not issue the feared (by the regime) call for Polish-German reconciliation. Alongside the meeting with Gierek at Belvedere, the Auschwitz visit was the event to which the communists devoted the most attention in their efforts to portray the papal pilgrimage as a success for the regime and an affirmation of much of what Poland's government stood for. However, like that earlier event, this one too gave John Paul ample opportunity to make statements that for Poles could apply not just to the wartime occupation but also to the ensuing three decades under communist and Soviet hegemony. Talk of violations of human rights and of national sovereignty, and specifically the subordination of human rights to the system to the point where such rights no longer existed, could easily sound to a Polish audience in summer 1979 as an indictment of the regime under which they were currently living. Moreover, the pope's appreciation of the Polish nation's age-old struggle "for its fundamental rights among the nations of Europe," as he put it when referring to the Polish-language tablet at Birkenau, also had a contemporary ring.

The next day, June 8, the pope visited the rural agricultural center of Nowy Targ. There, before a gigantic crowd consisting of large numbers of the local highlander population (the Górale), with their colorful costumes, characteristic music, carved wooden altar, and backdrop of the Tatra Mountains, he praised farmers and their work and spoke in defense of marriage and family and against abortion, among other things. Early in his homily John Paul expressed his regret that some pilgrims from across the nearby border (chiefly Slovaks and Czechs, presumably) were unable to enter the country to attend the papal mass.[96] Later in the day, the pope celebrated mass at Wawel Cathedral in Kraków to mark the conclusion of the archdiocesan synod, then gave a speech to representatives of the world of science and culture in the Pauline church at nearby Skałka. This was followed by a speech to tens of thousands of youth assembled outside the church, at which John Paul announced that he was discarding his prepared text; he instead gave a talk on the Church's ministry to academic youth in Poland, a rather light-hearted address filled with reminiscences more appropriate to the festive occasion.[97] The event included much singing, chanting, and bantering with the pontiff, who was in a jovial mood. Near the end of his talk, however, John Paul got more serious and included the concluding section of the talk he had prepared. He told Poland's youth that the future depended on them, and he exhorted them to fear not hardship but frivolity and pusillanimity and to be honest, sober, and faithful, "with freedom of spirit and force of conviction," to be consistent in their faith, confide in Mary, and follow Jesus Christ.

The prepared comments that the pope opted not to deliver are worth considering in greater detail.[98] Key portions of them were drawn from a letter that John Paul had written to Mexican youth who had participated in a meeting with him at the Shrine of Our Lady of Guadalupe on January 31. The letter spoke of how young people "deeply feel the evil that lies heavily over the life of the nations of which they are sons and daughters." These youth "fret over the need for change, the need to create a better world, more just and more worthy of man"; they "correctly express objections to the great injustices, discriminations, violence, and torments inflicted upon people." George Weigel surmises that John Paul may have set aside these prepared remarks because he had sensed or been warned that a political demonstration might break out. Indeed, some students hoisted a large cross near the end of the talk, which led thousands in attendance to pull out smaller crosses they had brought to the event.[99] After the event, a group of about 150 students proceeded with the cross to Kraków's Commons, the site of the big papal mass the next day, and planted it in the ground next to the altar.[100]

On June 9, the pope addressed the Council of the Pontifical

Theological Academy, as well as an assembly of the sick and their caregivers at the Franciscan church and a group of female religious. The high point of the day, however, was the mass he celebrated outside the monastery at Mogiła, on the edge of Nowa Huta, the mammoth settlement the communists had constructed adjacent to Kraków for those employed at the equally mammoth heavy industries nearby. Not permitted to visit Nowa Huta, the pope came as close as he could by visiting Mogiła, a famous pilgrimage site since the thirteenth century, with its shrine housing a reputedly miraculous image of Jesus Christ crucified. Haunting the event, however, was the Ark of the Lord Church in the district of Bieńczyce. As Archbishop Wojtyła, the pope had been instrumental in a two-decade struggle to get this church constructed in Nowa Huta, intentionally built without houses of worship.[101] After the reforms of 1956, the state granted the Church permission to erect a place of worship in Nowa Huta. In anticipation of the construction, local Catholics erected a cross on the site destined for the new church. When the regime later canceled plans for the church and sought to remove the cross in April 1960, thousands of Poles turned up to protest and to defend the cross, and violent clashes took place between protesters and police.[102]

Prevented on this trip from visiting this church he had helped found, John Paul threw a bouquet of flowers onto it from his helicopter. Meanwhile, two nights earlier, thousands of parishioners from the Ark of the Lord Church marched to Mogiła in a candlelight procession carrying one of the devotional treasures of their church—an icon of the Black Madonna, purportedly made from shrapnel removed from Polish soldiers wounded at the Battle of Monte Cassino during World War II.[103] John Paul would bless this icon as part of the service at Mogiła. Upon arrival, flanked by vast and exuberant crowds consisting largely of workers from Nowa Huta and their families, the pope made his way from the helicopter to the altar, even riding past a statue of Lenin draped in papal colors.[104]

The Mogiła homily was an exemplary illustration of John Paul's clever approach to his audience, as well as to the regime.[105] He expressed his "greatest respect and esteem" for the gigantic industrial complex at Nowa Huta and his solidarity with the directors, engineers, steelworkers, and ministers who built it. He also reiterated that the Church wanted to come to an understanding "with each regime of labor," asking only that it "allow the Church to speak to man about Christ and to love man with the measure of the dignity of man." However, in a manner not typical of Catholic discourse, John Paul interwove themes of evangelization with Catholic social teaching on labor. He included himself as one of Nowa Huta's builders, thanks to his work in getting that city a church. Moreover, he connected Nowa Huta with the cross of Christ, declaring several times that "Nowa Huta was built on the foundation of the Cross of Christ." Referring both to the ancient cross at Mogiła and the recent cross that the Ark of the Lord Church had brought to Nowa Huta, the pope noted that Mogiła's monastery, with its shrine of the Crucifixion, was a testament to the Christianization of Poland and that another cross now stood in Nowa Huta, testifying to a new evangelization. The pope then went on to link Christ's cross with the world of labor, noting that "the mystery of the Cross is deeply inscribed in the work of man." According to John Paul, "It is not possible to separate the Cross from human labor. It is not possible to separate Christ from human labor." Referring to his own experiences with manual labor during the war, when he worked at the Solvay firm's quarry and chemical plant near Kraków, the pope emphasized "the dignity of work as a measure of the dignity of man" and shared his view that the "problematic of the person of labor" cannot be ultimately solved without the Gospel, because "Christ will never agree that man is recognized—or recognizes himself—only as an instrument of production."

The crowd was smaller than normal for papal events, given the limitations of the venue, but it was in high spirits, interrupting John Paul on more than forty occasions.[106] Papal references to the connection of Jesus Christ, the Gospel, and the Church with human labor and with the defense of the dignity of the worker especially resonated with the crowd, as did the pope's words about building Nowa Huta on the foundation of Christ's cross and his own past experience as a worker. The ebullient audience sang "Sto Lat" and other festive songs, chanted "Long live the Pope," and engaged in banter with the pope for much of the homily.

The pope's address to workers on the threshold of Nowa Huta had several fascinating dimensions. First, he expressed no criticism of Nowa Huta itself, though he easily could have noted the ecological damage caused by such a great industrial complex, the economic problems with such industrial giganticism, or the social problems connected with vast and shoddily constructed housing estates. He focused only on the positive, praising Nowa Huta as a great achievement. Second, he was masterfully disingenuous in finding the meaning of Nowa Huta in the cross of Christ. This was a settlement built by the communists explicitly as an atheistic town devoid of churches or religious symbolism. In seizing on the ancient cross of Christ at the nearby monastery and making the thrust of his homily the connection between Nowa Huta, as well as labor in general, with Jesus Christ and his cross, John Paul was taking something the communists were proud of, sharing that pride, and then turning it into an evangelical statement. In professing that Nowa Huta was founded on the cross of Christ, that its history is written through the cross, he was in fact blatantly impinging on a realm in which the communists jealously guarded their ownership, and no doubt Poland's leaders were disturbed by the direction the pope took the address. Finally, the pope used the occasion to recall and highlight his own successful efforts to build a church in Nowa Huta, and he called on Poles to continue to build churches. Along these lines, he made reference to Father Józef, a local priest who had devoted the best years of his young life to attempts at establishing a parish church in the nearby district of Mistrzejowice.[107] Overall, John Paul at Mogiła demonstrated skillfully how a homily focusing almost exclusively on religious themes could still contest the regime in areas it felt were its own purview.

Later in the day, John Paul returned to the theme of Saint Stanisław when he addressed a delegation of bishops from abroad invited to Poland for the commemoration of Stanisław's martyrdom.[108] Again, John Paul's message was cleverly mixed—Stanisław was an example of "creative synthesis" between loyalty to the Church and fidelity to the fatherland (the latter being something the regime would welcome, though Poles surely knew that love of fatherland and love of its government or governing system were not synonymous), but he was also a model of courage for bishops engaged in transmitting and defending the faith, a model the authorities would surely not want to see emulated very much in Poland. Later that day, John Paul visited the graves of his parents at the nearby Rakowice cemetery, met with nuns at a church in Kraków's Old Town, hosted dignitaries at the archepiscopal palace, and attended a concert at the Franciscan church that featured the premiere of "Beatus Vir" by the great Polish composer and "holy minimalist" Henryk Górecki.

The next day the pope held his final large-scale event during the pilgrimage, a mass at the Commons in Kraków. The liturgical occasion was the feast of the Most Holy Trinity, or Trinity Sunday. The crowds may have been the largest of the entire pilgrimage, with some estimates even as high as two million or three million.[109] The homily kept largely to religious matters, though given the social dimension of Catholic theology, the particulars of the Polish situation, and the character of John Paul, it not surprisingly carried some political overtones.[110] For example, he noted that Poles were living in "a difficult epoch in our history," and he asked them to "pray for the victory of moral order." He also stated twice that "it is necessary to open the borders," and while greeting pilgrims in attendance from south of Poland's border, he expressed his solidarity with those Slavic peoples whose absence he felt and who were "all the more in our hearts and in our prayers."

A chief focus of the homily was Saint Stanisław. The pope, having already employed Stanisław in a variety of ways connected with the spiritual, political, and cultural points he wished to make (for example, as role model for bishops, patron of Poland's moral order, patron of Polish unity, and link with the rest of Western Christian Europe), added yet another dimension to the Polish understanding of that medieval saint. In this case, it was the bishop-martyr's connection to the sacrament of confirmation. In his homily, the pope took the concept of national baptism and added to it the concept of national confirmation. Just as the baptism of Prince Mieszko, leader of the Poles when he accepted Christianity in 966, was regarded symbolically as the baptism of the Polish nation, so Stanisław's martyrdom in 1079 was the nation's symbolic confirmation.[111] As John Paul explained, just as confirmation marks the passage of a young man or woman into adulthood in the faith, strengthening them so as to be courageous witnesses to Christ, so Stanisław's death marked the maturation of the faith of the young Polish nation, ripe enough in 1079 to bear witness to Christian morality to the point of martyrdom. Then the pope did something remarkable—he bestowed a "confirmation" on his audience, telling those present that he wished to transmit to them that same Spirit that the apostles, Saint Stanisław, and Poland's bishops down through the ages had passed on. Quoting a series of scriptural verses connected with the action of the Holy Spirit, John Paul performed a symbolic "laying of hands" on Poles, with the intent of strengthening their faith at this key moment in history.[112]

In his homily at the Kraków Commons, the pope also sought to inspire Poles and connect them to their traditional faith in other ways as well. He called on Poles to embrace the whole spiritual heritage of a thousand years of Christianity in Poland, a heritage that he could not imagine a Pole repudiating. For John Paul, one's national heritage was a "treasure," a "spiritual fund," a "great common good" confirmed "by each choice, by every noble deed, by every life lived in an authentically Christian way." This, in the pope's estimation, is what constituted Polish identity and sustained it over the centuries and what Poles rejected at their own peril.

As was so often the case during this visit, John Paul expressed kind words of gratitude to the regime for inviting him to Poland and to the local authorities for facilitating his visit. He also expressed his regret that, due to his busy schedule, he was unable to meet with the Polish Ecumenical Council, the body representing Poland's religious minorities, and conveyed his hope and desire for a future meeting. At the end of the mass, the pope was "nearly engulfed by ecstatic followers" as he made his way to the papal motorcade.[113]

Later that day, after giving a few short remarks to the journalists who had been covering his visit, speaking to them in English, French, Italian, and Polish, John Paul arrived at the airport at Balice outside Kraków.[114] John Paul concluded the pilgrimage on a number of positive notes. He once again thanked the government for its invitation and its kindness in helping during his visit. He mentioned in particular the meeting at Belvedere and expressed the hope that it would lead to a further favorable development of relations between the Church and the state, as well as between the Vatican and Poland. He commended both Church and regime for their courage in bringing this extraordinary visit about and said he regarded this cooperation as an "enormously needed" witness to the rapprochement between nations and the cause of world peace. The pope ended by wishing prosperity and success to Poland and bestowing his blessing.

John Paul's last contact with Poland during this visit was the message he sent from his departing plane. He yet again expressed his gratitude to the central and local authorities for their goodwill toward him and their efforts in making his visit possible. He wished continued progress for Poland "in the realms of spiritual, moral, cultural, societal, and economic life" and expressed his confidence that relations between Church and state and between the Vatican and Poland would improve.[115]

CONCLUDING ASSESSMENT

John Paul's optimistic concluding assessment of the visit, which masked far more than it affirmed, was mirrored by the regime's public assessments of the pilgrimage. The party presented its perspective on the visit to the Polish public in very positive terms. An article in the intellectually oriented Communist Party weekly *Polityka*, written by its editor in chief, Mieczysław Rakowski, summed up the visit in just such a way.[116] Reacting to a view ascribed to Western media, such as CBS News, that the communist regime had greeted the pope with "indifference," Rakowski noted the presence of Poland's head of state and other government ministers at John Paul's airport arrival and departure, Gierek's meeting with him at Belvedere, the large role played by state authorities in preparing and organizing the visit, and the "extensive" coverage devoted to the visit by the state's media.[117] Rakowski approvingly noted John Paul's realism, his avoidance of confrontation, his encouragement of Church-state dialogue, his obvious affection for his native land, his recognition of the achievements of Poland since 1945, his praise of labor, and his calls for rapprochement between different nations and systems. Rakowski rejected Western media reports that the large turnouts at the papal events were driven by religious, or even political motivations, arguing that popular curiosity, the desire to participate in extraordinary events, John Paul's charisma, and patriotic pride in a pope who was a Pole all contributed to the large audiences.

The Communist Party's chief daily newspaper, *Trybuna Ludu*, had a similar perspective on the papal visit.[118] Marian Kuszewski, in an article filled with communist self-congratulation, emphasized the well-organized nature of the trip and the discipline and cultured demeanor of the Polish audiences. He appreciated the pope's support for peaceful coexistence and international cooperation and his opposition to the arms race. He also liked John Paul's high regard for labor, in both its economic and its ethical dimensions, which to Kuszewski was in accord with fundamental socialist values. Of the major papal speeches, the article cited the ones at Belvedere, where John Paul expressed appreciation for the socioeconomic development of Poland since World War II and gratitude to Gierek for all he had done for Poland; at Jasna Góra, where the pope encouraged Poland's bishops to pursue Church-state cooperation and dialogue; and at Auschwitz-Birkenau, where John Paul recognized the Soviet role in the liberation of Europeans from Nazism and insisted that the crimes of genocide would not be forgotten. Both Rakowski and Kuszewski recognized that important differences existed between the pope (and Catholic Church) and the regime but regarded these as a normal feature of a pluralistic world. Both authors pointed to John Paul's Christological view of history as a major difference with the Marxists, Rakowski noting John Paul's assertion that Christianity lies at the heart of understanding European history and Kuszewski acknowledging "historiosophical" differences between the pope and the regime. Both articles, each in one of the very top-level Communist Party periodicals, attest to the importance the regime placed on presenting the papal visit as a success on many levels—organizational, political, and international, among others.

Certainly John Paul said and did a number of things that the regime appreciated. His words of gratitude to his hosts, his calls for peace and disarmament, his praise of Poland's accomplishments since 1945, his support for the country's northern and western borders, his commemoration of wartime Polish heroism and condemnation of Nazi atrocities, and his recognition of the Soviet role in defeating Germany were all in tune with the party's interests. Moreover, the fact that he did not emulate Charles de Gaulle's outburst in Quebec and that he jettisoned his prepared speech to youth at Skałka showed that John Paul was prudent enough to avoid outright provocation. The government, party, and police analysts commenting on the visit during or shortly after it noticed several other things they liked about the pilgrimage. It was noted that the pope's exhortation to Poles to live morally could boost public morality, strengthen the family, and increase Poles' obligation toward the common good. It could also contribute to fighting social ills such as alcohol abuse, shoddy work performance, theft of public property, and failure to honor commitments.[119] It was also noted that the pope kept Poland's political opposition at arm's length. One police report made the claim that the pope's clerical entourage was instructed to keep dissidents from having direct access to John Paul.[120] A government analyst, meanwhile, remarked that while the pope did meet with Catholic activists, for example, those from *Tygodnik Powszechny*, the Catholic journal *Więź*, and the Club of the Catholic Intelligentsia, his relationship with them seemed less close than when he was their archbishop.[121]

Still, John Paul said quite a bit that rankled Poland's political authorities. He brought up uncomfortable events of the past, namely, the Soviet Union's failure to aid the Warsaw Uprising in 1944 and the regime's refusal to allow Paul VI to visit for the millennial celebrations in 1966. He stressed the central role of Jesus Christ, Mary, and the

Catholic Church and faith in Poland's history and culture. He called for European unity on a Christian foundation and reached out to the Slavic and Orthodox peoples of Eastern Europe in a way that challenged Soviet cultural hegemony in the region. He expressed his solidarity with the "forgotten churches" of the Soviet bloc and openly complained that some pilgrims were being prevented from crossing national borders in order to see him. And he called on Poles, especially youth, to take risks. Also significant was what the pope did not say during his visit. Some analysts noted that he made no mention of the upcoming thirty-fifth anniversary of the Polish People's Republic. Moreover, when he did raise the kind of issues the regime wanted him to, such as peace, disarmament, and relaxation of international tensions, he did not do so "sufficiently concretely."[122] He failed to call ideologies, systems, or states by name, and he failed to point out the sources of social injustice, imperialism, and exploitation of the developing world (that is, the imperialist, capitalist West). As one analyst put it, John Paul spoke in terms of good and evil, "as if independent of the existing divisions and systems," and not in terms of socialist and capitalist.[123]

Apart from the content of his speeches and homilies, regime analysts commented negatively on John Paul's overall style. Reports from the Office of Confessional Affairs and the Ministry of the Interior noted that the pope would deviate from his prepared texts at times, playing to the audience, raising sensitive issues, and then letting the crowd use its applause to provide emphasis. The reports observed that John Paul used allusions, metaphors, and subtexts in order to provoke certain reactions from the crowd; he also cracked jokes and encouraged singing.[124] One police report stated that some Western journalists and diplomats saw the pope as seeking "cheap popularity" and that some clergy thought John Paul was transforming religious ceremonies into political rallies by including political subtexts in his addresses.[125] The pope, according to government and police reports, was accused of turning his events into "theatrical performances" and undercutting, through informalities, the dignity of the papal office.[126] These reports also claimed that even Wyszyński himself had concerns about the pope's unconventional approach to his high office, citing the cardinal's gentle admonition to John Paul at Gniezno in which he told him that "you opened your heart yesterday with such youthful freshness, as if at that moment you forgot the weight of responsibility for the entire universal Church weighing on you."[127]

Characteristic of John Paul's approach was that statements and gestures that on the surface might seem in harmony with communist objectives often contained a second edge that cut against the regime's views and interests. Yes, John Paul called for improved Church-state relations, but he also encouraged the Church in Poland to push for things like increased church construction and greater media access. Yes, he called for national unity, but he did so in a context in which the most imaginable national unity would be one where Poles united behind the pope and their Church in opposing the regime. Yes, he spoke of Polish heroism and suffering during the war, but he reminded his audience of the bitter disappointments of that time, most of which could be laid at the feet of the Soviet Union. Yes, he praised national sovereignty, human rights, and the rights of nations, but he did so with the implication that the regime was not effectively defending these goods. Yes, he praised Poland's industrial accomplishments over recent decades, but he coupled that praise with affirmations of the strong Christian faith of Poland's workers. Yes, he praised alliance systems founded on mutual respect, but he did so without pretending that Poland was a member of such. Yes, he spoke out to youth against being indifferent, but he did so in a context where engagement was far more likely to lead a young person to Catholic activism or political dissent rather than to Marxism or support for the regime. Yes, he had kind words for Vatican diplomat Casaroli, but he pushed an Ostpolitik far more challenging to the communists than the one Casaroli had been pursuing under Paul VI. When the pope thanked and praised Poland's leaders, he was actually challenging them. When he thanked the state militia for helping to keep order, he was in fact reminding them that they were Poles and should act in accord with that identity. Time and again John Paul, from the pilgrimage's beginning to its end, found ways to pressure the regime while remaining within the parameters for the visit worked out by Poland's government and Church leaders that spring.

During his visit, John Paul demonstrated how ostensibly or even genuinely religious words and gestures could carry political implications. For example, in calling down the Holy Spirit upon Poles at Victory Square, he made it clear that the country needed "renewal." One could easily infer that this meant more than spiritual renewal and could include economic and political renewal, among other kinds. His bestowing of a symbolic confirmation on his mass audience at the Commons in Kraków was aimed at strengthening Poles to meet their present challenges, a good deal of which could be ascribed to the practices and policies of the regime and Poland's situation in the Soviet bloc. The pope's statement that living the Gospel life entails risk could encourage Poles to challenge or resist their government in various ways, and his repeated affirmations that good fruits can come out of suffering could comfort those Poles who were paying a price for such resistance.

One further dimension of the pilgrimage worth exploring was the establishment of groups of "ecclesial crowd marshals" (literally, "ecclesial order service," or *kościelna służba porządkowa*), set up by the Church to aid with crowd management. On the one hand, it has been argued that the regime made a "strategic error" in having the Church participate in crowd control. As Weigel asserts, "People who had been told for thirty years that they were incapable of organizing themselves independently of the state or the party could now test that claim empirically."[128] On the other hand, regime analysts of the visit tended to justify the decision, seeing benefits coming to the regime from this case of state-Church cooperation. Not only did this set-up provide needed personnel for crowd management, but it also made the Church accountable for maintaining order and minimized the sort of tensions that might arise if the state alone was responsible for keeping papal audiences and spectators in line. Having the Church provide marshals, according to one analyst, also made it more difficult for the Western press to blame the regime in the event of pilgrims being obstructed.[129]

In the immediate aftermath of the papal visit, several Catholic periodicals, including *Znak*, *Tygodnik Powszechny*, and *Więź*, invited readers to send in accounts of their personal experiences and thoughts concerning the papal pilgrimage. In analyzing these materials, numbering 87 published and 132 unpublished reports, two psychology professors, one of whom attended six of the most important large-scale papal events of 1979 in Poland, provide some insight as to how Poles processed these events at the time.[130] These accounts attest to a feeling of unity among participants in the massive celebrations, a deep identification with others present, the feeling of being part of a greater whole, and a sense that the enormous crowd shared similar values—personal, Polish, Christian, and Western. Moreover, these values were regarded as reinforced during the events, in opposition to or alternative to many of the values of the regime. Participants reported that they did not feel lost in an anonymous multitude but instead felt a deep connection with John Paul and others. Their connection was enhanced by wave-like rhythms of clapping, cheering, and chanting flowing through the enormous crowds.

Similar conclusions were reached by Józef Makselon in his study of the papal pilgrimages.[131] Regarding the 1979 visit, he noted that "a hitherto unprecedented explosion of positive feelings took place." Each site visited by the pope produced "a unique psychosocial microclimate" where feelings of security and mutual affinity dominated. There was a sense that the crowds shared common values and were conscious of this. Makselon also noted that the level of applause, which punctuated many of the papal homilies, was unprecedented in Poland at religious services.

One also gets a sense of how particular Poles viewed the visit of John Paul, especially those prominent in cultural, intellectual, or political life, from the accounts published in Catholic journals such as the monthly *Więź*. For example, the distinguished poet Anna Kamieńska wrote that everyone seemed to be "carried away" by the experience.[132] "We lived through some kind of great visitation," she wrote. "It was as if a perpetually open place of longing and loneliness became filled." She added that everyone wept when John Paul left and that Poles felt "orphaned" by his departure. She too noted the break with precedent as crowds interrupted religious ceremonies with applause. Kamieńska summed up the visit as a "short therapy of joy and love" that was "very necessary for us," a people who had not experienced joy for a long time.

Other important figures added their perspectives. Jan Józef Lipski, a Warsaw Uprising veteran and longtime dissident as well as co-founder of KOR, wrote of how John Paul's visit had an impact on everyone in Poland—those faithful to, indifferent to, and even averse to the Church; the learned and the uneducated. He noted the feelings of unity, euphoria, and enchantment of a nation "spellbound" by the pope's presence.[133] Catholic activist Stanisław Stomma spoke of the "deep and serious rejoicing" of Poles as they experienced an event of historic proportions, one that made an "enormous impact" and brought a "deep ferment"; it was a "genuine confirmation."[134] The writer Jan Józef Szczepański also noted the gravity and historical scale of the events and remarked that the crowds seemed to sense this as well and behaved accordingly.[135]

Some of these contributors confessed that they had certain fears in advance of the pilgrimage, fears that as it turned out were unfounded. Szczepański, for example, had anticipated organizational problems— brutally jostling crowds, "communications disasters," lack of food provisions, overall messiness, and vandalism, and he was pleasantly surprised at how well things came off. Lipski feared an atmosphere of emotional triumphalism around the visit, and Szczepański worried about expressions of bigotry and fanaticism. None of their apprehensions came to pass. Lipski also had concerns about the possible limited impact of the papal visit—he feared the Poles would treat the pope's statements as sacrosanct and unassailable, letting John Paul do the thinking for them. He thought people would hear what they wanted to hear and not what the pope was actually saying. He feared that John Paul's summons to courage would remain an unheeded platitude and his teaching degenerate into a list of quotations rather than lead to understanding and action.

More hopeful was the view that had been expressed before the

start of the papal visit by leading Catholic activist Tadeusz Mazowiecki, who wrote that "the Pope's visit will inject new energy into society.
The masses will feel stronger; they will understand that they should
demand more. These nine days will be a religious event; of course,
they will also shape the consciousness of the people."[36] Events over the
next year would show that Mazowiecki's prediction would be closer
to the reality than Lipski's worries. John Paul's visit would serve as
the catalyst for upcoming upheavals.

2

COMFORTER

The 1983 Pilgrimage

IN THE IMMEDIATE AFTERMATH OF THE 1979 PAPAL VISIT, LIFE seemed to get back to normal. The regime carried on with business as usual, and Poles headed off for their summer vacations. Although certain features of the pilgrimage, such as the astronomical public interest in the events and the high and engaging participation of youth, bothered the regime, it was relieved that the pilgrimage went off without any serious public disturbances and that the political opposition remained on the margins during its course.[1] Although the authorities knew they had tough work ahead in trying to counter the growing social influence of the Church, there was little sense that the situation was irreversible or that the emergence of a mass political movement was on the horizon.[2]

Nevertheless, a lot had happened during the pilgrimage that would change Poles in fundamental ways, elevating their aspirations, increasing their confidence, and making them harder to govern. As a number of scholars and other observers have noted, the nine-day pilgrimage had a transformative effect on society. First of all, it had raised hopes. According to opinion surveys, 71 percent of Poles expected a postpilgrimage improvement in the Church's situation and influence in their country.[3] Such expectations were not misplaced, for the pilgrimage made it clear, as Andrzej Friszke and Marcin Zaremba put it, that the Church's social capital now outweighed the government's institutional capital.[4] Furthermore, Poles had gotten a taste of freedom. For the first time since communists took over their country, the public square was dominated by non–Communist Party voices. The regime's monopoly on public discourse was broken in dramatic fashion. Enormous crowds almost daily attended events, witnessed ceremonies, and listened to words that were beyond the control of the party and at times even inimical to its ideology and understanding. Poles also got a taste of self-government. The events were largely organized, managed, controlled, and peopled by members of the Church and society at large, with the government not playing its customary dominant role. Moreover, a strong sense of community and a mood of mutual benevolence and social solidarity reigned among the population.[5] It was an "intoxicating climate."[6] Jan Józef Lipski from KOR noted that "people acted different: kinder to one another, disciplined yet free and relaxed, as they enjoyed these few days of internal, shared freedom. It seemed as if people had been transformed. The nation showed its other face. These were truly unusual and extraordinary days."[7] Adam Michnik, one of the most prominent members of the democratic opposition, put it best in an observation that has become classic: "Something very strange happened here. The same people who are so frustrated in everyday life, so angry and aggressive when queuing for goods, suddenly transformed themselves into a buoyant collective of dignified citizens. Discovering dignity within themselves, they became aware of their own power and strength. The Police vanished from the main streets of Warsaw; as a result, exemplary order prevailed all around. A society deprived for so long of its rights suddenly recovered its ability to take care of itself. Such was the impact of Pope John Paul II's pilgrimage to Poland."[8] By attending and participating in these mass events, and responding with enthusiasm to John Paul and his words and gestures, Poles could make it clear that their sympathies and loyalties lay with the pope, the Church, and the nation, not with the state's communist rulers. Michnik called it "a national plebiscite," even a "second baptism" of the nation.[9] Lipski, writing in the early 1980s, noted that John Paul's pilgrimage to Poland "left its mark on the consciousness of the entire nation, above all on the young," and that "spiritually, Poland before June 1979 and Poland after June 1979 seemed to be two different countries."[10]

Also significant was John Paul's message. He encouraged Poles to not give up hope, and to "be not afraid!" He presented an alternative worldview to the regime's, speaking of concepts such as human rights, the dignity of the human person, and the dignity of labor in ways the political authorities did not and could not.[11] He approached history and morality from a Polish Catholic point of view, challenging conventional communist understandings and breaking certain taboos. For example, he spoke of the "unbreakable" link between the Polish nation and Catholicism, the primacy of Jesus Christ for Poland's history, the connection between the Blessed Virgin Mary and Poland, the European and Christian roots of Polish culture, and the unity of Europe based on Christianity. As Jan Kubik notes, he reinvigorated national and religious symbols and demonstrated that social and political problems could be articulated within a non-Marxist discourse.[12] His message clearly resonated with his audiences. It seemed that pope, Church, and nation were speaking the same language, and it was the party and state that were out of step. In fact, it can be argued that the overriding framework for understanding the visit and its impact was that it delineated clear lines in Poland between "us and them," *them* being the communists, and *us* the Church and nation aligned behind its native-born pope. It was this us/them dichotomy that, as Maryjane Osa points out, would frame the upcoming Solidarity revolution in Poland.[13]

Poland's economic woes—huge foreign debt, shortages, long lines—continued into 1980, but the context was rapidly evolving in the late 1970s, to the regime's detriment. Internationally, Poland needed good relations with the West, to whom it owed much money, so the government had an incentive to be especially concerned about its behavior and international reputation. Meanwhile, oppositional activity was on the upswing. An independent (or underground) press began to develop and spread rapidly. Although the chief initiative came from the intelligentsia, publications also emerged for and by workers, farmers, and students.[14] This publishing activity in turn fostered the development of social networks and helped lay the foundation for later political activism. By the late 1970s, oppositional groups were growing in terms of numbers of people involved, types of groups, and interconnection between them.[15] Some activists were developing ties with the working class and even organizing illegal labor unions. The Church, meanwhile, not only had ties with the opposition and the workers, but, more important, its symbols, long powerful in Poland, had achieved the status of rallying points for a vast proportion of the population thanks to the papal visit. And Poles now had an elite ally sitting in the Chair of Saint Peter at the Vatican. Thus, when the next round of economic crisis and labor unrest hit Poland in July 1980, things played out differently than in the past.

When the government announced a sharp rise in the price of meat at the beginning of July, strikes broke out at various enterprises across the country. From July 1 to mid-August, there were more than two hundred strikes, in fifty locales.[16] In mid-July, Lublin experienced a large-scale work stoppage, and by mid-August, strikes had spread to the Lenin Shipyard in Gdańsk as well as to Szczecin. On August 28, coal miners also went out on strike. By August 29, more than 640,000 Poles had gone on strike at 653 enterprises.[17] This wave of strikes differed from earlier worker unrest in several ways. First was the unprecedented scale— countrywide, involving immense numbers of workers. Second, the strikers coordinated with each other. In Gdańsk and elsewhere, they formed the so-called Inter-enterprise Strike Committee (Międzyzakładowy Komitet Strajkowy, or MKS) to coordinate actions of mutual support and represent workers in talks with the government. Third, the intellectual opposition rallied to the support of workers like never before. The Committee of Defense of the Workers (KOR) had already spoken out in support of strikes by early July, and advisors from Warsaw traveled to Gdańsk to help the MKS.[18] Finally, worker demands soon went well beyond issues of wages, prices, and working conditions to encompass a broad range of concerns, which then made their way into the settlements reached between strikers and the government in late August.

A particularly salient aspect of the strikes was the blatant religious symbolism. For example, workers decorated the gates and fences of the Gdańsk shipyard with crosses and images of Our Lady of Jasna Góra and Pope John Paul II. Priests held open-air masses for workers outside the shipyard gates.[19] Although the Church leadership was initially somewhat cautious in its support, in line with Cardinal Wyszyński's long-standing policy of doing whatever he could to spare Poland massive bloodshed, it gave the strikers crucial assistance during these dramatic days and after.

The unrest culminated in a set of agreements, the most prominent being those signed in Gdańsk on August 31 between MKS chair Lech Wałęsa, a labor activist who had emerged as the strike's top leader, and the government. Wałęsa signed with a large souvenir pen that bore an image of Pope John Paul II. These so-called Gdańsk Accords included, most significantly, the acceptance of "independent, self-governing" labor unions, as well as the right to strike.[20] However, besides economic demands such as wage increases and price cuts, workers also demanded and received the release of political prisoners, the rehabilitation of workers who had lost their jobs for participating in the workers' demonstrations in 1970 and 1976, access to the mass media for those with noncommunist viewpoints, and the broadcast of Sunday mass on state radio.[21]

The accords were impactful in a number of ways. They led to the fall of Edward Gierek and his replacement by Stanisław Kania as first secretary of the party. They also spurred the creation of an independent and self-governing labor union known as Solidarity, with Wałęsa at its head; it held its organizing convention on September 17. Solidarity grew into a mass social movement, eventually encompassing from nine million to ten million members and attracting a diverse cross section of Poles, from college professors to agricultural workers, and including urban, rural, patriotic, Catholic, working-class, and intellectual components.[22] The accords also spurred similar self-organization among other groups, with farmers creating Rural Solidarity (with more than half a million members), students starting the Independent Students' Union (with eighty thousand members), and organizations forming for artists, academics, and others.[23] Even party-controlled associations for journalists and writers were taken over during the ensuing months by members sympathetic to Solidarity.

For the next sixteen months, Poland was freer and more pluralistic than any communist-ruled country had ever been. The independent press grew exponentially. Public debate was open and direct, as reform-minded Poles sought to formulate and institutionalize a different vision for their country, one that would incorporate political, economic, and social changes while still remaining in the Soviet bloc and under the headship of the Communist Party. However, these ensuing months, which began with great joy and hopefulness, soon were fraught, and the country quickly moved to the edge of crisis. The economy continued to deteriorate. The party was divided between hard-liners pushing to roll back the concessions of August 1980 and reformers more open to accommodating societal desires. The Soviet Union and Poland's Soviet bloc allies were pressing Poland's leaders to take a tougher approach to Solidarity. Solidarity itself was divided between the more radical elements, who wanted to push even harder for change, with all the risk that entailed, and those more open to compromise, hoping to consolidate their gains and seeking a modus vivendi with the regime. The Catholic Church, in the delicate position of supporting reform while opposing violence and those opposition radicals who might provoke it, sided with the moderates.[24] These months saw procrastination and obstruction by regime officials in an effort to prevent implementation of the reforms, as well as occasional incidents of violence against the new trade union. Solidarity responded by calling short-term warning strikes to press the regime to keep its side of the bargain. The Solidarity period also witnessed two tragic events at the highest echelons of the Church—an assassination attempt on May 13 against Pope John Paul II in Rome and the death of Cardinal Wyszyński on May 28 in Warsaw. Bishop Józef Glemp replaced Wyszyński as primate.

By autumn of 1981, things were heading toward a showdown. In September, Solidarity held its congress, at which it issued a declaration expressing its hopes of meeting soon with representatives of independent labor movements elsewhere in the Soviet bloc. This only increased Soviet bloc pressure on Warsaw to crack down. Moreover, many Poles by this time were getting tired of the turmoil and feared the threat that disorder could bring to their country.[25]

During the months leading up to this crisis, General Wojciech Jaruzelski, minister of defense since 1968, rose to the head of the government and party. In February 1981 he became prime minister, and on October 18 he replaced Kania as first secretary. As outside pressure mounted and the domestic situation worsened, Jaruzelski took the fateful step of declaring martial law on the night of December 12–13. Deploying tens of thousands of troops and more than one hundred thousand security force and police officers, Jaruzelski seized control of the country, suspended Solidarity, interned thousands of its members, and placed Poland under military rule.[26] In the early days of establishing martial law (and over subsequent months as well), government forces even killed a number of Poles who resisted or protested, most notoriously in the massacre of nine miners at the Wujek coal mine in Katowice on December 16. To run Poland under martial law, Jaruzelski set up a provisional institution, the Military Council of National Salvation (Wojskowa Rada Ocalenia Narodowego, or WRON).

The Polish bishops responded quickly to the imposition of military rule. Primate Glemp's overriding priority was avoidance of bloodshed. On December 13, in a homily at the Jesuit church in Warsaw, he expressed sorrow over the break in dialogue that martial law represented, called for release of the "unjustly arrested," and appealed for calm and avoidance of "fratricidal conflict."[27] In the wake of the strike-breaking massacre at Wujek, Glemp's homily at the Gniezno cathedral on December 17 likewise implored Poles to set aside hatred, passion, and conflicts.[28] More stridently, Poland's bishops issued a communiqué on December 15 in which they blamed the imposition of martial law for squandering an opportunity to reach agreement between the government and society, condemned the "dramatic limitation of civil rights," and asserted that social peace would be preserved with the restoration of the rights of the Solidarity union, not the employment of tanks.[29] That same day, the Conference of of the Episcopate of Poland also issued a document calling on all of Poland's bishops to provide moral and material assistance to the interned and their families, including pastoral visits and provision of the sacraments, and asking them to intervene by calling for the release of the interned, especially for the sick and parents with children.[30] On December 17, lay Catholics founded an organization, headquartered on Piwna Street in Warsaw, to help the interned and their families, with similar initiatives emerging across Poland with support from the local bishops.[31]

John Paul was likewise quick to respond to the imposition of martial law. Right from the start he spoke out unequivocally against it and in support of the workers' right to form independent labor unions. In a series of addresses in the aftermath of the December 13 crackdown, the pope repeatedly called for respect for human rights in Poland, including the rights of persons of labor and especially the right of workers to form self-governing and independent trade unions.[32] John Paul expressed sympathy for those arrested and their families, and he asserted the right of Poles to live and address their domestic problems in accord with their own culture and national traditions.[33] He denounced martial law as a violation of the fundamental rights of the person and the nation, and he specifically noted its violation of freedom of conscience, as Poles were being compelled by the regime to sign statements that ran counter to their own convictions.[34] He also denounced the use of force in addressing Poland's problems, asserting that there must be no shedding of Polish blood, especially in light of that country's enormous losses in World War II.[35] Aside from his public pronouncements, John Paul also wrote a letter to Jaruzelski on December 18 calling on the general to desist from "actions which are bringing with them the spilling of Polish blood" and to return to "the road of peaceful dialogue" begun in August 1980.[36] The pope also informed the visiting Archbishop Bronisław Dąbrowski on December

22 of his full support for Primate Glemp's stance on the introduction of martial law.[37] On Christmas Eve, John Paul lit a candle in his window at the Vatican as a sign of solidarity with Poles.

Despite papal appeals, martial law continued. Although Wałęsa was interned with the imposition of martial law, Solidarity continued to operate as an underground organization. With the union outlawed, the Catholic Church's position in Poland became even more important. It was now the sole dialogue partner for the regime, as well as being what it had already been for some time in Poland—the most important guarantor of the social peace.[38] The Church did much for Solidarity and workers' rights, though it was somewhat ambivalent toward the now illegal union. While some bishops openly sympathized with Solidarity and maintained secret contacts with it, Cardinal Glemp and most bishops unequivocally supported the principle of independent labor unions but not necessarily in the form of a restored Solidarity. Part of this stance was due to caution, but part was due to an aversion by Glemp and many bishops to what they regarded as an extremist faction in Solidarity, and in the political opposition as a whole, which they felt was taking dangerous risks that could end in terrible violence.[39] Nevertheless, the Church gave considerable support to the victims of martial law and to the ideals that had inspired the Solidarity movement.

While urging caution, stressing national reconciliation, and opposing violence of any kind, the Church in Poland appealed for the release of Wałęsa and other internees, as well as for dialogue aimed at a "national agreement" based on "the social contracts that were concluded in 1980."[40] Dioceses undertook initiatives to provide food, clothing and medical supplies to internees and their families, including distribution of aid sent from abroad. Collections were taken up at masses to aid the interned. Some churches became "Solidarity fortresses," which were safe spaces where the union could be mourned, commemorated, and celebrated. In some parishes, masses were celebrated for patriotic occasions not on the communist calendar (such as the day celebrating the Constitution of May 3, 1791) or to commemorate victims of regime assaults on workers (e.g., the crushing of the unrest of December 1970 or the Wujek mine massacre). Artists and scholars not in good standing with the regime could find venues in Catholic churches to present alternative thought and culture. Priests ministered to prisoners and smuggled information to and from them past prison security.[41] Some helped hide Solidarity activists.

However, the biggest intervention by the Church into Poland's ongoing political crisis was the proposal for a visit by the pope. On May 3, 1982, while large-scale demonstrations were taking place in Poland against martial law and for Solidarity, John Paul told an audience of visiting Poles in Rome that he considered it his religious and patriotic duty to go to Poland for the six-hundredth anniversary of the appearance of the icon of the Black Madonna of Częstochowa, a long-awaited celebration scheduled for that August.[42] Poland's episcopate seconded this papal intention, inviting John Paul at its June 8 meeting for an August visit and expressing its desire to negotiate with the government over that.[43] However, while the Church, whether at the papal, episcopal, clerical, or lay level, was all for such a visit, it was controversial in other milieus. Both Poland's rulers and its oppositional circles were divided over the question. Some communists did not want to risk the social upheaval that could accompany a papal visit and the problems it could cause for Poland's relationship to the Soviet Union and its bloc; some intellectuals and Solidarity activists feared a visit by John Paul would lend legitimacy to the Jaruzelski regime and martial law.[44] The state authorities, however, decided that this potential legitimation was reason to support a visit, and they especially hoped that allowing the pope to come would help end Poland's international isolation and the sanctions imposed on Poland by Western countries.[45] However, they also believed that August 1982 was premature. They wanted to postpone the visit until sometime in 1983.[46] Figuring into these calculations was also the government's anticipation of popular protests during the second anniversary of the labor unrest of 1980 and especially of the Gdańsk Accords on August 31. Poland's bishops, on the other hand, insisted on the August 1982 date. Late spring and early summer saw the regime and the bishops in negotiation over the question, with the regime winning that round.

The primate made the case for an August 1982 visit in a letter to Jaruzelski of June 19. Glemp tried to convince the general that a papal visit would calm society and provide a way out of the current "abnormal" political-societal situation.[47] It would help lift the mood of weariness, anxiety, and insecurity bordering on desperation that plagued society, and it would provide opportunities for national agreement and understanding, thereby strengthening the process of renewal in Poland. Glemp assured Jaruzelski that Catholics would maintain order and peace during the visit. The general replied on June 30, arguing that the August date was "premature," that the visit needed to come at the "appropriate moment." Jaruzelski asserted that more time was needed for the visit to be "responsibly prepared," as public life was not yet fully back to normal. He noted that the visit carried with it the potential for emotions to get out of control and that there was no certainty that the Church could manage these emotions and guarantee that public gatherings retain a religious character and not turn into manifestations of political opinion.[48] Since much smaller religious ceremonies were already being utilized against the regime, with homilies preached and songs sung that were inimical to the authorities and demonstration marches emerging after masses, events on a papal scale could potentially trigger large-scale trouble.

While some might dismiss Jaruzelski's arguments as the self-serving excuses of a regime that sought to avoid any situations that might challenge its dominance, his position is certainly understandable. A papal visit had the potential to bring crowds of a million people each day into the public square at a time when the great majority of Poles were highly embittered against the government. Anticipating that things might get out of control, as well as concerns about what that would mean for Poland's domestic situation and its relations with the Soviet Union and the rest of the Soviet bloc, was not paranoia but a reasonable fear.

As Church and state negotiated over the date of the visit, the state added some arguments. On the negative side, it was maintained that the underground opposition would take advantage of any easing up by the regime in the present context and try to provoke widespread disturbances during the visit. On the positive side, the regime expressed the view that the overall situation would improve by 1983, putting stock in anticipated economic improvements and societal pacification through implementation of a degree of workers' self-government and new, purportedly autonomous trade unions that Jaruzelski was developing as an alternative to Solidarity.[49] The government also argued that it could not assure security for the pope on such short notice and in the context of an underground seeking to exploit social anger. As an alternative date, state negotiators suggested September 12, 1983, the three-hundredth anniversary of the siege of Vienna, a date not only close to Jaruzelski's heart as a military man but also one that could give a patriotic (and potentially regime-friendly) character to the visit.[50]

When Glemp visited John Paul in July to sound out the pope about a possible postponement of his pilgrimage, John Paul took a position that would make an early visit even more difficult to realize.[51] The pope, noting that he was aware that some people thought his visit would be an affirmation of martial law and the Jaruzelski regime, told Glemp that he set three conditions for a visit: the rescinding of martial law, the release of the interned, and the opening of a dialogue with society by the authorities. He also agreed to shift the visit to 1983; shortly thereafter, Poland's government agreed that a visit could take place that year.[52]

With a 1983 date in sight, government and episcopal representatives discussed the character of the visit. In November 1982, Poland's Catholic leadership agreed to certain demands of the government, laid out in a document entitled "Tenets Regarding the Preparations for the Second Visit of John Paul II to Poland."[53] According to these tenets, the pope was not to do or say anything that could disturb Poland's relations with the Soviet Union or the rest of the Soviet bloc; he was to talk about peace and disarmament; he was to condemn West German revisionism and emphasize the Polishness of the Recovered Territories of western and northern Poland; he was to oppose the sanctions imposed on Poland by the West; and he was to maintain the religious character of the visit and refrain from inflaming societal tensions and oppositional attitudes.

The regime's overriding concern, and the condition it set for approval of a visit and any accommodation to the Church's desires, was that the Church partner with the state in assuring societal peace and domestic order, both during the visit and in the months leading up to it. In practice, this entailed Cardinal Glemp speaking out against the general strike called by Solidarity for early November 1982, agreeing to the above-mentioned criteria for the visit, and preventing any official participation in the papal events (for example, serving as ecclesial crowd marshals or on welcoming delegations) of those deemed unreliable by the authorities.[54] As negotiations over the details of the visit continued, the state and Church authorities cooperated closely, at both the national and local levels. For example, the archbishop of Wrocław promised to counteract pro-Solidarity protests should they arise, while Church officials in Katowice agreed to keep persons the regime deemed undesirable from serving as crowd marshals or on delegations presenting gifts to the pope. They also promised to defuse any disruptions that might break out during papal events by having priests distract the crowd with songs and prayers.[55]

Poland's political opposition, including the underground leadership and activists of the banned Solidarity union, were uneasy and in some cases outright hostile to what they regarded as inappropriate accommodation of the martial law regime by the Church. For example, Glemp's failure to support Solidarity's strike action in November 1982 prompted some activists in Szczecin to label him "Red Glemp" and accuse him of betraying the union.[56] The Communist Party politician Mieczysław Rakowski took the same view, noting in his diary-memoir that the Catholic Church had "abandoned" Solidarity.[57]

Alongside concerns that the regime was blackmailing the Church into deserting Solidarity in order to procure the papal visit, Poland's political opposition and the Solidarity underground worried that John Paul's pilgrimage might legitimize the Jaruzelski regime as well as raise enormous hopes for Poles that would end only in frustration.[58]

An article by Teodor Ursyn in the Solidarity newspaper *Tygodnik Mazowsze* of April 14, 1983, expressed concern that John Paul's visit would bring "some kind of gleam of papal dignity to irradiate the regime's hateful faces" and asked, "If John Paul II is to serve as a chaperone for the rapists of the nation, should he come at all?"[39] A fear could be discerned among the Polish opposition that the papal visit might cement the changes introduced by the martial law regime and thereby damage the interests of nation and Church.[60] Some commentators took a strident approach to the papal visit. The underground periodical *KOS* urged Poles to act up instead of lying low in advance of the visit, which would thereby force the regime to either cancel the pilgrimage or allow it, but on "our terms."[61] The author felt that either of these outcomes would be preferable to a visit taking place on the government's terms. A number of voices from the opposition, however, took a more hopeful approach to the visit. The principal underground Solidarity organization, that of the Mazowsze region, issued a declaration on March 24 that saw the pilgrimage as an opportunity for Poles to assemble around the values that the pope was championing, predicting that it would be a pilgrimage of hope, of deepening and regeneration of faith, and of love, "teaching us to struggle for human and national rights in a peaceful manner."[62] In the same *Tygodnik Mazowsze* article in which he raised concerns about the visit, Ursyn balanced his reservations by giving John Paul the benefit of the doubt. He noted that because John Paul is "a great person, wise and full of intuition," he may be able to "avoid equivocation."[63] The very fact that the pope had decided to come to Poland, in Ursyn's view, meant that he thought his intervention was necessary and possible, that there was something he could do. The ambivalence, or even dilemma, of the opposition regarding the visit was likewise expressed by Wałęsa himself, who told Father Alojzy Orszulik, a leading representative of the bishops in their relations with the state, that "both the visit of the Pope during the period of martial law, as well as the nonvisit, are bad."[64]

As both Church and government prepared for the visit, a number of issues awaited settlement. Besides the decision on the precise dates, most of these pertained to how much access to the population the pope would be allowed to have. The regime wanted a system of tickets, passes, and authorization letters that limited who could get close to the pope or even into the venues. It wanted no individual pilgrims but only those in groups of thirty, each led by a Catholic priest who would be responsible for the participants' behavior, including any banners, shouts, and songs. It also wanted events to end before dusk, or no later than 9:30 p.m., and did not want the pope spending the night in Kraków. The Church pushed for easier access to the pope, and while agreeing to access passes for those in the zones closest to John Paul, it insisted on controlling the printing and distribution of such passes. It also insisted that state security personnel not enter papal residences or situate themselves between the altar and the congregation during papal masses. The Church also wanted the regime to provide sufficient transportation to the venues, as well as adequate parking, honest television coverage, and time off for employees and students desiring to see the pope.[65]

The state presented its argument for limiting access to the pope in terms of the danger of assassination (given that John Paul had just two years earlier been shot and nearly killed by an assassin in Rome) and the possibility that antigovernment forces would try to take advantage of the papal events to provoke mass disturbances. The Church argued that the state was being overly sensitive and that the pastoral nature of the papal visit necessitated that John Paul be accessible. A huge question in this respect was whether the pope would meet with Wałęsa.[66] The regime, fearing the boost in prestige that a papal meeting could give Wałęsa, wanted an unequivocal no; the Church argued that the state could not tell the pope with whom he could and could not meet. This question remained on the table and was not settled until John Paul was already in Poland.

On March 19, both Henryk Jabłoński (Poland's chair of the Council of State) and Primate Glemp sent John Paul official invitation letters. The pope replied on April 21, 1983, to Jabłoński's letter, expressing his "heartfelt gratitude" for the invitation and recalling positive encounters with Jabłoński during his 1979 visit. He noted that he wanted his upcoming visit to serve the common good, Church-state relations in Poland, and Polish-Vatican relations internationally, in addition to achieving religious goals. Then the pope let the other shoe drop. He requested the release of those incarcerated under martial law as a necessary step toward national understanding, and he used the term "solidarity" twice, albeit with a lowercase *s*, in speaking of the rights of individuals and social groups and in expressing his unity with the episcopate in calling for full social justice in Poland.[67] The regime was "unpleasantly surprised" by the pope's call for amnesty; in the government's view, release of the imprisoned would be a *fruit* of the visit, not a condition for it.[68] Also, by this time a number of detainees had already been released, and martial law itself had been suspended, although not removed, at the end of 1982.[69] Although John Paul's call for amnesty clearly annoyed Poland's communists, it was not enough to derail the approaching papal pilgrimage.

As the visit drew near, the Church got a significant amount of what it wanted. It would control the access passes, which would pertain only to those in the sectors closest to the pope. Individual pilgrims would be allowed, the pope would be able to overnight in Kraków, and Vatican security personnel alone would be inside papal residences.[70] The state got a commitment from the Church that it would contribute to preserving an atmosphere of peace and order in Poland before and during the visit and would assume responsibility for the behavior of crowds at papal events.[71] Even though there were continuing tensions between Church and state, especially at the local level, with communist officials in certain districts denying workers and students the opportunity to take time off to see the pope, failing to provide adequate transportation to events, or harassing would-be pilgrims, the visit went off as planned.[72]

As the date of the pope's arrival neared, the Solidarity underground changed its ambivalent tone toward the pilgrimage to one of predominantly "joyful expectation."[73] The union used the weeks leading up to the visit to come up with recommendations for greeting the pope, reiterate the crimes of the regime, and present advice to

Poles on how to conduct themselves during the visit. The Temporary Coordinating Commission (Tymczasowa Komisja Koordynacyjna [TKK]), Solidarity's underground governing body, issued an open letter to John Paul in which it stated that "a weary society waits for its meeting with you"; expressed the expectation that his visit would strengthen hope, faith, and love; spoke of the victims of martial law; and called for a "stable, democratic, and lawful Poland," where the dignity of the person and the nation was respected.[74] On March 23, the TKK issued a statement on the visit, noting that Poles were anticipating the pope's visit with joy and saw it as "a visit of peace and hope."[75] The Solidarity leadership spoke of Poland's current suffering, mourning those killed or imprisoned under martial law and condemning the regime's trampling on fundamental rights. They also called for an amnesty for the imprisoned and accused the regime of using the papal visit as blackmail. The statement exhorted Poles to create the proper climate for a worthy reception of the pope and announced that "for the time of the visit we will refrain from any protest actions." Wałęsa too issued an "Open Letter to Society" that called on Poles to demonstrate gravity, caution, calm, and moderation, as well as to resist provocation that might hinder the pilgrimage.[76] Various underground Solidarity newspapers and newsletters across Poland gave Poles advice and encouragement in the lead-up to the visit. Among other things, Poles were urged to be present in full force at papal events, to maintain dignity and calm, to refrain from consumption of alcohol, to decorate home and workplace in honor of the visit, and to dress appropriately for the occasion.[77] These appeals often included calls for amnesty for the imprisoned. The underground Radio Solidarity asked Poles to show that the Solidarity movement was still alive by turning out at papal events with banners conveying statements from Solidarity's first nationwide congress, the words of John Paul II and Cardinal Wyszyński, and pertinent Bible verses written in the characteristic Solidarity script.[78] Now that the Church and state had reached agreement on most of the essentials of the visit and the opposition had gotten its say, the stage was set for John Paul's arrival.

WARSAW

On June 16, 1983, John Paul touched down at Warsaw's Okęcie Airport, where he was greeted by Jabłoński, chair of the Council of State, as "an apostle of peace" and "a continuer of the work of John XXIII and Paul VI."[79] Jabłoński praised the visit as "evidence of the far advanced normalization of the life of the country" and as an occasion that could increase understanding and cooperation in Poland. In what seemed like a commercial advertisement for the Jaruzelski regime, Jabłoński applauded the government for improving its legal system, strengthening democratic institutions, reforming the economy, and correcting mistakes. Then, after Cardinal Glemp welcomed the pope, John Paul gave his arrival address.

In his speech, the pope made clear his identification with the suffering of his compatriots under martial law. He spoke of this "august and difficult moment in the history of the Fatherland."[80] Having planted his customary kiss on the Polish ground upon arrival, John Paul likened it to kissing the hand of his "earthly mother" and noted that this mother "has suffered through much and continues to suffer anew." He went on to raise a very sensitive issue, albeit somewhat obliquely—those imprisoned under the martial law regime. Citing Jesus's words in Matthew 25:36 ("I was sick and you visited me. I was in prison and you came to me"), he spoke of his closeness to those suffering, in particular the sick and those in prison. Although this could mean regular prisoners instead of the people interned under martial law, the audience surely knew to whom this term referred and burst into applause when the pope made these allusions.[81] The pope ended his short speech with a call for peace for his fatherland.

The next stop on the papal itinerary was the Cathedral of Saint John the Baptist in Warsaw's Old Town, to which John Paul proceeded from the airport along streets lined with perhaps hundreds of thousands of people, traveling in his bulletproof, bubble-topped "Popemobile."[82] At the cathedral, the pope celebrated a memorial service for the late Cardinal Wyszyński. In his homily, John Paul once again identified himself with the suffering of his compatriots.[83] In speaking of Jesus Christ's redemptive suffering on the cross, an event whose 1950th anniversary the Catholic Church was commemorating that year in the Jubilee of the Year of Redemption, John Paul affirmed that he "stands beneath the cross of Christ" with all his compatriots, especially with "those who most painfully feel the acrid taste of disappointment, humiliation, suffering, deprivation of freedom, injustice, trampling on the dignity of man." This remark brought a sustained outburst of applause from the assembly. In praising Wyszyński and thanking God for giving him to Poland, the pope quoted from the cardinal's writings during the time of his incarceration in the mid-1950s, a reminder of the past persecution of the Church under Poland's communist rulers. John Paul went on to note that "Divine Providence spared Wyszyński the painful events connected with the date of December 13, 1981," a clear reference to martial law. At this, more applause erupted from the crowd, prompting the pope to admonish them that henceforth they were not to interrupt him.

Later that evening, remnants of the enormous crowds that had turned out for the papal arrival coalesced into a group of several thousand at least.[84] Some carried Solidarity banners and chanted the name of the banned union and its leader, Lech Wałęsa, while marching south from the Old Town toward Communist Party headquarters. When police blocked their advance, the crowd veered off to the west and soon dispersed.[85] Thus concluded the pope's first day in Warsaw, passing without serious incident but also making clear that John Paul was not going to pretend his fellow Poles were not suffering under the martial law regime. The next day promised to be full of drama—John Paul was meeting Jaruzelski at Belvedere Palace, where each would give a public speech, followed by a lengthy private meeting. That evening, the pope would address Poles at an old soccer stadium, an event sure to bring the most Poles into the streets since the imposition of martial law a year and a half earlier.

At Belvedere, the pope gave his speech first and then the general followed with his own. The body language during the event was telling. John Paul was "cool and formal."[86] The two protagonists had a cursory handshake outside the door to the venue, then spoke from opposite sides of the room. Jaruzelski listened to the pope with a clenched fist. John Paul did not look at the general when the latter spoke. In a short address lasting barely more than fifteen minutes, John Paul, in carefully crafted words, placed on the Jaruzelski regime the responsibility for getting Poland out of its current domestic sociopolitical and international diplomatic crisis.[87] Some of the speech's content was welcomed, and expected, by the regime—namely, calls for arms control and world peace and unequivocal confirmation that Poland's "recovered" northern and western territories unambiguously belonged to Poland.[88] However, the thrust of the speech, in its carefully crafted wording, put the Jaruzelski regime on the spot on a number of fronts—the historical, the domestic, and the international. First, the pope raised the issue of Poland's sovereignty, always a touchy subject for the communists, who had to negotiate Poland's place within the Soviet orbit. John Paul spoke of past losses of independence for Poland, specifically the time of the Partitions, when Poland had to live for more than a century under "imperialisms contrary to our independence," and World War II, when Poland paid with "six million lives" for its right to a sovereign existence. Although John Paul named no names, it was surely not lost on Polish listeners that Russia, either as the tsarist partitioners or the Soviet partners-in-crime with Nazi Germany, played a role in both of these historical assaults on Polish independence.

The pope then went on to address the domestic situation, recognizing that he had come at "a particularly difficult moment," noting "the harsh rigors of martial law" and the suffering of Poles. But rather than simply comfort Poles in their distress, John Paul proposed a solution—one the regime surely did not welcome. For the pope, renewal could come only on the basis of the principles worked out in August 1980 in the agreements "concluded between the representatives of the state authorities and the representatives of the world of labor." Thus, while not calling specifically for the relegalization of the Solidarity union, John Paul was affirming the principles that had brought it into existence as the only way forward for both regime and society. Then, after speaking positively about the Catholic Church and its efforts on behalf of world peace, he went on to speak more generally about domestic peace. Drawing from his annual papal World Day of Peace message of January 1, 1983, John Paul spoke of the importance of the means of achieving social peace, stressing among other things dialogue, "structures of co-participation," and "manifold mediating institutions" in handling conflicts between employers and employees. Again, without mentioning Solidarity (or even Poland), the pope affirmed the indispensability of associations like Solidarity for solving the current crisis in his homeland.

Finally, John Paul indirectly raised and took a subtle position on an issue that was of especially great concern to the regime. Few issues meant as much to Poland's rulers as the question of the sanctions slapped on Poland by the NATO countries in the aftermath of the imposition of martial law, and few issues were as touchy for the pope. The regime would have liked nothing better than for the pope to call for the repeal of the sanctions during his visit. On the one hand, sanctions were hurting the Polish economy and society, but on the other hand, lifting them while Solidarity remained outlawed would be rewarding the detested Jaruzelski regime. As it turned out, John Paul sidestepped this sensitive issue by tossing the ball into the regime's court. The pope used his speech at Belvedere to present a vision of Poland's place in Europe and relations with the West that differed from the party's. Rather than confirm Poland's Eastern orientation, John Paul spoke of "Poland's place between East and West" and called for dialogue and cooperation with the countries of Western Europe and North America, especially the United States. And just as dialogue at home, in the pope's view, was to be based on respect for the social accords of late summer 1980, so too was Poland's international reputation to hinge on the regime's willingness to bring about renewal in Poland.

Several reports produced by government or party analysts after the visit addressed the question of sanctions, particularly within the context of John Paul's Belvedere speech. A report from the Administrative Division of the Party's Central Committee states that the pope did not take a stand on sanctions.[89] However, a report from the Office of Confessional Affairs notes that the pope's position was so amorphous that it was hard tell whether he was for or against sanctions.[90] The report noted that it was difficult to tell whether John Paul was criticizing the sanctions themselves or calling on the regime to take the steps needed for those sanctions to be lifted.

Now came the general's turn. He was visibly shaking as he began.[91] Jaruzelski's speech was as well crafted as the pope's, and, as British scholar Timothy Garton Ash has aptly pointed out, he spoke Polish, not "translated Sovietese."[92] Like John Paul, the general employed Polish history to make his points.[93] He opened by noting the traumas experienced by Poles over the centuries, their many defeats and futile insurrections, with generations going to their deaths like "stones tossed by God on the rampart."[94] He went on to mention World War II, when Poles were "sentenced by Hitlerite genocide to extinction," and how they regained their sovereignty thanks to the supreme sacrifices of countless Soviet soldiers. He noted that owing to Poland's present allies, its borders were secure for the first time ever—"Not one square centimeter of Polish land" was endangered, and places like Gdańsk, Wrocław, and Szczecin were now Polish cities. Later in his speech, Jaruzelski pointed out the enormous progress made by Poland under the communist regime; the country was no longer a land of "thatched roofs," millions of illiterate persons, and starving rural poor. Asserting that "the historical advance of the Fatherland is an undisputed fact," the general reminded the pope to consider how markedly the southern region of Podhale, which the pope knew well, had changed for the better over the course of his lifetime.

Woven into this larger historical context was Jaruzelski's defense of martial law. The general explained that it was not the government that had driven the country to the edge of catastrophe and that martial law had been imposed as "a last resort." While admitting that Poles were suffering under it, he asked rhetorically how much suffering, anguish, and tears had in fact been avoided because of it. Jaruzelski even quoted Tadeusz Kościuszko, a Polish military hero who in the 1790s had led an uprising against Russia, about the need to "sacrifice many in order to save everything." The general also spoke of the importance of the state, declaring that "when the state weakens or descends into anarchy, the nation pays the price" and adding that Poles knew this historical truth all too well. In addition, Jaruzelski argued that the Polish situation should be viewed in the context of the fact that much of the world was far worse off than Poland in terms of foreign oppression and violations of human rights, that even in powerful and rich countries there existed areas of poverty, crime, and hopelessness. On the positive side, the general expressed his optimism that "the worst is over," renewal was well under way, and martial law might be abolished in the near future if people showed sufficient prudence and civic responsibility.

Having staked out their positions publicly, John Paul and Jaruzelski then met privately for about two hours and twenty minutes, an hour longer than planned.[95] They discussed the domestic and international issues raised during their respective speeches, and John Paul was particularly concerned about potential amnesties for those still interned under martial law and about the prospects for a meeting with Wałęsa, which he raised three times during the discussion.[96] In explaining his reasons for insisting on a meeting with Wałęsa, the pope allegedly admitted that NATO countries were pressuring the Vatican toward this end, and he expressed his belief that, since he had readily met with Wałęsa at the Vatican at the peak of the latter's fame, it would be wrong to refuse him a visit now that he was under duress.[97] That afternoon, party press secretary Jerzy Urban informed journalists that the authorities had approved a "strictly private" meeting between Wałęsa and John Paul, though the details of when, where, and how long were not disclosed.[98]

That evening, John Paul had his largest event yet in Poland's capital: he celebrated mass for possibly a million or more persons at Warsaw's Decennial Stadium and the park surrounding it.[99] In his homily, the pope connected the readings from that day's liturgy with the Polish situation.[100] At a time when the Jaruzelski regime was hoping and calling for "renewal" in Poland, the pope cited the Book of Revelation and its reference to a "new heaven and a new earth," an eschatological domain in which "all death and sorrow and hardship will be no more" and everything will be made new. Along with these words of comfort to a nation in distress, John Paul used the Gospel story of the wedding feast at Cana, when Mary's statement about the lack of wine prompted Jesus to perform the miracle of changing water into wine; the pope connected the presence of Jesus Christ in Poland's history both to Mary and to his own impending visit to Jasna Góra in honor of the six-hundredth anniversary of the Black Madonna icon in Poland. At the heart of the pope's message, however, was a reflection on Poland's past, present, and future, which he connected with the passage from Saint Paul's Letter to the Hebrews stating that Jesus Christ is always the same, "yesterday and today and forever."[101]

Given that 1983 was the three-hundredth anniversary of the victory of European Christian forces over the Ottomans at the siege of Vienna and that Poland's King Jan III Sobieski was a hero of that victory, the pope spoke at length about the significance of that event. Although the regime welcomed papal praise for Poland's military achievements of the past, in particular against an empire whose successor was now a member of NATO, John Paul in fact cleverly addressed the anniversary in ways that worked against the regime's intentions. First, he used the siege of Vienna to connect Poland to the West, noting that the victory tied Poles to their neighbors to the south and west. Second, he spoke of the event in a way that made the Turks look good and, implicitly, made Russia look bad. He recalled that Sobieski's victory garnered respect and recognition for Poles among the Turks and that in the period of the Partitions, from the late eighteenth century until 1918, during ceremonial receptions of foreign envoys at the Ottoman court the Ottomans regularly asked, "Is the envoy from Lechistan [Poland] present?"; they would then receive the reply, "Not yet." Third, the pope presented Sobieski more as a Catholic than as a Polish patriot, noting that during the king's Vienna expedition he made a pilgrimage to Jasna Góra and to other Marian shrines. Finally, John Paul made much of the message Sobieski sent to the Apostolic See announcing the Christian victory—"Venimus, vidimus, Deus vincit," or "We came, we saw, God conquered."

Expanding on the theme of God's conquering, John Paul spoke of two dimensions of such conquering—personal and communal. On the personal level, we are called in Jesus Christ to victory over sin, over the "old Adam" rooted deep within us, a victory over ourselves. Such a victory means "life in the truth, rectitude of conscience, love of neighbor, the capacity to forgive, and the spiritual growth of our humanity." Such victories are inseparable from hardship and even from suffering, as Christ showed with his cross. In offering examples of such victories over the self in the face of adversity, John Paul referred to letters sent to him by people interned under martial law.

The pope went on to speak of the victories, as well as defeats, suffered by the Polish nation over the course of its history. He spoke of moral defeats as well as political ones, noting the corruption of the era of Saxon rulers and the times Poles' lack of concern for the common good went so far as to amount to culpable offenses against their own fatherland. He also spoke of those times of moral renewal—the education reforms of the late eighteenth century, the Constitution of May 3, 1791, the attempts at moral reconstruction and restoration of independence in the nineteenth century. In noting the renewal under way in late eighteenth-century Poland, one cut short by foreign occupation, John Paul called the Partitions "a terrible historical wrong, an infringement of the rights of the nation and the international order." Implicit in this statement was not just that Russia was a major culprit in that historical wrong but that Poland's current situation also involved an infringement of the nation's rights and the international order.

The pope then turned to a couple of other issues of the sort that normally the regime liked to see raised—world peace and the achievements of postwar reconstruction. However, once again John Paul addressed these issues in ways that undercut rather than bolstered the communist authorities. He noted the horrors of war and the Church's part in past and present efforts toward world peace. He then went on to recall the enormous destruction suffered by Warsaw in World War II, asserting that "Poland paid in full—with dividends!—its allied obligations that it took upon itself in the horrible events of 1939 to 1945." He reminded his audience of Poland's "right to a sovereign existence and normal cultural and socioeconomic development" and stated that "the fate of Poland in 1983 cannot be a matter of indifference to the nations of the world—especially of Europe and America." This was far from the preferred communist boilerplate for addressing peace. Similarly, with reference to postwar reconstruction, John Paul praised the "moral victory" achieved in Warsaw and across Poland but gave no credit to the regime. Rather, this was a "moral victory of the nation."[102]

Next came the most provocative part of his homily, in which the pope directly addressed Poland's present dilemma and spoke of the potential way forward. He noted that his present trip had come at a difficult time for the whole society, thus alluding to events of recent years "beginning from August 1980." At this reference to the month when Solidarity was born, the audience burst into applause, prompting the pope to admonish them not to interrupt him. He went on to express gratitude for all those who were helping Poland, "especially since December 1981," thus raising by implication the fact of martial law. At this point, John Paul started speaking of solutions. He asserted that the nation must live from and develop itself from its own forces. Reiterating the theme of "Deus vincit," the pope spoke of the victory to which God was calling Poles at this stage of history—not a military victory, but a moral one. This, for John Paul, must be the essence of the renewal that the regime was touting. This moral victory, which was the only thing that could lead society from breakdown and return unity to it, must entail respect for fundamental human rights. It must proceed from dialogue and agreement, "the only way for the nation to enjoy civil rights in their fullness and possess the appropriate and necessary societal structures" (an oblique reference to, among other things, independent trade unions). Only this would liberate the societal forces that the state needed "in order to be able to fulfill its tasks and through which the nation actually expresses its sovereignty." In other words, if the regime expected Poles to make the sort of sacrifices necessary to get the economy out of the doldrums, it would have to respect human rights and accommodate society's demands for independent trade unions.

At the end of the mass, John Paul greeted and blessed those

present, mentioning in the process the various dioceses that had sent representatives to the event. When he said "there are pilgrims here from the Diocese of Gdańsk," thunderous applause broke out among the crowd. Rather than admonishing the crowd not to interrupt him, this time John Paul said, "Anything I'd like to add to this designation will already be unnecessary in the face of this mass reaction. Greetings and blessings for the Diocese of Gdańsk!"

It was no surprise that the massive crowd seized this opportunity to show its support for Solidarity. Western media reported the presence of pro-Solidarity banners, upraised hands flashing the Solidarity-associated "V for Victory" sign, and welcome banners written in Solidarity-style script.[103] One banner read, "You Are the Father of Solidarity."[104] At the end of the event, some chanted the name of Lech Wałęsa. Still, incidents were much fewer and smaller than the evening before. John Paul contributed to the maintenance of peace, concluding his address after mass by expressing to the crowd his desire that "all the days of my pilgrimage visit to Poland will be days of peace, calm, and inner rest."

John Paul made several other appearances while in Warsaw. On June 17 he held an "ecumenical meeting" with representatives of Poland's Protestant, Orthodox, Jewish, and Muslim communities and attended a celebration at which he received an honorary doctorate from the Catholic University of Lublin. He also visited the Capuchin church, site of the sarcophagus containing King Jan III Sobieski's heart, and there met with individuals from the Catholic newspaper *Tygodnik Powszechny*, advisors to Solidarity, and Barbara Sadowska, the mother of Grzegorz Przemek, a student who had died the month before in Warsaw after being beaten severely by riot police.[105] The initial plan was for the pope to give a speech at the church, but he canceled that because his talks with Jaruzelski ran overtime. On June 18, he made two unannounced stops in a residential neighborhood of Warsaw—first to visit the monument to the victims of the Warsaw Uprising of April 1943, where he laid flowers and prayed silently, and then, not far from there, to stop at the remnant of the former Pawiak prison, where Poles were held before being taken to Nazi prison camps.[106] One of Pawiak's most celebrated inmates was the Franciscan priest and recently canonized Saint Maximilian Kolbe, to whom John Paul would devote the rest of the day as he was spirited off by helicopter to Niepokalanów, Kolbe's former headquarters, where he would give two addresses pertinent to Poland's newest saint.

NIEPOKALANÓW

The pope's visit to Niepokalanów provided a splendid example of one of John Paul's greatest strengths—the ability to speak about the saints in ways that made them relevant, exemplary, and inspiring for a contemporary audience. The pope had visited the site of Kolbe's martyrdom at Auschwitz during his 1979 visit, and now he was visiting the place where Kolbe did much of his life's work, a town of friars about thirty miles from Warsaw and headquarters of the Catholic media enterprise run by Kolbe in the interwar period. John Paul first addressed members of religious orders, then celebrated mass for nearly 250,000 persons who had gathered.[107]

In his homily, John Paul said nothing of direct political relevance but nonetheless intervened in Poland's current situation in several ways.[108] The first was through his discussion of Kolbe, the centerpiece of his talk. The pope used Kolbe's martyrdom at Auschwitz, where he had volunteered to replace a family man in a starvation bunker, to forcefully and dramatically convey a message of hope. Kolbe's death, according to John Paul, showed the power of love over death, "the central truth of the Gospel." Kolbe gave his life for a brother, experiencing a "spiritual victory," as Christ did on Calvary. The pope emphasized that Kolbe had agency—he did not "suffer death" but rather "gave his life." He was the "steward of his own death." He bore witness against the "civilization of death" exemplified by Auschwitz, and his sacrificial act amounted to a victory over death.

John Paul also emphasized that Kolbe was a saint of global significance, noting that at his canonization the previous October in Rome, pilgrims had come from all over the world but most notably from Germany and Japan.[109] The pope also expressed his view that Kolbe was an especially apt saint for the present, stating that he "confirmed in some especially meaningful way the drama of humanity of the twentieth century." Still, he was also a patron of Poland, one who shared his nation's "experiences, sufferings, and hopes." John Paul went on to recount Poland's own historic sufferings dating from the late eighteenth century to World War II—partitions, deportations, concentration camps, starvation bunkers. Quoting from the Easter Sequence of the Catholic liturgy, John Paul stated, in Latin, that "death and life have clashed in a miraculous duel" (Mors et vita duello conflixere mirando), then forcefully asserted that Kolbe's example shows that love is stronger than death. The homily, which in a number of spots entailed John Paul speaking loudly and dramatically, even shouting, climaxed with the pope quoting Saint Paul's Letter to the Romans: "Do not be overcome by evil, but overcome evil with good," which the pope called "a Gospel program. A difficult program—but possible. An indispensable program."

The homily's messages, all centered around Kolbe's life and death, contained a number of points pertinent to Poles suffering under martial law. The call for sacrifice, the reminder of the Christian belief that love and life conquer death, the exhortation to combat evil with good, and the emphasis on agency over passivity—all of this aimed to comfort, encourage, or inspire Poles in their present predicament. It was also significant that the pope recounted the litany of past traumas suffered by Poles, implying that martial law was yet the latest chapter in a history that had seen much suffering and sorrow but where suffering and sorrow did not have the last word.

Another intervention by John Paul in Polish politics at Niepokalanów came in the form of his outreach to Poland's farmers, building on initiatives taken by Poland's bishops since 1981.[110] This was his first rural stop on the 1983 pilgrimage, and, according to a government report, the pope met with activists from Rural Solidarity while in Niepokalanów.[111] The large number of people attending the mass included many farmers, both from the immediate vicinity and farther afield. Among the attendees that the pope welcomed during his homily were "participants of pastoral communities working for the renewal of the countryside in connection with the Church," groups in which some former Rural Solidarity members had found an outlet for their activism.[112] John Paul devoted a portion of his homily to farmers, during which he praised them for doing the Lord's work in cultivating the Polish land and providing the nation with its food. In celebrating Polish farmers, John Paul quoted the renowned peasant leader of the interwar period, Wincenty Witos, who had praised the Polish peasant for preserving "the three values that gave the foundation to the creation of the Polish state"—"land, religion, and nationality." Quietly reaching out to rural activists, praising rural religiosity, and quoting precommunist political leaders favorably were all evidence of the pope's continuing gibes at the regime, even if less overtly political than his words and deeds in Warsaw.

A final dig at the regime came at the end of the mass, when crowds sang the hymn "Boże coś Polskę," with a controversial line that called for a restoration of Poland's freedom. Specifically, the hymn's refrain changes depending on whether the Poles are experiencing national independence or not. When Poland is independent, Poles sing "Preserve for us a free Fatherland," whereas when Poland is living under foreign oppression, they sing "Return to us a free Fatherland." It was this latter refrain that was sung at this and other papal events in Poland, providing a safe and effective way for the population to express its disaffection with the Jaruzelski regime and imply that Poland's communists were servants of Moscow incapable of guaranteeing Poland genuine sovereignty. When Poles sang the hymn at the end of the mass at Niepokalanów, it was clear to observers that the pope responded positively, waving and spreading his arms, to the forbidden words.[113]

CZĘSTOCHOWA AND JASNA GÓRA MONASTERY

From Niepokalanów, the pope proceeded on to Częstochowa and the Jasna Góra monastery, the apex of his visit and the site of his most formidable challenges to the regime yet. His two-day visit there, on June 18 and 19, was packed with potentially dramatic and contentious events. Upon arrival, he would address a gathering of pilgrims from the Diocese of Szczecin-Kamieńska, one of the centers of the labor unrest that helped lead to the emergence of the Solidarity movement. Later that evening, he would speak to a massive assembly of Polish youth. These events would be held outside the monastery walls. The next day, among other things, he would celebrate mass in honor of the six-hundredth anniversary of the appearance of the icon of Our Lady of Jasna Góra in Poland, also adjacent to the monastery, and later address the Conference of the Polish Episcopate in Częstochowa. Taken together, these events caused considerable consternation among Poland's authorities, and Poland's Catholic hierarchy received a sharply worded rebuke from the government after John Paul's first day at Jasna Góra.

Because the pope was not permitted to visit any of the Baltic Sea ports during this pilgrimage, or even the regions around them, arrangements were made for pilgrims from the Diocese of Szczecin-Kamieńska to come to Częstochowa to see and hear him. As part of this visit, John Paul met with a delegation of workers from Szczecin.[114] In addressing the large crowd of pilgrims, the pope gave the regime something that it wanted—a positive reference to the restoration of "Polishness" to Western Pomerania, reincorporated into the Polish state after World War II.[115] However, he also gave the authorities much that they did not appreciate. The pope's words included pointed references to the events dating from August 1980. Specifically, John Paul noted that Poles had come to Jasna Góra with heavy and wounded hearts, and he remarked that the world was amazed as the Polish worker "stood up for himself with the Gospel in his hand and a prayer on his lips," a comment drawing sustained applause. He went on to connect Jesus Christ with the meaning of human labor, referring to "the Christ of workers" who stands before them and says, "Peace to you! Do not be afraid! Come, refresh yourself!" The pope then entrusted Poles in their distress to Our Lady of Jasna Góra and asked her to watch over them, including their actions "in accord with a right conscience and in accord with universally recognized rights." John Paul concluded by referring to that evening's event for youth, for which a number of participants were already assembling. He asked that that evening's liturgy "be full of dignity and peace" and told people "to have patience with one another." These remarks demonstrated the pope's concern lest upcoming events get out of hand, particularly given what he was planning to say to Polish youth that evening.

A vast crowd, mostly young, turned out to the meeting with the pope outside the monastery's walls.[116] This was the most spirited audience yet for a papal event, with one government report describing it as a "collective euphoria of religious rapture."[117] The regime took greater precautions than usual. It dropped the national radio and television coverage of the event.[118] It also brought in heavy police reinforcements, including the riot police known by their Polish acronym ZOMO, though their presence was restricted to the perimeters of the crowd and their intervention was minimal.[119] Sustained, thunderous applause greeted the pope, and his appearance underscored one of the problematic features of this papal visit—the cocoon of security placed around John Paul, which, unlike during the 1979 visit, kept him at considerable distance from the adoring crowds. As a result, the pope was met almost at once with various chants, including "Come closer to us," which he tried to indulge within the constraints of the situation, getting to within fifty yards of the enormous crowd.[120]

The first part of the pope's speech had a calming effect, with its praise for Mary and emphasis on love—of God, of Jesus Christ, and of the Mother of God, a love that "continually encompasses us" and that was present to Poles over the centuries.[121] Then the pope went on to direct powerful words toward Polish youth and the challenges they faced. He built the speech around the motto "Be vigilant!"—part of the Jasna Góra Appeal that John Paul and his audience would later be singing together to conclude the event.[122] He instructed his young audience that being vigilant means being "a person of conscience," to "call good and evil by name," and to work to overcome the evil in oneself. He warned against demoralization and asked Polish youth to build a barrier against it, noting how much such demoralization had cost Poland in the past. Although he had started off by speaking of values that transcended Poland's current situation even if they were quite resonant in it, the pope soon went on to make references, both direct and indirect, to Poland's sufferings under martial law. He first did this by connecting vigilance with love of neighbor—that it means, among other things, to not be shut in on oneself but rather open to others, to, as he put it, "fundamental interhuman solidarity." By speaking the word "solidarity," albeit with a small *s* and not as the title of Poland's banned labor union, John Paul evoked an outburst of applause, which only continued as he began to cite evidence of such solidarity. This evidence was seen, according to the pope, in the concern shown in the "difficult" recent months "for those who were interned, imprisoned, or dismissed from work, and for their families." He urged Poles to keep this concern from slackening. At this point, John Paul's words were being interrupted by applause at nearly every sentence or two, if not more frequently. Unlike at past events, however, he made no attempt to quell the applause or the cheering; if anything, he may have been using the cadence and gestures of his delivery to rouse his listeners.[123]

Toward the conclusion of his address, the pope explored yet another dimension of what it meant to "be vigilant"—the responsibility Poles have to Poland. John Paul noted that the value of a thing is determined by what it costs and that Poles sometimes envied those nations to which freedom came more easily (here the pope mentioned the French, the Germans, and the Americans). He then admonished his young audience to "not desire a Poland that costs us nothing." Then John Paul proceeded with words that bothered the regime as much as anything so far. He spoke of the feelings of injustice and humiliation felt by Poland's youth, the lack of a sense of prospects for the future, and the temptation even to flee to "a different kind of world."[124] Still, the pope concluded on a hopeful note, expressing his belief that the fundamental solution lies in the human person, who "cannot remain without a way out," and calling on Our Lady of Jasna Góra to intercede so that Polish youth could persevere in hope.

The course of the visit so far, especially the pope's speeches at Częstochowa on June 18 to the pilgrims from the Szczecin diocese and to Polish youth, displeased and even alarmed the regime.[125] The authorities had protested orally to the Church leadership after John

Paul's homily at Warsaw Cathedral, but they now decided to lodge an official protest, "emphatically, that is, not in a diplomatic manner," as one government report put it.[126] Delivered on June 19 by Adam Łopatka, head of the Office of Confessional Affairs, to Archbishops Franciszek Macharski and Bronisław Dąbrowski, the official statement read as follows:

> The Government with great bitterness and indignation has become acquainted with the content of the homilies to the Szczecin diocese and to youth.

> The text of the homily to youth has a political rather than a religious character. It leads to a disturbing of the peace and it incites. Its content is untrue and unfair. The emanating of a vision of hopelessness is an exhortation to rebellion against the authorities. No one has done more than the present system for the people and for the youth in Poland.

> The presentation of the current difficulties as calamities and situations without prospect, instead of exhortation to study and work, is immoral and harmful for the nation.

> We are reading yesterday's behavior by the Pope in Częstochowa as a unilateral breaking of the agreed-upon tenets of the visit. This is happening at a time when the Government is faithfully abiding by all the tenets, and even fulfilling additional desires on the part of the Church.

> We are treating the content of the homily to youth as an exhortation to rebellion and to religious war. Does the Church want rebellion and a religious war in Poland?

> The authorities made the point on December 13, 1981, that they are in a position to effectively oppose all attempts to destabilize the system and the state.

The Government has reserved for itself the right to introduce revisions into the program of the visit. This concerns especially television and radio transmissions, entering into polemics with statements of the Pope while the visit is still going on, and other appropriate steps.[127]

Government spokesperson Jerzy Urban informed the foreign media of the protest at a press conference in Warsaw.[128] Archbishop Dąbrowski, meanwhile, issued the Church's response that same day.[129] He stated that the episcopate and the pope shared the government's concern that the papal visit be proper and peaceful and that the bishops were in fact working for such an outcome. Dąbrowski went on to reject the government's interpretation of the visit as expressed in its protest. He asserted that "the statements of the Holy Father, though concerning problems connected with the difficult and complicated situation in our country," were "astonishingly cautious and measured." He noted that the large youth gathering of the previous evening took place in an atmosphere of peace and order and that one should not have been surprised at the exuberance of youth in the presence of John Paul II. Dąbrowski asserted that the pope had the right and obligation to pursue concrete dialogue and could not limit himself to general statements and that the content of his speeches the day before had been no different from earlier speeches in which he had expressed his concern for the future and security of the Polish state. Dąbrowski concluded by rejecting, in the name of the Polish bishops, the accusations that the pope was calling for rebellion and religious war and trying to destabilize the system and state. It was this kind of reaction, according to Dąbrowski, that was impeding the dignified and peaceful course of the papal visit.

The next day, June 19, John Paul had two major events, along with the Jasna Góra Appeal with which he concluded every evening at Jasna Góra. Thus, there would be an opportunity to see whether he "got the message" conveyed in the government protest. The first event was the centerpiece of the entire visit—the mass commemorating the six-hundredth anniversary of the icon of Our Lady of Jasna Góra, or the Black Madonna. In unseasonably cold weather, wind, and a steady light drizzle, a crowd of up to a million people gathered outside the walls of the Jasna Góra monastery for the event.[130] Solidarity banners were sprinkled throughout the crowd, along with other kinds of banners employing the Solidarity-style script.[131]

The pope opened his Jubilee homily by connecting the Catholic faith and Polish nation, especially through Jesus's mother, Mary, as Our Lady of Jasna Góra.[132] She is "Mother and Queen of our Nation," honored at this "national shrine of my Fatherland." John Paul connected Mary's presence at the wedding at Cana (the Gospel reading from that mass) with her presence in Poland since the Middle Ages, manifested above all in her icon at Jasna Góra. Her message, both at Cana and in Polish history, was that we should obey her son, to "do whatever he tells you." She brought, in the pope's words, a "maternal character" into Polish Christianity. Later in the homily, John Paul developed the idea that Mary is particularly present to Poles during difficult times, especially given their "very difficult geopolitical position." Among these times he included not only the Swedish invasion of 1656 and the Partitions but also the present-day troubles. No matter what their situation, Poles could always go to Jasna Góra and ask Our Lady to return to them, as the famous hymn put it, a free fatherland.

John Paul developed two themes in this homily that were potentially political—freedom and sovereignty. With respect to freedom, the pope reiterated basic Catholic teaching about freedom being both a gift and a task, and he reminded his audience that it can be used well or badly. People can use freedom "to build or to demolish." The other theme, sovereignty, was more problematic for the regime. In discussing the freedom of the nation, John Paul asserted that "the nation is genuinely free when it can form itself as a community defined by a unity of culture, of language, of history. The state is essentially sovereign if it governs with society and at the same time serves the common good of society and if it allows the nation to realize for itself its own subjectivity, its own identity." Although the regime would have liked Poles to think that it in fact was living up to this standard of sovereignty, the loud outburst of applause at the end of this statement

made it clear that Poles saw the pope's words as an indictment of communist rule.[133] Implicit here was that the regime was not governing
"with society" nor serving the common good when it denied Poles
the freedom to organize independent trade unions. This became even
clearer later in the homily, when John Paul included among human
and national rights "the rights of human labor."

John Paul's Jubilee homily departed significantly from his addresses the day before in that it made no mention of the events of
August 1980 or December 1981, nor of martial law, the interned and
imprisoned, nor of "solidarity," whether with large *S* or small. The
first time applause broke out, the pope admonished his audience not
to interrupt him, and it never happened again. This more cautious
approach by the pope can be attributed both to the protest issued by
the government that morning as well as to the solemn religious nature
of the anniversary mass.

Later that day, the pope spoke at another major event, the Conference of the Episcopate of Poland.[134] Here John Paul got more specific
about Poland's situation, praising the Church's work in visiting the
imprisoned and interned and providing help for their families. He
noted the "gloomy and painful image of life of society formed over the
course of recent years," to which the Church was responding with love
of neighbor. He also made an effort to connect Catholic social teaching with recent events in Poland, quoting from an address he gave in
1982 to the International Labour Organization in Geneva, using the
term "solidarity" six times, with references to the solidarity of workers
with each other; the need for society's solidarity with them; solidarity as an antidote to hatred, egoism, and injustice, and to division
and opposition; and as a means toward dialogue and cooperation. In
making this case, John Paul included a number of statements critical
of Marxism, both in theory and in practice. He did this by noting
that "hatred, egoism, and injustice are too often raised to the dignity
of ideological principles or fundamental laws of social life"; that solidarity "opposes seeing society in categories of struggle 'against,' of
seeing social relations in categories of uncompromising opposition of
classes"; and that one can solve contradictions through dialogue and

cooperation "without pursuing the destruction of opponents." All of these tenets were repudiations of Marxist notions of inevitable class struggle as the sole road to justice for workers.[135]

John Paul concluded another eventful day with the customary Jasna Góra Appeal, drawing what the state authorities estimated was a crowd of one hundred thousand to the environs of the monastery.[136] The pope approached the sensitive political situation with caution, including words of hope and reconciliation. After citing Jesus's words from the Gospel about visiting prisoners (Matthew 25:40), he told his audience, "I cannot ignore matters that occupy many hearts," acknowledging the difficulty of speaking aloud "about painful matters." He then went on to ask Mary's intercession for those who suffer and for those who cause suffering, evoking a lengthy outburst of applause. He also triggered applause a few minutes later with a reference to "social solidarity" and then with one to August 1980. After this third incident, John Paul asked the crowd to stop interrupting his prayer. The pope commended to Our Lady the "truths, principles, values, and attitudes" worked out in recent times, "especially since August 1980," and asked her intercession in favor of "genuine moral and social renewal" and "a dialogue through which the nation could regain the hope of full participation in the making of the shape of its common life." In effect, John Paul was calling for dialogue between state and society on the basis of the resolutions that launched the Solidarity era in late summer 1980. He followed by also commending to Mary the state authorities and went on to speak out against revenge and hatred and for forgiveness and reconciliation.

In assessing the impact of the government's protest on John Paul's behavior, a party analyst noted that the pope's Jasna Góra Appeal of June 19 was "significantly softened" from what had been expected.[137] There is no doubt that John Paul's talks before public mass gatherings on June 19 were of a different nature than those of a day earlier. He was far less indulgent of applause, far more circumspect about events of August 1980 or the sufferings under martial law, and put far more stress on forgiveness and reconciliation than he had at his two major events on June 18. Moreover, John Paul's warning at the

Jubilee mass against the misuse of freedom struck a note of favor with the regime, with a government analyst calling the pope's thesis "useful from our point of view."[138] The implication was that it was the Solidarity movement that had recently misused freedom and brought Poland to the brink of anarchy. (Jabłoński, who chaired the Council of State, would include this insinuation in his brief speech on June 23 at the pope's farewell at the Kraków airport.[139]) However, this does not mean that the pope abandoned or even tiptoed around sensitive issues. He spoke of sovereignty in a way that implicated the regime in its attenuation, spoke positively of the accomplishments of August 1980 as the foundation for future renewal, and continued to make it clear that he recognized and sympathized with the current sufferings of Poles. Also, at a nonpublic event (the bishops' conference) that same day, John Paul spoke again of the imprisoned, the interned, and those dismissed from their jobs, and he repudiated core tenets of Marxism in the name of social solidarity.

POZNAŃ AND SILESIA

On June 21, the pope bade farewell to Jasna Góra and headed on to the western Polish city of Poznań for a two-day visit, then on to sites in the region of Silesia. On June 20 in Poznań, the pope beatified Mother Urszula Ledóchowska, who founded an important religious order, the Gray Ursulines, and he then helicoptered off to southern Poland to address a huge crowd at the Upper Silesian industrial center of Katowice. After overnighting back at Jasna Góra, John Paul then paid a visit to Lower Silesia, first to its chief city of Wrocław, then to the nearby shrine of Góra Świętej Anny (Saint Anne's Mountain). All of these events provided occasions for the pope to raise sensitive issues connected with recent events in Poland, especially regarding the situation of workers. He did not disappoint.

At Poznań, John Paul celebrated the beatification mass for Mother Urszula before hundreds of thousands of onlookers at a local field.[140] Among the crowd could be seen banners written in the familiar Solidarity script, as well as people wearing round blue badges displaying the so-called "Madonna of Martial Law," a local artist's rendition of the Black Madonna of Częstochowa dedicated in the Dominican church in Poznań the day martial law was declared.[141]

The visit to Poznań opened a foray by John Paul into that part of Poland that had belonged to Germany during World War II and to Germany/Prussia during the century and a quarter of partition, when Polish lands were incorporated into neighboring empires. The communist regime wanted the pope to affirm the Polishness of these areas, and one of the expectations of his visit, made clear beforehand, was that the pope would make such affirmations. This the pope clearly did, but he did so in a way that undercut other interests of the party. Pleasing to the communists was John Paul's emphasis on the Piast origins of the Polish state and nation, for during Poland's genesis in the tenth century the Piast dynasty held those parts of Poland later claimed and/or occupied by German states (and, significantly, not the parts that Russia later took from Poland).[142] Likewise, the pope spoke with a patriotism shared by the regime, making celebratory references to Poland's independence in 1918 and lamenting the injustice of the Nazi invasion in 1939. Gearing his homily toward a rural audience, John Paul alluded to the movement by Poles in the late nineteenth century to keep agricultural land out of German hands, an important chapter in the history of Polish patriotism. In this vein, he noted the famous case of Drzymała's wagon, the story of a Polish farmer who circumvented Prussian law against Poles building homes on their own land by living in a circus wagon that he moved every day, an episode that became well known across Europe, to Prussia's humiliation. Finally, when speaking of Blessed Urszula Ledóchowska, John Paul connected her with the German government's assault on the Catholic Church and Polish nation, reminding his audience that her uncle Mieczysław, as primate of Poland and archbishop of Gniezno-Poznań, had been imprisoned by the Prussians during the anti-Catholic *Kulturkampf* launched by the new German state in the 1870s.

Although the government was pleased by these affirmations of anti-Prussian Polish patriotism, John Paul's homily combined them with insinuations that ran counter to regime interests.[143] First, in hailing Poland's Piast past, the pope explicitly connected the origin of the

Polish state and nation with the Catholic Church. He then went on to note once again Poland's connection with the West by mentioning the presence of the German (Holy Roman) emperor Otto III and two papal representatives at the congress in Gniezno, which established the Polish hierarchy in the year 1000. The crowd applauded when the pope noted that, because of this connection with Rome, "Polish culture possesses characteristics that are above all West European." Second, John Paul's references to Poland gaining its independence in 1918 and losing it in 1939 were problematic for the regime in two ways. First he reinforced the historic Catholic religiosity of Poles by connecting these events specifically with a monument to the Most Sacred Heart of Jesus that once sat in the center of Poznań, erected after the war in gratitude for Poland's restoration of independence and destroyed by the Nazis. He then went on to speak of another monument erected later on the same site to honor the dozens who perished during clashes between protesting workers and government forces in Poznań in 1956. The authorities wanted to keep the pope and the crowds a safe distance from this monument, built during the Solidarity era to commemorate worker resistance of an earlier time. To this end, the papal motorcade was not permitted to drive past the monument on its way to the mass, and after the mass riot police cordoned it off lest protesters congregate around it.[144] The regime might have been able to keep the pope and crowd from the monument physically, but it could not prevent him from referencing it in his homily: "Today on this spot [that is, where formerly stood the monument to the Most Sacred Heart of Jesus expressing Poles' gratitude for independence] stand two crosses as a monument to the victims from 1956." The veneration of this place by local Poles for reasons past and present led the pope, as he put it, "to want to kneel at this place in spirit and pay homage." This comment too brought outbursts of applause.

The two major themes of the homily—rural life and the beatification of Blessed Urszula—provide the further examples of how the pope undercut regime interests. While praising Poles' past efforts to keep land in Polish rather than German hands, John Paul noted the prominent role played by Catholic bishops and priests in that campaign. He went on to discuss more recent issues in Poland's agriculture and quoted Cardinal Wyszyński, especially his April 2, 1981, speech to Rural Solidarity, the farmers' union established in 1981 as a country cousin to Solidarity and likewise banned under martial law. Wyszyński's defense of rural and agricultural life, as John Paul noted, was akin to Pope John XXIII's call in his 1961 encyclical *Mater et magistra* for the protection of rural standards of living. Although John Paul did not explicitly praise or promote Rural Solidarity, its mere mention was significant and was appreciated as such by the crowd, which met it with sustained applause. With respect to Mother Urszula, John Paul noted in passing that after seven years of ministering in St. Petersburg she was forced to leave Russia in 1914 and thereafter worked in many ways "on behalf of her agonized Fatherland"—comments that reminded Poles that it was not just Germany or Prussia that had oppressed Poles before 1918 but Russia as well.

After his brief stay in Poznań, the pope flew by helicopter to the Upper Silesian industrial center of Katowice, where a crowd of perhaps a million or more people awaited him in the pouring rain at an airfield outside town, at Muchowiec.[145] In the heartland of the coal-mining region, Katowice had been a Solidarity stronghold where resistance to martial law was particularly bitter in December 1981. Consequently, security was much tighter than at previous venues, and police confiscated all banners and placards from arriving participants, even those of a purely religious nature.[146]

John Paul used this opportunity to speak in an industrial center to address worker-related issues at greater length and in greater depth than at any time previously on the visit.[147] As the event was a Marian devotion, the pope made reference to Mary under the title of her image at the shrine in nearby Piekary—Mother of Justice and Social Love—which he then connected with human rights, especially rights for workers.[148] In a lengthy homily that included about thirty interruptions by applause, only one of which the pope cut short, John Paul raised a number of sensitive issues that resonated with his audience. About halfway into his address, John Paul brought up "the events that took place in Poland from August 1980," speaking about them quite favorably. He asserted that these events were not just about pay raises but about the moral order itself in connection with human labor, that they were without violence, and that they had "an expressly religious character." He then went on to affirm and defend human rights, especially the right to form trade unions. In so doing, he quoted from his recent encyclical on labor, *Laborem exercens*. John Paul noted that he had spoken in a similar spirit to a delegation of visiting members of Solidarity at the Vatican in January 1981, his first direct reference to Solidarity by name during the visit. The pope went on to quote Cardinal Wyszyński, saying that this right of association is given by God; it is not up to the state to bestow it but rather to recognize and protect it.

A major theme of the papal homily was the meaning of labor, and the pope pointed to what he saw as a close connection between labor and God. Drawing from *Laborem exercens*, John Paul spoke of labor as a "fundamental vocation," linking it with God's work of creation and Jesus Christ's work of redemption. In the Silesian greeting of "Szczęść Boże!" with which the region's working people traditionally greeted each other, John Paul saw a further indication of these connections.[149]

Near the conclusion of his homily, John Paul made a passing reference to a politically charged issue. In remembering all those workers who had lost their lives in mining accidents and other workplace disasters, the pope mentioned "those who recently perished in tragic events," a clear if indirect reference to the nine miners killed by the regime's strikebreakers in the nearby Wujek mine in December 1981. In fact, a delegation from the Wujek pit was in attendance at the papal event.[150]

Communist analysts had much to dislike in the Katowice homily. The USW report noted that while John Paul was not calling for the restoration of Solidarity, he was asking that the agreements that brought Solidarity into being be the starting point for dialogue between regime and society and was thereby rejecting regime-sponsored alternatives to the independent union.[151] The report went on to note that the pope was quoting selectively from *Laborem exercens*, leaving out those portions of the encyclical that seemed to indict Solidarity, for example, that trade unions must take into account the limits imposed by the general economic situation of the country; that they are not to have a politically partisan character, or take up the practice of politics; and that strikes should be used only as a last resort.[152] For the regime, Solidarity was failing John Paul's standards on all three counts. The USW report also took note of the pope's words about the dignity and meaning of labor but argued that these concepts originated not with the Church but with socialism.[153] The KC report expressed irritation at Western news coverage of the visit, noting that the French press covered the speech at Katowice with headlines such as "The Pope Enrolls in Solidarity," "The Pope in Solidarity with Solidarity," and "The Pope Places Emphasis on His Support for 'Solidarity.'"[154]

After overnighting back in Częstochowa, John Paul headed the next morning, June 21, to Lower Silesia, where he gave a major address in the chief city of Wrocław, then went on for a Marian event at the shrine of Saint Anne's Mountain, a popular Silesian pilgrimage site dating to the late Middle Ages. On the day of the pope's visit to Lower Silesia, the government followed up its earlier statement on John Paul's speech to youth at Jasna Góra with a widely publicized interview with Deputy Prime Minister Rakowski.[155] On the front pages of state and party newspapers across Poland, Rakowski rejected the notion that Polish youth "lack prospects for the future," a rebuttal to John Paul's assertion to his young audience at Jasna Góra. In a further indirect dig at the pope, Rakowski criticized certain "educators" who treated history uncritically, feeding "myths, legends, and half-truths" to Polish youth in an effort to fascinate them with the heroic past while avoiding mention of anything bad in it. Such an approach, Rakowski warned, created the impression that Poles are "a special and chosen nation." It also ignored the unemployment and "depravity" of youth in the capitalist West. The deputy prime minister also took on Solidarity indirectly by accusing certain "demagogues" over the past three years of trying to manipulate Polish youth into a "struggle against socialism." That same day, in a friendly gesture to the Polish regime, the Vatican press office issued a statement by its chief spokesperson, Father Romeo Panciroli, accusing "certain international news organizations" of interpreting John Paul's words and visit as having a political character rather than the "exclusively religious and moral" nature that the pope intended.[156] This was clearly an example of Cardinal Casaroli trying to smooth the feathers that John Paul was ruffling.

Despite the renewed pressure from the regime and the Vatican effort to downplay political interpretations of the pope's words, John Paul in his homily at Wrocław was no less inclined to raise politically sensitive issues than he was the day before at Poznań and Katowice.[157] Wrocław too was a Solidarity stronghold and scene of pro-Solidarity protest activity under martial law. Immense crowds, possibly numbering one million, gathered at a local racetrack for the papal mass.[158] John Paul built his homily around the beatitude "Blessed are those who hunger and thirst for righteousness" and the figure of Saint Hedwig (ca. 1174–1243), repeating and expanding some of his comments about her during his 1979 visit. The pope recalled that in 1979 he was not permitted to visit Silesia, so the relics of Saint Hedwig were brought to him at Jasna Góra. He spoke of his special bond with Hedwig, as the day he was elected pope coincided with her feast day in Poland. He praised her as a woman of multiple vocations, first as wife and mother, then as widow and founder of a monastery at which she lived the religious life. He connected her with Polish history in two important ways. First, her son, Henry the Pious (Henryk II Pobożny), perished fighting the Mongols at the Battle of Legnica in 1241, a key historical event that Poles traditionally regarded as saving western Europe from Mongol invasion and laying the foundation for the perception of Poland as the "bulwark of Christendom."[159] John Paul reminded his audience of these accomplishments, even going so far as to parallel Hedwig with Jesus's mother Mary, both of whom lost a son so that others might be saved—western Europe from the Mongols in the case of Hedwig, humankind from its sins in the case of Mary. Second, John Paul used Hedwig to argue for reconciliation between Germans and Poles. He noted that Hedwig, as a German marrying into the Polish ruling family, served as a link between the two nations, as well as intercessor for Polish-German reconciliation over the centuries.

He recounted the words of Wrocław's former metropolitan, Cardinal Bolesław Kominek, who in 1967 referred to the statue of Hedwig on a bridge in Wrocław linking the eastern and western banks of the Odra (Oder) River, on whose western banks lived the Germans while the Poles lived on the eastern bank; he called the statue a reminder "that everyone are brothers, no matter on which side of the river they live."[160] John Paul then went on to add that "this idea of mutual understanding and reconciliation, *Versöhnung*, had as you know many exponents also on the German side," and he then noted his own participation in past reciprocal visits between the Polish and German bishops.[161]

John Paul's evocation of Piast times, which reminded Poles that these western territories of their country had been under Polish rule centuries ago, was welcomed by the regime. Government and party reports noted that the papal event at Wrocław made "a great impression with its patriotism" and "forcefully displayed the Polishness of these lands."[162] To underscore this theme, the altar at the papal mass was flanked by the seals of the major cities Poland had recovered or obtained from Germany in 1945.[163] However, regime analysts expressed displeasure that the pope "too strongly accentuated reconciliation between Poles and Germans," failed to condemn growing calls for border revision from nationalist groups in West Germany, and used the German word for reconciliation.[164] Furthermore, the M-L report found disfavor with John Paul's reference to the Battle of Legnica. This was surely because any reference to defense against "the enemy of the East" was taken by many Poles, as well as by the regime, to imply that the Soviet Union was the latest in a long series of such enemies that Poles had had to face over the centuries, beginning with the Mongol invasion.[165]

John Paul went on in his homily to use Saint Hedwig as an example of marriage and family life, and, after emphasizing the importance of trust for marriage and family relationships, he began to discuss the necessity of trust for addressing Poland's current crisis. This shift to contemporary events roused what had been to that point a calm crowd, especially when the pope returned to the theme of the beatitudes and spoke of those in Poland who were at present hungering and thirsting for righteousness—agricultural workers, those active in culture and education, miners and steelworkers, administrators, all the people doing hard daily labor. He expressed to them his and the Church's "solidarity" and pledged that he would protect and defend those hungering and thirsting for righteousness from any attempts to weaken their efforts or to accuse and slander them. Although John Paul did not refer to the Solidarity trade union by name, he said the word "solidarity" twice, to outbursts of applause. In fact, this part of the homily was interrupted repeatedly by applause, which John Paul made no effort to quell. Then, at the end of his homily, he made reference to those Poles who had died during World War II and in the forty years since, including "all those who perished in the events of recent years." Thus, for the third homily in a row to a mass audience, the pope made reference to Poles, especially workers, killed by the communist regime. By the event's end, the pope's words had transformed a rather sedate crowd into a boisterous one, albeit one that avoided violent confrontation. The only notable incident after the event was when several hundred protesters tried to march with Solidarity banners from the racetrack to the cathedral in town, where John Paul was to address local clergy, and riot police dispersed them with water cannon.[166]

After a brief address at the cathedral, the pope helicoptered to the mountain region and Góra Świętej Anny (St. Anne's Mountain), where an enormous crowd met him at a medieval monastery.[167] The crowd was exuberant right from the start, even breaking out into the celebratory Polish song "Sto Lat" during Marian vespers. In a lengthy address, the pope covered an assortment of religious themes—Mary, the incarnation, redemption, divine filiation, prayer, and the sacraments, among others—and spoke of a number of local and national saints and heroes.[168] The pope avoided references to recent events but continued to speak on themes addressed in his other appearances in Silesia—namely, an affirmation that these western regions were an integral part of Poland, as well as a call for German-Polish reconciliation. The venue itself added to the patriotic dimension of the event, for it was near a monument to the Silesian Insurrectionists, who rose up in the early 1920s against the occupation of Silesia by Weimar Germany as part of the border disputes between Poland and Germany in the aftermath of World War I. John Paul specifically commemorated these insurrectionists in his homily. He also made five references to the Piasts, who as rulers of the medieval Polish state with which the communists liked to identify and that had ruled over these western territories in medieval times, served as a symbol of Polish lordship over the region. The visit to Góra Świętej Anny was the closest thing to a sop for the regime that John Paul carried out during his pilgrimage. His original intent had been to visit Lublin, the home of Poland's Catholic University, but the regime vetoed that and proposed Góra Świętej Anny instead.[169] The event itself, religious and patriotic but not political, was the best the Communist Party could expect in the circumstances and what they had hoped against hope would have characterized the entire pilgrimage.

John Paul clearly got the better of the regime during his brief visits to Poznań and Upper and Lower Silesia. Although chastised by the government for his words to youth at Jasna Góra, the pope did not shy away from raising sensitive issues and alluding to recent problematic developments—the principles of August 1980, workers' right to independent trade unions, Solidarity, Rural Solidarity, and the killing of workers by communists. He also combined something the state very much wanted—a patriotic assertion of Poland's right to possess the formerly German western territories—with things that disappointed it, namely, positive calls for German-Polish reconciliation and avoidance of direct criticism of West Germany. Furthermore, he alluded to Poland's *antemurale* tradition, ostensibly against the Mongols but implicitly against other threats to Poland's welfare and identity coming from the East. It was furthermore a tradition that Poles were dying to protect; it not only distinguished Poland from the East but tied the country to the West. There remained now for John Paul only the final stop on his visit, Kraków. His visit to Silesia completed, John Paul headed off by helicopter to his beloved former home, where enormous crowds were expected to gather and listen to what he would have to say to them during this stormy and stressful time.

KRAKÓW

John Paul had two major public events in Kraków—a mass before an enormous crowd on Kraków's Commons, at which he beatified two Poles from the nineteenth century, followed by a visit to the Mistrzejowice district of the nearby working-class suburb of Nowa Huta, where he consecrated a church in honor of Saint Maximilian Kolbe. He also received an honorary degree from Kraków's Jagiellonian University, spoke to the Papal Theological Academy, and addressed a synod of local bishops. However, it was what the pope did privately during his visit to Kraków that carried the most significance, namely, an unscheduled second meeting with Jaruzelski at Wawel Castle and a private meeting with Lech Wałęsa and his family at a resort in the Tatra Mountains.

The event at the Commons was first on the agenda, drawing what may have been the largest crowd of the entire pilgrimage.[170] The two persons chosen for beatification, significantly, had been participants in the 1863 Polish uprising against tsarist Russia, and both suffered on account of it. Father Rafał Kalinowski, a young engineer and officer in the Russian army at the time, joined the failed revolt and paid with a prison term in Siberia; Brother Albert Chmielowski took part while a student and lost a leg in the fighting. John Paul held up both men as examples of the Gospel call to "lay down one's life" and saw their self-sacrifice for the uprising as a stage on their road to holiness, a road that carried them to the religious life of service to the faithful and the marginalized.[171]

John Paul's homily was designed to give encouragement and comfort to his compatriots. He spoke out against "demoralization, indifference, and despondency" and reminded Poles that Jesus Christ the Good Shepherd would be with them as they walked through the "dark valley," as Christians interpret the Twenty-Third Psalm. These comments drew the most sustained applause of the event. The crowd also responded enthusiastically to the pope's hopeful conclusion, in which he spoke of the recently beatified as "signs of victory" for the nation, a victory "by the power of faith, hope, and love," a "victory by the power of truth, freedom, and justice." At this point, many in the audience raised their hands in the "V for Victory" sign in support of the banned Solidarity union.[172] Although the pope said nothing about the Solidarity movement, it was not hard to see the connection between heroic veterans of the 1863 uprising against Russia and the Poles' current conflict with their own Soviet-backed government on behalf of workers' rights. At the end of mass, the pope again indirectly raised the current situation by expressing his regrets that some were unable to take part in that day's mass, including the sick and "persons deprived of freedom."

At the end of mass, protesters unfurled dozens of Solidarity banners and began marching the approximately seven miles to John Paul's next event—the consecration of a new church in the district of Mistrzejowice in Nowa Huta, the large working-class suburb of Kraków the pope had not been allowed to visit in 1979.[173] Built as a model communist town adjacent to vast industrial enterprises, Nowa Huta was the site of a decades-long struggle by workers and their priests to get the regime to allow Catholic churches there, a struggle in which John Paul, as Archbishop Karol Wojtyła, had been instrumental. The pope was on hand to consecrate what was now Nowa Huta's eighth church.

As the protesters marching from Kraków in a group of several thousand arrived, they joined the crowd already assembled at Mistrzejowice, producing a sizable gathering of several hundred thousand.[174] As the pope addressed this crowd, he alluded to the past difficulties of Catholics trying to get churches built in Nowa Huta, and he singled out for praise the late Father Józef Kurzeja, who had devoted his life to that struggle. Quoting from his 1982 address to the International Labour Organization in Geneva, John Paul's homily emphasized the dignity of labor, as well as other favorite themes—the connection between truth and freedom, the meaning of labor, and the connection between work and prayer.[175] He made no direct reference to the Solidarity movement; however, he did pronounce the term "Christian solidarity" to much applause, and the content of the homily was in accord with the values that produced and were represented by Solidarity. The event ended on a very upbeat note, with John Paul singing and joking and the crowd chanting phrases such as "Long live the Pope!" and "Stay with us!" The festive atmosphere reemerged later that evening in Kraków, where a large crowd gathered outside the archbishop's residence, where John Paul was staying, with the pope speaking and joking with them from his window until nearly midnight.[176] Meanwhile, a group of protesters proceeded to march, carrying both Solidarity and papal banners, from Mistrzejowice to the Ark of the Lord Church in Nowa Huta, where they laid flowers in commemoration of Bogdan Włosik, a young worker killed in protests that past October against the banning of Solidarity. They then attempted to continue their march to Kraków but were diverted by police roadblocks into a field, where church officials convinced them to disperse.[177]

After the consecration in Mistrzejowice, John Paul faced what would be the most talked about parts of his visit—a second meeting with Jaruzelski, followed the next day by a meeting with Lech Wałęsa. The former must be understood in relation to the latter: whether John Paul would meet with Wałęsa was arguably the most sensitive issue of the entire visit. The regime very much preferred that no such meeting take place and made its position quite clear in the negotiations before the trip. The pope, on the other hand, insisted he had the right and freedom to meet with whomever he desired. As the visit ran its course, there was daily speculation as to if and when John Paul and the head of the banned Solidarity union would meet. The *Washington Post*, for example, speculated that Wałęsa would meet John Paul at Jasna Góra.[178] That did not happen, and the pope's words to youth at Jasna Góra in fact threatened to derail the meeting altogether. The sharp government protest against alleged Church attempts to foment rebellion included a threat to revise the papal itinerary, which could be read as an attempt to quash the anticipated meeting.[179] The protest did not seem to constrain John Paul, who in its wake continued to raise issues sensitive for the regime (workers' rights, trade unions, Solidarity's values, etc.). However, it did prompt him to ask for a second meeting with Jaruzelski. Such a meeting was a gesture of enormous importance to the regime.[180] Above all, it could be interpreted as John

Paul affirming that Jaruzelski indeed was the acknowledged leader of Poland, that the pope was not just doing an end-run around him and talking directly to the people but that he was concerned also for what the general thought.[181] It remains unclear as to what John Paul and Jaruzelski discussed, but several immediate results were evident. First, the regime celebrated the meeting in its media, affirming that the pope and Jaruzelski had reached some important agreements.[182] Second, the pope's meeting with Wałęsa was now definitely on and would take place the next day at a resort in the Tatra Mountains. Third, John Paul's concluding speech the next day at the Kraków airport was positive in tone and avoided the kinds of digs at the regime that had characterized other parts of the visit. And finally, just what John Paul discussed, or did not discuss, with both Jaruzelski and Wałęsa touched off extensive speculation in the media, including insinuations that the pope had cut a deal with Jaruzelski at Wałęsa's expense.

The meeting with Jaruzelski took place on June 22 at Wawel Castle. It came as a surprise to the press and the public. There was speculation that Jaruzelski had asked for the visit, but the predominant view then and now was that it came on John Paul's initiative, which is how the Polish press presented it.[183] The provenance of the meeting seems more complicated, however, as Rakowski notes in his diary-memoir.[184] According to Rakowski, the initiative came from Press Bureau chief Mirosław (Mirek) Wojciechowski, who conveyed to Cardinal Glemp that the general was dissatisfied with certain aspects of the papal visit. Glemp then persuaded John Paul to propose a meeting.

The meeting lasted about two hours and twenty minutes, and no indication was given to the press or public of its content. It is possible that the meeting did not achieve any sort of specific agreement between the general and the pope but only a reiteration by Jaruzelski that martial law could be lifted soon, provided Solidarity refrained from street demonstrations and provocations. The Polish Press Agency's brief communiqué on the visit was positive and foresaw a positive future for Vatican relations with the Polish People's Republic.[185] The Polish media's coverage of the visit included photos and film footage of Jaruzelski and John Paul smiling and shaking hands, and the pope was clearly in a good mood when he engaged the crowd outside the window of the archbishop's palace shortly after the meeting.[186] Jaruzelski presumably also came out of the encounter feeling better, as the meeting could be presented as a success for the regime and might help the general withstand the criticism of those in the party upset with the way the visit had been going and with the upcoming papal audience with Wałęsa.

In the swirl of speculation about how the meeting proceeded, an account from a source close to Wałęsa stated that John Paul had pointed to the validity of the Gdańsk Accords, with Jaruzelski replying that he respected them but had to suspend them on account of Solidarity and was seeking to realize them via government-sponsored trade unions and the Patriotic Movement of National Rebirth (Patriotyczny Ruch Odrodzenia Narodowego, or PRON).[187] He may have also tried to impress on the pope the difficulty of his situation, caught between Solidarity and the Polish public on one hand and party critics and the Soviet Union on the other.[188] Rakowski claims that Jaruzelski told him the meeting was basically a continuation of the discussion at Belvedere and was largely ethical-philosophical in nature, not mentioning martial law or Wałęsa.[189] According to Rakowski, Jaruzelski reported that the pope accepted Polish realities, telling the general, "I understand that in Poland socialism is a permanent phenomenon."[190] John Paul also allegedly sought to explain what the regime regarded as his strident interventions in Poland's political and social situation. According to Rakowski, the pope told Jaruzelski that he must speak about dignity and identity in order to be faithful to himself and his vocation but that he had been doing this "delicately," seeking with "great caution" not to worsen the situation in Poland.[191]

The next morning John Paul was off by helicopter to a Tatra Mountain hostel to meet Wałęsa. The venue was chosen by the regime and no doubt full of listening devices. The event was regarded as an unofficial visit, and it was the pope's final stop before he was to head for Balice Airport in Kraków and his departure for Rome. Neither Wałęsa nor the Polish authorities spoke in any detail about the meeting, and the Vatican customarily is silent about private meetings of the pope. Wałęsa's memoirs say very little of substance about the encounter. Based on Western press reports of the time, as well as later remarks by General Jaruzelski and Bishop Tadeusz Gocłowski, who accompanied Wałęsa on behalf of the Polish bishops, the accounts we have are conflicting—one has the meeting lasting approximately forty minutes and covering the situation in Poland, the popular mood, and Solidarity's future; the other has the meeting lasting for fifteen to twenty minutes and consisting mainly of John Paul speaking with Wałęsa's wife and children and surveying the mountain landscape.[192] The fact that Wałęsa had so little to say about the meeting and that both Vatican and Solidarity sources reported that he left the meeting with an air of disappointment, lend credence to the view that John Paul either failed to tell him what he wanted to hear or told him something that he did not want to hear.[193] Observers at the time also noticed that the Vatican elected not to release any photos of John Paul with Wałęsa.[194]

Of the interpretations at the time, the one that holds up best is the view that John Paul wanted Wałęsa to refrain from public activity while the Church sought to negotiate an end to martial law and an amnesty for the interned, hence the cold shoulder in the Tatras.[195] Adding to the mystery and confusion about the meeting was a front-page editorial appearing two days later in the Vatican newspaper *L'Osservatore Romano*, by deputy editor Virgilio Levi, entitled "Honor to the Sacrifice." The article stated that "officially Lech Wałęsa once more leaves the scene. We can say that he has lost his battle. . . . Sometimes the sacrifice of uncomfortable people is necessary so a higher good can be born for the community."[196] In praising Wałęsa for stepping aside for the greater good, the article was endorsing the view that John Paul had asked him to withdraw from political activity. The article, either because it was misleading or because it was too true, led to Levi's resignation the next day and to the newspaper management publishing a notice that the article had reflected Levi's "own journalistic opinion."[197] It also led to charges that the pope had abandoned Wałęsa in order to "cut a deal" with Jaruzelski, an accusation most famously leveled in an op-ed piece by William Safire in the *New York Times*. Safire accused the Church of "backing away from moral heroism," noted that Wałęsa had to "wait in publicized ignominy" for his meeting with the pope, and accused John Paul of presuming to substitute himself for the not totally controllable Wałęsa as "the exclusive symbol of Polish freedom." Safire concluded that "the Pope should uphold and protect Mr. Wałęsa, not try to replace him."[198] Other sources soberly noted that Levi was likely ill informed or misinformed about the actual meeting or that his article reflected the opinion of Vatican elements unhappy with John Paul's "excessive" concern about developments in Poland rather than an actual papal policy to abandon Wałęsa.[199] Still other sources, for example, Deputy Prime Minister Rakowski, believed that Levi got in trouble for stating too boldly a view that was circulating at the Vatican.[200]

Regardless of what transpired between Wałęsa and John Paul, Safire's critique of John Paul is unfair and exaggerated. Unlike observers in the Western media, the pope did not see Wałęsa as the only possible embodiment of the principles of workers' rights championed by the Solidarity movement. For John Paul, it was the principles that lay at the foundation of the Gdańsk Accords, including the freedom to organize independent trade unions, that were essential, not the identity of the movement's leader. In fact, Wałęsa's role as head of Solidarity was not uncontested. Many younger Poles preferred the more radical Zbigniew Bujak, and some prominent Polish intellectuals and cultural figures kept Wałęsa at arm's length.[201] Still, John Paul had been determined, since the visit's planning stages, to meet with Wałęsa, and he did what he could to see that goal realized. That in itself demonstrates papal support for the Solidarity movement.

It is entirely consistent with John Paul's career-long concern for the freedoms and welfare of his compatriots, as well as for peaceful, constructive change and responsible exercise of freedom, for the pope to seek a way to get martial law lifted and labor activists and dissidents out of jail, even if that meant that Wałęsa might have to reduce his profile or even step aside as the process developed. This is hardly a "sell-out" of the movement or its principles. If anything, it could be seen as a way to get things moving in a delicate situation. Likewise, given that Jaruzelski was under pressure from hard-liners in Moscow, from elsewhere in the bloc, and from within his own party, in part for being too accommodating to the Church and for permitting the second pilgrimage, it made sense that John Paul would not want him to come away with nothing from the visit.[202] By requesting a second meeting with Jaruzelski, by minimizing his contact with Wałęsa, by avoiding any explicit endorsement of the Solidarity leader, and by toning down his comments at the pilgrimage's conclusion, the pope gave Jaruzelski the possibility of presenting the visit as beneficial for the regime rather than as a big mistake. John Paul seems to have successfully maneuvered between the needs of Jaruzelski's team on the one hand and the welfare of his compatriots and the rights of workers on the other.

We know from subsequent developments that Wałęsa did not step aside and that although certain important elements in the Church in Poland were interested in a cooperative agreement with the regime that left Solidarity on the sidelines, John Paul remained firm in his commitment to the tenets on which the Solidarity movement was based, as manifested in the Gdańsk Accords, and he was thus unwilling to bless abandoning them for the sake of better relations with the Polish regime. At the same time, his commitment to a peaceful evolution of the situation makes it plausible, even likely, that he sought the lifting of martial law, along with sufficient restraint on the part of Solidarity necessary to make that a reality. Unlike both the Polish communist regime and the Western media, the pope did not obsessively focus on the person of Wałęsa, or even on the institution of Solidarity, but on the principles that inspired it. These are what he wanted to see come to fruition in his native land, and he was careful not to compromise these principles while seeking improvement in the lives of the Polish population, including those still interned.

After this short meeting, John Paul was helicoptered to the airport in Kraków, where he spoke his final word to Poles before departure. Also speaking were President Jabłoński and Cardinal Glemp. The pope's speech, as the *Washington Post* observed, contained "careful, non-controversial language" and appears to have been toned down from an earlier draft in the wake of John Paul's meeting with Jaruzelski.[203] Indeed, there was no mention of even "solidarity" with a small *s* in his speech, let alone of Wałęsa. The pope expressed gratitude to everyone who had assisted in making the visit possible, including even those responsible for his security and for keeping order.[204] He called on the whole of society to work to overcome Poland's present difficulties, and in a subtle plug for Polish sovereignty he stated that "the nation . . . must live and grow by its own powers." He affirmed human rights, as well as the dignity of the human person and human labor. He called for mutual trust and a spirit of social love, and he expressed his wish that good would prove to be more powerful than evil in Poland. Without being blunt, John Paul made his points, and the subtext of his comments presented challenges to the regime, whether it wanted to recognize them or not. Anyone who had been listening to John Paul's words over the previous seven days knew that when he expressed his desire that the authorities work toward building the common good and restoring the deserved place of Poland among the nations of Europe and the world, he was setting goals that he believed could be achieved only through respect for the rights of workers, including their right to independent trade unions. Likewise, any affirmation of Polish sovereignty by John Paul implied criticism of outside, primarily Soviet, pressure. The government, its reputation hinging upon a papal visit that could be seen as beneficial to the regime, played up the positives and put its own interpretation on the pope's words. President Jabłoński, with whom John Paul "chatted animatedly" at the event, stated in his speech that "we find in many statements of Your Holiness judgments convergent with ours."[205] For example, Jabłoński quoted favorably the pope's warning in Jasna Góra that humans can use freedom to build or destroy, the implication being that this could be applied to Solidarity's alleged abuses of the greater freedom Poles had achieved after August 1980.[206] The government also liked the fact that John Paul had noted in his farewell address that "rights and obligations are closely connected with each other," something that could be used to encourage Poles to eschew strikes and demonstrations and take up the hard work needed for economic recovery.[207] Still, as noted above, the speech presented subtle challenges to the regime and in no way abandoned the principles that had inspired the Solidarity movement and the Gdańsk Accords. At the end of the event, the pope got on board a LOT Airlines plane and departed for Rome.

CONCLUDING ASSESSMENT

As with the 1979 pilgrimage, if not even more so, the government of Poland wanted to present the 1983 papal visit as a great success for the regime. Toward this end, Adam Łopatka, as director of the government's Office of Confessional Affairs, gave a lengthy address to the Polish Sejm on June 24.[208] He played up healthy Church-state relations, extolled John Paul's meetings with government authorities, especially the two with Jaruzelski, and accused the Western press of distorted reporting and overly politicizing the visit, noting that the Vatican had complained earlier about the same things. Łopatka hailed the successful execution of the visit, highlighting the work of crowd control marshals, medical personnel, transportation services, and the police. He noted the close cooperation between the government and the Church in the successful execution of the visit. The director summarized the negotiations with the Vatican and with Poland's bishops in advance of the visit, putting emphasis on expectations that the trip would contribute to national reconciliation in Poland, improved relations between the Polish People's Republic and the Apostolic See, and world peace. Łopatka saw success in all three areas. Although he acknowledged that it was too soon to present a deep and comprehensive analysis of the visit, he shared a number of observations with the aim of presenting the visit in as positive a light as possible. According to Łopatka, the visit contributed to national agreement and national revival as well as to improved Church-state relations. He cited in particular some examples of Western opposition to the visit as evidence of its benefit to the Polish regime. According to Łopatka, despite efforts by the opposition to exploit the papal gatherings for political ends, the visit took place in an atmosphere of calm and dignity. He noted with satisfaction the contribution to international peace that John Paul's visit occasioned, claiming that it demonstrated the convergence of views between Poland and the Apostolic See with respect to peace, the arms race, and nuclear catastrophe. He also credited John Paul for affirming the inviolability of Poland's borders and the Polishness of the western and northern territories, a papal rejoinder to revanchists in West Germany. John Paul's visit also affirmed the "realistic" policy of cooperation by the Church in Poland with the state. Although the director recognized that the full picture of the visit was not unequivocally rosy, he contended that the differences between the regime and the pope did not leave a "dominating imprint" on the visit. Łopatka concluded by informing the Sejm that with the pope's second visit, the confessional policy of the Polish People's Republic had "passed the historical test."

How did Łopatka's assessment line up with the reality of the visit? The Church and state did cooperate successfully in planning and executing the pilgrimage, and the pope did refrain from words or actions that might directly provoke the Soviet Union and its allies.[209] John Paul also affirmed the legitimacy of Poland's western borders and the Polishness of the Recovered Territories. However, a number of the positives that Łopatka mentioned were far more equivocal than he pretended, and he left a lot unsaid that would otherwise paint a very different picture of the visit.

With respect to the events of August 1980 and December 1981, John Paul found ways to let his affection for Solidarity and dislike of martial law be known. Throughout the course of his trip, the pope made it obvious that his heart lay with his compatriots, who were suffering under the martial law imposed by the regime. He repeatedly expressed his sympathy toward those Poles who were interned, imprisoned, dismissed from work, or otherwise suffering in the wake of the December 1981 crackdown on Solidarity. He also made clear his support for the values and principles that animated the workers' movement and served as the basis for the accords it reached with the government in late summer 1980. On several occasions he outright affirmed the workers' right to independent trade unions. Although he mentioned Solidarity by name only once, he made numerous references to "solidarity" with a small *s*, insisted on meeting with Wałęsa, and met with Solidarity advisors and supporters, including workers from Szczecin, the mother of a victim of police violence, and representatives of Rural Solidarity. John Paul also used indirect means to evoke the spirit of the outlawed labor union without naming it, for example, by a timely employment of words such as "victory" that prompted crowds to flash Solidarity's two-finger "V-for-Victory" sign.

The pope dealt especially cleverly with the question of sanctions. To affirm them could be seen as backing a policy that was hurting Poles economically. To oppose them could be construed as support for martial law. John Paul managed to do neither. Reminiscent of Jesus Christ, who evaded the Pharisees' efforts to trap him over the issue of whether to pay taxes to the Romans and force him to come out as either a toady supporting Roman oppression or a tax rebel liable to prosecution, John Paul avoided having to choose between supporting Jaruzelski or inflicting pain on ordinary Poles. Rather, he expressed his hope that the conditions would materialize for cooperation between Poland and the West, especially the United States. This meant the regime must hold a dialogue with society, in accord with the social agreements concluded in the wake of the events of August 1980 "by the representatives of the state and the representatives of the world of labor."[210]

Despite his finesse, the pope did disturb the regime in some ways, such as his references to the dismal state of Polish youth, his allusions to the massacres of workers in 1956 (Poznań) and 1981 (Wujek mine), or his stress on the deep connection between the Polish nation, the Polish workers, and the Catholic faith, to name a few. He also made several references to repression of and resistance by Poles while living under Russian rule in the pre–World War I era, as well as to Poland's historical connections with the West and defense of Europe against enemies from the East in past centuries. Even when accommodating communist wishes, the pope often did so in a way that provoked the regime. For example, along with asserting a patriotic defense of Poland's borders, he upset the government with his appeals for German-Polish reconciliation. Moreover, any praise of Poland for its accomplishments after 1945 went to the nation, not the state or government or party, and John Paul's emphasis on the importance of Polish sovereignty was more a subtle indictment than a commendation of the regime.

When it became clear that the papal visit would be about much more than religious commemorations and that John Paul would be testing the limits of the tenets agreed on prior to the visit, the government pushed back, chiefly through interventions with Vatican diplomats and Polish bishops, as well as press commentary and media briefings. In this context, the pope knew how to retreat effectively when necessary without sacrificing his credibility and authority in the eyes of his fellow Poles. We see this, for example, in how he treated bursts of applause from his audiences at key points in his homilies and speeches. Generally, he cut applause short or asked the crowd not to interrupt him. He did this in Warsaw at Saint John the Baptist Cathedral and at Decennial Stadium, as well as in Częstochowa at the anniversary mass and the Jasna Góra Appeal. The latter two events came in the immediate aftermath of a government intervention. However, at other times the pope let the applause ring out, in particular during his speech to youth at Jasna Góra (which helped prompt the government intervention of June 19) and when addressing largely working-class crowds at Katowice and Wrocław a few days after the intervention, which was evidence as sure as any that John Paul, while sensitive to the regime's concerns, was not going to be cowed by them. The same holds for the content of his addresses in the aftermath of the June 19 intervention. In his Jasna Góra Appeal, the pope was more subtle than previously in addressing the current situation in Poland, and he included calls for dialogue, reconciliation between state and society, and forgiveness along with warnings against hatred and revenge. But neither then nor subsequently did he cease talking about human rights, the principles of August 1980, the right to independent labor unions, the present and past suffering of his compatriots, and solidarity (directly) and Solidarity (indirectly).

John Paul's skillful handling of the complex and sensitive situation in his homeland is very evident in his approach to Jaruzelski and Wałęsa. He agreed to a second meeting with the general and came to some sort of modus vivendi with him, ending his week in Poland in a good mood and with an upbeat farewell, subtle in its challenge to the regime. Wałęsa, on the other hand, was sidelined by the pope, who staunchly defended Solidarity's principles throughout his visit, especially the workers' right to independent labor unions, and insisted on meeting the outlawed union's leader, but without treating Wałęsa as an indispensable player in Poland's immediate political future.

Overall, John Paul operated adroitly during the second pilgrimage, making the most of a critical situation, accommodating the regime when he had to but also pushing beyond the pre-agreed tenets and going places where the regime did not want him to go. Contra Vatican diplomats, as well as those Polish bishops who, like Cardinal Glemp, were reluctant to rock the boat, the pope pressured the government by his repeated expressions of concern for the victims of martial law and of support for the ideals that inspired Solidarity.[211] Still, he was careful not to hitch the Church to Wałęsa's falling star or to undermine Jaruzelski's authority in the face of pressure from critics in his own party and his position in the eyes of the Soviet Union. In John Paul, Poland was dealing with a formidable personality, a leader who was diplomatically astute, yet eager and able to advance views critical of the regime and sympathetic to its victims, while careful not to provoke violence from either population or regime.

Poland's opposition, as represented above all in the Solidarity union, expressed great satisfaction with John Paul's visit. On July 3, the Temporary Coordinating Commission issued a statement referring to the visit as "days of great religious, moral and social upheaval," during which John Paul conferred "a proper sense to the words Truth, Freedom, and Justice." The papal events brought together all those Poles who valued "the sovereignty of the nation, the subjectivity of society, the dignity of the person and the meaning of his labor, and the right of free association."[212] In an interview in *Tygodnik Mazowsze's* July 14 issue, Zbigniew Bujak, one of the most important leaders in the Solidarity underground, elaborated on the impact of the pope's visit.[213] He called John Paul's teachings "a fundamental inspiration for our life, of our work and struggle," with his homilies serving as "an

essential guidepost for our activity." Bujak noted that the locales of
the papal events became "enclaves of freedom" where Polish society
could show its authentic face. Banners emblazoned with "Solidarity"
and cheers for the union were ubiquitous, making it clear that despite
months of repression, Solidarity remained "a universal symbol of society's efforts and aspirations." Its supporters received during these
momentous days "a feeling of strength flowing from the conviction
of the justness of our efforts."

The Solidarity press across Poland gave extensive coverage to the
papal visit, including copious excerpts from papal speeches, and it
provided often insightful analysis. The underground publication *KOS*
celebrated the impact of the pilgrimage by noting that "we recovered
our voice, we stood erect. We again became subjects in our own history, something unprecedented in a totalitarian state." Although the
pilgrimage was "a religious and moral event" and not a political one
per se, the pope came to give witness to the truth, and in a totalitarian
country "there is nothing more political than truth."[214] A number of
Solidarity publications mentioned the pro-Solidarity chants, banners,
flags, and two-fingered victory signs that repeatedly popped up during
the visit.[215] *Wola* mentioned that Poles lost their fatigue and anxiety
during the pilgrimage.[216] Kraków's *Kronika Małopolska* wrote that "we
obtained moral support for the fundamental values of the movement,
a confirmation of its rightfulness, and encouragement to confidence
and dialogue . . . based on precisely these very values."[217] Several publications compared the days of June 1983 with those of June 1979 and
August 1980. The Solidarity newspaper in Gdańsk stated that in June
1979 John Paul had awakened Poles to a moral renewal of society,
which bore fruit in August 1980. John Paul had now come in June 1983
to call for faithfulness to those values.[218] Another underground journal
compared the "togetherness" felt by Poles in June 1983 with the similar
experience in June 1979 and August 1980.[219] An especially apt summation of the 1983 visit came from the publication *Solidarność Walcząca* of
the radical anticommunist splinter group Fighting Solidarity, which
observed that "this whole visit became a great nationwide referendum.
We voted with our feet—coming to [meet] with the Pope from town

and country, and with our hands—applauding Him for words and statements the closest to us."[220]

For most Poles, the 1983 visit was probably about comforting them in their distress more than anything else. John Paul shone like a candle amid the gloom of martial law, with a message of hope in a time of despair. He could assure Poles that they were not forgotten, that their current woes were but another phase in a long tradition of Polish suffering, and that they could live in the hope that their suffering would bear positive fruit in the future, that love, life, and good would ultimately prevail. Along with comfort and hope, the pilgrimage also brought inspiration and encouragement, both in the expressed views of the Polish opposition noted above and, as we shall see later, in actuality. If the first pilgrimage of John Paul II helped lead to Solidarity, what, if anything, would this second visit lead to? As one Catholic intellectual hoped in advance of the pope's arrival, "The first visit broke through a barrier of fear. Perhaps this one can break through the barrier of hopelessness."[221] Indeed it did, though not immediately. Garton Ash, speculating about Poland's future after the second papal pilgrimage, concluded that "for all the depression and repression, Poland may be said to be in a better condition than any of its neighbors—including even Hungary. This transformation of consciousness, this moral revolution, is a lasting achievement of the Pope and Solidarity." Garton Ash continued, "Whatever develops in Poland over the next few years, it will be different from anything we have seen before. Though the police rule the streets, the country cannot be 'normalized'—i.e., returned to Soviet norms. Though the totalitarian Communist system remains in outward form, in reality it is still being dismantled from within."[222] Soon, Jaruzelski himself would begin implementing reforms that contributed to this dismantling. Then John Paul would make his own contribution to the process with a visit in 1987, during which he would criticize and condemn communist policies more forcefully than ever. Finally, wildcat strikes would break out in 1988 and 1989 and prompt the government to share power with a relegalized Solidarity. With this one-two punch from John Paul and Polish laborers, communism's days in Poland were numbered.

Father Karol Wojtyła, in the early 1950s, on one of the many mountain excursions he took with young adults from his parish and students from Kraków's Jagiellonian University. Archive of Adam Bujak.

Cardinal Wojtyła blessing a child with its mother in front of Wawel Cathedral in Kraków in the 1970s. Adam Bujak.

John Paul II, as pope, in 1985. Photo by Rob C. Croes / ANEFO.

John Paul arrives at Okęcie Airport in Warsaw for his first papal pilgrimage to Poland in June 1979. Alamy Stock Photo.

John Paul addresses an enormous crowd at Częstochowa during his 1979 visit to Poland. Institute of National Remembrance.

(*Above*) The Pope gives Holy Communion to the leader of the banned Solidarity trade union, Lech Wałęsa, during the Mass at Zaspa. The district was home to Wałęsa, whose flat was in one of its extensive housing developments. Arturo Mari / AP Photo.

(*Opposite page, top*) John Paul at his meeting with Poland's leader, General Wojciech Jaruzelski, during his 1983 visit. Poland was under martial law at the time. United Press International.

(*Opposite page, bottom*) The enormous crowd at the papal Mass for the World of Labor at the working-class district of Zaspa in Gdańsk in 1987. Banners of the outlawed independent labor union Solidarity can be seen among the audience. Alamy Stock Photo.

The pope meets with hierarchs of the Ukrainian Eastern Rite Catholics in Poland during his 1991 visit. Outreach to Eastern Christians, including Ukrainians, was a major goal of that pilgrimage. Alamy Stock Photo.

3

CRITIC

The 1987 Pilgrimage

SHORTLY AFTER THE 1983 VISIT, THE GOVERNMENT, AS EXPECTED, lifted martial law. Still, the population was embittered, and economic conditions remained distressed. The outlawed Solidarity movement, albeit significantly weakened organizationally, persisted in illegality. Underground publishing and oppositional organizations also continued to operate. Jaruzelski had an enormous task before him in overcoming widespread societal hostility or indifference toward his regime, as well as in meeting the challenge of improving Poland's image abroad, getting its economy back on keel, and mastering serious divisions within the Communist Party, which he continued to serve as first secretary. Poland faced something of a stalemate, with the regime unable to win over a largely hostile or indifferent population and get it to cooperate in Poland's recovery and Poles, now without a legal independent trade union, unable to bring sufficient pressure on the government to make desired changes. By 1986, however, the logjam had begun to loosen, largely on account of changes in the Soviet Union. In March 1985, the reformist Mikhail Gorbachev became general secretary of the Communist Party of the Soviet Union. After consolidating his power, he launched a reformist program at home and encouraged one abroad, which spurred the Jaruzelski regime to embark on its own series of reforms in hopes of reconciling Poland's leaders with its people.[1]

Soon after lifting martial law, Jaruzelski amnestied most of Poland's seven hundred–plus political prisoners.[2] His administration then tried a number of things to get Poles to support the government. It eased censorship, promoted government-sponsored trade unions as a replacement for Solidarity, created new associations for artists and intellectuals, facilitated the construction of hundreds of churches, and launched a crackdown on "speculators," on whom Poland's economic problems were blamed. There was also an attempt to attract those Catholic activists and members of the political opposition most amenable to cooperation with the government through the establishment of an advisory council to the chairman of the Council of State. In November 1985, Jaruzelski resigned as prime minister, though retaining decisive power and prestige by remaining on as first secretary of the Communist Party and by succeeding Jabłoński as chairman of the Council of State.

Despite these efforts, Jaruzelski had meager success in restoring public trust and faced a number of related problems as well. The economy continued to deteriorate—prices rising, shortages persisting, foreign debt increasing. Opinion polls showed a steady increase in the proportion of Poles who thought the economic situation was bad, from 38 percent in December 1985 to 69 percent in spring 1987. Moreover, the Communist Party had become increasingly factionalized, with some reform-minded members pushing for more than the basically cosmetic changes proposed by the government and others intent on tougher measures against the opposition. The martial law regime especially targeted priests who were actively supporting Solidarity. One such figure was Father Jerzy Popiełuszko, who was vicar at Saint Stanisław Kostka parish in Warsaw's Żoliborz neighborhood. Father Popiełuszko was chaplain of Solidarity for Warsaw steelworkers, an organizer of support for the interned and their families, and the initiator of the pilgrimages of working people to Jasna Góra, among other things.[3] He was perhaps best known, and most troublesome to the communists, for the "Mass for the Fatherland" that he had celebrated one Sunday each month since February 1982; it was an occasion to pray for those killed under martial law, as well as for those interned, arrested, or fired from their jobs. Popiełuszko and other pro-Solidarity clergy were targeted by the security services in a series of operations, which for Father Popiełuszko culminated in his abduction and brutal murder by security agents in October 1984.[4] The regime held its breath as more than two hundred thousand people attended a martyr's funeral in Warsaw, albeit without incident.

Solidarity, meanwhile, along with other elements of Poland's opposition, remained active in the underground. When parliamentary elections were held in autumn of 1985, Solidarity called for a boycott, and somewhere between 66 and 79 percent of Poles voted, well below the near total participation typical of elections in communist states.[5] Nevertheless, Solidarity's capacity to mobilize society was greatly diminished at this time. Its leaders were in prison, in hiding, or inactive. Poles were apparently psychologically exhausted, tiring of the struggle, losing faith in the prospects of success, and caught up in daily hardships. The union's occasional calls for strikes found little support. Nevertheless, the organization continued to operate under its Temporary Coordinating Commission, or TKK, and a number of other small but active political groups sprang up, while the underground press flourished. Solidarity estimated that fifty thousand to seventy thousand Poles were actively engaged in its activities, with an additional two hundred thousand as occasional helpers; the police put the numbers at thirty-four thousand and one hundred thousand, respectively. Even the lower estimates constituted a considerable problem for the regime, and they explain why rallies connected with the opposition could draw upward of ten thousand participants on national holidays and days of commemoration, almost always in connection with a Catholic mass.

Thus, state and society were locked in a stalemate. The opposition could not be shut down, but it lacked the power to extract concessions from the regime. At this juncture, a big influence came from the outside. Gorbachev's rise to power in the Soviet Union, as well as Jaruzelski's decision to bind his future to the Soviet leader's reformist agenda, meant that Poland set itself on the path to reform in greater earnest than in the years immediately after the lifting of martial law. In summer 1986, Gorbachev visited the Polish Communist Party congress and boosted the general's confidence. Another amnesty soon followed, and oppositional groups took advantage of the loosening of restrictions to emerge into the open. While most Solidarity structures opted to remain underground, some began to operate in public, and a number of clubs began to hold open meetings. This easing of repression and revival of political life had international ramifications. In early autumn, Wałęsa and some leading Polish intellectuals and activists called on U.S. president Ronald Reagan to lift the remaining sanctions against Poland.[6]

Change was clearly in the air. The international context had improved considerably since the early 1980s. The Soviets were not only encouraging reform in Poland but getting along better with the United States, which also welcomed Jaruzelski's easing of tensions at home. Poland began to improve its status internationally. Some sanctions had already been lifted, and Warsaw was holding meetings at the foreign minister level with the West. A September 11, 1986, amnesty only improved Poland's standing. Still, this was not enough to bring social reconciliation and economic renewal or to assuage hard feelings about martial law.

This improving but still troubled Poland was the context of John Paul's third pilgrimage, in June 1987, to his native land. In January that year, Jaruzelski himself went to the Vatican to meet with the pope and settle certain issues related to the visit. The more conciliatory attitude that prevailed among Poland's leaders, as well as the new course emanating from Moscow, created conditions for a papal visit like none before. John Paul would be coming to a Poland where he could speak more openly than during his previous visits, about Poland's past, present, and even future. The opposition also took advantage of the new atmosphere and the upcoming papal visit, as we shall see below.

Hopes for a 1987 visit by the pope began to be raised soon after his second visit, when Cardinal Glemp suggested that John Paul visit Poland for the statewide Eucharistic Congress planned for that year.[7]

By late 1985, Church and government officials had begun discussing such a visit, principally through the Joint Commission, made up of government officials and the episcopate, which handled contacts between Church and state leaders in Poland. The chief negotiators for the government were Kazimierz Barcikowski, representing Jaruzelski as chairman of the Council of State, and Adam Łopatka, minister and director of the Office for Confessional Affairs. Those for the Church were Cardinal Franciszek Macharski, archbishop of Kraków, and Archbishop Bronisław Dąbrowski, secretary of the episcopate. At the Joint Commission meeting of December 23, 1985, the government presented its expectations for such a visit: it had to contribute positively to consolidation in Poland and to the reputation of Poland internationally; the pope's speeches were not to complicate Poland's position in the Soviet bloc nor provide material that Western media could use against Poland; John Paul would visit the western territories, thereby affirming their Polishness; he was not to visit Gdańsk, given the "complicated climate"; government and Church were to act in tandem and avoid any kind of "surprises"; and the visit could not last too long, given the impact on production caused by lost labor and the problems with mass transit of pilgrims.[8]

As talks proceeded over the next year and a half, the two sides settled an array of issues, with each making important compromises, giving up certain desiderata, and achieving key objectives. The Church proposed that the visit, scheduled for early June 1987, begin in Kraków and end in Warsaw. The state authorities saw this as a violation of protocol, one that threatened to undermine the prestige of the regime, and they insisted that the visit begin in Warsaw and include a meeting between Jaruzelski and John Paul very early on.[9] The Church agreed to this, and a meeting between the pope and the general was slated for the Royal Castle on day one. The Church also conceded to government wishes that John Paul not visit Rzeszów, as it was located in the eastern part of the country and too close to the Soviet border for comfort.[10] Both sides agreed that the visit would not be "overpacked," the regime wanting to avoid the disruption to the work day and the challenge of transporting such huge crowds (as well as its unspoken desire to not give too much opportunity to the pope to connect with the population), and the Church agreeing because John Paul himself did not want to be so overburdened with events as in past pilgrimages and because he needed to be back in Rome in time for the Corpus Christi celebrations there.[11] The Church was also anxious that the regime not deploy an excessive number of uniformed security forces during the visit.[12]

The government authorities had anxieties of their own, as one might imagine. They worried about what kind of "accent" John Paul would put on the beatifications to be carried out during his visit, in particular that of Karolina Kózkówna, whose case (she was the victim of attempted rape by a Russian soldier) needed to be handled delicately.[13] They also expressed concern over links between certain clergy and the political opposition, in particular Father Henryk Jankowski, who was pastor at Saint Brigida's in Gdańsk and a staunch supporter of Solidarity.[14] Although willing to allow the pope to visit the grave of the priest-martyr Father Popiełuszko at Saint Stanisław Kostka Church in Warsaw, the state representatives insisted that this be an "unofficial" visit and that the pope not appear to be blessing the pro-Solidarity and antiregime activity that had been undertaken at the parish at the time of and since Popiełuszko's murder.[15] The regime was also open to the pope meeting with Wałęsa, but "without surprises." In negotiating with the Church, communist spokespersons betrayed their deepest fears—that the pope would lift a kneeling Wałęsa to his feet in an act of solidarity with him or that the crowds would hoist Wałęsa up to the altar during the ceremony.[16]

Most of these issues were settled to the satisfaction of Church and state during the preliminary negotiations. The Church assured the government that the beatifications would be handled carefully, noting that a similar situation came up in 1983 with the beatification of Father Rafał Kalinowski (another victim of Russian aggression), which John Paul had treated with care.[17] It also agreed that the visit to Popiełuszko's grave would be unofficial.[18] On other issues, the Church would not back down. It refused to agree to remove Father Jankowski from his position as pastor at Saint Brigida's parish in Gdańsk, and it affirmed that the Holy Father would meet with Wałęsa when and where the pope wished. With regard to alleged support by clergy for the opposition, the Church held its ground, arguing that the links that particular clergy had with the opposition should be treated as a separate issue from the papal visit and rejecting any interventions against such clergy as a condition for the visit. After Jaruzelski's trip to the Vatican on January 13, 1987, the questions of Wałęsa and Jankowski receded from discussion, suggesting that the general and the pontiff had worked something out.[19]

Jaruzelski's meeting with the pope also opened the way for the regime's acceptance of a stop by the pope in Gdańsk, probably the thorniest issue up to then. Negotiators on both sides devoted more attention to this issue than to any other. The regime had a number of reasons to fear and discourage such a visit. Gdańsk was the site of major labor unrest in 1970 and 1980, it was the birthplace of the Solidarity movement, and it was the home of both Wałęsa and the troublesome Father Jankowski. In the government's view, the climate was not yet right for a visit to Gdańsk.[20] The state feared above all that the event would degenerate into a political demonstration and that keeping order might be beyond the capability of the local church.[21] The ecclesial representatives, on the other hand, presented their case for Gdańsk by stressing themes in line with the interests of the regime.[22] First and most important, the bishops played to the regime's patriotism, especially its desire to present itself as defender of Poland's western borders against alleged German revanchism. Along these lines, the bishops stressed that Gdańsk, where World War II began with a German invasion, was the ideal locale for commemorating Polish heroism. They pointed to celebrated acts of resistance at the Polish military base at Westerplatte and at the Polish Post Office in Gdańsk. They noted the proximity of the Stutthof concentration camp, where many members of Gdańsk's Polish minority arrested by the Nazi regime had perished. They connected the upcoming eight-hundredth anniversary of Oliwa Cathedral and the Order of Cistercians associated with it to the preservation and defense of Polish identity in the Pomeranian region. They argued that should the pope bypass Gdańsk, it might confirm the belief that the city really should be regarded as German and not Polish. Second, the Church sought to connect the papal visit with the "peace" policy of the time in the Soviet bloc, noting that there was nowhere better than Westerplatte from which John Paul could appeal for peace. This argument got a huge boost when Jaruzelski concluded after his January meeting with John Paul at the Vatican that the pope's views on peace were the Church's own and not part of the American vision of international order.[23] Third, the Church noted the potential damage to Poland's international reputation should the pope not visit Gdańsk, as the foreign press would speculate that the government was keeping him away. A successful visit, on the other hand, would drive home to the world that social conditions in Poland had indeed become stabilized. The Church noted that the mood in Gdańsk had been calm since the amnesty of 1986 and that the residents there had sufficient religious self-awareness to keep events from turning into a political demonstration. In fact, a papal visit would only reinforce the calm, whereas should the pope not visit, there would be a clamor. The Church also expressed confidence in the ability of the bishop of Gdańsk to maintain order.[24]

As the negotiations in preparation for the visit proceeded, the Church refused to back down on Gdańsk. The pope even made it a condition for his visit, on the ground that his credibility would be at stake should he not stop there.[25] Ultimately, the regime conceded on Gdańsk, while insisting that the pope hold an event at Westerplatte while there, to which the Church obliged. The government also let it be known that should the visit to Gdańsk come off well, it would be more forthcoming in accommodating some of the desires of the Gdańsk diocese regarding permission for church construction and other issues related to the functioning of the Church there.[26]

Besides the Church and the state, Poland's opposition, especially the Solidarity underground and representatives of alternative culture, had a stake in the upcoming visit and expressed their feelings about it. In May, the Solidarity newspaper *Tygodnik Mazowsze* published a roundtable on the papal pilgrimage that included, besides an editor from that publication, a Catholic journalist, an independent publicist, and a member of the Club of Catholic Intelligentsia.[27] Their discussion raised a number of concerns about the upcoming visit. Since this was the third time in eight years that the pope was visiting, the event carried less intrinsic interest. On top of this was the perception that the regime was using the visit to (over)emphasize improving relations between state and Church, which was off-putting to Poland's population. For example, it was noted that not just local administrative authorities but even local party leaders were meeting with local bishops in preparing for the visit and that the culminating event, the mass in Warsaw to conclude the Eucharistic Congress, was taking place "in state space," in the center of town adjacent to the Stalin-era Palace of Culture. Along with fears that society was being pushed to the margins by state and Church leaders in the planning for the visit, there was also concern that the Church might cut a deal with the regime without taking the citizens into account. One roundtable participant noted that it was difficult to find volunteers to be ecclesial crowd marshals. There were also concerns that, at some events, the audience would be cherry-picked to suit regime preferences (especially in Łódź) and that neither a meeting with Wałęsa nor a visit to Popiełuszko's grave was on the agenda (at least yet).[28] Aside from these many concerns, one of the participants expressed the expectation that, whatever the degree of accommodation the Church in Poland made to the state in preparing for the visit, the pope himself would not avoid social issues and could be expected to endorse society's negative attitudes toward the Jaruzelski regime. He also hoped that John Paul would remind Poles of the moral and spiritual dimensions of their social and political struggles. It was also noted that the bishops seemed to be neither encouraging nor discouraging Poles to display Solidarity banners during the events, though they also understandably did not want the papal mass and altar to be merely backdrops to crowds with banners of the banned union.

The official documents produced at this time by the Solidarity leadership avoided the concerns and anxieties that were prevalent in the *Tygodnik Mazowsze* roundtable and mentioned in later issues of the newspaper.[29] On May 23, Solidarity's provisional leadership, including its chair, Wałęsa, sent an open letter to Pope John Paul welcoming him and congratulating him on his upcoming visit.[30] The letter proclaimed, "This will be a great holiday for us all, a consolation for the abused and humiliated, for those living in poverty." It went on to say that Poland needed "bread and freedom" today but that above all it needed hope, and the Solidarity leaders expressed their conviction that John Paul's visit would indeed "regenerate Polish hope." The letter expressed special appreciation that the pope's itinerary would include visits to Gdańsk, given its symbolic importance as "the capital of 'Solidarity,'" the place most closely associated with the accords of August 1980, and the site of the monument to protesting workers killed in 1970, and to the grave of Father Popiełuszko in Warsaw, who gave his life for the Solidarity movement.

Eight days before the pope touched down in Poland, a few dozen activists met at a Warsaw church to draw up a public statement in advance of the visit. Participating were the top brass of Solidarity, including Wałęsa and Zbigniew Bujak, as well as notable figures from Polish alternative political and cultural life—the historian and activist Bronisław Geremek, dissident Adam Michnik, Catholic editor Jerzy Turowicz, world-renowned journalist Ryszard Kapuściński, and activist and hero of the Warsaw Ghetto Uprising Marek Edelman, among others. The statement was endorsed by an equally illustrious set of Polish figures, such as dissident Jacek Kuroń, Catholic activist Tadeusz Mazowiecki, philosopher and theologian Father Józef Tischner, and renowned filmmaker Andrzej Wajda. The signatories expressed their conviction that "the third pilgrimage of John Paul II to the Fatherland will be an event of momentous importance and far-reaching effects."[31] The statement then went on to call for a number of rights, freedoms, and conditions they hoped could ultimately come to fruition in Poland. These included genuine state sovereignty; democracy; equality before the law; the elimination of "social caste privileges" (an implicit reference to the special perks that came with being a Communist Party member); political and societal pluralism; independence of the courts; freedom of thought, information, education and culture; and an economic order that valued the meaning of labor, fostered human initiative, shared the profits of development, and provided decent living conditions. The statement also emphasized the renunciation of violence, which it saw as a fundamental feature of the Solidarity movement, in line with the papal admonition to "overcome evil with good." In conclusion, the signatories affirmed, "our deep desire is that the June pilgrimage of John Paul II become a stimulus for the settlement of the most difficult Polish problems in the name of the common good," something that requires "courage and imagination on both sides." They expressed their conviction that "the presence of the Holy Father will strengthen Polish aspirations, and make Polish hopes real."

WARSAW

After what turned out to be the smoothest preparatory period of all three visits, John Paul's pilgrimage was set. The pope landed at Warsaw's airport on June 8 and was greeted there by General Jaruzelski, in his role as chairman of the Council of State, and by Cardinal Glemp. Each gave a brief welcome address stressing only the positive.[32] The general spoke fondly of his recent visit to the Vatican and expressed his hopes that the papal visit would contribute to peace and positive developments in Poland. The cardinal stressed improvements in the Church's situation in Poland—greater freedom in public life for Catholics, holiday camps and pilgrimages for youth seeking spiritual growth, hundreds of new ecclesial buildings. John Paul, for his part, thanked his hosts for inviting him and greeted his "Fatherland," as well as his compatriots, noting that they "know the joy and bitterness of living on this land."[33]

As in the previous two visits, John Paul's first stop in Warsaw was the Cathedral of Saint John the Baptist. There, John Paul spoke to cloistered nuns, among whom was an extraordinary guest from abroad, Mother Teresa of Calcutta, whom the pope warmly and jovially greeted. Then, after holding an ecumenical meeting with leaders of Poland's non-Catholic religious communities at the primate's residence, the pope left for the day's most politically charged event—a meeting with Jaruzelski at the Royal Castle in Warsaw's Old Town.

The meeting opened with public remarks by both leaders, followed by a private meeting lasting approximately seventy minutes. Jaruzelski was the first to speak at the public portion of the event. His speech emphasized what he regarded as significant positive changes in Poland since 1983: "The stormy waves have calmed down. The fires have faded."[34] He claimed that national dialogue had broadened in scope since then and that new, even path-breaking institutions were being created as "socialist pluralism" advanced in Poland through various new forms of association and self-governance. Although not giving details, the general was obviously speaking about the steps the regime had taken to replace the Solidarity union with its own new associations for labor as well as to draw the Church and other noncommunist Polish groups into cooperation with the regime and thereby isolate the political dissident opposition. Jaruzelski spoke in celebratory terms about Poland's "irreversible" process of renewal and reform, and he expressed his openness to "realistic initiatives." By "realistic," Jaruzelski meant "respect for the Polish raison d'état and acceptance of the socialist principles of our state." This was another way of emphasizing sensitivity to Poland's place in the Soviet bloc and affirming the permanence of the communist system. Jaruzelski thus made it clear that there were certain lines that could not be crossed.

In affirming the need for progress and renewal in Poland within the above-noted parameters, Jaruzelski's speech included acknowledgments that there were important differences and divisions in Polish society, as well as much skepticism, bitterness, and distrust. He noted that many families were living in difficulty, with shortages and sometimes in outright poverty. To leave the current mess behind, he called for societal engagement with his regime and its plans for renewal. The general proposed that, instead of "sterile martyrdom" or "passive expectation," the Poles needed to have initiative, work diligently, and contribute to the strength and prosperity of their country. He welcomed the assistance of the Church in this endeavor.

Although Jaruzelski did not mention martial law by name, he justified his action in 1981 indirectly. He noted that the troubles in Poland were "often stirred up by foreign hands" and argued that "yesterday" was a matter of national survival. The general also raised the question of national sovereignty, a sensitive one given that many Poles saw him as selling out the self-determination they had expressed through the Solidarity movement by giving in to Soviet pressure. Jaruzelski acknowledged Poles' sensitivity to the issue of sovereignty due to their tragic history, during which they saw that sovereignty trampled many times. But then he went on to warn against "imperial illusions" and to laud the accomplishments of communist Poland in securing and defending the borders. He noted that the Polish People's Republic had achieved broad access to the Baltic Sea and restored to the nation the cities of Wrocław and Olsztyn, as well as Western Pomerania. He praised the great work of the Polish Left in reintegrating these Recovered Territories and noted that their return to Poland came through the blood of Polish and Soviet soldiers. He triumphantly concluded that Poland was now more safe and secure, and with more dependable allies, than ever before.

Jaruzelski also spoke optimistically about the development of church-state relations. He acknowledged the "indispensable" role that Christianity had played in the nation's history, as well as the special position of the Roman Catholic Church in Poland. He credited believers and nonbelievers together with building the People's Poland over the past forty-three years and expressed the party's appreciation for the Church's contribution to strengthening patriotic attitudes, civic consciousness, and ethics in Poland.

Some of his praise for the Church came in a backhanded way. For example, Jaruzelski expressed satisfaction that the Church's social doctrine had evolved to become open to the problems of the "ethos of labor," while noting that Polish communism had stressed the dignity of the worker from the beginning and brought social justice to a Poland where working people were brutally exploited and treated unjustly. Jaruzelski also commended John Paul for his ardent defense of peace, coupling that with praise for the efforts of the "socialist" countries to free humanity from the "curse of the arms race."

To sum up, Jaruzelski presented a speech designed to justify the regime's perspective on the past decade or so in Poland—that the people had legitimate economic grievances, which had been exploited by domestic and foreign enemies to the point that the state had to step in and restore order so as to spare Poland outside intervention by Soviet bloc allies anxious to defend the communist system. Now the country was on an irreversible course of reform and renewal, and the regime looked forward to the Church's cooperation with it in promoting economic development and social stability in Poland and peace abroad. Such renewal, however, had to take place within the limits of membership in the Soviet bloc and dominance of the communist system, led by the Communist Party, which had rescued Poland's working people from past exploitation and had restored and secured Poland's borders like never before.

A Western journalist at the event noted that the pope stared grimly at the floor as the general justified his regime and its policies.[35] Now it was John Paul's turn.[36] The pope was speaking in a milder tone and in a less confrontational atmosphere than at his last speech in Jaruzelski's presence, in 1983.[37] Nevertheless, John Paul presented a forceful challenge to the general by taking up the issue of peace and making it the centerpiece of his remarks in a way that undercut Jaruzelski's objectives. The general, aware that John Paul was an advocate of world peace and disarmament in a manner independent of and distinct from that of NATO and the United States, was hoping that talk of peace would be a central part of the papal visit. The government had insisted, for example, that John Paul visit Westerplatte during his trip to Gdańsk and that he make a statement there advocating peace, something that Jaruzelski had also mentioned in his speech at the Royal Castle in Warsaw. Also, the emphasis on peace surely made the papal visit more palatable to Poland's Soviet bloc allies, who were all enlisted in Soviet-sponsored attempts to advance the communist perspective on East-West relations and disarmament.

John Paul, however, took up the issue of peace in a way most detrimental to the Jaruzelski regime—he connected it strongly with the issue of human rights. The pope said that the Charter of Human Rights of the United Nations was unambiguous about this connection.[38] John Paul said, "If you want to maintain peace, keep in mind the person. Keep in mind his rights, which are inalienable, because they emerge from the very humanity of each person." He went on to enumerate some of these rights specifically—every person's "right to freedom of religion, of association, and of expression of one's views." Then he added, "All violation and disregard of the rights of man constitute a danger for peace." Given that Jaruzelski's regime, in shutting down the Solidarity movement, was violating the right of association, John Paul was in effect implying that the general standing opposite him was himself a danger to peace. The pope, a bit later in his speech, returned to the connection between peace and human rights, then segued into the issue of popular participation in governance. Quoting the Second Vatican Council's *Gaudium et spes*, John Paul applauded those political systems that "allow the largest number of citizens to participate in public affairs with genuine freedom." He also contended that peace begins with people, people who are not just objects to be governed by the authorities but subjects in their own right with a voice in the commonwealth.

John Paul then extended this vision to labor, noting that it is only when people have a sense that labor and the economy are for them, and not they for the economic system, will they work to further economic progress. This, in effect, was the pope's solution to Poland's current economic problems and societal malaise—not the co-opting of society into the Jaruzelski regime's new, largely cosmetic institutions but the establishment of a relationship between state and society based on the priority of the human person and that person's right to a voice.

John Paul's final event in Warsaw was at the Church of All Saints, where he celebrated the mass opening the Eucharistic Congress, which was the professed reason for his visit to Poland. His homily avoided political content, staying focused on topics such as the Eucharist, Mary, sin, and suffering, as well as on the congress's motto: He Loved Them till the End. The pope did refer in passing, however, to Poland as "this wearied, afflicted land" and quoted from Father Popiełuszko on the meaning of the cross.[39]

LUBLIN AND TARNÓW

The next day, John Paul left for the second leg of his tour of his wearied, afflicted homeland—the city of Lublin. His first stop was Majdanek, the nearby former Nazi concentration and death camp, and while there he held a brief commemoration of that camp's wartime martyrs and met with some of its survivors. Then he proceeded by Popemobile to the Catholic University of Lublin (KUL) for an address to "representatives of the world of scholarship" in the university's aula.[40] In the audience were not only members of the academic community at KUL but representatives of many educational institutions across Poland and of the Polish Academy of Sciences, as well as foreign guests. In a speech geared toward an academic audience, the pope focused on issues such as human subjectivity, the philosophical implications of the biblical creation story, and the relationship between science and religion. Despite the erudite content and diplomatic tone of his comments, John Paul landed several blows to the regime and its policies and ideology. In what was to become a theme of the pilgrimage, the pope spoke with concern about Poland's future, in this case that Poland's university students and young scholars might be unable to bear the full fruit of their talents and education in their homeland. He wondered about their prospects of finding work, adding that this was also a problem in many countries of the European West.[41] He also noted the dire housing situation that hung over the future of Polish youth. Expressing his dismay that "so many young, promising people" may not see for themselves a future in Poland, he said that "it is necessary to think over the many issues of societal life, structures, organization of labor, all the way down to the very foundations of the contemporary state organism, from the viewpoint of the future of the young generation in the Polish land." John Paul further challenged the communist regime by speaking of the importance of academic freedom and the autonomy of the universities and other educational institutions. Finally, the pope disputed the thesis that science and religion stood in contradiction to one another, a view that he noted dated to the Enlightenment and was developed further in the nineteenth century, by followers of Marxism, among others. For John Paul and the Church, this was a reductionist denial of the transcendent dimension of the human person and meant not just the "death of God" but also the "death of man." This was one of the few times in any of his visits to Poland thus far that the pope took aim at Marxist teachings as opposed to communist policies. More of both was coming on the current visit.

After his meeting with the academics, John Paul held a Liturgy of the Word on the KUL campus for its students. In his homily, he avoided anything political and focused on KUL, its contribution to Poland, and the nature of a Catholic university. Afterward, as was typical at youth-oriented papal events, John Paul joked with the crowd as it chanted "Long live the pope" and sang "Sto Lat." Next came the big public event of the day, an open-air mass in the Czuby district of Lublin. State security was anticipating a large crowd (the police claimed 650,000 were in attendance, the Western media put the number at "close to a million").[42] They were thus out in full force, with hundreds of police vans parked at strategic locations and thousands of riot police ready should disturbances break out.[43] The papal route was lined with regular police officers. The mass, which included the ordination of forty-six young men to the priesthood, was low key in terms of its political profile. The pope stuck mainly to religious topics, in particular the sacraments and the priesthood, especially the latter's vocation of service.[44] The crowd, though large, was subdued. In contrast to 1983, there were few Solidarity banners among the crowd. The only sustained applause was after John Paul mentioned Father Popiełuszko as an example of a priest who sacrificed his own life in serving others.[45]

Several factors might explain the lower fervor seen in Lublin in contrast to venues visited by the pope on previous pilgrimages. First, there was the overpowering police presence. Second, the context had changed since 1983. Martial law had been lifted, political prisoners amnestied, and the government was undertaking a series of reforms aimed at winning over Polish society, however grudgingly, to the Jaruzelski regime. Third, relations between Church and state were on the mend. As the pope himself noted in his homily, the number of churches was increasing in the Lublin diocese. In this improved atmosphere, Church authorities were reluctant to criticize the large police presence. Moreover, the ecclesial crowd marshals strove to maintain the religious character of the papal events, and at least some clergy had apparently urged their parishioners to refrain from bringing political or pro-Solidarity signs.[46]

From Lublin the pope headed to Tarnów, a smaller city in southeastern Poland about fifty miles from Kraków. The next day, on June 10, he addressed a crowd of close to a million people gathered on a muddy suburban field.[47] The occasion was the beatification of Karolina Kózkówna, the Polish peasant killed while resisting rape by a Russian soldier in 1914. A diverse audience included workers, artisans, former prisoners from Auschwitz, veterans, members of Catholic youth organizations, boys and girls from scouting groups, pilgrims from Hungary, Slovakia, and Moravia, and Poles from America. But above all, the crowd was dominated by rural people, many in traditional costumes. In obedience to admonitions from their parish priests, few brought political banners or symbols, and many waved small yellow-and-white papal flags and red-and-white Polish banners.[48] Nevertheless, John Paul chose this venue to make the most overt political statement thus far during his pilgrimage. It came in the second half of a homily that devoted considerable attention to rural issues and problems.[49]

After a lengthy elaboration on Blessed Karolina herself, the pope went on to emphasize the dignity of rural labor, which he then tied the production of bread and to the Eucharist, a fitting connection given that John Paul was in Poland for the nationwide Eucharistic Congress. He noted that the Mass refers to bread as "the fruit of the earth and work of human hands" and that Jesus called himself "the bread that comes down from heaven and gives life to the world." He then went beyond this religious message to address Poland's agricultural past and present. After first noting that he was not an expert on farming and was thus bringing no solutions, he acknowledged problems in the contemporary Polish countryside, which had experienced "a manifold economic and moral crisis." John Paul spoke of "the mistakes committed in the past and those which continually last and attest to the failure to value agriculture, which became the terrain of ill-considered experiments, a lack of trust, and even discrimination." He spoke of the "deformations of rural life," the "second-rate status of the farmer," and the "manifold threat" to Polish farming. The pope then went on to speak of Polish farmers as constituting an element of stability and continuity, citing the great peasant leader of the interwar period, Wincenty Witos, who had called the independent Polish peasant the strength and infallible mainstay of the state. Then, despite his disclaimer, John Paul presented a solution—the Rzeszów-Ustrzyki Agreements, concluded in February 1981 between the government and Polish farmers to address the country's many agricultural problems. The pope noted that these agreements were being ignored, so he could not remain silent about them. He went on to call for the implementation of the agreements, as well as for the replacement of the "peasant" or "peasant-worker" model with that of the "productive and independent producer."

These papal comments packed considerable political punch. John Paul was essentially calling for the restoration of the outlawed Rural Solidarity, a union of private farmers established under the Rzeszów-Ustrzyki Agreements. The region around Tarnów, long known for a fierce attachment to private agriculture, had plenty of such farmers. In noting Poland's agricultural problems, John Paul mentioned the regime's past and continuing discrimination against private farmers to an audience fully aware that seed, fertilizer, and machinery typically went to state farms, to the detriment of private ones. The evocation of Witos also raised political flags, with its harkening to the precommunist period and affirmation of private farming. The crowd, listening quietly for most of the homily, broke out in applause at least a dozen times, especially when John Paul addressed the problematic situation in agriculture, quoted Witos and the renowned poet Cyprian Norwid on the Polish peasant, and defended the Rzeszów-Ustrzyki Agreements. The unspoken context behind the crowd response was the effort since 1981 by the Polish bishops to aid private agriculture in Poland through funds provided by Western governments, the so-called Agricultural Foundation of the Episcopate of Poland, and the apparently successful efforts by the regime by the mid-1980s to encumber and stifle the aid program, effectively paralyzing the bishops' efforts.[50]

That evening the pope celebrated a vespers service for priests and members of male and female religious orders.[51] The homily was geared toward those in religious vocations, referencing their calling and ministry. John Paul instructed priests to remain close to the people and their experiences, not aloof from them. He mentioned the Polish tradition of clergy suffering with their compatriots, sharing the fate of the nation, as "among the Siberian deportees in the times of national bondage" and in the prisons and concentration camps in the recent period of occupation. To give an example of such a priest, the pope mentioned Father Popiełuszko, making this the third day in a row that he referred to Poland's recent and prominent priest-martyr.

The security services characterized John Paul's homily as "tough-minded and conservative" and found several things about it they disliked.[52] Their primary objection was to his support and sympathy for Rural Solidarity through his emphasis on the importance of the Rzeszów-Ustrzyki Agreements and his call for their implementation. The security services' report also noted unfavorably the pope's criticism of state agricultural policy and his reference to Witos and support for the continuation of the movement of independent farmers that Witos had promoted in the past.

KRAKÓW

The next stop on the papal itinerary was Kraków, where the pope arrived in late afternoon for a service of the Liturgy of the Word at the Commons. Anywhere from seven hundred thousand to more than a million people turned out to welcome him.[53] This visit to Kraków was smaller in scale than the 1979 and 1983 stops in terms of crowd size and number of events (the pope had only two public appearances in Kraków this time). Nevertheless, as reports from state security observed, there was a different atmosphere than at the earlier mass event in Lublin and one "could notice a growing excitement."[54] While oppositional sentiment and activity were at a minimum in Lublin and Tarnów, in Kraków a crowd heavily composed of students came ready to flash "V-for-Victory" signs and unfurl pro-Solidarity or anti-government banners. Still, disturbances were limited—a few scuffles when police pulled those with such banners out of the crowd and a postevent march that was quickly dispersed. Forty-six were arrested for these actions.[55]

The event itself featured an address by John Paul to the residents of his beloved Kraków.[56] This homily was heavily pastoral in tone, eschewing any direct references to Poland's politics, featuring discussion of scripture, the Eucharist, and Poland's spiritual traditions and offering Poles the comfort and encouragement they needed as they faced the challenges of the day. The pope said, "We cannot surrender to a breakdown of spirit, to depression. Frustration—spiritual or social—must not dominate us." John Paul went on to say that each Pole was being called upon "to write a new chapter, a new part, a fragment" of their land's difficult history. He then recited a prayer attributed to the great Jesuit of Poland's Catholic Reformation of the sixteenth and seventeenth centuries, Piotr Skarga.[57] The prayer called on God to keep his hand and discipline on the Polish nation and thanked him "that you have taken our fruits from the hands of oppressors, invaders, and enemies . . . that after years of bondage you have bestowed upon us once again freedom and peace." It asked God through the power of his Holy Spirit to "quiet the heart, encourage confidence in Your love[,] . . . arouse in the nation the desire for patient struggle for the maintenance of peace and freedom." The prayer asked God's help for the Poles in maintaining his kingdom in their personal and family life and in national, social, and governmental life. To this end, it asked for the protection from the vices and cultivation of the virtues that would enable Poles to face these challenges: "Defend us from individual, familial, and social egoism. Do not allow the more powerful to despise the weak. Protect us from hatred and prejudice toward people of different convictions. Teach us to fight against evil, but to see a brother in the person who behaves evilly and not to take from him the right to conversion. Teach each one of us to perceive our own faults, so that we don't begin the work of restoration with the removal of the mote from our brother's eye." The prayer went on to ask God for "the courage of life in truth" and to teach Poles to see the good wherever it is, protect it fervently, and defend it courageously. It also asked God to preserve Poles "from participating in the hypocrisy that is corroding our world." Although the prayer has a certain timeless character, it without doubt was particularly apt for the Poland of the 1980s—its challenges, its temptations, the virtues it needed to cultivate and vices it needed to avoid. The call for living in truth overlapped with the messages of prominent Polish critics of the regime such as Adam Michnik and the exiled philosopher Leszek Kołakowski (as well as being at the heart of the message of prominent critics of communism elsewhere, such as Russian writer Aleksandr Solzhenitsyn or Czech playwright and human rights activist Václav Havel). And a certain magnanimity toward the communists could be read in the prayer's warnings against hypocrisy, its openness to conversion of evildoers, and its recognition that everyone has faults. The prayer triggered applause from the audience at three points—namely, its calls for patient struggle to maintain peace and freedom, for protection against hatred and prejudice toward people of different convictions, and for the courage to live in truth.

The pope's next event in Kraków was mass at Wawel Cathedral, which he celebrated that evening. The homily centered on Blessed Jadwiga, whom John Paul had beatified in August 1986 and whose relics lay beneath the celebrated "Black Cross" at the cathedral.[58] Like Skarga, whom the pope had referenced earlier in the day at the Commons, Jadwiga is associated with responsible leadership in service to the common good. John Paul used this occasion to raise an important dimension of his Eastern policy, namely, his desire to strengthen connections with and help nurture the Church inside Soviet borders. Because Jadwiga's 1386 marriage to Lithuanian leader Jogaila (Jagiełło in Polish) placed Polish and Lithuanian lands under a joint leader and established the centuries-old link of Poland to Lithuania and the "Ruthenian lands," she was an ideal figure for highlighting the Eastern policy.[59] In discussing Blessed Queen Jadwiga, John Paul expressed both his regret at being unable to be in Lithuania for the celebration that year of the six-hundredth anniversary of the "baptism" of the Lithuanian nation into Christianity and his gratitude at being at least able to commemorate that event at the site of the relics of the woman who was Lithuania's first Christian queen. In this vein, the pope also mentioned Saint Kazimierz, the patron saint of Lithuania, who was born at Wawel Castle and prayed at the Wawel Cathedral.[60]

Although the mass at Wawel concluded the pope's official agenda for the day, one of the more significant events of the entire visit ensued after John Paul returned for the night to the archbishop's residence. It got little attention in the Western media, probably because the remarks were not prepared beforehand and distributed to the press in the languages of West European and North American journalists. Crowds of Polish youth congregated outside John Paul's window, and the pope addressed them in an impromptu speech.[61] Such assemblies outside wherever the pope was overnighting were not unusual during his pilgrimages, but this one stood out because John Paul spoke at greater length than ever before at one of these unplanned meetings; in fact, he said more than he had said at the mass gathering at the Commons or in his homily at Wawel. Moreover, in contrast to the jovial banter that typically marked such encounters, this time John Paul had much of substance to share.

He spoke first about the "problematic of youth," noting that youth was a great gift from God, "beautiful and difficult—perhaps beautiful precisely because it is difficult." He asserted that "if a society thinks about its future, it must think about the conditions of life for its youth." This must be a high priority. Still, even the best of conditions may not help and may even hinder youth in their development. Lest one think that John Paul was merely continuing his ongoing critique of contemporary Polish conditions, he noted that young people in Italy and elsewhere also faced challenges, especially unemployment. The pope called on young people to allow the Eucharist to empower them to be stronger than the conditions they face—to not retreat before them prematurely, nor give up, nor lose hope about their prospects for the future. Recalling his own youth spent in part under Nazi German occupation, John Paul said that he had gotten strength from the Eucharist to be stronger than the conditions he had to face.

In assessing the situation in his homeland, the pope relayed to his young audience that he had heard that Poles were loving less, that "egoisms and antagonisms" were being voiced more and more, that people were contending with each other more and tolerating each other less. He then expressed his hope that the Eucharistic Congress might contribute to transforming such a climate. Finally, John Paul raised the question of freedom, about which the Catholic Church held a substantially different view than either communist or Western liberal societies. Here the pope both cited warnings from Poland's past and anticipated future challenges. He told his audience that their generation once again faced the question of freedom. He spoke of how their Polish ancestors were guilty of abusing freedom, the so-called "golden freedom" that "turned out to be rotten!" This allusion to the internal decay of the Poland of the seventeenth and eighteenth centuries, when Polish noblemen belonged to one of the freest and most privileged social classes in the world but neglected the common good in order to each freely pursue his own interest, served as an admonition to Polish youth to not do likewise as they faced this question of freedom. Putting things in theological perspective, John Paul argued that freedom is not something that one possesses but rather something that one must continually acquire. He noted that God gave humans free will, without regard for the consequences, and when they used that freedom badly, God had to pay for it through the sacrificial death of Jesus Christ. Poland's young generation now had to face the question of freedom—it was not a settled question, nor could one run from it; it had to be faced honestly. Everyone was obliged to take up this task because everyone belonged to the nation. The Church, according to the pope, could help. In speaking of the Church's "special consciousness of what freedom is," John Paul was alluding to the view, which he elaborated in his own writings, that the Church understands freedom not in the liberal sense of freedom as choice but rather as the liberation one attains by choosing to live in accordance with God's moral truth. It is thus a task and a responsibility, not a precondition for choosing but the result of wise and good choices. As John Paul told the young people assembled outside his window, God did not give humans freedom for license. He told his audience that one cannot have a healthy society if freedom, be it personal, communal, or national, is not accompanied by a sense of responsibility.

In the course of the speech, John Paul said "solidarity" several times, though always with a small *s*, which evoked several of the many bursts of applause during his address. His exhortation to his audience to seek and exercise a responsible freedom would be relevant to any audience in any context, but the tone of the pope's address and some of his other statements during this visit reflected a sense that changes were in the air, an anticipation that more freedom was coming to Poles, both individually and as a nation, and that Poles should not misuse it. This in fact turned out to be a foretaste of the theme that dominated his fourth papal visit to Poland, in June 1991, in the aftermath of the collapse of communism in Eastern Europe and the establishment of a liberal parliamentary regime.

THE BALTIC PORTS OF SZCZECIN, GDYNIA, AND GDAŃSK

The next morning, June 11, John Paul paid a private visit to the grave of his parents at Kraków's Rakowicki cemetery, then headed off to the Baltic coast for the portion of his trip that promised to be the most momentous and dramatic. The first stop was the port city of Szczecin, on the East German border. The pope celebrated a mass at eleven o'clock in the morning, at Jasna Błonia Square, in honor of Polish families. The government put the crowd at 350,000, so it was surely larger than that.[62] The attendees were orderly, and few banners were displayed containing content inimical to the regime. The pope's homily focused on marriage and family.[63] He spoke of the nature of marriage, the virtues it needs and fosters, its connection to the Eucharist, and the problems and dangers it faced in contemporary Poland. He stressed the Church's role in defending the rights and sanctity of the family in Poland, noting that threats came from both outside and inside. He reminded Polish families not only of their obligations and rights but also of the obligations of society and state toward the family. He spoke of the moral decline threatening the family, society, nation, and state and asserted that harm to the family harms the whole society and nation. Among the threats to the family, the pope included divorce, broken homes, children raised by institutions, egoism, permissiveness, and moral relativism. He also included the situation whereby mothers work outside the home to the detriment of their family life and called for the "just treatment of women who are mothers" so that they are not economically compelled to take up paid labor outside the home at the cost of their "irreplaceable family obligations." The pope also cited as detrimental a lack of sensitivity to values beyond material ones, even at times "a desire to seek, at the price of family life, earnings and prosperity abroad." Finally, John Paul noted the material difficulties facing families in Poland, including those connected with housing, as well as the need for proper remuneration for one's labor. The Church in Poland, according to the pope, defended the family against such usurpations of its rights by society and the government. Some of what John Paul noted as problems facing the Polish family could be laid at the feet of Poland's government (for example, an economic system that required women to work full time outside the home and lack of adequate housing for families). Other problems Poles brought on themselves through bad moral choices (for example, seeking one's fortune abroad at the expense of one's family). Still others were endemic across Europe and North America, not just in the Soviet bloc (for example, the problem of divorce and the ensuing family breakdown).

Although his focus in Szczecin was on marriage and family, the pope did not let the opportunity pass to raise the issue of the Solidarity movement, noting that "in the 1980s Szczecin was a place of momentous events—and momentous agreements between the state authorities and the representatives of the world of labor." These accords concluded in Szczecin during the Solidarity revolution, as John Paul stated, and concerned the dignity of labor, and of the laborer. He called Poles to the task of "working on work." The crowd responded positively to the pope's references to the dignity of labor, as well as to his references to the material difficulties facing Polish families and his defense of the family against the contemporary problems plaguing it, interrupting him with applause more than a dozen times.

After a speech to seminarians at the local cathedral, the pope headed by plane to the next stop on his three-city tour of the Baltic coast—Gdynia. There he addressed "people of the sea." These included fishermen, sailors, shipyard workers, and others whose lives were connected to the sea. He celebrated mass at Kościuszko Square, near the water and with a backdrop of ships at anchor in the port.[64] Hundreds of thousands turned out for the event.[65] Security was tight, with the city sealed off for hours before the pope's arrival and sharpshooters posted atop the apartment blocks adjacent to the square.[66] The crowd was peaceful, with many waving yellow-and-white papal flags and only a few displaying the Solidarity banners that were ubiquitous at large papal events.[67]

In his homily, John Paul raised the issue of solidarity numerous times, both with a small s and a capital S.[68] After mentioning the need for solidarity between peoples and nations, he harkened back to when "precisely this word 'solidarity' was declared here, at the Polish sea," proclaimed in a new way yet in confirmation of its "eternal" meaning. The pope went on to address world peace and then turned his discussion of it into an affirmation of the principles of the outlawed Solidarity union. It was solidarity, according to John Paul, that the world needed in order to counteract the conflict between systems and nations. Instead of "everyone against everyone," humanity needed "everyone with everyone," "everyone for everyone." He went on to note that "solidarity was proclaimed on the Baltic coast in a new way and a new context," recalling the events of the 1970s and 1980s in this region as the "glory of the people of the Polish sea." John Paul took an issue that the regime dearly wanted him to raise—world peace—and combined it with a celebration of the Solidarity union it feared and despised. He warned that the world, through its dizzying armaments race, was headed toward war and mutual destruction, even "collective self-destruction." To move forward from this situation, one needed a social solidarity that respected the rights of each person, including providing space for the development of one's talents and initiatives, and above all one's labor. He noted the central role of solidarity in the social teaching of the Catholic Church, manifested in a series of papal social encyclicals dating to the late nineteenth century and continuing through his predecessors John XXIII and Paul VI and up to his own time. Departing from his prepared text, he called for a solidarity that respects human diversity and pluralism, thereby presenting an implicit challenge to a regime that favored political uniformity at home and the subordination of Polish interests to Soviet ones abroad. After presenting solidarity as an antidote to combat between nations and social systems, John Paul noted that solidarity also involves combat, but a combat *for* people and their rights, not against people as enemies. This combat for people should be governed by "truth, freedom, justice, and love." Clearly, the pope regarded the Solidarity movement as embodying this combat for the person, and he recalled that during his trip to India the previous year, the grandson of Mahatma Gandhi had approached him to thank him for Poland, purportedly because of what Poland's experiences in the 1970s and 1980s meant for the struggle for human rights. John Paul had not yet gotten to Gdańsk and already he was challenging the regime's view of Poland's recent past more stridently than he ever had before in his native land. For the pope, "solidarity" was a rich and profound concept, operative on many levels and connected with the Solidarity movement, with Catholic social teaching, with peace, with pluralism, and with the human person.

Aside from connecting his comments to the region's recent past as a center of the Solidarity movement, the pope also localized his homily by speaking of the sea and the livelihoods related to it—livelihoods that involved many sacrifices (such as long separations from loved ones while at sea) or dangers (such as maritime or industrial accidents). He celebrated Gdynia as "a symbol of our second independence," given that it was built after 1918 as a Baltic port to give the newly resurrected Polish state crucial access to the sea. He also devoted a section of his homily to the local Kashubian minority, a Slavic ethnic group in northern Poland, praising their past struggle against germanization, their fidelity to Catholicism, and their resistance during World War II. Finally, the pope spoke of the region's great suffering during the war, noting that the Diocese of Chełmno had lost more than 350 priests and that thousands of Poles in the region ended up in mass graves. He also referred to the many who had died at the nearby Nazi concentration camp at Stutthof (in Polish, Sztutowo).

When John Paul first raised the concept of solidarity in his homily, the crowd responded with thirty seconds of applause, after which he instructed them not to interrupt him, as he had "important and essential" things to say. The crowd controlled itself for nearly ten minutes, then applauded again when the pope made reference to the glory of Poland's events being felt as far away as India and yet again when he said that even a pope who was not a Pole would have to raise these matters while on the Baltic coast. John Paul also prompted applause during his praise of the Kashubs and when he spoke of the symbolic importance of Gdynia in Polish history. The mass ended, as was typical for large papal events, with a joyful exchange of gifts, chants of "Stay with us," the singing of "Sto Lat," and papal joshing with the crowd.

Late that evening, John Paul had an unofficial meeting with Lech Wałęsa at the archbishop's residence in Gdańsk. Although the forty-minute visit was more symbolic than substantive, Wałęsa was elated afterward, calling the meeting "great," stating that the pope had told him to "endure," and indicating that he had told the pope all that he had wanted to say.[69] Although Wałęsa gave few details about the meeting, people close to him told the Western press that his mood had shifted in the course of the papal pilgrimage from near despair to "hopeful enthusiasm."[70] This surely reflected the moral support John Paul had been giving to Solidarity over the course of the week, of which the meeting with Wałęsa was a part.

The papal pilgrimage was now at its midpoint, and the regime took the opportunity on the eve of the gathering in Gdańsk to make it clear to the Church in a private discussion that it was not happy with the course of the visit so far. Minister Władysław Loranc, the new head of the Office of Confessional Affairs, met in Warsaw the morning of

June 11 with Bishop Jerzy Dąbrowski to convey the government's concerns.[71] Besides some minor complaints, for example, that choirs were singing "Boże coś Polskę" at papal events with the offensive (to the government) lyrics that implied that Poland had lost her sovereignty, he raised two major grievances. First, he said that the pope was not acknowledging the positive changes the government had carried out since 1983, such as the amnesty for political prisoners and the various administrative reforms. Second, he said that John Paul, who frequently spoke out for peace in other contexts, seemed to be avoiding the topic in Poland, including in the text of his upcoming talk to Polish youth at Westerplatte, near Gdańsk. Dąbrowski defended John Paul on both counts. He argued that the pope had been engaged in getting the American sanctions against Poland lifted, had received Jaruzelski "in great style" at the Vatican, and certainly had noted the amnesty. He also claimed that the pope simply had a different approach to peace than did the Polish government, preferring to see human rights as a precondition for peace rather than vice versa, as the government did. Loranc conceded that the visit still had several days remaining but indicated that if certain topics continued to be absent from the pope's remarks, the government could only regard this as a failure to acknowledge the positive steps it had been taking. He reminded Dąbrowski of the risk the regime was accepting in hosting a papal visit. Dąbrowski promised to pass these concerns on to Cardinal Glemp.

We also see the regime's discomfort with the course of the pilgrimage in a midvisit assessment by the security services after John Paul's fourth day in the country.[72] The report observed that the pope's speeches were becoming increasingly political, heating up the atmosphere and helping to increase tensions at particular venues. Lublin, Kraków, and Tarnów were noted as places where the political emphases were most pronounced, and the pope's raising of the issue of human rights at the Royal Castle in Warsaw, of the Rzeszów-Ustrzyki Agreements in Tarnów, and of the Szczecin Agreements in Szczecin were cited with displeasure. The report further observed that the Western press was suggesting that the pope was failing to support the regime's suppression of oppositional activity by Catholics and criticizing government policy in his speeches, even to the point of becoming an advocate for Solidarity. Among the few positives in the regime's assessment of the visit was John Paul's affirmation of the Polishness of the northern territories and allusions to the suffering its inhabitants had experienced during the war and their historic resistance to germanization.

It is no surprise that the government expressed discomfiture at the visit's midpoint, as the next stop was Gdańsk, potentially the most explosive meeting of the visit. John Paul met in the morning at Gdańsk's cathedral in the Oliwa district with representatives of professional and occupational groups, after which he departed by boat from the pier at Sopot to Westerplatte, one of the first places attacked by Nazi Germany in its invasion of Poland on September 1, 1939. During the interwar period, the League of Nations allowed Poland to maintain a garrison there, and during the invasion a small number of Polish soldiers (fewer than two hundred) were able to hold off more than three thousand German soldiers for nearly a week in a heroic resistance. The government very much wanted the pope to visit Westerplatte, and its expectations were that he would give a speech there promoting peace, something that the Church itself had alluded to in its earlier arguments for why the pope should visit Gdańsk. In his homily at the Liturgy of the Word held at Westerplatte, however, an event geared to an audience of Polish youth, John Paul said almost nothing about peace. Instead, he addressed problems relevant to Poland's youth—a topic sure to annoy if not disturb the regime. John Paul recognized that Poland's youth were facing difficult material conditions, at times accompanied by feelings of hopelessness.[73] The way to face these and other sorts of difficult situations, he said, was to be faithful to the truth and to duty, to a right conscience formed in line with God's commandments. "The guy or girl who communes with God on the basis of the inner truth of his or her conscience is powerful," John Paul asserted. He also alluded in the homily to human rights, which he saw as providing to all persons the space to be able to fulfill their tasks and obligations and thereby grow as a person.

The pope went on to exhort Poland's youth to avoid evil and

accomplish the good made possible by the empowerment that can come to them through the love of Jesus Christ. He admonished them against succumbing to resignation, indifference, despair, and internal emigration (whereby one flees from the world, society, and life), as well as literal emigration (whereby one deserts the fatherland). He urged them to resist the temptation of hopelessness and the self-destruction that can lead to "alcoholism, drug addiction, sexual wrongdoing, the seeking of sensations, and finding one's outlet in sects or other associations that are foreign to the culture, tradition, and spirit of our nation." He encouraged his audience to get to know the genuine teaching of Christ and the Church, "especially at a time when there are attempts in various ways to convince you that that which is 'scientific' and 'progressive' contradicts the Gospel, when liberation and salvation without God, or even against God, is being offered to you." John Paul urged Poland's youth to avoid the "fashionable conformism" of the day and to not remain silent when harm happens to another person but rather to have the courage to express appropriate objection and take up their defense. He called on them to live courageously, not to flee from difficult situations, to evangelize their surroundings with joy and hope, and above all, to be demanding of themselves, to "be more," to "work on themselves."

John Paul, in reminding his audience that Poland's future depended on them, drew inspiration from Poland's past, as he so often did. He spoke of how each Pole for the last thousand years, and especially the last two hundred years, stood before the challenge of "working on oneself" and how many Poles took up the challenge of their times rather than flee from it. As a powerful example of this, the pope recalled the group of young Poles under the command of Major Henryk Sucharski, who in September 1939 heroically resisted Poland's invader (Nazi Germany) against long odds right there at Westerplatte. The pope told young Poles that each of them had his or her own personal "Westerplatte," some task they must undertake and fulfill, some rightful matter for which it was not possible *not* to fight, some duty or obligation from which it was not possible to flee or "to desert," some truths and values that one had to maintain and defend, for oneself and for others, just as those young Poles did in their heroic resistance at Westerplatte in 1939. Drawing from one of his favorite Gospel accounts, the story of Jesus and the rich young man, John Paul told his audience that responding affirmatively to Christ's call to "come, follow me" is a "Westerplatte moment" that they, unlike the rich young man of the Gospel, should answer, not flee.[74]

The crowd responded enthusiastically to the pope's address, interrupting more than a dozen times with applause, for example, when John Paul called on youth to be demanding of themselves and focus on "being more" instead of "having more" and when he said that young people want "a world of truth, freedom, justice, and love." In the eyes of the regime, John Paul at Westerplatte was continuing to commit the sins of omission that Minister Loranc had raised with Bishop Dąbrowski the day before. The pope said nothing about the regime's accomplishments and next to nothing about peace. Even more noticeable were the pope's sins of commission. He spoke of the difficult life for youth in Poland, of their poor material conditions and hopelessness, resignation, indifference, and despair. He noted the existence of social problems plaguing youth, such as alcoholism and drug abuse. All of this made communist-run Poland seem a bleak and unpromising place. John Paul also, in warning against those who claim the Gospel contradicts whatever is scientific and progressive and that liberation comes without or even against God, was raising an issue not only globally relevant but pointing a finger at communist viewpoints in Poland. His admonition to not be silent when another person is harmed was subversive, given the fact that Poland's communist regime for decades had counted on precisely such silence as it sidelined its real and imagined enemies. The call to courage and responsibility, valid everywhere and at every time, had a special poignancy in Poland, where encouraging young people to rise to meet their own personal "Westerplatte moments," in the given context, could inspire youth to stand up to an unjust regime at the cost of personal sacrifice.

The next stop after Westerplatte was a Liturgy of the Word for the sick at Gdańsk's historic Marian Basilica. In a homily aimed at commending and encouraging Poland's health care professionals and comforting and inspiring the suffering, John Paul also spoke of the unsatisfactory state of health care in his native country.[75] The pope cited increases in illnesses of the circulatory system and tumors, an insufficient number of adequately equipped hospitals and hospital beds, long waits for medicines and operations, and a shortage of adequate drugs and outpatient clinics. With an eye toward Poland's future, he criticized the continuing dependence of many of its young people on alcohol, narcotics, and nicotine, the unsatisfactory state of the health of its children, and the massive number of abortions performed in Poland's hospitals. By now, it was clear that the pope was not missing any chances to point out the regime's shortcomings as they pertained to the various audiences he was addressing.

The next stop was the monument in Gdańsk to the shipyard workers killed by government troops during the labor unrest there in December 1970. The regime, careful to avoid any public disturbances, sealed off the center of the city for many blocks, so that nary an automobile or pedestrian was to be seen as the pope made his visit to the monument to pray and lay a wreath.[76] The awkwardness of the situation was underscored by the fact that only Communist Party officials and the police constituted the audience at the commemoration.

It is not surprising that the regime was doing everything it could to ensure that its risky gamble in allowing the pope to visit Gdańsk did not blow up in its face.[77] John Paul had to travel by boat and helicopter in the region, so as to minimize the crowds that a land route would attract. Television coverage was local, not national, and the Gdańsk homily was not broadcast live. There was also a huge police presence in Gdańsk during the papal visit, with the *Washington Post* noting that the city was "virtually under police siege."[78] There were countless barricades, roadblocks, tens of thousands of police personnel, armored vehicles stretching for miles, and preventative detentions of potential troublemakers. The government justified the show of force by claiming that provocateurs could disrupt the events, as they had allegedly tried to do two days before in Kraków, where police and demonstrators scuffled after the pope's event at the Commons. More important, however, was the fact that John Paul was coming for the first time to the epicenter of the Solidarity revolution of 1980 and had been intensifying his criticism of the regime and celebration of the heritage and values of Solidarity in recent days.

The high point of the Gdańsk visit, and in fact of the entire 1987 pilgrimage, was the pope's "Mass for the World of Labor" celebrated that afternoon at the site of a former airport runway in the workers' district of Zaspa. The site itself was loaded with symbolism and significance—the venue was surrounded by workers' housing, not far from the apartment of Wałęsa himself. The altar was 28 feet high, built by shipyard workers to resemble a ship's prow, with three 114-foot-high crosses rising above it like masts.[79] The resemblance to the city's monument to the shipyard workers killed during the 1970 unrest was intentional, and the regime had managed to obstruct the altar's construction until just a few days before the pope's arrival.[80] Crowds were estimated at between 700,000 and a million.[81] Practically every window in the housing developments around the square bore the image or insignia of the pope, and Solidarity banners were ubiquitous among the crowd. Wałęsa and his wife Danuta were in attendance, as were other Solidarity activists.

The pope's concern for labor issues, the problems of the working class, and the recent worker unrest in Poland, evident in his homilies in Szczecin and Gdynia, were fully apparent at the mass in Gdańsk. There, John Paul raised a host of sensitive issues, to a degree yet unmatched in this or his two previous pilgrimages. In his homily, John Paul referred to the shipyard monument and his visit to it earlier that day. He also had much to say about Solidarity: he praised Gdańsk as the city "in which the need of renewal of man through labor, the liberation of man through labor, was born anew."[82] He referred to the enormous effort undertaken in Gdańsk, along the whole Baltic coast, and elsewhere in Poland "aimed at restoring to human labor its full personal and social dimension." He praised the historic significance of the Gdańsk Accords as "an expression of the growing consciousness of people of labor carried to the whole social-moral order in Poland," which had their genesis in the tragic events of December 1970 and "remain as a task for fulfillment." Applause broke out repeatedly as the pope mentioned these issues and events that were so significant to his audience.

John Paul used the homily to elaborate on workers' rights. He emphasized that humans were not a commodity and that thus "labor cannot be treated . . . as a commodity." The worker, according to the pope, "has a right to decide about his workplace." This includes the right to "independent and self-governing trade unions," which, as John Paul noted, "was emphasized right here in Gdańsk." The pope took his advocacy of workers' rights even further, however, when he stated that because labor contributes to the common good of society, the people of labor "are entitled to decide about the affairs of the entire society, which lives and develops from their labor." If this was not a call for democracy, it certainly came close.

To a degree unprecedented in past visits, John Paul incorporated a direct critique of Marxism into his homily, an indication that the times were indeed changing in Poland. The pope used the second epistle reading from that day's mass, Saint Paul's letter to the Galatians, to argue against the Marxist dogma of class struggle. Paul's words, "Bear one another's burdens," were for John Paul the inspiration for social solidarity, which never means "one against the other." (At this point, bursts of applause were becoming frequent and sustained, coupled with the chanting of "Solidarity! Solidarity!" and prompting John Paul to ask the crowd, successfully, to allow him to speak without interruption). According to the pope, conflict cannot take precedence over solidarity; if it does, then struggle ensues in which others become seen as enemies to be conquered and destroyed rather than persons with whom to reach agreement. In a final poke at the communists, the pope expressed his great pleasure at the close connection between Polish workers and the Catholic faith, noting from the days of Solidarity's birth the images of workers going to confession and mass on the grounds of the plants at which they worked. As if to underscore the close connection between labor activism and Catholicism, Walęsa and his wife Danuta received Holy Communion from John Paul himself during the mass.

After the mass, John Paul addressed some additional words to his sizable audience. He told the crowd, "I tried in my own words to speak about you and speak for you," taking up his earlier praise of the Solidarity movement. The pope asserted that what had transpired in Gdańsk and the Baltic region and in other centers of labor in Poland had "great significance for the future of human labor," not only in Poland but everywhere. He once again expressed his pleasure at the sight of workers praying at the Gdańsk shipyard during the decisive days of summer 1980 that had given rise to the Solidarity movement, and he promised to pray daily for workers and "especially for the great inheritance of Polish 'Solidarity.'" The reference to Solidarity brought sustained applause.

After John Paul's departure by helicopter, around ten thousand demonstrators, many carrying Solidarity banners and chanting Solidarity slogans, undertook a protest march. Their goal was the 1970 monument in town. Police intervention, however, was able to thwart the march and disperse most of the crowd before it met its goal.[83] During dispersal operations, demonstrators were beaten by police wielding batons, and some demonstrators in turn threw bottles and rocks at police.

Although the events in Gdańsk came off relatively peacefully, there is no question that John Paul took his challenge to the communist regime to a new level of intensity. Whether it was his references to the events of 1970 and 1980, his championing of workers' rights, including the right to form independent trade unions, his critique of Marxist class struggle, or his playing up of themes of both Solidarity and solidarity to an eager crowd, the pope thrust ample provocative material in the face of a worried regime. At the same time, however, he kept within certain parameters. For one, he made no reference to martial law. When the pope brought up the past, it was summer of 1980, not December 1981, on which he focused. He also did not call specifically for the restoration of Solidarity. Rather, in accord with the approach he had been taking since his visit in 1983, he pointed to the principles that the Solidarity movement represented, as manifested in the Gdańsk Accords and other agreements of 1980–1981, as the indispensable condition for Poland to get out of its current economic and political mess. And fundamental among these principles were independent and self-governing trade unions.

None of this pleased the communist authorities. A police report lists quite a number of things the regime did not like about John Paul's homily and actions at the mass in Gdańsk: his reference to the worker unrest of December 1970; his stress on the right of workers to independent and self-governing trade unions; his praise of Gdańsk as a wellspring of the struggle for workers' rights; his numerous direct references to Solidarity; his presentation of Catholic social solidarity in opposition to the theory of class struggle; his criticism of the regime's new trade unions, meant to replace Solidarity; and his giving Holy Communion to both Lech and Danuta Wałesa.[84] That John Paul was attacking not just government policy but Marxism itself was noted in the official report. It also said that the pope "clearly provokes the chanting of 'solidarity' slogans" and riled the people up instead of calming them down. Except for the final contention, which contradicts the fact that John Paul concluded his comments after mass by urging the crowd to "let this day remain to the end a day of prayer, let no one disturb its special character, the kind which your cause deserves," this appears to be an accurate report on the pope's appearance in Gdańsk.[85]

CZĘSTOCHOWA AND ŁÓDŹ

Later that day the pope arrived in Częstochowa, where he hosted that evening the first of three events over the next twenty-four hours. The papal visit to this premiere Marian center of Poland, with its Jasna Góra monastery and celebrated icon of the Black Madonna, was less prominent than in pilgrimages past. However, even though the events had smaller attendance, were shorter in duration, and were fewer in number than in 1979 and 1983, and though Western press coverage was scanty, John Paul's day in Częstochowa represented a significant new direction in his approach both to the Poles and to the regime. Upon arrival, the pope conducted the Jasna Góra Appeal outside the walls of the monastery. He opened by telling the crowd (numbering somewhat more than eighty thousand) that he had promised those assembled earlier that day in Gdańsk that he would carry their prayer intentions for labor and its renewal to Jasna Góra, to the feet of Our Lady of Częstochowa.[86] He went on to pray for all people who labor, whether physically or intellectually, and all who were suffering from distress of varying kinds—two topics surely on the minds of Poles. John Paul's address included vigorous moral exhortation, including speaking out in particular against abortion and alcohol addiction. He admonished those who made fun of efforts to promote sobriety and impugned a "poorly understood" freedom, a freedom that meant license. He stated emphatically, "God did not give man freedom in order to destroy himself and others." The pope also stressed the necessity and power of hope, the power that makes a person strong in the midst of suffering and obstacles. He quoted a poem by Jan Kasprowicz called "Błogosławieni" (Blessed ones), celebrating those who maintain hope and faith in times of storm and darkness. Woven through the pope's words was devotion to Mary, whom he referred to as "Queen of Poland" and "Tutor of our consciences" and to whom he appealed for the needed hope. The crowd was especially lively, interrupting John Paul with long bursts of applause several dozen times, including a nearly four-minute interval consisting of clapping, chanting, and off-text banter from the pope.

John Paul spent the night at the monastery, which was a scheduled stop for prayer and meditation. Meanwhile, Jaruzelski sent a pair of leading Communist Party officials, Deputy Chairman of the Council of State Kazimierz Barcikowski and Central Committee member Stanisław Ciosek, to express dissatisfaction over the pope's "so unambiguous political engaging" in his homilies up to that point.[87] According to Vatican officials, they conveyed to Cardinal Agostino Casaroli their "anxiety" over the impact of the pope's words and their concern for how his visit was being received in the Soviet Union.[88] John Paul apparently wanted to discuss the concerns directly with Barcikowski, but the latter declined to engage him on the issues and left it to Casaroli to inform the pope.[89] That night, at a press conference, government spokesperson Jerzy Urban acknowledged that the meeting between party officials and Church officials had taken place, but he presented it as a normal part of church-state relations.

However, he refused to deny reports that the pope had been given a warning.[90]

Although his final two addresses in Częstochowa did not mention Solidarity, they challenged the regime in a perhaps even more profound way. The first event on June 14 was mass at the Chapel of the Miraculous Image (that is, of the Black Madonna), where the pope once again brought up the question of freedom.[91] He again warned that "freedom can be transformed into license." He meant this not only in the sense that one can choose to enslave oneself to the vices of pride, avarice, lust, envy, sloth, egoism, and hatred but also that "license—as we also know from our own history—can beguile man under the pretext of 'golden freedom.'" By referring to a time in Poland's past when Poles abused freedom to the point that they lost their independence, John Paul seemed to be anticipating a time when Poles would once again enjoy the challenges of political independence and political freedom.

John Paul developed these ideas further in his farewell address at the Częstochowa airport, where he made freedom of various kinds the centerpiece of his speech.[92] He spoke out on the importance of freedom of conscience, confession, and religion and noted that such freedom was under assault in many parts of the world (the communist world being unmentioned but obviously included here). However, John Paul then went on to argue against seeing this issue as "black and white." Rather, in places where the Church was indeed free to carry out its mission and ministries, its freedom was threatened in other ways. What he had in mind were those parts of the world that were "completely secularized," with an ideology "proclaiming human life without God," propagating a way of life for the person and for society "as if God did not exist." We see this in the "otherwise free countries" where freedom is misused to transgress God's laws, especially concerning respect for life and the sanctity of marriage, with people exhibiting a "utilitarian, permissive mentality" that leaves no place for human dignity while often doing so in the name of freedom of the person.

After what was obviously an attack on the "freedom" in Western societies, the pope went even further in universalizing the problem, seeing its roots not in any particular ideology or system but in humankind itself. As he put it, the Church's struggle for freedom in the contemporary world was "not only with programs, ideologies, and systems which are enemies of religion, but also with the weakness of man, a weakness that is manifested in various ways. After all, it was not ideologies, not regimes, not systems, but only the person who gave rise to the sin which takes place throughout the course of human history. Man succumbed to the satanic illusion that he himself can be as if God, that he himself can decide about good and evil, and that only he is the sole and ultimate measure of all that belongs to the world, to the creation."

One could imagine that Poland's communist leaders appreciated John Paul's omission of references to Solidarity and his focus on what he regarded as the flaws of the West and on problems that transcended political systems and ideologies. He indeed stepped away from the approach he had taken consistently during the first half of the pilgrimage—attacking Poland's present problems, blaming the government for them, celebrating the Solidarity movement and its ideals, and championing them as the solution to Poland's problems. However, at Częstochowa the pope seemed to be anticipating a post-communist future—recognizing that the West too held dangers for Polish Catholics and that many of the problems that plagued them were not communist problems but human ones that would not go away even if the regime disappeared. While the government might welcome the pope's universalizing the problem, and his pointing out that the West was far from perfect, the subtext appears to be the expectation that freedom, both national and personal, was in Poles' near future—a supposition that any communist regime would find terrifying.

Concluding his short stay in Częstochowa, John Paul flew by helicopter to the industrial city of Łódź, where he spoke at three events. First, he celebrated mass at a local airport before a large crowd.[93] At this mass fifteen hundred children received their First Holy Communion, including one hundred from the hand of the pope.[94] This festive occasion was followed by a short impromptu meeting with representatives from the world of scholarship and culture at Łódź Cathedral. Finally, the pope paid a visit to a large textile enterprise, Uniontex, where he spoke at length to a crowd of fifteen hundred workers, most of them women.[95]

Early in his speech at Uniontex, John Paul cleverly turned one of the regime's attempts to celebrate its achievements into a criticism. Jaruzelski in his speech at the Royal Castle in Warsaw on the first day of the pope's visit had noted that John Paul would be visiting Łódź, and the general spoke of that city's history of labor struggle and of the "brutal exploitation" of the workers there by the ruling bourgeoisie in the days when Poland was a "semi-colony of foreign capital."[96] In addressing the textile workers at Uniontex, John Paul recalled these comments of the "Chairman of the Council of State" about Łódź's history of "economic contrasts and social tensions," but he went on to add that industry-related problems continued to be keenly felt in Łódź, including those connected with ecology, housing conditions, and work that harmed the health of workers and their offspring.[97] He acknowledged the positive initiatives the government had been taking toward the protection of the health of laborers but expressed concern that these did not extend to all enterprises in Łódź and thus needed to be expanded. In continuing to tailor his comments to a female workforce, the pope spoke out against the undervaluing of the work in the home that many women do as mothers, including serving as the first educator of their children, passing on the faith, and guarding the "domestic hearth." He also noted the problem of women being overworked, which led to occupational illnesses, broken marriages, and consequently overwhelmed single mothers.

John Paul, with apprehension, accepted women's labor outside the home as a reality and called for discerning how to draw the greatest possible good from the situation. He reiterated his view that work is for the person and not vice versa, and he emphasized that this was particularly important in terms of women's labor outside the home. He affirmed that "the equal dignity and equal responsibility of men and women justifies in full the access of women to public occupations." At the same time, he stressed the priority of maternal and family tasks over those of occupational labor. He called on women to integrate home, family, marriage, children, and work into a complete vocation, not putting work in opposition to domestic concerns. He called on society to assure the structures and conditions that would make this possible. John Paul also made passing reference to the contributions the women of Łódź's textile factories had made to the "great call of solidarity" that had passed through Poland in recent years, with its goals of the dignity of labor, autonomy for the worker, and freedom of conscience and religion.

John Paul's words at Łódź were not as dramatic or poignant as those at some of his other stops on this pilgrimage, nor were his criticisms as sharp. He did continue his previous approach of pointing out problems in contemporary Poland related to the nature of his audience, but he was less forceful than he had been earlier in asserting workers' rights and even acknowledged positive initiatives taken by the regime on behalf of the health and safety of workers. In comparison to speeches earlier in the pilgrimage, he underplayed his support for Solidarity and its values but did include them. The crowd received him warmly, with the women singing and joking, especially near the end. A police report notes that they were "clearly moved" by the visit, with some of them crying.[98]

WARSAW

John Paul then departed for Warsaw for his final two days of the visit. They promised to be interesting ones and included meetings with Poland's "creators of culture" and with Jewish community leaders, a visit to the grave of Father Popiełuszko, a beatification mass on Defilad Plaza, a speech to the Conference of the Episcopate of Poland, a second meeting with Jaruzelski, and a farewell address at the airport. Although the zenith of the pilgrimage was the pope's visit to the Baltic coast and meeting with Poland's workers, John Paul also devoted considerable attention to Poland's political and cultural elites, culminating in his "speech to the representatives of the world of culture" at the historic Church of the Holy Cross in Warsaw the evening of his arrival in the capital city. An invited crowd of "about

2,000 persons" from various milieus of Polish culture attended, including believers and nonbelievers.[99] In his address, John Paul spoke of the crucial role played by culture in the survival of the Polish nation during the Partitions and occupations of the past.[100] In a challenge to the economic determinism endemic in Marxism, the pope stressed the primacy of culture over economics, that is, the primacy of what was deepest in the human person. In this respect, though economic and cultural values ought to complement each other, it was the "human, humanistic, moral" values that should take the lead: "The economy must listen to culture! It must listen to ethics!" John Paul noted that these truths had implications for Polish labor, itself threatened in terms of these fundamental values. He also expressed his great joy "that intellectuals, artists, people of culture are finding in the Church a space of freedom, which sometimes is lacking for them anywhere else."[101] This was a clear reference to the support the Church had been giving to intellectuals and creators of culture in recent years, such as providing a venue for lectures and theatrical performances involving nonbelievers as well as believers. John Paul saw these practices as helping Poland's creators of culture to discover the Church "from the inside," and he made it clear that he expected the Church in Poland to continue along these lines.[102]

The regime paid considerable attention to this papal outreach to Poland's leading intellectual and cultural figures, and reports on the event at the Church of the Holy Cross contained extensive negative commentary.[103] Analysts noted that the overwhelming majority in attendance represented the intellectual opposition, that is, those active in the alternative culture or so-called "second circulation of culture" (*drugi obieg kultury*). Half of them were from Warsaw. Demand for tickets was intense, with the Church authorities and leaders of the alternative culture determining who got the coveted entry, attainment of which was regarded as a badge of honor among the elites of Polish culture.[104] Police reports accurately depicted John Paul as providing encouragement to Poland's intellectual opposition and alternative culture, providing a great boost to their confidence. They noted his assertion of the indissoluble bond of Polish culture and national identity with Catholicism, as well as his great satisfaction over the identification of intellectuals and people of culture with the Church.

Much more than the pope's words disturbed the regime about the Warsaw event. The evening was rife with "long-lasting ovations," "demagogic gestures," adulatory words, outbreaks of applause "bordering on hysteria," and persons kneeling before the pope and kissing his hand. There were also blatantly political manifestations—gifts of illegally published books presented to the pope; the singing of the traditional patriotic-religious hymn "Boże coś Polskę" with the alternative refrain offensive to the regime; a near-unanimous display of the Solidarity salute (two fingers raised to make a *V*). Outside the church, an additional five thousand persons gathered, and upon the pope's exit from the church they unfurled a banner that included the word "Solidarity" and bade John Paul farewell with fingers raised in the "V-for-Victory" sign. This whole event, according to a report by the authorities, was "a sad reflection on the political and artistic, and especially moral face of this forum representing Polish culture."[105]

The next morning, the pope met with representatives of the Jewish community.[106] Next, John Paul paid a private visit to the Church of Saint Stanisław Kostka in Warsaw's Żoliborz district, the site of the grave of the martyred Father Popiełuszko. Given that the visit was anticipated but unannounced, some Poles had been keeping vigil outside the church while others monitored John Paul's moves in hopes of finding him at the church.[107] By the time of his arrival, several thousand persons were waiting for him near the church, though appropriate security preparations kept them from getting close to John Paul.[108] Reports from the security services characterized the crowd as "aggressively" pro-Solidarity, flashing the Solidarity "V-for-Victory" signs with their fingers, shouting pro-Solidarity slogans, and carrying banners with political content.[109] The crowd had grown to twenty thousand by the end of the visit, as people learned that the pope was at Popiełuszko's grave and hurried to the venue. John Paul's visit began with prayer inside the church, then he went outside and knelt, prayed, and laid flowers before and kissed Popiełuszko's tombstone.

After that, he kissed and spoke briefly with the martyr's parents and then left, as did the crowd, for his next stop—mass at Defilad Plaza.

Before the mass, however, the pope made a stop at the church of the Basilian Fathers in Warsaw, on the site of a monastery of the Greek Catholic Rite (popularly known in Poland as the Ukrainian Rite).[110] This outreach to a subgroup of Catholics associated with Poland's Ukrainian minority foreshadowed what would be a predominant theme of John Paul's next pilgrimage, in 1991.[111] Two priests from the monastery joined with the pope in concelebrating the upcoming mass on Defilad Plaza.

That mass was the final huge event of the visit, celebrated by the pope on the plaza adjacent to the enormous, Stalinist-style Palace of Culture, which dwarfs much of downtown Warsaw. A crowd of half a million, if not more, had gathered.[112] The mass marked the conclusion of the Eucharistic Congress that had taken place across Poland during the papal visit and that had included the beatification of Bishop Michał Kozal. John Paul's homily highlighted religious issues, such as the Eucharist, sacrificial and redemptive love, and evangelization.[113] He held up Kozal, who had been bishop of Włocławek at the start of World War II and martyred by the Nazis at Dachau in 1943, as an example of love "amid the madness of violence, destruction, contempt, and hatred," a love that even included love of enemy. John Paul called Kozal a "patron of our difficult times, full of tension, hostility, and conflicts." As befit the conclusion of a papal visit focused on the Eucharist, the event concluded with a Eucharistic procession across the heart of Warsaw, in which tens of thousands of Poles marched to the square beside the Royal Castle, where the pope blessed the crowd with the monstrance.[114] Overall, the mass and procession proceeded peacefully. Although hundreds, or as many as a few thousand, protesters carrying signs and chanting slogans for Solidarity held a procession after the mass on Defilad Plaza, there was minimal disturbance or police intervention.[115]

John Paul's next stop was a dinner and meeting with Poland's bishops, at which he addressed important questions concerning relations between Church and state in Poland and between Poland and the Holy See internationally. The context for the pope's remarks was the pending efforts by both Church and state in Poland to regularize their relationships both at home and internationally. Jaruzelski was hoping for a quick establishment of diplomatic relations between the Polish People's Republic (PRL) and the Apostolic See.[116] Formal diplomatic relations would contribute to the legitimacy of his regime internationally. Domestically, he anticipated that improved relations with the Church would make it easier for him to draw important Catholic circles away from the dissident and Solidarity opposition and into cooperation with the regime. It would also potentially soften the societal mood.[117] Cardinal Glemp and the Polish bishops, with some exceptions, were eager that the regime accord full legal status to the Church, which, among other things, would allow it to regain control of some of the charitable institutions the state had deprived it of back in the early 1950s. Vatican diplomats shared these goals, and all sides hoped that the new atmosphere under Gorbachev would provide openings to settling these questions. John Paul, however, had other ideas, as he made clear in his meeting with the bishops.[118]

The pope's address placed the Church's efforts into a broad historical context.[119] He spoke of the challenges that the Church had faced in the past, in particular in the Poland of the twentieth century. One such challenge was the ideology of dialectical materialism, which regarded religion as something that alienated humans from the fullness of their humanity because it meant that people renounced what is human for the sake of God, who, according to the presumptions of the materialist system, was only a creation of the human mind. John Paul noted that this could be a destructive challenge but in fact was also a creative one. The Second Vatican Council took up this challenge, read the "signs of the times," and gave testimony to the truth about God and humankind "with new depth and power of conviction." He then went on to charge dialectical materialism with reducing the human person to a reflection of the prevailing socioeconomic conditions, thereby depriving humans of their subjectivity. This led John Paul immediately into a consideration of the establishment of formal diplomatic relations between the Apostolic See and the PRL. He noted that the Apostolic See had relations with 116 countries worldwide, including Muslim states in Africa and Protestant states in Scandinavia. Thus, it was "abnormal" that it did not have relations with a Catholic country such as Poland. Such a situation was also harmful for the Polish nation. John Paul acknowledged that the authorities of the PRL had proposed that formal diplomatic relations be established with the Apostolic See and that Poland's Conference of Bishops had responded positively to the idea.

Next, the pope made clear the connection between the Church's call to defend the human person and its institutional relations with the Polish state both internationally and domestically. At issue was the credibility of any agreement regarding relations between Church and state, particularly in the eyes of the nation. This credibility was possible only if the bishops fulfilled their mission of speaking the truth about the human person, which included human rights and the rights of society and the nation. The pope's understanding of human rights also extended to the right to participate in political life without discrimination. In effect, he was calling on the bishops to support and defend principles that, if applied, would mean the end of the Communist Party's monopoly on political power in Poland. He affirmed that state sovereignty was only ethical when it expressed the sovereignty of the nation, that is, when society was the authentic lord in the state. In John Paul's view, these were issues that the Church was obliged to take up and make its own, and he added that the bishops of many Latin American countries, among others, were doing precisely this.

John Paul's address to the bishops, coming at the climax of a visit in which he had already done a number of things that annoyed the regime, added yet another layer to the multifaceted challenge he presented to the Jaruzelski government. The pope was placing human rights and political pluralism ahead of the potential advantages the Church in Poland would receive from the regularization of relations between Church and state domestically and internationally, and he was urging Poland's bishops to proceed accordingly. On June 23, little more than a week after the pope departed the country, Poland's Conference of Bishops issued a statement supporting the calls by John Paul for respect for human rights and greater political freedom in Poland.[120]

Given that General Jaruzelski was without question dismayed, or even agitated, by the way John Paul's visit turned out, their upcoming private meeting at Warsaw's airport and successive speeches promised a dramatic conclusion to the pilgrimage. The pope and the general met for fifty-five minutes at the airport. Although the meeting was of course closed to the public and the media, one newspaper reported that Jaruzelski seemed upset after the meeting and had slammed the door of the car as he departed.[121]

Next came the pope's official departure ceremony. Jaruzelski, Cardinal Glemp, and the pope each gave a short speech in turn. Sandwiched between the general and the pope, Glemp's words were an anodyne recounting of the stops on the visit, with not a word about Church-state or Vatican-PRL relations. Jaruzelski, on the other hand, made the most of his opportunity, raising sensitive issues, defending his record, and taking a few pokes at John Paul.[122] He opened by expressing his hope that the visit would have positive fruits—an increase in Poland's prestige, advances toward national agreement, and improved work and morals. He stated that for many millions of Poles, religious faith and socialist values coexisted, and he called for the engagement of all Poles "of honorable motivation." The general offered "permanent, constructive relations" between the socialist state and the Roman Catholic Church, in the interest of the fatherland. He then took a swipe at the pope, pointing out that John Paul was taking back to Rome an image of Poland in his heart, but not Poland's actual problems, which Poles back home would have to face. While the general admitted that Poland, like any other country, was "not a paradise on earth," it was "secure in its own just borders" for the first time in its history. Implicit in Jaruzelski's words was that Poles had the Soviet bloc to thank for this "priceless good," and he blamed "derogatory foreign manipulations" for attempting to damage Poland's reputation. The general spoke of contemporary Poland being "on a path of renewal, democratization, and reform . . . in convergence with the current deep transformation in the world of socialism." Jaruzelski noted that John Paul, in all his travels, was surely aware of the social ills, misery, injustice, and contempt for human rights in the world. The general then, putting his own twist on the "solidarity" that the pope often spoke about, expressed Poland's solidarity with all those people around the world suffering as a result of "racism and neocolonialism, exploitation and unemployment, persecution and intolerance." He expressed the hope that the world would choose the path of peace, not a "civilization of fear." He went on to contrast the PRL's peace initiatives with the calls for confrontation emanating recently from West Germany.

Like a boxer in the final round, far behind in points but desperately ending with a flurry of punches, Jaruzelski made a not unimpressive attempt to salvage some self-respect and political capital from the papal visit. Much was packed into this short speech, all of it aimed at either defending, praising, or justifying the regime and its policies and ideology. His offer of Church-state cooperation was premised on his belief that Poles had not just Catholic values but socialist ones as well. His trumpeting of communist successes implied gratitude toward the Soviet Union and its bloc, as well as accusations against Western media and governments that failed to appreciate Poland's accomplishments. His evocation of "solidarity" was aimed squarely at the injustices and problems of the noncommunist world, such as those found under right-wing regimes in places that enjoyed American support (e.g., Latin America), or those that inhabitants of Western countries suffered, such as discrimination, poverty, or joblessness. His call for peace was a defense of Poland's borders against alleged threat from Germany and in line with the long-standing Polish Communist Party policy of exaggerating the threat from West Germany in order to justify a close alliance with the Soviet Union. Jaruzelski also challenged John Paul's authority to criticize Poland's situation, dismissing him the way natives often dismiss emigrants. The general suggested that although the pope might hold a special place in his heart for his homeland, he did not have to live there and personally deal with its problems. The general depicted his own regime as one pursuing the reform and renewal currently in vogue in the Soviet Union. However, despite his best efforts, Jaruzelski was far from able to undo the damage John Paul had been doing to his interests and regime over the past week.

The Western media observed that Jaruzelski "bristled with frustration" and "bluntly" expressed "his bitterness" over the papal visit, while John Paul stood with his head bowed, eyes sad, mouth fixed in an ironic smile.[123] Then the pope's turn came. The papal address was more or less upbeat.[124] He did little to reply to Jaruzelski's assertions, perhaps not wanting to dignify them with comment. What he did say was largely positive. He called for dialogue and cooperation between government and society and for the virtues associated with it, including patience, perseverance, farsightedness, and courage. He expressed pleasure over the construction of so many churches in Poland in recent years. He conveyed gratitude to everyone who had made his visit possible, at all levels. This included Jaruzelski, whom John Paul singled out by thanking the general for his invitation, for greeting him upon arrival, for hosting him at the reception at the Royal Castle, and for holding talks with him and attending his farewell ceremony. The speech was not all praise and gratitude, however. Near the end, the pope reiterated, albeit a bit less bluntly, the calls for human rights that had been a motif of his visit. Acknowledging that Poland was facing a difficult challenge, he called for a Poland where life would become more and more human, more and more worthy of humankind, echoing the teaching of the Second Vatican Council. He also connected peace to human rights, citing Pope John XXIII's encyclical *Pacem in terris*, which spoke of the "four fundamental rights of the person at the root of genuine peace on earth"—the rights to truth, freedom, justice, and love. These, in John Paul's view, were the conditions for genuine progress, whether personal, social, spiritual, or economic. The pope also repeated a statement by Pope Paul VI that he had quoted in each of his two earlier visits, making it his farewell wish—"A prosperous and happy Poland is . . . in the interest of peace and good cooperation between the nations of Europe."

In addition to again mentioning human rights and connecting them with peace, John Paul also perturbed the regime by what he did not say. The Polish press noted that the pope omitted any response to

Jaruzelski's offer of cooperation between the state and the Catholic Church, saving that for a dispatch from his plane as it departed.[125] Specifically, the pope stated in the dispatch, "I harbor also hopes that my visit to the fatherland will serve the successful development of relations between Church and state and between the Apostolic See and Poland."[126]

CONCLUDING ASSESSMENT

The 1987 visit, at least on the surface, lacked the import of John Paul's previous two pilgrimages as well as his next. Indeed, it would be hard to compete with the dramatic homecoming of 1979, the riveting visit in the wake of martial law of 1983, and the return to a newly free Poland in 1991. However, one could argue that the 1987 pilgrimage was just as unique and noteworthy as those other three visits. What set this pilgrimage apart from the earlier two, along with its strong Eucharistic motif, was the openness with which the pope addressed political issues, the directness with which he chose to talk about Poland's troubled recent past and present, and even his anticipation of a postcommunist future. This situation can be attributed to a number of factors—the growing crisis in the Soviet bloc as the Soviet Union began to undertake its own reforms under Mikhail Gorbachev and allow the bloc's member states expanded autonomy; the desire of Poland's regime to woo a Catholic Church whose support it desperately needed to carry out its own reforms aimed at restoring economic production and social peace at home; and John Paul's desire to distance himself from those Polish bishops who were willing to pursue accommodation with the regime at the expense of the principles of workers' rights and sociopolitical reform that underlay the Solidarity movement.

On many levels and in many ways, John Paul II's 1987 pilgrimage to his native land challenged the Jaruzelski regime and the whole communist system. First, John Paul cataloged Poland's manifold socioeconomic problems—rural-agricultural, industrial, familial, moral. Right from the start he hit the regime with criticism after criticism—of agricultural policy, of working conditions, of cultural and educational policy, of health care. He spoke of the sad state of

Poland's youth, of family breakdown, addictions, and unfulfilled promises. During no previous visit did the pope speak so pointedly and comprehensively about what was wrong with Poland or of the limitations of its ruling ideology. He also had very little to say about any of the government's proposed reforms nor did he offer any praise for its meager accomplishments over the past few years.

Second, John Paul broke earlier taboos by speaking at length of the triumphs and tragedies of the Polish working class over the past two decades, placing himself squarely on the side of the Solidarity movement and its ideals. Along lines particularly embarrassing to Poland's Marxist regime, he noted the global reputation of the Polish working class as committed to their Catholic faith. Although he did not mention martial law, John Paul brought up examples from Poland's recent past that were uncomfortable for the regime or that contradicted or challenged its goals—the assault on workers in 1970; the emergence of Solidarity in 1980 and Rural Solidarity in 1981; the broken agreements of 1980–1981; and the martyred Father Popiełuszko, whom he even held up as a model for Poland's priests.

Third, John Paul made efforts to affirm and deepen the Church's relationship with and influence among those social groups the communist regime traditionally tried to identify itself with—peasants, workers, youth, and the intelligentsia. He praised and defended the Polish farmer before a massive crowd of rural Poles in Tarnów, criticizing Polish agricultural policy and calling for the implementation of the agreements that had resulted in Rural Solidarity. He addressed an enormous crowd of workers in Gdańsk, affirming their past labor activism and similarly calling for the implementation of the accords of the Solidarity period. He spoke about youth and offered words of advice and inspiration to them at the campus of Catholic University in Lublin, outside his window in Kraków, and at Westerplatte. He met with academics, artists, and other cultural figures, encouraging Poland's Catholic Church to continue providing them with support. On a number of occasions, the pope reminded his audience (and the authorities) of the close connection farmers and workers maintained with the Catholic faith in Poland, the central role that Catholicism had historically played in Polish culture and identity, and the support the Church and the intellectuals and creators of culture were giving to each other.

Fourth, John Paul challenged the Marxist view of reality several times, criticizing its reductionism, its penchant for conflict, and its materialism. In its place, he offered an alternative that had profound implications for the place of labor in society. The pope directly repudiated key Marxist doctrines and trumped them with Catholic ones. For example, in speaking against class struggle, he appealed to the Catholic understanding of solidarity (with a small *s*). In opposing the atheistic reduction of the human person to material forces, he presented the Catholic concept of a human person composed of body and soul, influenced by but still able to transcend his or her environment.

Fifth, and most important, John Paul chose to make human rights the centerpiece of his pilgrimage. He presented human rights as the foundation for domestic and international peace. He made respect for human rights a precondition for any future agreements between the Church and the regime, so that such agreements would have credibility with the people of Poland. Among the rights he stressed was the one that had inspired the Solidarity movement—the workers' right to independent and self-governing trade unions. He made his support for these values abundantly clear and was even bold enough to call for political pluralism in his assertion that Poles be able to participate in the governance of society without discrimination. The pope made these principles a crucial part of his vision for how Poland could get out of its current mess. While he did not explicitly call for the return of Solidarity, he praised its legacy, hailed its values, met with its leader, and called for the implementation of the agreements that had launched it in 1980–1981. The emphasis on human rights was all the more disappointing for the regime in that the two things the government most wanted John Paul to do—talk about world peace and encourage an agreement between the Church and the regime—the pope ended up connecting closely to an issue the regime hoped he would avoid altogether.

Finally, John Paul seemed to be already looking past the communist era to a postcommunist Poland. He called attention to Poland's future and projected a confidence that the old system was on its way out. He exhorted Poles to be courageous and hopeful (not surprising for a pope who counted "Be not afraid!" among his most favorite Gospel passages and who titled his most important work of public outreach *Crossing the Threshold of Hope*), and he called on them to stand up for justice and in defense of those wrongly persecuted. His words to Poland's youth were especially powerful in this respect. He also gave greater prominence than in his earlier visits to the sort of issues that promised to outlive communism and confront whatever regime might replace it—abortion, addiction, egoism, democracy, emigration, and "brain drain," among others. The pope struck so many nerves as he traveled around Poland that it is no surprise that Jaruzelski took the extraordinary step of trying to defend his own government and rebut the pope's critiques in his speech at the pope's farewell.

John Paul's visit confounded expectations in a number of ways.[127] Jaruzelski anticipated that the pope would avoid raising politically sensitive issues and reciprocate the general's hospitality by affirming the government's recent attempts at reform, praising Polish and Soviet efforts on behalf of peace, and smoothing the way for official relations between the PRL and the Apostolic See. Rakowski noted in his diary-memoir on June 16 that Jaruzelski was "dumbfounded" by the way the visit turned out, having gotten the impression during his January visit with the pope in Rome that John Paul would take care to maintain the religious character of the pilgrimage.[128] Cardinal Glemp also expected the visit to steer clear of politics and bear fruit in improved Church-state relations. The opposition, on the other hand, had some anxieties in the period leading up to the pilgrimage, fearing that the Church and state were marginalizing Solidarity and the rest of the Polish opposition. John Paul toppled these worries right from the start. During his pilgrimage, the pope had clearly, as in Luke 1:52, "cast down the mighty from their thrones and lifted up the lowly." In other words, the visit could be seen as a significant defeat for the general, an assessment confirmed by the party itself, according to Rakowski's diary-memoir.[129]

Solidarity and its supporters, by contrast, were delighted. On June 14 the TKK issued to the union's members a communiqué containing several points that turned up regularly in many of the postvisit assessments at the time. The first point was that because Poland was not a free country, the pope "spoke about us and to us, and also . . . for us." Second was that Solidarity was not just a Polish affair but one that inspired people of labor throughout the world in their struggle for freedom, dignity, and justice. Third was that the pope's message was a source of "encouragement and hope," obliging Poles "to endurance, to a sustained resistance."[130] In a postpilgrimage interview in *Tygodnik Mazowsze*, Zbigniew Bujak reiterated these and other themes, adding that things had gone much better than expected. He correctly noted that John Paul had made it clear that "we can count on him as our spokesman." Bujak also stressed the symbolic importance for Solidarity of the pope demonstrably visiting the grave of Father Popiełuszko, a martyr for the banned trade union.[131]

Two commentaries on the papal visit are worth considering in some detail. Shortly after the visit, Dawid Warszawski published an article entitled "Three Polands" in the underground journal *KOS*.[132] Warszawski argued that there were three "Polands"—the Poland of the Jaruzelski regime, the Poland of the tired and apathetic masses, and the Poland of Pope John Paul. In his estimation, the greatest success of the pilgrimage was that this second Poland drew closer to the third one, leaving the first in oblivion for a few days. Warszawski went on to provide a litany of things he appreciated about the pope's teachings and actions in Poland, including his praise for the Solidarity movement and the principles of the Gdańsk Accords, his support for the implementation of the agreements that established Rural Solidarity, his emphasis on "solidarity" as an essential part of Catholic social teaching, his holding up of Father Popiełuszko as a model for Poland's clergy, his call for academic freedom while visiting KUL, his assertion that Poles should be not just objects but also subjects in deciding about their common affairs, and the teaching that humans are not to be treated as a commodity.[133] Right after the papal visit, another key article appeared in *Tygodnik Mazowsze* under the byline "W.K." and the headline "A New Catechesis: Reflections on the Papal Pilgrimage."[134] The article covered much of the usual ground in postpilgrimage assessments by the opposition—the worldwide significance of the Solidarity movement, the importance of solidarity for Catholic social doctrine, how John Paul "freely and consciously" took on the role of voice for the voiceless, and so forth. The author framed the pilgrimage, however, in terms of what it could teach the Church in Poland. In this regard, W.K. put emphasis on John Paul's call for a "servant priesthood," with clergy living lifestyles close to those of the common people and siding with the persecuted and powerless instead of those with wealth and power. He also appreciated John Paul's statement to Poland's Conference of the Episcopate that the Apostolic See would not cut a deal with the government at the expense of Polish society, as well as the pope's open support for the Church's providing "spaces of freedom" for creators of culture and engaging in dialogue not just with the segment of culture that is expressly Catholic but with creators of culture understood more broadly. Finally, the author noted that on the final day of his visit the pope reached out to three groups that were not Polish Catholics—Ukrainians, through his visit to the Eastern Rite monastery of the Basilian Fathers; Jews, through his meeting with representatives of Poland's Jewish community; and Belarusians, because when the pope visited Father Popiełuszko's grave, he mentioned that the priest-martyr came from Belarusian stock and grew up in a Belarusian household.[135]

By using the greater degree of freedom and more relaxed conditions in late communist Poland, John Paul was able to challenge the regime and its system more directly and thoroughly than he had in his more cautious visits of 1979 and 1983. The profound critique of the communist ideology and regime often attributed to John Paul's 1979 visit was in fact more fully manifest in 1987, though the former visit was unmatched in terms of drama and societal impact. At the same time, the pope was anticipating the sorts of problems that could take center stage as Poland transitioned into postcommunism. Some commentators have argued that John Paul's disillusionment with the Poland that emerged after the fall of communism had led him to become angry, bitter, and moralistic by the early 1990s.[136] In fact, an examination of the 1987 pilgrimage reveals a pope who was already concerned about the direction that a postcommunist Poland might take and thus integrating moral exhortation on issues like abortion and addiction into his speeches, warning Poles that freedom can be abused, and recognizing that human problems were older than and bigger than any ideology—that sin would be with us whether communism was or not.

John Paul in 1987 clearly hoped for a different kind of Poland than the one he was visiting—one free of the domination of Marxist ideology, communist social and economic policies, and Soviet pressure. He and his Polish compatriots would not have to wait long. Police reports noted that at one of John Paul's rallies in June 1987, a banner was unfurled among the crowd that read "Let the Fourth Pilgrimage Be in an Already Free Poland."[137] When the pope returned in June 1991 for that fourth pilgrimage, it was to a newly democratized Poland liberated from decades of communist rule.

4

PROPHET

The 1991 Pilgrimage

EACH OF THE POPE'S VISITS TO COMMUNIST POLAND TOOK PLACE in a significantly different context—the twilight of the Gierek regime, then Jaruzelski's state of martial law, followed by the Gorbachev era of reforms, but the changes between the 1987 and 1991 pilgrimages provided a dramatically new context for the fourth pilgrimage.[1] By 1991, communist rule had ended. Poland was a multiparty democracy with civil liberties and in rapid transition to a market economy. Lech Wałęsa, amazingly, was president. The Soviet outer empire had collapsed, the Warsaw Pact military alliance had dissolved, and negotiations were under way for the removal of Soviet troops. The new Polish government was now eagerly seeking closer ties with and eventual incorporation into the institutions of the European and North American democracies.

General Jaruzelski's demise came relatively quickly and proceeded apace as communist regimes collapsed across East-Central Europe in the "miraculous year" of 1989. His attempts in the late 1980s to repair the broken system by reaching out to society and trying to stanch the economic hemorrhaging had come to naught. His referendum on economic reform in late November 1987 had failed due to low voter turnout. Then, after sharp and widespread price increases on February 1, 1988, strikes broke out in Nowa Huta, Gdańsk, and elsewhere in April and May, followed by further unrest in August in dozens of coal mines, as well as at the port of Szczecin, the shipyard in Gdańsk, and the industrial complexes of Nowa Huta. Driven by younger workers, the strikes focused on wage increases to keep pace with price hikes, as well as the relegalization of the Solidarity union. Desperate to calm an explosive situation, Jaruzelski reached out to Wałęsa, who met on August 31 with General Czesław Kiszczak, who was interior minister, and agreed that a "round table" would be convened to discuss the situation in Poland and how to deal with it. In September, Jaruzelski appointed Mieczysław Rakowski, a leader of the reformist wing of the party, as prime minister, and Solidarity began coming out into the open. It established the one-hundred-person Civic Committee (Komitet Obywatelski), led by Wałęsa, as well as more than a dozen working groups to prepare for the upcoming round table. Solidarity cells sprang up like mushrooms across Poland's enterprises, its organizational structures began to operate publicly, and its newsletters circulated openly. Beginning on February 6, the Round Table Talks between Solidarity and the regime began. They continued until April 5, and their work culminated in an agreement to hold semidemocratic elections in June.[2] In April, the union was officially legalized. In a very short period of time, Solidarity fielded and campaigned for a complete slate of candidates for the Sejm seats up for grabs, and in two rounds of elections in June it won all of the 161 seats contested in the lower house and 99 of the 100 seats in the newly re-created Senate. In July, the newly elected parliament, as part of the Round Table Talks agreement, chose Jaruzelski as president, by a margin of only a single vote. After this landslide defeat, the Communist Party became marginalized at extraordinary speed. The new Polish government that was established in September, with Catholic activist Tadeusz Mazowiecki as prime minister, contained only four Communist Party members, and in July 1990 three of them were dropped. As the party continued to fragment and decline, Jaruzelski resigned as president and Wałęsa succeeded him by winning a popular election in December 1990. Along with these profound political changes that transformed Poland into a multiparty democracy came a rapid economic transition to a market economy, in accord with a policy called "shock therapy," which caused a good deal of disruption and brought pain to large numbers of Poles, especially the industrial working class.

During this dramatic transition, the Catholic Church played a crucial role. From 1981 on, it spoke out as a voice for reconciliation between the regime and society, open to cooperation with the government but not at the expense of society's desire for independent trade unions. This was a policy very much affirmed by John Paul, who had made it clear to Poland's bishops during his 1983 visit that the Church was not to abandon the principles and ideals that had inspired the Solidarity union and its accords with the government of August 1980. Thus, while some bishops and priests kept Solidarity at arm's length, the episcopate as a whole continually called for the release of any Solidarity leaders who were in prison or detention, and some clergy courageously embraced the underground union even at the cost of their lives.[3] The Church also was able to construct hundreds of new churches and church-related buildings at this time, seizing the opportunity presented by Jaruzelski's hopes of winning it over to partnership with his regime. As developments accelerated in the late 1980s, the Church exercised two highly important functions. First, it was the honest broker in talks between the regime and Solidarity. All negotiations between the authorities and the opposition were mediated by a Catholic bishop or priest, something that both sides wanted and needed. Second, the Church mobilized voters on behalf of Solidarity in the June election. Many priests encouraged parishioners to support Solidarity, and churches provided a key locale for collection of signatures for candidates. In 1990, the Church threw its weight behind Wałęsa in the presidential vote.[4] However, as clerical involvement in politics, much appreciated by Poles in 1989, continued on into the new democracy, many became alienated by it, as we shall see below.[5]

Clearly, much had happened in Poland by the time the pope made his visit in 1991, even if the writing on the wall could already be seen back in 1987. Despite these changes, most of them arguably positive, John Paul chose to make his 1991 visit not a triumphal celebration of communism's fall and Poland's liberation but rather a visit marked by admonitions against immorality and abuses of freedom within Poland and expressions of concern and anxiety over the lack of faith found in much of the western part of Europe to which Poland was eager to attach itself. In this vein, John Paul decided to draw the principal themes of his preaching from the Ten Commandments. During each day of his visit, the homily at mass was built around a commandment, as the pope worked through the Decalogue in order, opening with the first commandment on June 1 in Koszalin and culminating with the tenth commandment in Płock on June 7. For the visit's final leg, in Warsaw, the pope focused on what Jesus Christ called the "greatest commandment"—to love God and neighbor. The "guiding thought" of the visit, drawing from Saint Paul, was "Do not quench the Spirit!" (1 Thessalonians 5:19), which John Paul associated with gratitude, courage in the face of difficulties, and freedom from enslavement to a materialism that diminishes the dignity of the human person.[6]

When John Paul arrived in Poland on June 1 for his fourth papal pilgrimage, he faced a country in the midst of a dramatic transformation, with all the hopes and anxieties that such processes entailed. This period of transition saw the breaking open of questions that had long lain dormant, as well as intensification of issues already growing under communism. Abortion, the media, education, relations between the Church and state, economic policy, relations with the West and with Poland's immediate eastern neighbors—all these issues were up for renegotiation, and the Church had something to say about each of them. John Paul managed to touch on all of these issues, and more, during his 1991 pilgrimage. This chapter focuses on those issues of greatest concern to the pope during this visit: (1) abortion, (2) the economic transformation and its social implications, (3) relations with Eastern Christians, both Orthodox and Eastern Rite Catholic, in Poland and to the east, and (4) the place of Christianity, and of Poland, within Europe. It also examines the pope's approach to a number of other issues involving relations between the Church and state (such as education and the media) and relations with Poland's ethnic and religious minorities, including Lithuanians, Ukrainians, Lutherans, and Jews. Finally, it examines a teaching that lay at the foundation of much of the pope's discourse in Poland—the connection between freedom and truth.

Although the pope chose not to make the heroism of the struggle against communism, the damage that system had brought to Poland, and the many positive changes Poland was undergoing in the aftermath of its collapse into central themes of his visit, he did not ignore these things altogether.[7] Upon arrival at the airport, he greeted Poles as a newly sovereign nation and society whose newly regained sovereignty was achieved at the cost of much effort and sacrifice (559). He spoke of the "fall of totalitarianism" as a "gigantic historical process" and "great good" (560). Throughout his visit, John Paul spoke of the problems inherited by contemporary Poland from the communist past, especially "a deep economic crisis" that went hand in hand with a no less acute ethical one (645). He recalled the communist era as a time when human talents were wasted and the whole of socioeconomic life was out of balance and when "the greatest injustices" were organized "in the name of a great devastating utopia that was supposed to realize 'a paradise of absolute justice on earth'" (647). He noted that freedom, especially of speech and religion, was denied to Poles under that system (670).

Throughout the pilgrimage, John Paul intermittently made reference to the benefits that communism's collapse brought to Poland and surrounding countries. These included the end of the promotion of "intense atheism" by the government (625); the abolition of the office of censorship (667); the release of political prisoners and establishment of more humane conditions in prisons (704); the revival of Catholic charities that had been suppressed after the war (609); fewer obstacles to the Church's ministries to prisoners, soldiers, and students (683, 705); and the establishment of full diplomatic relations between Poland and the Apostolic See (728). The pope summed up the transformative events of 1989 as a time when whole nations found their voice, people conquered fear, and "inexhaustible stores of dignity, courage, and human freedom were revealed" (730).

Although emphasizing the daunting challenges facing Poland at the time, the pope praised the "great historical achievement" of 1989 (648). He depicted the struggle against communism as being "in defense of the subjectivity of a society destroyed by totalitarianism" (714). He noted Poles' successful "war for the liberation of the nation from the fetters of the totalitarian system" (672) and acknowledged the key roles played by the working class (especially Solidarity) and the Catholic Church in the process that brought down communism (620, 672, 715). With respect to the Church's role, the pope celebrated how that institution became "the one unfailing point of reference in a situation of distrust" (729), stood up to the regime's efforts to undermine religion as it promoted dialectical materialism (729), and provided asylum to the creators of culture, giving them access to society that the regime had denied them (737).

Despite the Church's crucial contribution to defending Polish society and culture during the communist period, by 1991 Poland was experiencing a significant change in public perceptions of the Church and its role. Under communism, the overwhelming majority of Poles embraced the Catholic Church as an alternative, both ideologically and institutionally. Now, the Church was increasingly seen as one of many players in a significantly more pluralistic society. Its moral-political agenda was no longer regarded mainly as a welcome antidote to communism but, for increasing numbers of Poles, as something out of step with the sort of modern, liberal, Western society that they hoped to establish. Because Poland now had institutions of genuine self-government, important issues could presumably be addressed through the proper constitutional, legal, and political channels. The Church began trying to shape the new Poland in accordance with its social and moral vision, as its bishops pushed for a ban on abortion, limits on contraception, catechism classes in the public schools, restrictions on the media, freedom to use churches for political campaigning, and opposition to a separated Church and state. While the bishops were having a fair measure of success, the Church's perceived pushiness was provoking a backlash, with many Poles increasingly wary of the Church's influence.[8]

Indicative of the growing tensions between the Church and state was the co-called Kapera Affair in spring 1991. On May 7, Kazimierz Kapera, who was deputy minister of health, made a number of controversial statements in a television interview. In speaking of AIDS, he stated that widespread availability of condoms was not necessary to combat the disease, because its spread was limited mainly to "deviant" groups, namely, homosexual men and drug users. He justified his position on religious grounds. He also expressed his opposition to contraception, both for religious reasons and because it allegedly took the joy out of sex. Responding to calls from the press for Kapera's dismissal, Prime Minister Jan Bielecki fired him on May 11. The next day, Cardinal Glemp defended Kapera in his Sunday homily, claiming that he had been dismissed "for his religious convictions" and likening the move to past communist persecution of the Church. Bielecki in turn publicly defended his action.[9]

According to polls at the time, most respondents thought the Church had too much political influence and should leave politics and policy to society and its elected leaders. Significant percentages opposed the Church's education and media policies, and most of the country's population differed with its views on abortion. Thus, opposition was growing to the Church's positions and to the ways in which it tried to influence public policy. As far as the latter was concerned, the Polish government in 1989 began taking a number of steps that implemented the desires of the Polish bishops not through public debate, parliamentary legislation, or public referendum but rather through administrative orders. For example, some restrictions on abortion and contraception, as well as the inclusion of religious catechesis in the school curriculum, were instituted initially by orders of the pertinent ministries, not through legislation.[10] When Parliament did take up issues such as abortion, education, media law, and electoral law, the bishops lobbied hard for their positions and thereby became major players in a number of increasingly contentious debates taking place in Polish politics in the early postcommunist years. Consequently, when John Paul arrived in Poland on June 1, 1991, he was returning to a country caught up in several social and political conflicts over the shape of the new Poland. The Church itself was playing an important but contested role in those conflicts.

OVERVIEW OF THE TRIP

The pope's visit lasted from June 1 to June 9. He arrived in the north-western town of Koszalin, where he spoke at the local military base. On June 2 he flew to the southeast corner of Poland for a series of events in the towns of Rzeszów, Przemyśl, and Lubaczów. In this region, the pope raised issues connected with relations between the Roman Catholic Church and Eastern Rite Catholics, as well as Eastern Orthodox Christians and Ukrainians, and he beatified Przemyśl's former bishop, Józef Sebastian Pelczar. Then John Paul went on to the cities of Kielce and Radom, the former notorious for the 1946 pogrom there, the latter a key center of labor unrest in 1976. In both cities, the pope celebrated mass at the local airport, preaching on the fourth and fifth commandments ("Honor your father and mother" and "You shall not kill"), respectively, and putting heavy stress on the issue of abortion. On June 4, John Paul traveled on to northeastern Poland, addressing Lithuanian pilgrims in Łomża and beatifying Mother Bolesława Lament in Białystok, where he also took part in an ecumenical service at the Orthodox Cathedral of Saint Nicholas. In Olsztyn the pope spoke at a pediatric hospital and celebrated a mass in honor of the laity, among other things. On June 6, John Paul headed for the central Polish cities of Włocławek and Płock, celebrating the feast of the Sacred Heart at both venues on June 7 and preaching on the ninth and tenth commandments ("You shall not covet your neighbor's wife" and "You shall not covet your neighbor's goods"), respectively. In Włocławek, the pope also addressed educators, while in Płock he visited a prison.

John Paul's pilgrimage culminated with a two-day visit to Warsaw, after having spent a full week in the country. As the highlights of a heavy schedule of events (fourteen public addresses in Warsaw), the pope spoke to Poland's political leaders at the Royal Castle; celebrated the two-hundredth anniversary of Poland's renowned Constitution of May 3, 1791, at the Cathedral of Saint John the Baptist; met with those parliamentary representatives who supported antiabortion legislation; opened and addressed the plenary conference of Polish bishops; hosted the diplomatic corps in Warsaw at the Nunciature; addressed representatives from the world of culture at the National Theatre; met with representatives of the Jewish community; took part in an ecumenical service at the Lutheran Church of the Most Holy Trinity; and beatified an eighteenth-century Franciscan from Kraków, Father Rafał Chyliński.

Two features of this itinerary are particularly worth noting. First, most of the trip took place in eastern Poland, giving John Paul ample opportunity to raise issues connected with Eastern Christianity and with Poland's eastern ethnic minorities and neighbors. Second, the decision to make preaching on the Ten Commandments the framework for the pope's travels was both understandable and controversial. The Decalogue motif was chosen on the grounds that, as Poles built the new, free, democratic, postcommunist Poland, they needed God's guidance more than ever. As John Paul pointed out in his homily in Płock, God's commandments protect the human person and bring peace and joy.[11] If the newfound freedom of Poland and Poles was not anchored to the moral truth of the commandments, then freedom would become a new form of slavery and cause the enslavement of others. After their long experience under a repressive system, Poles must learn to be free, a difficult task. The teachings of the Decalogue, according to John Paul, were the best service that he could provide to his compatriots at this critical time of transition. This approach subsequently came under much criticism, even from some of John Paul's biggest supporters and admirers. George Weigel, for example, argued that the theme "was not well-suited to the psychology of the moment" and that the pope's words were often perceived as "scolding and nay-saying."[12] Jonathan Kwitny wrote that "on previous trips home, the pope had captured Poland's mood and hopes in his hand; this time, he grasped only air" and that "the encouragement that had been JP's trademark seemed to have curdled into negativism."[13] According to Ewa Kulik, a Solidarity activist quoted by Kwitny, "It was like he had lost touch with the country. . . . Instead of trying to understand us and teach us, he was wagging his finger."[14] Carl Bernstein and Marco Politi note that John Paul experienced being out of touch with his audience for the first time during a visit to Poland, and they quote Father Józef Tischner as later noting a "certain emotional discord between him and his audience."[15]

No issue played a bigger role in setting the mood for the papal visit than abortion, and the controversy over abortion in Poland in the months and weeks leading up to John Paul's arrival presented the pope with the opportunity to throw himself into a contentious moral-political battle raging among his fellow Poles. He did not hesitate to do so.

ABORTION

A strong movement to ban abortion reemerged in 1989, with those opposed to the procedure seeking to overturn a 1956 law and its subsequent modifications that established abortion as legal and readily available in Poland.[16] Under communism, Poles experienced acute shortages of contraception (and of just about everything else), and abortion was relied upon as the principal means of "birth control," giving Poland one of the highest abortion rates in the world.[17] During periods of relative liberalization, when Poles were freer to make their opinions heard, pressure mounted for repeal of easy access to abortion. This was the case, for instance, during the "Polish Spring" of 1956–1957 and the Solidarity period of 1980–1981. With the breakdown of the communist regime in spring 1989, opponents of abortion made their strongest push yet. Lawyers commissioned by the Episcopal Commission for the Family drafted an antiabortion bill, which around seventy-five deputies endorsed in Parliament. Called the Unborn Child Protection Bill, it granted full personal rights to the fetus and stipulated punishments of up to three years in prison for doctors who performed abortions and women who procured them. These initiatives took place in the aftermath of the famous Round Table Talks, held from early February to early April 1989 between the communist government and the Solidarity opposition, and the talks produced an accord that Poland would hold elections in June. As part of the Round Table Agreement of April 4, Poland's unicameral legislature would be transformed into a bicameral one, with free elections to the new Senate and open competition for 35 percent of the seats in the lower house, the Sejm. In this context, the Communist Party members welcomed the antiabortion agitation as a way to divide Solidarity between its more traditionally Catholic and its more secular liberal supporters.[18] By June, demonstrations, petition campaigns, and media debates over abortion were under way. These were soon superseded, however, by the Polish elections and subsequent political maneuvering, and abortion moved to the margins for a time. It returned to center stage, however, in 1990, when deputies in the newly created Senate raised the issue.

In summer 1990, the Senate took up the abortion issue energetically, drafting, debating, and ultimately passing, on September 29, a law banning it. Unlike the 1989 draft, the final version did not include punishment for women who had abortions. The right to life was guaranteed from conception, abortionists could receive up to two years in prison, and exceptions were limited to threats to the life of the mother and pregnancies resulting from rape. The law also outlawed IUDs and birth control pills deemed abortifacient.

Next it was the turn for the lower house of Parliament, the Sejm, to take up the abortion question. In January 1991, after a stormy debate, the Sejm set up an "extraordinary commission" to deal with the issue. The forty-six-member committee was sharply divided over what to do about abortion or even how to decide what to do. By a narrow vote, it decided to solicit "public opinion" on the issue. Between February 15 and March 31, Poles could send their views to the commission. That 89 percent of those who did so supported a ban on abortion was more indicative of the ability of the Catholic Church to organize a campaign for the ban than a reflection of public opinion, as polls at the time showed Poles much more divided or even ambivalent about abortion. Eventually, the commission approved, by a narrow vote, a draft bill banning abortion in all cases except when the mother's life was in danger.[19] This draft then headed on to the full Sejm for debate.

Certain features of the context of the abortion debate are crucial for our purposes. First, because the Sejm was elected in accordance with the Round Table Agreement, whereby the communists and their allies were guaranteed 65 percent of the seats, it was a body less amenable to the Church's positions than the Senate. Also, with elections coming in the fall, many deputies would have liked to skirt this controversial issue altogether. Second, Poland's bishops from the start were lobbying heavily for a ban on abortion, and they issued an appeal on May 2 asserting their positions on a number of issues facing Poles at the time. With respect to abortion, the bishops affirmed their opposition to any compromise, and they flatly rejected proposals that the law on abortion be put to a public referendum on the grounds that the right to life can never legitimately be a matter of public opinion. To do so could lead to further wicked acts—for example, to depriving sick persons of life—and in the past such a questioning of the right to life had led to concentration camps.[20] Although the bishops were no doubt sincere in this belief, there was another, more practical reason for opposing a referendum, one that provides the third important dimension to the context—Poles themselves were divided over abortion, and the total ban favored by the bishops would not have come close to passing in a nationwide popular vote. Polling data from mid-May had 31 percent of Poles supporting abortion without restrictions; 19 percent supporting a total ban; and 49 percent favoring permission for abortion in some cases.[21] Other polls reflected similar though not identical results.[22] A final dimension of the context was the upcoming visit of Pope John Paul II on June 1. Opponents of abortion in Poland, and especially the Catholic bishops, were hoping to welcome him with the gift of a ban on abortion. Defense of the unborn had been close to

John Paul's heart for most of his life and was a prominent issue during his pontificate. He had welcomed the passage of the antiabortion bill by the Senate in fall 1990, when he told a group of Polish pilgrims visiting Rome that the Senate bill was "a worthy initiative . . . a first step on the way to overcoming the evil inheritance weighed down with the stamp of totalitarian materialism."[23] He had also spoken of the defense of "the right to life from the moment of conception" at his meeting with the visiting president of Poland, Lech Wałęsa, in February.[24] In order to greet the pope appropriately, his supporters believed that a ban on abortion not only had to be enacted but that this had to happen relatively quickly.[25]

As the full Sejm took up the issue in mid-May, it faced at least three options. It could vote yes or no on an antiabortion bill, either as proposed, as modified, or in alternative form. It could call a national referendum on the issue. The third option would be to find a way to shift the issue to the future, presumably after the upcoming parliamentary elections in the fall. It was this latter option that, after stormy debate, won the day. The Democratic Union (Unia Demokratyczna), a party with roots in the Solidarity movement and a liberal Catholic orientation, proposed a nonbinding resolution that would substitute for a vote on the ban on abortion. By a vote of 208 to 145, the Sejm postponed consideration of the antiabortion bill and then endorsed the Democratic Union's proposal. Among other things, the resolution urged that the 1956 abortion law be repealed and that abortions no longer be done in the private offices of doctors. It asked the government to take measures to "restore respect for human life and a feeling of responsibility for parenthood," including better sex education. It also asked the government to explain how it planned to deal with the increased birthrate and other social consequences (for example, the increased need for orphanages) that would ensue from a ban on abortion.[26]

Although many of Poland's parliamentarians could now breathe easier, having ended a contentious debate and put off a fateful decision, the Catholic bishops and other opponents of legal abortion were disconcerted. The resolution was far short of what the antiabortion forces, including the Catholic bishops, desired and served mainly as a way to put the issue off until the autumn. The bishops were also surely concerned that in a country where at least 90 percent of the population identified as Catholic, they could not count on majority support for unequivocal defense of the unborn. The fact that this resolution was proposed by the Democratic Union, a party with its roots in the Solidarity movement and with important Catholics among its leadership, also stung the Church. Worst of all, however, was that this parliamentary maneuver foiled one of their fondest hopes—to present a ban on abortion as a gift to John Paul during his upcoming visit.

This failure was widely regarded as a blow to the Church's prestige and influence. People were increasingly annoyed with the Church's political activism, as opinion polls of the time showed. The bishops were not only pushing for a law out of step with most of public opinion but were apparently using "nondemocratic" means toward that end. Specifically, they preferred to work through a Sejm in which 65 percent of the representatives were holdovers from the communist period, elected in June 1989 to those seats unopposed by Solidarity, rather than to support a popular referendum, even though upwards of 70 to 75 percent of Poles regarded a referendum as their preferred approach to the abortion issue.[27]

The drawn-out and acrimonious conflict over abortion, postponed but far from resolved, helped set the stage for John Paul's June visit to his native land. Poles across the social and political spectrum were stirred, and debate over the place the Church should occupy in society and politics had come to the forefront. John Paul's presence would only magnify these issues, and how he chose to address them would be an important part of his message to his compatriots during this first papal visit to the new, postcommunist Poland.

It was not until the third day of his pilgrimage that the pope raised the question of abortion directly. John Paul delivered a one-two punch against legalized abortion during back-to-back masses celebrated at airports in Kielce and Radom, respectively, on June 3 and 4. Before a congregation of 150,000 at Kielce, he preached on the fourth commandment ("Honor your father and mother"), addressing abortion within the context of the family.[28] Elaborating on what he called the crisis currently facing the Polish family, the pope reiterated that children should be "regarded and accepted as a gift of God," indeed, a gift sometimes difficult to accept but always "priceless." Even an unexpected pregnancy "is never an intrusion or an aggressor." Rather, it is a human person with a claim to special sacrifice from its parents. According to John Paul, the world would turn into a nightmare if married couples who find themselves facing material difficulties see in their newly conceived child only a burden and a threat to their stability or if married couples who are well off see in the child an unnecessary and costly expense. "This would mean," according to the pope, "that love no longer counts in human life," that human dignity is totally forgotten.

The next day at Radom, John Paul returned to the topic of abortion, this time in connection with the fifth commandment, "You shall not kill."[29] Before a crowd of 250,000, he described the commandment as one that affirms the right of every person to life—"from the first moment of conception through to natural death."[30] It intercedes in a special way for the innocent and defenseless. John Paul's admonitions against killing the innocent were not narrowly focused on the unborn, however. Reciting a litany of the horrors of the twentieth century (mass killing of noncombatants in wartime; aerial bombing, including with the atomic bomb; concentration camps; mass deportations; the deaths of millions of innocents), the pope put special emphasis on the systematic and categorical murder of entire nations and groups, above all the Jews and Roma. He noted how these genocidal acts were preceded by whole programs of racial and ethnic hatred that repudiated the absolute and universally binding nature of the fifth commandment. These "mad ideologies" gave individuals the right to decide about the life and death of persons, groups, and nations. They replaced God's command against killing with a human freedom to kill, even regarding killing as a necessity. Consequently, an enormous stretch of the European continent became the graveyard of innocent people, victims of humans' usurping for themselves the authority over life and death that belongs to God.

The pope then remarked that added "to this graveyard of human cruelty in our century" is "yet another great cemetery—the cemetery of the unborn, the cemetery of the defenseless, whose faces not even their own mothers know, mothers who agree to or succumb to pressure to take away their lives before they are born." John Paul reminded his audience that the unborn were already alive, "conceived beneath the heart of their mothers, not suspecting this mortal threat." Here the pope made reference to a film that showed a fetus desperately trying to defend itself against the threat to its life posed by abortion. John Paul spoke of how his memory remained haunted by the image of this "horrible drama" played out in the womb and witnessed in the film.[31]

The pope then brought the issue back to current developments and controversies in Poland. He referred to those pressure groups and legislative bodies working to make abortion legal, and he asked, "Is there such a parliament that has the right to legalize the murder of an innocent and defenseless human being?"—to authorize killing precisely in the situation where life most needs to be protected and assisted?

After this powerful statement against abortion, and indeed against all taking of innocent human life, John Paul shifted to the positive aspects of the fifth commandment and encouraged Poles to help those facing inopportune pregnancies. He noted how the prohibition against murder protects the life and health and dignity of each person, regardless of race, religion, level of intelligence, degree of consciousness, age, or state of health. He exhorted his audience to accept other persons, especially their own children, as gifts from God and to render assistance to those faced with pregnancies coming at difficult times. The pope stressed the need for greater social concern not only for the unborn child but also for its parents, especially its mother. He called for the creation of institutional forms of support for parents who feel overwhelmed by worries and difficulties in conjunction with a pregnancy, and he asked parishes and monasteries to join in this movement of social solidarity with the unborn child and its family.[32]

As he continued his circuit of Poland, John Paul came back to the issue of abortion on at least five other occasions, a frequency without precedent in earlier papal visits. He especially emphasized abortion during the final two days of his visit, in Warsaw. At an event on June 8 in the Royal Castle commemorating the two-hundredth anniversary of Poland's Constitution of May 3, 1791, John Paul spoke of human rights and solidarity.[33] He affirmed that the most important human right is the right to life, and he underscored that genuine solidarity must be integral, meaning that it must include everyone, especially those unable to defend themselves. Thus, said John Paul, "we are not free to exclude from it [solidarity] the unborn children."

That same day the pope demonstrated his unequivocal support for antiabortion legislation by addressing those parliamentarians who had sponsored the bill banning abortion.[34] He thanked them for taking the initiative to draft and promote legislation defending the unborn, asserting that the first and fundamental right for a human being is the right to life. John Paul went on to identify what he saw as some of the reasons for the failure of many to resist abortion: human weakness, becoming used to abortion being legal, a "deeply disfigured" social consciousness. Lest one regard opposition to abortion as a strictly religious position, the pope noted that non-Catholics, and even some ardent adversaries of the Church, shared its position on the right to life for the unborn, and he cited the Italian legal and political philosopher Norberto Bobbio as an example.[35] For John Paul, this was a matter of the common good and of the moral and physical health of the nation. Alluding to the failure of Poland's Parliament to address the issue to his satisfaction in the weeks leading up to his visit, he expressed his view that at least a starting point had been reached, as well as his hope that a fuller result would come about in due time. John Paul also used this occasion to reiterate one of his favorite points about abortion—that though some women, especially in the international feminist movement, had come out in support of legalized abortion, abortion in fact is against women and that behind the female voices of the pro-abortion movement hides the man.[36] In raising this issue, John Paul endorsed the call of Poland's primate, Cardinal Glemp, for dioceses and parishes to undertake various initiatives toward enhancing and strengthening the position of women as wives and mothers.

On his final day in Poland, John Paul came back to abortion yet again. At his Angelus reflection that day, he spoke of the "destructive effects" of the communist period on Polish women as mothers, an oblique reference to the easy access to abortion since 1956.[37] He also continued his implication of men in the tragedy of abortion, stating that "behind the sins of the woman usually stands the man. Because often in the moment when she especially needs courage and help from him, he egoistically leaves her to herself or even pushes her to commit that sin that later will constitute a heavy reproach of conscience for the entirety of her life." According to the pope, the man bears responsibility for this burdening of the woman's conscience, and he expressed his indignation that many would like to continue this situation, establishing it as something normal.

Finally, the pope raised the issue of abortion yet again when he spoke to the Conference of the Episcopate of Poland, the climax of his visit.[38] In commenting on the issue, John Paul indirectly admitted the widespread support in Poland for legal abortion. He blamed the Polish Constitution of 1956 for its legalization of abortion, noting that people all too easily equate what is legal with what is moral, making it harder for the Church to convince people that abortion is wrong. It was therefore important that the law be changed in order to facilitate the changing of people's minds on the issue. Thus, it was not so much a question of changing public attitudes in order to bring about a change in the law but rather of changing the law in a way that would reshape public attitudes.

John Paul encouraged the bishops, in the spirit of Saint Paul, to proclaim the Church's teaching against abortion whether people wanted to hear it or not.[39] In his words to the bishops, the pope mentioned a recent Vatican document that noted an increasingly widespread mentality supporting legal abortion, "even among persons by nature noble-minded."[40] In this admission, John Paul was touching on one of the most formidable obstacles to the outlawing of abortion—that legalized abortion was being supported by some quite decent people. The Church thus faced a big task in trying to reshape public attitudes on the issues.

MORE ISSUES OF CONCERN TO THE CHURCH IN POLAND

Abortion was not the only concern of the Polish bishops and their Catholic supporters in Poland. Education, the media, the elections, and the constitution itself were all among the matters of interest at the time. In fact, the first cause that Poland's bishops championed in a big way was getting religious education into the public schools. As with abortion, this matter also roused public controversy, not so much because of the substance of the issue (most Poles favored voluntary religious education in the public schools) but because of the way the policy change was implemented.[41] In August 1990, the joint commission of representatives of the bishops and the government, established under the communist regime but remaining in place after its fall, instructed the minister of education to add religion to the curriculum from kindergarten on up. The Church regarded this move as a necessary step in undoing the decades-long communist exclusion of religion from the schools, as well as recognition of the crucial role Catholicism played in the preservation of Polish identity over the ages. Opponents of the measure complained that religion courses took class time away from other subjects, that the education budget was already tight and could not afford the additional course, and that children whose parents had them opt out of the courses had to sit out the catechism hour in the hallway. Efforts by the bishops to get the policy anchored in legislation, including the provision of state salaries to religious education teachers, including clergy, kept the issue in the spotlight.

John Paul addressed education on June 6 during a meeting in Włocławek, when he spoke to catechists, teachers, and students.[42] After noting the importance of education for the nation and how teachers helped Poles to maintain themselves as a nation under foreign occupation by helping to pass on "authentic Christian and national values," the pope spoke about religious education in particular. He expressed his personal happiness over the return of religion to the educational system decades after the communists had forced it out. His words, however, were far from triumphalistic. He recognized the need for goodwill on all sides, indirectly acknowledging the controversy swirling around the policy. He denounced attitudes of fanaticism and fundamentalism, both secular and religious; he called for vigilance against xenophobia and intolerance that contradicted the spirit of the Gospel. He tried to finesse the complex relationship between parental rights to raise their children in the family's faith and the child's freedom to follow his or her conscience, calling for respect for the rights of children and young persons at school to form and express their consciences in accord with the faith formation received in the family and their own honest, personal spiritual searching. John Paul ended his talk by alluding again to the controversy, asserting that "the Church—I don't know why—is suspected of wanting something else. The Church wants to serve. This is its calling. The Church wants to serve, it wants to serve the person, it wants to serve society."

Another issue on which many Polish Catholics, along with their leaders, collided with the emerging postcommunist system was with respect to the media.[43] Here again the bishops let their views be known, calling for those wishing to share religious perspectives to have greater access to the media while lamenting the dissemination of opinions hostile to the Church as well as what they deemed pornographic material. The bishops accused the media of waging a "battle against Christian values" as well as creating a "pro-abortion atmosphere."[44] Here again, Polish society was divided, with a public opinion survey in July 1990 disclosing that 62 percent of respondents believed the Church should not have influence on television programming.

John Paul paid homage to this issue as well during his visit, on at least two occasions.[45] In an address to laity on June 6 in Olsztyn, the pope spoke of the responsibility to provide honest information in the media. In his view, the media ought to defend freedom but also respect the dignity of the person and support an authentic culture. As John Paul put it, "Society should be informed in an honest way, in accord with the truth and with the dignity of the nation. The press, film, radio, television, and theatre ought to form society, to create and cultivate a culture that contributes to its progress and not to its weakening or destruction. They ought to be imbued with the Gospel, the saving word of Christ." Earlier that day, he spoke at mass on the eighth commandment ("Do not speak false testimony"), and used that theme to comment at length on freedom of speech. John Paul welcomed its restoration in Poland as a great social good, but he noted that even "free" speech can remain unfree. Although no longer suppressed by the government's office of censorship, which had been abolished, it could be "shackled by egocentrism, lying, deceit, perhaps even hatred or contempt for others—for example, those of a different nationality, religion, or opinion." Truth can become degraded by being expressed without love or by being used in the service of lies. John Paul called for "goodwill, mutual trust, and respect for all those distinctions that enrich our social life." He spoke of the great need for an *odkłamanie* (that is, "a rectification of lies" or "undeceiving") in various spheres of Polish life—social, cultural, political, economic, and media. Rather than listing off the typical churchman's grievances against the media (anticlericalism, pornography, etc.), the pope exhibited a more profound grasp of the problems connected with greater freedom of speech and expression and gave Poles admonishments and exhortations appropriate to their situation.

Policy toward the media, education, and abortion were all connected with the question of Poland's new constitution, then being drafted.[46] The bishops lobbied the parliamentary commission that was working on the draft constitution, calling for a constitutional affirmation of the right to life from conception, a guarantee of religious education, and protection from morally dissolute and offensive publications. They also argued against a continuation of the communist-era separation of Church and state, calling instead for cooperation between the two institutions, albeit with respect for the autonomy of each. The bishops also wanted churches to be able to take part in political campaigns, something that two years earlier had been essentially noncontroversial. In the June 1989 elections, many churches had served as campaign headquarters for Solidarity, with some priests helping to select candidates and promoting them in their homilies.[47] This Church support for Solidarity was widely popular and appreciated at the time. However, by 1991 the context in Poland had changed considerably, and increasing numbers of Poles were uneasy with such heavy political involvement by the Church, especially now that the "us-versus-them" character of politics under communism had given way to a wide spectrum of permissible political views, currents, and parties that contended with each other over the shape that Poland's present and future would take.[48]

John Paul raised the issue of relations between the Church and state on several occasions during his visit. As this relationship was in a state of renewal and flux, the pope had an opportunity to present his own vision of how it ought to play out in Poland. On June 3, in a homily on the third commandment ("Keep the Lord's Day holy") at Lubaczów, he addressed the question of whether the state should have a so-called "neutrality of worldview."[49] For the pope, this depended on what one meant by the phrase. Legitimate neutrality of worldview was when the state protected the freedom of conscience and confession for all of its citizens, regardless of their particular worldviews. But this concept could also be used illegitimately, as a means for the atheization of state and society, as was the case under the communists. For John Paul, if the state jettisons God on the pretext of worldview neutrality, it would be making Catholics feel ill at ease in their own fatherland and return them to the ghettoization they experienced under the former regime. The pope went on to endorse a warning Cardinal Glemp had given against an "easy and mechanical imitation" of Western models or a continuing acceptance of certain forms that were appropriate in the communist era. These comments on Church-state relations evoked several interruptions by applause from the crowd. John Paul returned to the controversy over the proper place of the Catholic Church in Polish public life on June 6 in Olsztyn.[50] Acknowledging the growing anxiety in Poland over the political role of the Church, the pope noted that he heard misgivings, fear, and criticism of the Church, as if it were aspiring to dominate and threaten the autonomy of various spheres of public and governmental life. He assured his audience that this was not the case and quoted the Second

Vatican Council's document *Gaudium et spes*: "the Church . . . in no way identifies itself with the political community nor binds itself with any political system."[51] It only wanted to witness to the Gospel in the life of society and had no "aspirations to capture any of the spheres of public life which do not belong to it," he stated.

In tune with the Decalogue theme, John Paul spoke out on a host of moral issues as he made the rounds in his native country. He warned against excessive and vulgar nationalism and intolerance.[52] He admonished Poles for neglecting the religious obligation to attend Sunday mass. Above all, marriage, family, and sexuality got their due. In his homily on the fourth commandment ("Honor your father and mother") at the airport in Kielce on June 3, John Paul spoke at length about the crisis in the Polish family.[53] He lamented the high divorce rates, tensions and decaying interpersonal bonds within families, long separations when a spouse lived abroad, abuses related to alcohol, and insular families that closed themselves off from others. Near the end of his homily, the pope launched into an angry tirade against what he regarded as the abuses of freedom currently plaguing the Polish family. He asked, nearly shouting, "Are we free to recklessly expose the Polish family to further destruction?"—a comment that triggered one of the few rounds of applause from the audience. He demanded a mature freedom, not a fictitious one "that supposedly liberates man but actually constrains and debauches him." He called on Poles to examine their consciences on this threshold of the Third Republic and asked them to cease the reckless destruction of the Polish family and instead work intensively to rebuild it. At Łomża on June 4, the pope preached on the sixth commandment ("Do not commit adultery").[54] Here he spoke of the dignity of the human body and against lust, which reduces the other person to an object. In line with his theme of denouncing illusory freedom, the pope condemned so-called "free love" as nothing but a veil for adultery and dissipation, a costly illusion that hurt children, among others. On June 7 at mass in Włocławek, the pope preached on the ninth commandment ("You shall not covet your neighbor's wife").[55] He admonished Poles to refrain from involving themselves in that "civilization of lust" that was running rampant and calling itself "Europeanness." John Paul deemed it an anticivilization, an anticulture—one that works to waste the humanity of its adherents.

Although John Paul's addresses during this visit to Poland contained an abundance of harsh words, condemnations, admonitions, and warnings, much of what he said to Poles about marriage and family was positive. He spoke of the deep communion that binds a family together. He reminded his listeners that "every child is a gift of God."[56] He spoke of the unity of soul of the married couple and the capacity of Jesus Christ to provide them light and strength in their relationship. He noted the "beautiful, lasting, faithful, and indissoluble" love of a marriage strengthened by Christ.[57] Thus, though John Paul gave far more stress to the negative and the critical during this trip than in previous ones, there was still enough that was affirmative and encouraging to at least partly sweeten the bitter cup he was asking Poles to drink.[58]

SOCIOECONOMIC TRANSFORMATION

Although the pope addressed a number of important moral issues during his 1991 pilgrimage, only one issue rivaled abortion for pride of place in his discourse to his fellow Poles. That issue was the economic transformation taking place, or more precisely, its moral and social implications. John Paul was returning to a Poland in the midst of a serious economic, social, political, and cultural transformation, elements of which we have already seen in the debates over abortion policy and other issues. With respect to the economy, the country was transitioning from the reformist communist regime of the late 1980s to the nascent capitalist one of the early 1990s. In January 1990, the Polish government began implementing what was called the Balcerowicz Plan, which stressed tightening fiscal policies, cutting state subsidies, and looking toward the eventual privatization of much of the state sector of the economy. In what turned out to be a painful transformation for many Poles, inflation reached astronomical proportions; unemployment was rising, with at least 256,000 unemployed

Poles receiving no unemployment benefits; productivity was in decline; privatization had stalled; and consumer goods were more readily available than before but at prices many Poles could not afford. The semicommunist Sejm, which included many representatives whose prospects for reelection were slim and who thus had little incentive to work quickly or well, was dragging its feet, failing to act on more than one hundred economic reform bills awaiting resolution. Public trust in the government was dropping quickly, with one poll noting a decline from 56 to 42 percent in one month. Solidarity called a "Day of Protest" for May 22, and the result was a series of demonstrations and strikes across the country. Whether all of this was simply the birth pangs of a much-improved Polish economy or indications that Poland was on the wrong path was unclear at the time. What was clear was that the economy was on many people's minds when the pope arrived for his fourth pilgrimage on June 1.[59]

Economic transformation was an issue with many dimensions, touching the lives of Poles in countless ways, and John Paul referred to it at least a dozen times during his 1991 visit, though he stressed it the most during his homilies at masses in Lubaczów, Białystok, and Płock, when he focused on the third, seventh, and tenth commandments, respectively, and in his speech to government representatives at the Royal Castle in Warsaw. As is typical for papal teaching, John Paul avoided the technical details of economic reform and focused instead on the larger moral questions associated with economic policy and behavior. He also had advice, warnings, and exhortations with respect to the political transformation and addressed related issues of the environment and the situation in Poland's prisons.[60]

John Paul's first serious presentation of Catholic social teaching and its implications for Poland was on June 3 during mass at Lubaczów, when he preached on the third commandment ("Keep the Lord's Day holy").[61] Because John Paul's visit to Poland came in the wake of the release of his most important encyclical on Catholic social teaching, *Centesimus annus*, of May 1, 1991, he stressed some of the major themes from the encyclical in his addresses to his compatriots. At Lubaczów he went on to make one of his signature points—that "it is more important to 'be' than to 'have.' More important is who you are, rather than how much you own." In the proper "hierarchy of values," material goods are not ends in themselves but need to be used in accordance with God's will, the pope reminded his audience, warning them against the "error of consumerist attitudes." Moreover, John Paul affirmed as he took up another theme of *Centesimus annus*, the economic reform in Poland must be accompanied by the growth of a "social sense," an increasing concern for the common good. In particular, there should be concern for those people in greatest need, as well as benevolence toward "foreigners who have come here in search of bread."

John Paul would return to these themes again and again as he addressed Poles during this critical period. While dedicating a new seminary building in Łomża on June 5, he urged priests and seminarians to live a life of material poverty in imitation of Jesus Christ and his disciples.[62] Eschewing material riches not only makes a priest a better witness to the spiritual kingdom of heaven, but a simple lifestyle also protects him from the temptations of luxury and excessive comfort. Poland needs such a witness today, the pope urged his audience. Quoting his own words from an address in 1980, John Paul said that "the mission of the priest is to show that the destiny of man is not the accumulation of earthly goods, when there exist other, far more valuable goods for which it is worth doggedly aspiring—that is, the values that ennoble the person and connect him in a communion of life with God." The pope also called on the seminarians to have an attitude of sympathy and love for those most in need.

When addressing representatives of the world of culture on June 8 at Warsaw's National Theatre, John Paul asserted yet another theme from *Centesimus annus*—that culture has primacy over economics.[63] He noted that the communist system had tried, mistakenly and without success, to understand culture in terms of production and consumption. John Paul returned to his "being" versus "having" schema, first acknowledging that "having" is important in that there are human needs that the economy must meet but going on to affirm that this task of meeting needs would be realized effectively only on the foundation of the primacy of "being." As John Paul laid it out, "having" related to the economy, while "being" related to culture. In the proper hierarchy of values, culture has primacy over economics just as "being" has primacy over "having." The economy is realized through culture, in particular through that dimension of culture that is morality, meaning that the ethical dimension is crucial. Only in this way is the dignity of the human person protected. In a controversial statement in line with the suspicion of the West that, as we shall see, the pope displayed throughout this visit, John Paul said that "individuals accustomed to seeing their existence according to the primacy of 'to have'—and thus the primacy of material values—often seek a place in the West, where that primacy of the human 'to have' is better grounded." He quickly added that this is not the only or the decisive reason why someone moves to the West.

John Paul's second major address on Catholic social teaching took place at mass in Białystok on June 5, when he preached on the seventh commandment ("Do not steal") and beatified Mother Bolesława Lament as, among other things, a model of concern for the poor and marginalized.[64] Here the pope emphasized above all the connection between economics and ethics, a crucial component of Catholic social teaching. John Paul noted that the deep economic crisis inherited from the communist period went hand in hand with a grievous ethical crisis, with the latter conditioning the former. He referred to the "greatest injustices" committed by the communists in pursuit of what was supposed to be a "paradise of absolute justice." In the pope's view of things, Poland needed "to overcome the consequences of a regime that showed itself not up to the task economically, and pernicious ethically, in order to build within the framework of a new regime a just order, in which human talents will not be wasted and the whole of socioeconomic life will find the necessary balance." He warned Poles not to try to achieve a new economic system by a shortcut, by omitting moral guideposts, and quoted the words of Jesus Christ: "For what will it profit a man if he gained the whole world but brought harm to his soul?" (Matthew 16:26). John Paul called for the "scrupulous observation of the principles of justice" in the economic transformation, whereby all persons consider not just their own interest but that of society as well, in particular those who are poorest and most needy. He also called for an even deeper dimension of morality, that of merciful love. Thus, Poles stood before not only a great organizational and institutional effort but a moral one as well.

John Paul also took this occasion to address the ongoing economic transformation in terms of the Church's teaching on property, which dated to Pope Leo XIII's 1891 encyclical *Rerum novarum*. On the one hand, it was not wrong for the private individual to possess productive property. The commandment "Do not steal" in fact presupposed the right of the human person to possess things, and John Paul added that people have not only the right but the obligation to produce new goods for themselves and for others. However, God's commandment means that one is not permitted to abuse one's ownership of property to the detriment of those in need. As Leo XIII taught, goods produced privately are meant to enrich the whole of society, and no one should be excluded from the wealth created by private production to the point where they become destitute. It is the government's responsibility to make sure this does not happen. John Paul pointed to the West as an example of such misuse, evoking some applause from those assembled. He asked why the system of private property and private production there had not served the universal use of these goods, leaving not only a poverty-stricken Third World but also many people living in poverty and hunger within the West itself. According to John Paul, Poles needed to learn how to own and produce privately, which was not only a technical matter but a deeply ethical one as well.

John Paul continued the lessons in Catholic social doctrine on June 7, when he preached on the tenth commandment ("Do not covet your neighbor's goods") at mass in Płock.[65] This commandment provided a great opportunity for the pope to revisit the hierarchy of values. He reaffirmed that money, riches, and worldly comforts are transient goods that should never occupy the highest place in one's scale of values. He stressed that the human person is more important than things. He noted that with economic development many needs can be met but warned against becoming a slave to one's possessions. He stated forcefully that "no one is ever free to aspire after material goods in violation of the moral law, in violation of the rights of another person." John Paul expressed his wish "that none of you ever tries to enrich yourself at the price of your neighbor." He urged Poles, as they aspired to an improvement of their material condition, not to "lose common human sensitivity to the poverty of others. Take great care that we do not become a society in which everyone begrudges another something." The audience applauded these remarks, as well as John Paul's call for fairness (*uczciwość*) across Polish society—within families, between neighbors, in the workplace, in business, in government. Reiterating the overall theme of his 1991 pilgrimage, the pope argued that Poland needed God's law in order to prosper—that the Ten Commandments protected the human person and brought joy and peace.

Connected with John Paul's catechesis of his fellow Poles was his hope that Poland could and should become an example of Catholic social teaching in action. He brought this message to the government on June 8, when he addressed Poland's political leaders, including the president, cabinet ministers, and parliamentary representatives, at the Royal Castle in Warsaw.[66] On this occasion, John Paul quoted the Italian political scientist and politician Rocco Buttiglione with respect to Poland's future. Buttiglione wrote in the Polish Catholic journal *Ethos* in 1990 that Poles could either simply enter consumerist society, occupying the bottom spot, "or they can contribute to the renewed discovery of that great, deep, authentic tradition of Europe, offering to it simultaneously an alliance of the free market and solidarity." John Paul noted that he himself had spoken on this theme in 1987 along the Baltic coast, as well as in his encyclicals *Sollicitudo rei socialis* (1987) and *Centesimus annus* (1991), and conveyed his hope to Poland's leaders that in transitioning to the free market, Poles would continue and even deepen attitudes of solidarity.

FREEDOM AND TRUTH

At the foundation of much of what John Paul said during his visit was his steadfast belief in the connection between freedom and truth, a fundamental Catholic position that soon found lengthy expression in the pope's encyclical *Veritatis splendor* (1993). If there was one thing more than any other that tied together the pope's teachings and exhortations with respect to the emerging new Poland, whether it be in terms of abortion, education, the media, economic and social policy, or most anything, it was John Paul's firm belief that freedom needed to be grounded in truth. In this context, truth for the pope was more or less synonymous with morality. The understanding of freedom held and elaborated by John Paul and many Catholics differs considerably from the Western liberal perspective and therefore deserves a closer look. From the Western liberal perspective, freedom means the freedom to choose; *what* is being chosen is not at issue. From John Paul's perspective, freedom means the freedom that one attains by making the right choices. What is crucial is not the fact that one *can* choose but rather *what* one in fact does choose. It is the substance, not the process, that is paramount. Making the wrong choices does not result in freedom but in a self-enslavement to one's vices and passions and to the dire consequences of immoral decisions. This latter understanding of freedom implies virtuous thinking and living, which is why the moral law, including the Ten Commandments, is a crucial component of the concept of freedom. Persons who try to do the right thing, and societies that structure themselves in accord with God's law, are on the path to genuine freedom. This is sometimes explained in terms of playing a musical instrument—in the liberal sense, we are all free to pick up a musical instrument and try to play it. We can make that choice. But only the person who learns and follows the requisite rules and techniques, and who puts in the hard hours of disciplined practice, truly has the freedom to really play the instrument.[67] This latter freedom implies a development of personal virtue that leads to excellence. Thus, as John Paul presents his Catholic perspective on freedom, the persons or societies that follow the rules (that is, the moral laws of God and nature) and discipline themselves to live virtuously, are truly free, while those persons or societies that neglect and violate the moral law end up encumbered by their own ignorance, error, and lack of virtue and discipline. John Paul's worry for Poland was that, in exercising the first type of freedom, Poles would make wrong choices that would keep them from realizing the second, more fundamental type of freedom.

From this perspective, freedom indeed was difficult, as John Paul reminded his audiences.[68] It had to be learned, and implemented in accord with God's law, lest it become slavery, both an inner enslavement of oneself and an external enslavement of others. Thus, Poles stood before a test of freedom. Will they, the pope asked, make good use of it? Will they use it in truth? Although this freedom comes as an enormous gift from God, it comes along with a task, John Paul reminded his audience.[69] This is why John Paul placed such a premium on the Decalogue during this visit—it was the guide for how to pursue genuine freedom and how to avoid its counterfeits. In typical Wojtyłan fashion, the pope placed the question of freedom and truth into the broad sweep of Polish history, identifying those periods when Poles sought genuine freedom, often at great price, and those times when Poles abused what freedom they had. On the positive side, there was the great Constitution of May 3, 1791 (see below); the November Uprising against the Russian occupiers that began in 1830; the contribution of Poles to nineteenth-century liberation movements under the motto For Your Freedom and Ours!; the successful struggle for independence during World War I and the ensuing defeat of Soviet Russia in 1920; the struggle against Nazi Germany during World War II, especially the 1944 Warsaw Uprising; and the defense of society under communism, especially with the Solidarity movement. On the negative side, John Paul noted the abuses of freedom that had led to Poland's demise by the late eighteenth century, "a painful lesson of freedom misused to the point of madness. Misused to madness!" as he forcefully shouted to his audience in Płock.[70] For John Paul, if freedom means that one chooses selfishness, self-interestedness, venality, indifference to the needs of others, and trampling on the common good, then this is no freedom at all.

Again in Wojtyłan fashion, John Paul drove this point home with reference to the life of a Polish saint during his beatification mass for

Father Rafał Chyliński in Warsaw on June 9.[71] The pope presented Blessed Rafał's holy life of service as a protest against the corrupt times in which he was living, the so-called Saxon period of Polish history (1697–1763), which was a notorious period of thoughtless, self-destructive selfishness and corruption among the noble class that helped prepare the way for Poland's ultimate destruction by the end of the eighteenth century.[72] Although Blessed Rafał was no politician, his selfless devotion to the poor and to the sick stood out in stark contrast to the self-centeredness of the other noblemen of his time. John Paul even likened Blessed Rafał to Tadeusz Rejtan, the Polish parliamentarian who blocked the door of the Sejm in 1773 in a symbolic attempt to prevent the departure of delegates who had just voted to hand over large pieces of Poland's territory to Russia, Prussia, and Austria and who was thus remembered as one of Poland's greatest patriots.

It is no wonder that John Paul had the eighteenth century on his mind when speaking to Poles, since his visit came during the two-hundredth anniversary of the Constitution of May 3, 1791, one of the most celebrated documents in Poland's history. Poles are especially proud of this historic document. Dating from a time when Poland was threatened by external aggression and internal dissolution, it was the product of reform-minded patriots seeking to correct the constitutional problems that had accounted for Poland's precarious situation. Although that constitution was never implemented, later generations of Poles accorded great symbolic importance to it. As Norman Davies writes, "It was the Bill of Rights of the Polish tradition, the embodiment of all that was enlightened and progressive in Poland's past, a monument to the nation's will to live in freedom, a permanent reproach to the tyranny of the partitioning powers."[73]

In the spirit of the commemorations, John Paul spoke at length about that constitution, as well as its historical and present significance, during his first two appearances in Warsaw on June 8. The first was his address to the representatives of Poland's government, including President Wałęsa, at the Royal Castle in Warsaw's Old Town.[74] The second was at a thanksgiving service at the nearby Cathedral of Saint John the Baptist.[75] After reciting the preamble of the constitution, John Paul praised it as an expression of civic wisdom and political responsibility and asserted that it not only became the foundation of the newly independent Poland that emerged in 1918 after the defeat of the partitioning powers but that it should also be a point of reference for Poles in the wake of communism's demise, as they drafted their latest constitution. In accord with his connection of truth and freedom, the pope noted that the constitution opened with an invocation to God as Trinity, was presented on the altar in Saint John's Cathedral at a Te Deum service on May 3, 1791, and was acknowledged with approval by Pope Pius VI (1775–1799). Although the document is best remembered as the work of young men inspired by the Enlightenment and the French Revolution, for John Paul this recognition of God's authority was critical, enabling him to use the document to argue for the importance of grounding post-1989 Poland on the principle that authority should be exercised on the foundation of truth, for as Jesus Christ said, "The truth will free you" (John 8:31).[76]

RELATIONS WITH EASTERN CHRISTIANS

One of the most significant features of John Paul's 1991 pilgrimage to Poland was the outreach he undertook to Eastern Christians, both Eastern Orthodox and Eastern Rite Catholic.[77] To a considerable extent, the pope was on a mission of damage control. This was an especially troubled time for relations between these three dominant Christian groups in northeastern Europe.[78] The collapse of communism across the region led to what one scholar called an "ecumenical Chernobyl," a situation "in which a critical mass of long suppressed Roman Catholic, Orthodox, and Eastern Catholic antipathies were detonated by a potent charge of political freedom." Western Ukraine, where Eastern Rite, or so-called Greek Catholics, were especially numerous, was ground zero in this metaphor.[79]

There are a number of important features of this situation that set the stage for the papal visit. First, there were three interconnected relationships that needed to be considered—between the Roman Catholic Church and the Eastern Orthodox Church, in this case especially the Russian Orthodox Church but also with the Orthodox as a whole; between Eastern Orthodox Christians and Eastern Rite Catholic Christians; and between Roman Rite (also known as Latin Rite) Catholics and Eastern Rite Catholics. Each of these relationships was troubled at this time, even critically troubled in spots. Second, these relationships operated on multiple levels—they were a key part of the Catholic Church's ecumenical outreach and thus had global significance. At the same time, they were specifically connected to the religious and ethnic history and current political and diplomatic situation of the Baltic region in which Poles, Russians, Ukrainians, and Lithuanians, among others, were key players. They were also connected with local politics and ethnic tensions in Poland, particularly in the southeastern city of Przemyśl. Third, because religious and ethnic identity were largely synonymous in this region, relations between Orthodox, Eastern Rite Catholic, and Roman Rite Catholic Christians roughly paralleled relations between Russians, Ukrainians, and Poles, respectively. Thus, the Russian Orthodox Church from the one side and extreme Polish nationalists from the other looked on Eastern Rite Catholicism as a seedbed for Ukrainian nationalism. Finally, in his approach to Eastern Christians, John Paul was confronted with an apparent zero-sum game. On the one hand, the pope wanted to heal the millennium-long rupture in Orthodox-Catholic relations and bring these two ancient branches of the Church as close as feasible; on the other hand, John Paul wanted to protect the Eastern Rite Catholics from persecution and defend their right to exist with their own ecclesial leadership and infrastructure. However, any moves on behalf of the Eastern Rite Catholics upset the Orthodox, who regarded the Eastern Rite Catholics as the illegitimate offspring of earlier Catholic attempts to "Catholicize" the East, and any attempts to accommodate the Orthodox alienated Eastern Rite Catholics, who feared being sold out by Rome as the price for rapprochement with the Orthodox.

Przemyśl itself, where the pope paid a visit, was the site of a fierce dispute between Roman Rite and Eastern Rite.[80] John Paul had long been a friend of the Greek Catholics. He started defending them almost at once after his election in 1978. He wrote letters of encouragement to Eastern Rite leaders, he complained to Soviet authorities about persecution against them, he convened meetings of Ukrainian Eastern Rite bishops in diaspora, and he participated in Eastern Rite events in Rome. There were also attempts by the Catholic Church in Poland to improve relations with its Eastern Rite component. Since the Greek Catholics were not welcome in the Soviet Union at the 1988 celebrations of the millennium of the conversion of the medieval land of Kievan Rus' to Christianity, the Catholic bishops in Poland helped organize a commemoration at Częstochowa that featured the Eastern Rite Catholics.[81] At the same time, however, not all Polish Catholics were so positive about the Eastern Rite. In Przemyśl in southeastern Poland, conflicts broke out between a reassertive Greek Catholic Church and local anti-Ukrainian Polish nationalists. Among the contentious issues were how to remember the region's past, which included much violence between Poles and Ukrainians. These two nations had fought against each other in this region in 1918–1919, when Poland held on to Przemyśl in the face of Ukrainian attempts to annex it; during the interwar Polish Republic, when Ukrainian armed resistance units contended with government armed forces; and during World War II, when Ukrainian and Polish nationalist partisans bitterly fought each other in a vicious conflict that entailed mass actions of ethnic cleansing of each other's ethnic kin, which included the torching of villages and the mass murder of civilians.[82] The worst killing took place in the region of Volhynia, across the border in Ukraine, but there was also substantial deadly ethnic cleansing in eastern Galicia, on the western edge of which sat Przemyśl. After the war, the Polish government uprooted large numbers of Ukrainians from this region and resettled them in western Poland.

At the center of the tensions in Przemyśl was the local Church of Saint Teresa, which had been the Eastern Rite cathedral for more than 150 years until the government confiscated it in 1946; it eventually ended up in possession of the Roman Catholic Carmelite order. John Paul "had consistently upheld the right of the Greek Catholics to full equality with the Church of the Latin rite."[83] Continuing in this path, he gave the Eastern Rite Catholics their first local bishop since 1946 by appointing Jan Martyniak as Greek Catholic bishop of Przemyśl in January 1991. The new bishop, however, was without a cathedral. Under communism, the Greek Catholics worshipped in a local Roman Catholic church, but with communism's fall they requested the return of their former cathedral. The Church leadership in Poland, along with the Vatican's representative, Papal Nuncio Józef Kowalczyk, decided that Saint Teresa's should be returned to the Eastern Rite Catholics for the next five years, during which time the Greek Catholics would build a new cathedral with the support of the Roman Rite, a settlement endorsed by John Paul. However, while Poland's Church leadership was willing to accommodate the Eastern Rite Ukrainians, a small group of lay Catholics in Przemyśl organized the Association for the Defense of the Carmelite Church. They reacted against the proposed settlement with protests, media campaigns, candlelight vigils, a hunger strike, and ultimately the seizure of the church, barricading themselves inside so that it could not be handed over to the Ukrainians. These tensions were in play during the time of the pope's June 1991 visit, and even though local Polish activists decided to cease acting up for the period of the papal visit, there was enough trouble that John Paul elected not to pay a visit to Saint Teresa's.[84]

Relations with Eastern Orthodoxy were not much better at this time, which was particularly unfortunate given that harmony with Eastern Christianity was a matter very close to the pope's heart. John Paul had long been pursuing a positive relationship with the Eastern Orthodox Church, targeting it as the most desirable partner of all the Christians with whom the Catholic Church was seeking closer ecumenical relations. His 1985 encyclical *Slavorum apostoli* was an exhortation for Christian unity between East and West, and his naming of the Orthodox missionaries Saints Cyril and Methodius as co-patrons of Europe underscored both his outreach to the East and his belief that despite the religious divisions of the past, Europe should be united spiritually. John Paul sometimes spoke of the Church as breathing "with two lungs," an Eastern one and a Western one.[85]

He spoke out for reconciliation between Eastern Rite Catholics and Eastern Orthodox Christians, as well as between Ukrainians and Russians.[86]

The biggest issue in Catholic-Orthodox relations at this time was the question of the Eastern Rite Catholics, or what the Orthodox liked to call "Uniatism." The revival of Greek Catholic churches across the region horrified the Orthodox, who feared that Rome would use them as the spearhead of efforts to proselytize the formerly communist East. Eastern Rite Catholics, meanwhile, had been victims of severe Soviet repression, with their church essentially outlawed by Stalin after World War II, its property confiscated, and its clergy imprisoned. The Orthodox Church at the time supported this repression and benefited from it, acquiring many Eastern Rite churches as well as having its main religious rival removed from the picture. By the mid-1980s, Eastern Rite Catholics had begun to demand legalization, restoration of church property, and restitution. They particularly wanted the Orthodox Church to repudiate the so-called Lviv Sobor of 1946, an exercise in Soviet-sponsored propaganda and coercion in which the Soviet NKVD coerced those Greek Catholic representatives they had not imprisoned to dissolve their church and merge with the Orthodox.[87] Very importantly, Eastern Rite activism was closely tied to Ukrainian nationalism, and western Ukraine by the late 1980s had become a hotbed of ethno-religious agitation. When Ukrainian nationalists won the elections in their major urban center of Lviv in March 1990, they helped the Greek Catholics regain control of Saint George's Cathedral there by August, against Orthodox opposition. Meanwhile, hundreds of other churches were being seized by Eastern Rite Catholics throughout western Ukraine. The Vatican, in attempting to deal with the resurging Ukrainian Eastern Rite Catholicism and its own ecumenical objectives regarding the Orthodox, found itself sandwiched between two seemingly irreconcilable forces.

In October 1989, John Paul sent Vatican secretary of state Angelo Sodano to Moscow for negotiations with the Soviet leadership about religious matters, especially the Eastern Rite question, and in January 1990 Vatican representatives held talks with Russian Orthodox leaders in Moscow to attempt to resolve the issue. In these and subsequent talks with the Orthodox, Rome renounced any intentions to proselytize the Orthodox and agreed to Orthodox insistence that "Uniatism," understood as the creation of Eastern Rites within the Roman Catholic Church, was an unacceptable model for church growth and reunification.[88] At the same time, the Catholic Church insisted on the right of Greek Catholics to exist with their own church structures and leadership and their right to exercise their faith freely.[89] John Paul made it clear that religious liberty was a fundamental human right. In seeking accommodation with the Orthodox on the "Uniate" issue, John Paul harbored hopes that the Orthodox would attend the European Synod of Bishops that he was planning for autumn 1991.

If the question of the Greek Catholics was not problem enough, tensions over the Roman Rite Catholic presence in the Soviet Union reached new levels. With the Soviet government becoming far more accommodating in the waning months of communism, the Catholic Church seized the opportunity to establish two dioceses, in Pinsk and Grodno, in Soviet Byelorussia (now Belarus) and to appoint three "apostolic administrators" to handle church affairs for Roman Catholics in Russia and Kazakhstan.[90] Although the Vatican believed it was taking Orthodox sensibilities into account by, for example, appointing apostolic administrators instead of bishops and limiting its concerns only to Catholics in the Soviet Union, the Orthodox Church saw the Vatican policy as a threat. To make matters worse, Rome announced the appointment of these bishops and administrators without consulting or even informing the Russian Orthodox Church leadership, even though one of its metropolitans had been visiting the Vatican while these decisions were being made. Because these unfortunate events were playing out in spring 1991, a cloud hung over Catholic-Orthodox relations during the pope's June visit to Poland.

To add yet another dimension to the complex inter- and intra-Church relations of this time and place, Rome was having increasing problems in its relations with Greek Catholics. Although

John Paul defended the right of the Eastern Rite Catholics to exist and to worship freely under their own bishops, he left them dissatisfied by making certain favorable gestures and accommodations toward the Orthodox Church. For example, Rome's insistence that property issues be settled in harmony with the Orthodox grated on Eastern Rite nerves, as did John Paul's appointment of an archbishop for Roman Rite Catholics in Lviv and the tensions brewing in Przemyśl over the Church of Saint Teresa. The situation reached the point where the pro-Eastern Rite Lviv city government denied permission for a plane carrying Primate Glemp and a number of other Polish bishops to land in their city on an ecclesial visit in spring 1991. This was the situation as the pope prepared for his visit to Poland.

As John Paul embarked for Poland, he had his work cut out for him in terms of ecclesial relations with the East. Given all these tensions, John Paul arrived in Poland in June with inter-Christian relations high on his agenda. To underscore these concerns, his trip was geared toward the eastern part of the county. John Paul made only one stop west of Warsaw, that being his arrival at Koszalin in the northwest, and he gave a number of addresses close to Poland's eastern borders, sometimes only miles from the Soviet Union. Not only was the pope visiting those parts of Poland that had Lithuanian and Belarusian minority populations, he was also able to address large crowds of pilgrims from the Soviet Union, as the Polish authorities allowed tens of thousands of visitors from Lithuania, Ukraine, Byelorussia, and other parts of the Soviet Union into Poland without visas in order to hear the pope as he visited the border regions.[91]

During his visit, John Paul gave three addresses that bore heavily on relations between Roman Catholics and Eastern Christians. At Przemyśl on June 2 he spoke to Eastern Rite Catholics, both those in that city who were under siege from nationalistic Polish Catholic extremists and those of Ukraine and Byelorussia who had crossed Poland's border to hear the pontiff speak. At Białystok on June 5 he held an ecumenical service at the Orthodox Church of Saint Nicholas. In Warsaw on June 9 he devoted considerable attention to Eastern Christians in his speech to Poland's bishops. He also revisited these questions in some of his other appearances in Poland's east.

Arriving in Przemyśl on June 2, after earlier in the day having beatified former Przemyśl bishop Józef Sebastian Pelczar at mass in nearby Rzeszów, the pope first went to the local cathedral to visit Blessed Pelczar's tomb. In addressing the audience, John Paul spoke of the local population as "people of God of both rites."[92] He alluded to the Eastern Rite–Roman Rite tensions in that city, expressing his hope that the Diocese of Przemyśl would become "a model of cohabitation and unity in pluralism" where "love, benevolence, and mutual understanding show themselves stronger than all the artificial divisions and conflicts." He asked for Blessed Józef Sebastian's intercession toward this end, calling him "a man of reconciliation, a sower of fraternal unity."

John Paul next addressed an assembly of Eastern Rite Catholics, including many visiting from Ukraine, at a Roman Rite church in Przemyśl, where Greek Catholics had been worshipping unofficially for decades in the absence of a church of their own.[93] Before his Polish-language address, the pope greeted the audience in the Ukrainian language. Then he went on to speak at length about the millennium of the baptism of Saint Vladimir in 988. He referred to that event as the beginning of the Christian faith in this land, both for the Orthodox as well as for Eastern Rite Catholics, and he affirmed that the present-day Ukrainian Greek Catholic population had the medieval state of Kievan Rus' and its faith as their heritage. John Paul spoke of his own participation in events commemorating 988 and the fact that Eastern Rite Catholics, though strictly prohibited by the Soviet regime from taking part in the commemoration events in the Soviet Union, could do so in Poland at Jasna Góra, as they did in September 1988. The pope noted that the Eastern Rite, while not officially recognized by Poland's communist government, was nonetheless able to exist openly in Poland with the support of the Roman Rite. John Paul stated that the 1988 commemorations were prophetic in that they augured a new freedom and a revival for Eastern Rite Catholics. He also spoke of his hope that the joint Roman Rite–Eastern Rite celebration at Jasna Góra would serve "as a symbolic seal of the reconciliation and genuine brotherhood of Ukrainians and Poles."

John Paul then addressed Ukrainian-Polish relations in greater detail. He lamented the bitterness and torment the two nations had experienced over the previous decades and called for Poles and Ukrainians to distance themselves from all this conflict and distrust and seek "the mutual forgiveness of former wrongs." Based on their common faith in Jesus Christ, they should seek "reconciliation, brotherhood, and mutual respect." With an eye toward the recent exacerbation of ethnic tension in Przemyśl, the pope asserted that "the kindling of former nationalisms and antipathies would be an action against Christian identity; it would also be a glaring anachronism, unworthy of two great nations." He then exclaimed, "Oh how I heartily desire that Catholics of both rites mutually love each other!" Tying his words to the person beatified earlier that day, the pope mentioned Blessed Józef Sebastian Pelczar's fraternal feelings toward Eastern Rite Catholics.

John Paul then went on to express his great joy that the Church in Ukraine had emerged from the catacombs. He recalled the forty-five years of persecution the Greek Catholics experienced in Soviet Ukraine, where all of their bishops along with hundreds of priests and thousands of lay faithful ended up in prisons, labor camps, or lifelong exile; where all the church buildings, seminaries, and publishing houses were confiscated by the regime; and where the Catholic Church of the Eastern Rite was not permitted even to exist. The pope praised the courage of the large number of Eastern Rite martyrs of this period and the fact that none of its bishops had renounced their fidelity to Rome despite this persecution.

John Paul next took up the matter of the distinctiveness of Eastern Rite identity, speaking of the two attributes that constitute it—faithfulness to the Eastern Christian tradition and full unity with Rome—attributes that the Greek Catholics succeeded in preserving despite persecution. Quoting the Eastern Rite leader, Cardinal Myroslav Lubachivsky, the pope called the Eastern Rite "an inseparable part of the universal church . . . the Church of the Kievan tradition, united with Peter-Rock."[94] He then noted that all Orthodox churches had been in union with Rome through the first thousand years of Christianity. John Paul spoke of the "sacred obligation" the Church had to the Eastern Rite Christians, especially given their past difficulties and persecutions.

After devoting considerable attention to Roman Rite–Eastern Rite reconciliation, the pope raised the matter of Orthodox–Eastern Rite relations. He spoke of the communion (*communio*) of love within the Church and how it does not close in on itself; rather, it is open to all baptized Christians. Thus, the Church opens its heart in a special way "to the brother Orthodox Church of the Christian East." The pope expressed the hope that the Orthodox would share in the joy of the Eastern Rite revival, accepting its existence on moral grounds and as a reminder of the unity of the Church before the East-West schism. At the same time, John Paul made clear his expectations of his Eastern Rite audience: "I trust also that you will be able to exult in your freedom in such a way that does not trouble or disturb the priceless ecumenical peace with the Orthodox Church." He concluded this attempt to put a damper on Eastern Rite triumphalism with a recitation of Jesus Christ's call for Christian unity in his high priestly prayer from the Gospel of John (17:20–24).

At the end of his address to Greek Catholics in Przemyśl, John Paul told his audience that he was handing over to them permanent possession of the church in which they had been meeting; it would henceforth be their cathedral. This was in lieu of the church that was supposed to have been built for them in accord with the earlier agreement that had to be revised.[95] In his words to the Greek Catholics, John Paul took care to give Przemyśl's Roman Rite bishop, Ignacy Tokarczuk, credit for this act of generosity. The pope's concluding comments brought long rounds of applause from those present. After speaking, John Paul "plunged into a crowd of Ukrainians" who had turned out to hear him speak.[96]

On John Paul's June 5 visit to the northeastern Polish city of Białystok, he took up the thorny problem of Roman Catholic–Eastern

Orthodox relations. At the beatification mass there for Mother Bolesława Lament, the pope praised her for, among other things, her ecumenical spirit in promoting Catholic-Orthodox reconciliation.[97] In comments at the end of mass, the pope greeted visitors in the Belarusian and Russian languages, and he then continued in Russian to welcome the current revival of Christianity in Russia, speaking of the spiritual goods that both Catholic and Orthodox churches brought to humanity. These comments in Belarusian and Russian evoked much applause from the audience. John Paul also celebrated the establishment of new dioceses and other apostolic structures by the Catholic Church in the East, a sore spot for the Orthodox, but he was careful not to present this as some sort of competition with them.

Later that day, the pope addressed Catholic-Orthodox relations in more detail and with greater vigor when he paid a visit to the Cathedral of Saint Nicholas to take part in an ecumenical service with the Orthodox. After greeting his audience in Church Slavonic, he spoke of the "spiritual brotherhood" existing between the two churches.[98] He cited commonalities between East and West, in particular the veneration of many saints in common and the participation in the sacraments, especially the Eucharist. The pope thought it fitting that they were meeting in a church named for Saint Nicholas, because not only is he venerated in both East and West but he was a bishop in the fourth century, when the Church was not yet divided. John Paul went on to speak of the Catholic and Orthodox as "sister churches." He also recognized that their relationship had been painful in the past and that deep roots of distrust had still not been overcome, at least not completely. The pope acknowledged that "everyone carries the burdens of historical guilts, everyone makes mistakes" and went on to ask God's forgiveness for past injustices, regardless of which side was at fault. After this call for mutual forgiveness, John Paul spoke of the importance of dialogue. His speech recounted past accomplishments, quoted joint declarations of the two churches, and looked forward to further progress, including over "the very difficult issue of unionism." He expressed the hope that obstacles to unity would eventually be removed. John Paul reiterated the intentions of both churches, as stated in a 1987 declaration, to repudiate proselytism of each other, along with any attitudes that could be construed as lack of respect. The pope stressed the importance of educating youth in an ecumenical spirit and called for benevolence and a Christ-like, disinterested love in the relations between Catholics and Orthodox. Finally, John Paul made reference to some recent attacks on the Orthodox in Poland— the burning of an Orthodox church on Mount Grabarka and thefts at two Orthodox monasteries. Expressing his "deepest compassion" in connection with these painful events, the pope said that "these sacrilegious acts evoke deep pain in my heart and in the hearts of all Catholics. Everything that disturbs the good, fraternal living together of Christians of various traditions comes from the Evil One." John Paul ended by blessing the Orthodox.

Having addressed both the Eastern Rite Catholics and the Orthodox, the pope next turned his attention to the Roman Catholics when he spoke at length on East-West church relations to the bishops gathered in Warsaw on June 9, the climactic event of his visit.[99] In a talk that covered a number of important issues, John Paul devoted considerable attention to Eastern matters. In his presentation, the pope dealt jointly with the new opportunities that recent political changes provided the Catholic Church for strengthening its presence in the Soviet Union and with the implications of these initiatives for ecumenical relations with the Orthodox. He welcomed the fact that there was now a Roman Rite Catholic bishop in Lviv, two new bishops in Byelorussia, and new apostolic administrators for Russia, including Siberia, and Kazakhstan. He looked upon these regions as pioneer territory ripe for missionary activity, and, while noting that these developments were strengthening Poland's relations with the East, he remarked that this was not about the Polish nation or the Church in Poland but about the Church in its universal mission. John Paul noted that some were concerned that the Church had undertaken this Eastern initiative too quickly, and he stressed that it must be carried out "in a spirit of dialogue and ecumenical cooperation." As he put it, "It is an enormously important matter that we find understanding among our Orthodox brothers on the territory on which they above all for whole centuries were responsible for evangelization." The pope reiterated that "the Catholic Church, the Latin Church, absolutely does not want to take over this evangelization from their hands; it is not thinking of proselytism." According to John Paul, it only wanted to evangelize those communities that define themselves as Catholic, whether of the Roman Rite or Eastern Rite.[100] As far as the Orthodox Church was concerned, the Catholic Church only wanted to help it evangelize its own believers. In other words, with the newfound religious freedom that the Soviet Union was beginning to enjoy at this time, John Paul's hope was that both Western and Eastern churches would each work to bring their own believers back into active participation in their respective churches, with the Catholic Church willing to help the Orthodox in this endeavor, while eschewing any kind of "sheep stealing."

DIPLOMATIC, ETHNIC, AND RELIGIOUS OUTREACH

In addition to his outreach specifically to Eastern Christians, John Paul worked to heal wounds, build bridges, and strengthen relations with a number of other partners during the 1991 visit. He sought better ties with the Soviet Union and repeatedly expressed a desire to visit there. He tried to calm tensions with Ukrainians and Lithuanians in Poland and build up relations with Lithuania and Ukraine, which at the time were increasingly autonomous Soviet republics (soon to be independent). He addressed Protestants in Poland at an ecumenical gathering at the Lutheran Church of the Most Holy Trinity in Warsaw. Finally, he met with representatives of the Jewish Community, also in Warsaw.

In contrast to the John Paul who sternly lectured his fellow Polish Catholics on the troubling direction in which their country was heading, the pope's discourse with non-Catholic, non-Polish partners was upbeat and conciliatory. Moreover, it was clearly designed to strengthen bonds. At his very first mass in Poland in 1991, he greeted audience members who carried a banner calling on him to visit Russia.[101] At times during his travels, he expressed his hope that he could someday visit Ukraine, Lithuania, and Moscow. When speaking to Poland's Conference of Bishops, he noted that Soviet leader Mikhail Gorbachev on both his visits to the Vatican had "insistently" invited the pope to visit Moscow.[102] These comments reflected the rapidly improving state of Vatican-Soviet relations dating from the late 1980s.[103]

Alongside his efforts to heal Ukrainian-Polish tensions in Przemyśl and to reach out to the inhabitants of Ukraine itself, as we have seen above, John Paul likewise sought similar goals with respect to Lithuania and the Lithuanians. Here the critical event was his visit to the city of Łomża in northeastern Poland, where he addressed an assembly of visiting pilgrims from nearby Lithuania, including government officials such as the vice president, deputy prime minister, and minister of culture.[104] John Paul began by praising Poland's Lithuanian minority, expressing satisfaction that the Lithuanian language, culture, and identity were being kept alive in Poland through institutions such as the lyceum in nearby Punsk that taught in the Lithuanian language. He praised Poland's Lithuanians for enriching Poland's society with their culture, living "here on the land of your fathers." The pope then went on to address the visitors from Lithuania proper, repeating the words he had used at Saint Peter's in 1987 at the commemoration of the six-hundredth anniversary of Lithuania's "baptism," calling Lithuania a "Baltic bastion of the Church." He quoted one of his predecessors, Pius XI, who as papal nuncio to Poland called Lithuania the "fatherland of saints, martyrs, and heroes!" and "land of Mary!" John Paul noted the close connection between the histories of Lithuania and Poland, and he expressed his hope that the two nations would enjoy a harmonious and fruitful future together in the region. He evoked patriotic-religious symbolism for the Lithuanians by mentioning the Austos Vartia (Gate of Dawn) in Vilnius, the city gate that stood as a symbol of "the indestructible spirit of the nation" and that housed the famous icon of Mary, Mother of Mercy. During his speech, the pope twice embraced the octogenarian Cardinal Vincentas Sladkevičius, himself a living icon of Lithuanian patriotism and Catholicism and former inmate of a Soviet prison camp. The latter part of John Paul's talk evoked repeated bursts of applause from the crowd. Afterward, the pope met privately with a delegation of Lithuanian officials, one of whom subsequently told the *New York Times* that the pope had sympathy for the Lithuanians' desire for self-determination.[105] These words and gestures came at a time when Lithuania was engaged in a fierce struggle with the Soviet government for recognition as an independent state, and although the pope did not openly call for Lithuanian independence, the warm support he did give the Lithuanians was seen as an encouragement for their national cause.

Another group to which John Paul reached out during his 1991 visit was Protestants, in particular Poland's Lutheran minority. On June 9 in Warsaw, while attending an ecumenical service at the Lutheran Church of the Holy Trinity as guest of the Polish Ecumenical Council, he addressed ecumenical issues relating to the Protestants rather than Orthodox.[106] In his remarks, John Paul used Polish patriotism to connect with Lutherans. Challenging the stereotype that the true Pole had to be a Catholic, whereas Lutherans identified more with Germany, John Paul noted that the church at which they were meeting had been treated no better by the occupying Nazis than were Warsaw's Catholic churches. He praised a former pastor at Holy Trinity who perished in a Nazi prison camp, as well as a former Lutheran bishop decorated for the defense of Warsaw in 1939. The pope then went on to denounce intolerance, including the practice of offering or denying privileges and rights as a way to induce a change of religion, and he affirmed the right to practice one's faith publicly. With respect to his Protestant "brothers and sisters in Christ," he called for going beyond tolerance—for mutual forgiveness of the wounds incurred over the past four centuries of division and for cooperation between their churches in areas such as the defense of human life and dignity, efforts for peace and justice, and protection of the environment.

The final group that the pope took pains to address during his 1991 visit to Poland was the Jewish community. At certain stops on his trip, he made reference to past Jewish suffering. At the conclusion of mass at the airport in Kielce, for example, John Paul referred to the notorious pogrom carried out in that city in 1946, when a local mob killed several dozen Jews.[107] John Paul referenced the memory of this crime in praying for love and unity between people of all nations, races, religions, and convictions in Poland and throughout the world. On June 9, not long before meeting with the Lutherans, John Paul met with representatives of Warsaw's Jewish community. He spoke of the shared heritage between Jews and Christians in terms of figures such as Abraham, Moses, and David. He referred to the "splendid but also tragic thousand-year past of the Jewish community in Poland." In referring to the Shoah, John Paul repeated his words from his 1987 meeting with Warsaw's Jewish leaders, stressing the common threat that Jews and Poles both faced during World War II, while acknowledging that this threat was realized against the Jews to a degree that it was not against the Poles. He quoted a recent statement by Poland's bishops that spoke of Poland as a common fatherland for Jews and Poles and called for the past sufferings of the two peoples to unite, not divide them. John Paul noted that much good, as well as much evil, had happened over the centuries in Poland, all of which was surpassed by the genocide during World War II. The pope acknowledged the role that genocide played in mobilizing Christian Europe to redress the past crimes against Jews and to take up the work of uprooting from its mentality all unjust prejudices against Jews, a process the Catholic Church actively took part in, especially with the Second Vatican Council's declaration on the Church's relations with non-Christian religions, *Nostra aetate*. John Paul urged the Church, twenty-five years since the issuing of that path-breaking document, which fundamentally reoriented the Catholic Church's attitude toward Jews as well as other religions, to make a special effort to implement these teachings.

EUROPE, CHRISTIANITY, AND POLAND

The final theme taken up repeatedly and forcefully by John Paul during his 1991 visit was Europe—Europe's Christian heritage, its departures from that heritage, its current spiritual crisis and need for redemption and re-evangelization, the call for a spiritual integration of Europe East and West, and Poland's supposed need to gain entry to (western) Europe. Europe came up in various ways, especially in the pope's homilies at masses in Olsztyn, Włocławek, and Warsaw; at his addresses to the Polish government and to the foreign diplomatic representatives; at the bishops' plenary conference; and in his farewell comments at Warsaw's airport.

First, the pope made it clear that Europe had a Christian heritage. At the mass on June 9 in Warsaw during which he beatified Father Rafał Chyliński, John Paul argued that the seeds of freedom were brought to Europe by Saint Paul, in that the Gospel message of liberation through Jesus Christ "formed the history of Europe for 2000 years."[108] Thus, Christ is "the author of the European spirit." The previous day, in speaking to the diplomatic corps, John Paul had repeated the warning he had given to the European Parliament in Strasbourg in October 1988: that if Europe's Christian inheritance was not accorded influence in the present, this would not only mean the denial of the heritage of the past but would also threaten a worthy future for the inhabitants of Europe, believers and nonbelievers alike.[109] At the same time, he noted that Europe was facing a spiritual crisis. In his June 6 homily at Olsztyn, John Paul argued that Europe was simultaneously traveling along two paths—the path of its Christian inheritance of freedom through Christ and the path of freedom from Christ.[110] Europe, he said, has a special historical connection with Christ but also has given birth and continues to give birth to various programs of departure from Christ. The pope told his Polish audience that they now stood at a crossroads—the way of freedom through Christ's truth or the way of freedom from Christ. In his homily in Warsaw on June 9, he spoke of how in modern times, Jesus Christ had been bracketed off as Europeans began to think and live as if God did not exist.[111] This, too, according to John Paul, was part of the European spirit, part of the modern European tradition. He called on his audience to reflect deeply on the manifold meaning of Europeanness. With this in mind, the pope spoke of the need for a new evangelization of Europe.

Poland's place in this Europe was an issue of paramount importance for the pope, and nowhere did this manifest itself more than in his homily on the ninth commandment ("You shall not covet your neighbor's wife") at Włocławek on June 7.[112] In a part of Poland where more than half of diocesan clergy had perished under the

Nazis and near where Father Jerzy Popiełuszko, the pro-Solidarity priest and activist, was murdered by communist police agents, the pope confronted the question of Europe and Poland's place in it in dramatic and emotional fashion. After mentioning a number of the famous martyrs from the region, as well as the wartime losses of clergy, the pope, almost shouting, denounced "the whole civilization of lust and exploitation that runs rampant among us and gives itself the name 'Europeanness,'" asking rhetorically, "Is this civilization or anticivilization? Is this culture, or rather anticulture?" In John Paul's estimation, culture is what makes a person more of a person, not what consumes his or her humanity. The pope was especially adamant that the acceptance of libertine sexual values was not a measure of how European one was, and he resented the implication that Poland somehow had to "enter" Europe, to earn its place there by accepting such values along with protecting legal access to abortion. To a positive reaction from the audience, he pronounced that Poland *is* in Europe and always had been; that it did not need to *enter* Europe, because it had helped create Europe; and that it did so with greater effort than those self-appointed arbiters of what is and what is not European. John Paul angrily denounced the notion that freedom meant taking the life of the unborn child. He spoke of the great sacrifices that Poles had made for Europe, especially in recent decades, again evoking applause.[113] He then noted some of modern Europe's problems and evils—the killing of people because of their ethnicity, be they Jew, Rom, or Pole, and the "myth of class," another European heritage. For John Paul, Europe needed redemption, and "the world needs a redeemed Europe." Aware that he had gone off-text in unleashing a tirade against modern secular Europe, the pope was quick to ask his audience's pardon for these torrid words, blaming the cool weather and the emotion evoked by the martyrological significance of the venue.

Notwithstanding this critical stance toward a number of modern tendencies in Western Europe, John Paul's overall position remained that of full support for European integration, and his view was one that conceived of Europe in a broad sense, encompassing East and West. The pope noted past support of the Vatican for European integration, citing the efforts of Popes John XXIII and Paul VI to relax East-West tensions during the Cold War, and the heightened concern for Central and Eastern Europe under his own "Slavic" pontificate.[114] He noted the great contribution that Christians made after World War II to the blossoming of European civilization.[115] He encouraged the foreign diplomatic corps in Warsaw to work for a Europe based on fundamental values such as "ideological neutrality, the dignity of the person as the source of rights, the primacy of the person over society, respect for democratically recognized legal norms, pluralistic societal structures," and for spiritual and material development and integration to advance hand in hand, thus fostering a "continent of culture."[116] In addressing Poland's bishops on June 9 in Warsaw, John Paul spoke of a Europe stretching "from the Atlantic to the Urals" and of the great hopes he placed in the upcoming synod of European bishops, to which the Orthodox bishops were invited as guests.[117]

CONCLUDING ASSESSMENT

Postvisit assessments of John Paul's 1991 pilgrimage addressed the apparent rupture between the pope and a significant portion of Polish society. It had been more than twelve years since Wojtyła had lived in Poland, and that country had undergone momentous changes in the meantime, especially over the preceding two years. Father Tischner, writing in *Tygodnik Powszechny*, remarked that John Paul had come to a new country in June 1991, one he did not know quite so well as the Poland of the past, and that Poles on their end did not know him as well as they once did.[118] Tischner felt that many Poles, caught up in the current political feuding, heard John Paul's words as more ideological than the pope intended. Józef Makselon, who surveyed one thousand Poles from the Archdiocese of Kraków in 1994 on the papal pilgrimages, noted that the fault-finding with John Paul focused not on his person but on certain of his (and the Catholic Church's) teachings, especially those connected with sexual morality, and that this was without precedent in the earlier visits.[119] Writing a series on the pilgrimages in *Tygodnik Powszechny* in 1997, Janusz Poniewierski recalled some of the indications of the new rift opening between the pope and significant numbers of Poles in the early nineties.[120] He noted that attendance at the papal events in 1991 was lower than in earlier pilgrimages.[121] He suggested that fewer people seemed to be talking about the pope's words and that there was considerable carping about the cost of the visit. He cited criticism of John Paul in the liberal media of the time, with those critics accusing him of not understanding liberal democracy, as evidenced by his alleged failure to respect the autonomy of the political and legal realms. Poniewierski then went on to assess the situation. One the one hand, he felt that the pope's critics were interpreting his message too much within the immediate context of Polish politics and reading it in a selective, fragmentary manner. At the same time, it did not help that some politicians were appropriating John Paul's words in support of their own policies, and a number of bishops were indeed intervening in political affairs. Poniewierski ascribed the rift to fears on both sides—some Poles feared a "new totalitarianism," with the Church stepping in to threaten the freedoms that the nation had recently won back from the Communist Party. Other Poles feared that the Church was under siege and Catholics would be facing increasing discrimination. Some Poles were too optimistic about democracy and put off by the pope's warnings about the dangers of freedom misused, while other Poles were too pessimistic about the future, seeing more threat than hope and opportunity. As to the pope's approach, Poniewierski wondered whether John Paul was insufficiently sensitive to the fears of many Poles about clerical influence on the new Poland and whether he could have chosen his words and topics more aptly.

John Paul's record on political interventions is complex. On the one hand, he made his views clear on a number of issues of current debate (abortion, education, Church-state relations, the media) and even met with parliamentary representatives who supported antiabortion legislation. On the other hand, he did not support or condemn any particular Polish political party, and much of the criticism, warning, encouragement, and advice he conveyed to his compatriots transcended political boundaries and addressed the issues in their complexity.[122] As Father Tischner noted, John Paul's "speeches were directed to

consciences, not to parliamentary factions."[123] A notable example of
the way the pope could keep distant from politics was his reticence
on one of the more pressing issues of the moment—what to do about
former communists. Should they face justice or be left alone? Should
those in public office be vetted for links with the former communist
security services, or should a "thick line" (*gruba kreska*) be drawn between present and past and baggage from the communist period not
be carried into the future? These issues became bitterly divisive in
Poland (and it became impossible for them not to hang over Poland's
future). Nevertheless, during his 1991 visit John Paul refrained from
offering any opinion on such matters.[124]

In assessing John Paul's 1991 pilgrimage to his native land, we can
learn several things about the pope and his relationship to Poland
and to the broader issues raised by developments there. Above all,
John Paul made it clear that his aim was to speak the truth "in season
and out of season." Instead of congratulating himself and his fellow
Poles for bringing down communism, John Paul chose the prophetic
approach—bearing witness to the problems and choices of the time
from a Catholic Christian moral perspective. The pope pulled few
punches during this visit. He made it clear that he was not interested in winning any popularity contest in Poland but rather wanted
to speak frankly to his compatriots. His message of human rights
and human dignity was just as forceful, and in some ways even more
forceful, in a free Poland than it had been under the communists. This
can be attributed not only to the fact that the postcommunist context
allowed for freer expression but also because democracy meant that
Poles could shape their fate as never before, and they thus could be
held accountable for choices that violated moral law, be these constitutional, legal, political, or personal choices. Momentous decisions
were in gestation during John Paul's visit, and the pope treated this
period not so much as a time to celebrate but as a time to get to work
on shaping a new Poland in accord with Catholic Christian moral
principles.

With this in mind, John Paul shared with Poles a few things that
significant numbers of them did not want to hear. He urged a country

where many people were eager to share the freedom and secularism of the West to ban abortion and accord the Church and Christianity an influential role in public life; he counseled a nation hungry to share in the fruits of a Western-style economy to eschew a consumerist mentality, to show concern for those harmed by the economic transition, and to avoid moving to the West in pursuit of economic advantage; he encouraged a country where radical nationalism was resurgent to get along better with its own minorities and the peoples to the east, especially Eastern Christians. During past visits to Poland, when John Paul took a stand on the problems of the time, his message had resonated with the broad masses of his fellow Poles. In 1979, the native son had returned soon after his election as pope to an exuberant nation. In 1983, the Holy Father came to succor a Polish population demoralized and embittered by the trauma of martial law. In 1987, he devoted his attention to celebrating the Solidarity movement, criticizing the many problems with the communist regime, and preparing Poles for a postcommunist future.

This time, however, his message generated less enthusiasm, reminiscent in a certain sense of Jesus Christ's own words that "a prophet is not without honor, except in his own country, and among his own kin, and in his own house."[125] For the first time in a visit to Poland, John Paul seemed to recall this criterion of the prophetic vocation. While it would be too much to say that John Paul was being "dishonored" during this visit, he surely was not honored to the degree experienced in past pilgrimages, especially the first two. In true prophetic fashion, the pope's aim was to tell Poles not what they wanted to hear but what he believed they needed to hear. While some of John Paul's critics, as well as his defenders, blamed the tenor of his trip on inadequate or misleading advice given him by his own advisors or by the Polish bishops, everything that John Paul did and said during this trip was consistent with his past views on the pertinent issues and was important in laying out a Wojtyłan vision for a postcommunist Poland.[126]

John Paul also presented his vision for a post–Cold War Europe. Above all, he made it clear during this visit that he conceived of Europe holistically and integrally. First, Europe was not secular—it had a body and a soul, and thus the spiritual dimension of European society as part of the Christian heritage was non-negotiable. Likewise, because of this spiritual dimension, Europe was not just Western Europe, even if one defines Western Europe to include the Catholic countries east of Germany, such as Poland and Lithuania. Rather, Europe was East *and* West united, bound together through a common Christian heritage manifested in the Western and Eastern churches, hence the heavy emphasis the pope placed on outreach to the East during this visit. In fact, it is remarkable that during this visit John Paul spoke more favorably of the East than of the West. Toward the East, he spoke words of reconciliation, encouragement, and bridge building; the West, on the other hand, was treated more as a model to avoid, the realm of abortion, sexual libertinism, consumerism, secularism, and practical atheism. John Paul made it as clear as ever that he had little regard for the reductionist concept of a Europe that was merely Western and secular.

In summing up the 1991 pilgrimage, Bernstein and Politi set forth the analogy of Pope John Paul as a modern-day Moses. Spurred by Peter Hebblethwaite's observation that Cardinal Glemp compared Poland's liberation from communism to the Israelites' crossing of the Red Sea, these authors presented John Paul as reminiscent of Moses on several levels.[127] First, just as Moses led the Israelites out of slavery in Egypt through the Red Sea toward the Promised Land, so too did John Paul (albeit in conjunction with other factors) "lead" Poles out of communism toward the promised land of freedom and democracy. And just as Moses gave his people the Ten Commandments to guide them in their newfound freedom, so too did John Paul come to Poland to preach the lessons of this same Decalogue to his compatriots as they constructed a new republic, economy, and society.[128] The pope's visit took on yet another Mosaic dimension, however, when John Paul's words rubbed up against certain tendencies in postcommunist Poland. Reminiscent of the angry Moses coming down from Mount Sinai to find his people worshipping a golden calf, John Paul emotionally denounced what he saw as contemporary forms of idolatry by many Poles.[129] This may not have been the best approach in terms of public relations, but it stands as a manifestation of the prophetic position that the pope elected to take toward his compatriots at this crucial time of transition, with all its hopes and anxieties. For John Paul, the only freedom that would set Poles free was the one built on the foundation of God's law, and driving that point home was the chief priority of his 1991 pilgrimage.

CONCLUSION

By examining Pope John Paul's first four pilgrimages to his native Poland, we learn much about the person and pontificate of this major historical figure of late modern times. Over all four visits, we see which themes—human rights, the meaning of suffering and sacrifice, the connection between Poles and their Church past and present—meant the most to John Paul. We get insight into how he dealt with Poland's foreign and domestic "others," in particular Germans, Russians, Jews, and, in his fourth pilgrimage, Ukrainians, Eastern Orthodox Christians, and Eastern Rite Catholics. We also see his thoughts about Poland's place in Europe, his ambivalent views of the West, and his complex attitudes toward the East. In the third visit we get the fullest dose of his criticism of the communist regime and its policies, as well as a growing concern for his homeland's uncertain future. The fourth visit laid out his vision for the future more fully. Far from the triumphal tour that many expected, this fourth pilgrimage placed its greatest stress on what was going wrong or could go wrong in postcommunist Poland. From 1983 onward, John Paul placed increasing emphasis on the connection between freedom and truth, to the point that it became the overarching theme of his 1991 visit and, along with human rights, one of the driving forces behind his engagement with his fatherland.

THE PILGRIMAGES DURING THE COMMUNIST PERIOD

Because the contexts of the visits during late communism differed significantly from the postcommunist situation, the following assessment will treat the first three visits separately from the fourth. From the first three visits, we get a deeper sense of the pope's dealings with the communist regime. At various times and in various ways he challenged it, accommodated it, annoyed it, and outmaneuvered it. We see how he used the events of Polish history, Poland's saints and heroes, the liturgical season, and sacred spaces, places, and objects to drive home his major points. We note how he tailored his appeal to various societal subgroups—youth, the working class, farmers, the intelligentsia, the world of culture—in ways that challenged communists on turf they considered their own.

John Paul's way of dealing with Poland's communist regime deserves particular attention. First off, he was his own man in this respect. The Vatican diplomats and many Polish bishops were more cautious than the pope, more loath to offend the regime, and concerned, even alarmed at times, that John Paul might undercut efforts to achieve a treaty between the Polish People's Republic and the Apostolic See and scuttle potential agreements between the Church in Poland and the government. Government, Vatican, and the Polish episcopate often shared an interest in getting the pope to soften some of his more provocative words and deeds.

John Paul was obviously firmly committed to pressing the regime for concessions and, especially in 1987, to pointing out its errors and mismanagement of the country. His human rights advocacy, particularly when it concerned the rights of workers to self-governing, autonomous trade unions, no doubt rattled the governing authorities. However, at the same time that he was pushing the regime to reform and admonishing it for its shortcomings, he was careful not to cross certain boundaries. For example, though he raised a host of issues from Poland's past, he did not mention the Katyń Forest Massacre nor did he make direct negative references to the Soviet Union. Also, though speaking favorably of the principles of the Solidarity movement as expressed in its August 1980 agreements with the government and insisting on meeting with Lech Wałęsa, he never called for the restoration of Solidarity per se. Moreover, John Paul did respond to some of the communists' concerns, often conveyed to him through Vatican diplomats and/or Polish bishops. For example, during the 1979 pilgrimage he inserted into his speech at Birkenau words acknowledging Russia's contribution to the victory over Nazism during World War II, and he opted to set aside most of the text of a provocative speech to youth outside the church at Skałka in Kraków. In 1983, in the wake of a vigorous protest by the government, he omitted or minimized politically sensitive references in his next two mass public addresses, proposed a second meeting with General Jaruzelski, marginalized Wałęsa, and gave an upbeat farewell address at Kraków's airport. In 1987, the government intervened right before the dramatic papal visit to Gdańsk, to little avail, and then again afterward, prompting John Paul to ease up a bit on a regime that he had been clobbering during that pilgrimage, basically by sidestepping Poland's present problems to focus on ones that transcended sociopolitical systems.

Still, after some of these interventions John Paul seemed either unfazed or even more defiant. Soon after the government's energetic intervention in 1983, he was back to being a gadfly to the regime—emphasizing human rights, workers' rights, and the ideals of August 1980; referring multiple times to "solidarity" and even once to "Solidarity"; letting applause run on instead of cutting it short; and mentioning, at three large-scale events in succession, workers murdered by the regime. In 1987, John Paul gave one of his most provocative talks ever right after the government expressed its disappointment over the early course of the pilgrimage on the eve of his visit to Gdańsk. Although he backed off somewhat after a subsequent intervention, the pope was not going to let the chance pass to speak his mind in the birthplace of the Solidarity revolution.

These interventions are an important window into what bothered the regime most about the pope, and John Paul's responses deepen our appreciation for the clever and thoughtful ways in which he engaged that regime. To the extent that the pope was willing to meet the regime's concerns part way, we see several reasons for his caution. First, the pope had to face the fact that Vatican diplomats, such as Cardinal Casaroli, and Polish episcopal leaders, particularly Cardinal Glemp, wanted him to get along with the regime. Second, John Paul, while at times chastising the regime, did not want to embarrass its leaders too much, given that they had taken considerable risk in approving the visits and had to show the Soviet Union, Poland's Warsaw Pact allies, and hard-liners in the Polish Communist Party that the papal pilgrimages were benefits, not disasters, for the government. Finally, John Paul surely wanted to avoid the sort of bloodshed that might break out were a crowd, numbering in the six or seven digits, to let itself get incited at a papal event or by a papal address.

However, even when accommodating regime concerns, John Paul often did so in a way that his hosts found disconcerting. For example, in 1979 the government got the Church to agree that the pope would speak of Saint Stanisław in terms of national reconciliation instead of church-state division. John Paul, however, while affirming Stanisław as the patron of Polish national unity, emphasized that genuine national unity meant that no Poles, not even Poland's rulers, were above the law. In 1983, the bishops and the government agreed that John Paul would condemn West Germany's "revanchism" and emphasize the Polishness of the western and northern territories that Poland had acquired from Germany after World War II. The pope did affirm the Polishness of the regions, but instead of condemning West German revanchism, he spoke warmly of Polish-German reconciliation, even using the German word *Versöhnung*, to the dismay of the authorities. In 1987, the government wanted John Paul to speak at the Westerplatte site near Gdańsk and expected him to use the occasion to appeal for peace. Instead, to the regime's chagrin, the pope used the event to address Polish youth on the need for moral courage and heroic resistance in defense of truth, freedom, and justice.

The pope also found other ways to perturb the regime. His charismatic personality, the fact that he was a figure of great interest to the global media, and his ability to work a crowd all presented challenges to Poland's political authorities. John Paul's theatrical background surely contributed to his sense of timing, his ability to elicit crowd reaction (be it applause, laughter, or singing) verbally and nonverbally, his knack for leading his massive audiences in the direction he desired, and his capacity for maintaining control lest an aroused audience cross the line into violence or disruption. Another problem the pope presented for the regime was that even when he said something that the authorities could interpret as supportive, it had a second edge when considered in a Polish context. Talk of national sovereignty implied that the government was a compromiser rather than a defender of it. Affirmation of alliance systems founded on mutual respect similarly implicated the Soviet-sponsored Warsaw Pact. Allusions to Poland's accomplishments over the previous four decades, if mentioned at all, were typically ascribed to the nation rather than to the state or Communist Party. John Paul's words impinged on the authorities in other ways as well. His calls for courage and risk taking could be seen as implying resistance against the injustices perpetrated by the regime. Any support for human rights cast aspersions on a state with an established record of violating them. Furthermore, John Paul was generous with references to Poland's past suffering under Russian, Soviet, or communist oppression. Although he did not mention hypersensitive topics such as the Katyń Forest Massacre, he did bring up the Partitions, the 1863 revolt against Russia, the assassination of Father Popiełuszko, and the killing of Polish workers in 1956, 1970, and 1983, and, indirectly, the failure of the Soviet Union to effectively aid the Warsaw Uprising in 1944.

John Paul was especially adroit in handling two of Poland's most prominent and important public figures of the time—General Wojciech Jaruzelski and Solidarity leader Lech Wałęsa. In connection with Jaruzelski, the pope pushed the boundaries of the permissible in 1983 to encourage and inspire his massive Polish audiences and assure them that he stood behind the ideals that animated the Solidarity revolution that Jaruzelski had extinguished two and a half years earlier. In 1987, John Paul went even further, taking advantage of the looser atmosphere to rail at the multitude of problems Poland was experiencing under a regime that had not yet come to terms with a society disgruntled over the country's direction since 1981. Nevertheless, during the fraught 1983 visit, the pope met the general part way so as to not leave him completely exposed to pressure from the Soviets and his critics in the Polish Communist Party. An important feature of this accommodation was the sidelining of Wałęsa. For John Paul, the principles of Solidarity were what mattered most, not the actual organization, and even less so its former leader. Thus, the pope could adhere to his own long-standing commitment to human rights, and in particular workers' rights, as well as maintain credibility with Polish audiences by championing the right to independent and self-governing trade unions and other Solidarity tenets, while not unnecessarily antagonizing the regime or riling up the population with calls for the specific restoration of the original union and its former leader. For John Paul, it was the principles that mattered, not the particular form or personalities through which they were incarnated at a specific point in time.

In terms of how the government appraised the papal visits, there was much that it found especially disconcerting, such as John Paul's repeated emphases on the centrality of the Catholic faith in Polish history, in Polish culture, and among citizens of the Polish nation and particularly its working class; his stinginess with praise for what the communists regarded as the accomplishments of the Polish People's Republic and his refusal to support or even recognize Jaruzelski's attempts at reform in the mid-1980s; his energetic and apparently successful outreach to Poland's youth; and his raising of a host of touchy issues—human rights, especially workers' rights, past Polish problems with Russia, workers killed or imprisoned by the communist regime, failed government policies, the failure of the state to adhere to the social accords of late summer 1980, the bleak future of Polish youth, and the murder of Popiełuszko, to name just the most important ones. At the same time, the government needed to put a good face on the pilgrimages, given reservations from Moscow, other Soviet bloc allies, and those in the Polish Communist Party who questioned the wisdom of allowing such visits. Thus, state authorities, spokespersons, and analysts pointed to John Paul's affirmation of Poland's western borders and the Polishness of the Recovered Territories, his condemnation of Nazi atrocities and commemorating of Polish heroism and suffering during World War II, and his exhortation to Poles to build strong families, eschew alcohol abuse, work hard, and commit themselves to the common good as examples of how the papal visit was meeting regime expectations. But, as we have seen, even when the pope did something the government appreciated, it was often coupled with something that annoyed Poland's leaders. For example, Communist Party authorities noted that alongside the pope's defense of Poland's borders and condemnation of Nazi war crimes went a cordial appeal for reconciliation with Germany and Germans. There was also the issue that when John Paul called for world peace, he refused to blame the United States and the West for current international tensions. And, of course, his refusal to call for the reestablishment of Solidarity or to champion Wałęsa went hand in hand with a staunch defense of the principles that Solidarity stood for and a firm insistence that he meet with its former leader.

There are three broad dimensions of John Paul's visits that merit special attention, given their prominence in his approach to his native land during the papal pilgrimages. These are (1) his uses of history, of the saints and heroes of the past, and of the concepts of sacred time and sacred space; (2) how he spoke about those states or peoples with whom Poles had problematic relations in the past, in particular Germany, Russia, Jews, and Ukrainians; and (3) how he spoke of Poland's place in Europe, in its relation both to the West and to the East.

HISTORY, SAINTS, AND SACRED TIME AND SPACE

Right from the start, John Paul demonstrated adeptness in his employment of sacred time, sacred space, and the sacred personalities of Poland's past, all standard components of Catholic discourse. The

1979 visit was rich in such papal use of the past. The feasts of Pentecost and the Holy Trinity, as well as the nine-hundredth anniversary of Saint Stanisław's martyrdom, provided John Paul with the framework within which to convey important messages, as did his presence at the tomb of Saint Wojciech in Gniezno, the Wall of Death and Saint Maximilian Kolbe's death cell at Auschwitz, the memorial tablets at Birkenau, and Saint Stanisław's tomb in Kraków. In some cases, as in the procession of the Marian icon from the Ark of the Lord Church to Mogiła, the sacred object was brought to him. Moreover, the pope organized his pilgrimage around two major saints for Poland (Wojciech and Stanisław) with others (Maximilian Kolbe and Hedwig) also playing an important role. Also prominently featured was Jesus's mother Mary, with John Paul scheduling a stop of several days at Częstochowa, the site of the Jasna Góra monastery with its famous image of the Black Madonna.

Saint Stanisław stood in many ways at the heart of this pilgrimage. He was Wojtyła's ancient predecessor as bishop of Kraków and the reason why both the pope himself and Poland's bishops initially asked for a papal visit. Stanisław also presented a sensitive issue for the regime, given his potential use as a figure of church-state conflict. Although John Paul accommodated regime concerns by not visiting on the actual feast day of the saint and by stressing Stanisław as a symbol of national reconciliation and "creative synthesis" of faith and fatherland, the pope also employed the medieval saint in ways that ran counter to the regime's interests. As patron of Poland's moral order, Stanisław teaches us that no one, not even the government, is above or outside the moral law. As patron of Poland's hierarchy, he serves as a model of courage for the country's bishops. He is also a way to connect Poland, situated in the Soviet bloc for more than forty years, with the West, as Stanisław's conflict with the political authorities had parallels with the cases of Thomas Becket in England or Gregory VII's battle against state intervention in the Holy Roman Empire.

Other saints accompanied Stanisław in underscoring particular papal teachings. John Paul also pointed to Saints Wojciech and Hedwig in making his case for Poland's place in Western civilization—

Wojciech's tomb was the site of the Act of Gniezno, which linked the nascent Polish state to the pope in Rome and the emperor in the German lands, while Hedwig's son was connected with the saving of western and central Europe from the Mongols. Wojciech's influence also reached in the other direction, as the pope referenced him to discuss the Christianization of the Slavs and to reach out to Eastern Orthodox Christians. Hedwig, meanwhile, reinforced Poland's connection with central Europe, given her Bavarian ancestry. Maximilian Kolbe was used as the most contemporary and dramatic example of a message that John Paul pounded home during the visit—that suffering and death can bear good fruit, as we see with Christ on the cross at Golgotha. Wojciech was murdered by pagan Baltic tribes but had helped bring Christianity to northeastern Europe; Stanisław was executed by the king but had demonstrated the maturity of the Church in Poland and reinforced its claim that even the top political authority stood under God's law; Hedwig lost a son, but her loss helped save Europe from enemy invasion; and Kolbe showed that the light of love could shine through, even in one of the very darkest times and places in human history.

The 1983 visit continued the approaches John Paul displayed in 1979, as well as combining earlier and newer themes. The pope was visiting for a triple anniversary—it was 600 years since the appearance of the famous icon of Our Lady at Jasna Góra, 300 years since the breaking of the Ottoman siege of Vienna by Christian forces led in part by Polish king Jan Sobieski, and 1,950 years since the crucifixion of Jesus Christ. As in 1979, John Paul chose particular figures to emphasize prominently during the pilgrimage, in this case the late primate of Poland, Cardinal Wyszyński, who died in May 1981, and Saint Maximilian Kolbe. The pope, upon his arrival, celebrated a mass commemorating Wyszyński at Saint John's Cathedral in Warsaw; visited Warsaw's Pawiak prison, where Kolbe was held after his arrest in 1941; and celebrated a mass at Kolbe's former headquarters at Niepokalanów, for 250,000 people. As he did with Saint Stanisław in 1979, John Paul used Kolbe to make a number of points pertinent to Poles in their current, seemingly dire, situation. Kolbe's self-sacrificial martyrdom at Auschwitz represented for John Paul the light of hope in the midst of horrible darkness, a triumph of love over the "civilization of death," and of human agency over fate—all messages the pope wanted to get across to his forlorn compatriots.

John Paul also referenced other heroes of the faith over the course of his pilgrimage. As in 1979, mentions of Saint Hedwig once again played an important role. Addressing a gigantic crowd in Silesia, John Paul spoke of her son's contribution to the defeat of the Mongols at Legnica in 1241, thereby reminding his audience of Poland's role in defending the West against dangers from the East (an image that resonated with modern Poles). He additionally presented her as a key model and intercessor for German-Polish reconciliation. The pope also beatified three figures from the Partition era during his visit, each of whom suffered under the Russian partition, with two of them even having participated in the 1863 revolt against Russia.

John Paul's addresses during this pilgrimage made generous reference to historical events, both the recent ones of the early 1980s, as well as some from earlier periods of Polish history. In one of the premier events of the visit, the mass at Decennial Stadium in Warsaw during his second day in the country, he used the siege of Vienna and the heroism of Jan Sobieski to connect Poland to the West, recall violations of Polish sovereignty under the Partitions, and affirm the primacy of God in history. He also spoke of times of moral defeat, as well as moral renewal, in Poland's past, offering comfort and hope, as well as some admonitions, to the multitudes living under the gloom of martial law. Finally, he affirmed that Poles, through their sufferings during World War II, had more than earned the right to national sovereignty.

Unlike the first two visits, the 1987 pilgrimage did not coincide with any significant historic anniversary. However, it was organized around a nationwide Eucharistic Congress that John Paul addressed and that included a huge Eucharistic procession through Warsaw, as well as other Eucharist-centered events, and the pope worked Eucharistic themes into many of his homilies and speeches. He also continued his practice of highlighting particular heroes of faith and nation and visiting places of historical import. Two historical periods dominated papal discourse—World War II and the later communist period. In commemorating the war and its horrors, the pope visited the remains of the Nazi death camp at Majdanek and the site of Poland's military resistance to German invasion at Westerplatte, and he beatified a Polish priest who died at Dachau. He spoke on a number of occasions of Polish heroism, resistance, and suffering during the war. With respect to the communist period, John Paul took advantage of the less constrained atmosphere to visit the port cities along the Baltic coast and speak at length of the momentous events in that region from 1970 through the early 1980s. The pope also elected to give special prominence to the recently martyred Father Popiełuszko, mentioning him on several public occasions and paying a visit to his grave in Warsaw. Finally, John Paul presented Poles with an especially apt historical warning during this visit. Anticipating that Poland would become freer, he noted how Poles' ancestors back in the pre-partition days had abused their freedoms to the point that Poland lost its independence.

DIPLOMATIC, ETHNIC, AND RELIGIOUS OUTREACH

John Paul also distinguished himself in his dealings, largely skillfully and meaningfully, with those neighbors and minorities with whom Poles have had problematic relationships historically. Above all, this concerned Germans, Russians, Jews, and, in the 1991 visit, Ukrainians.

During the 1979 pilgrimage, John Paul acknowledged some painful episodes in Poland's past relations with Germans (the Partitions, wartime occupation, Auschwitz) and Russia (the Partitions, Warsaw Uprising), though generally without using the terms "German," "Russian," or "Soviet." For the most part, his approach to both Germans and Russians was sensitive and conciliatory. Regarding the Germans, not only did he celebrate Saint Hedwig as a patron of Polish-German reconciliation and note Poland's historical connection to the West through Germany (the Act of Gniezno), but he was accompanied by West Germany's Cardinal Hermann Volk during his visit to the Wall of Death at Auschwitz, and he made it clear in his homily at Birkenau that he had not come to name names or accord blame but only to remember and to treat all nations as brothers—remarks that drew the most applause of all on that occasion.

Regarding the Russians, the pope did make passing reference to the Partitions, to Poles' historic role in defending Europe from enemies to the east, to the Allied failure to assist the Warsaw Uprising, and to the bitter disappointments Poland experienced in the aftermath of the war but again without naming Russia or the Soviets directly as culprits. He did, however, recognize the Russian role in the struggle against the Nazis, and his treatment of the Eastern Orthodox in his address at Gniezno made it clear that he regarded his Christian brothers and sisters to the east not as some "oriental other" but as partners in building a spiritually unified Europe.

John Paul's engagement with Poland's Jewish community included words and deeds of sympathy and remembrance, most notably a reference in his speech at Victory Square to the "hundreds of thousands who perished within the walls of the Warsaw Ghetto," and a stop at the Hebrew-language commemorative tablet at Birkenau.[1] In his homily at Birkenau, the pope mentioned several of the motives for the killings, citing war, an "insane ideology," and the violation of national rights. Certain omissions, though, as well as certain references, could be off-putting to Jews. For example, the pope made no mention of antisemitism, nor of the fact that Jews constituted the vast majority of the victims killed at the site, while his references to Auschwitz as the "Golgotha" of our times and to the martyr Maximilian Kolbe were not likely to sit well with Jews. Although the pope did not meet specifically with Poland's Jewish community during his visit, nor with representatives from any of Poland's other religious or confessional minorities, he expressed his regret in his homily at the Kraków Commons that he was unable to meet with the Polish Ecumenical Council due to his busy schedule.[2] He added that he carried such a meeting in his heart "as a living desire and expression of hope for the future."[3] That meeting, which would have included Jewish representatives, would have to wait until the pope's next visit.

The 1983 pilgrimage saw the pope continue his practice of referring to past Polish suffering under Russian and German rule (the Partitions, occupation) without naming names, but with some alterations in his approach to these two historic hegemons. Regarding the Germans, the pope emphasized even more strongly than in 1979 the rightfulness of Poland's northern and western borders and the Polishness of the Recovered Territories. He spoke at length about the medieval Polish Piast state, which included much of that area, and noted several cases of Polish resistance to German domination in the nineteenth and twentieth centuries, including Drzymała's wagon and the Silesian Insurrectionists. At the same time, however, he balanced this by saying nothing negative about contemporary West Germany and by repeating in even stronger terms his calls for German-Polish reconciliation. Regarding Russia, given the sensitivity of the context the pope not surprisingly was careful not to antagonize the Soviets. Still, his beatification of two veterans of the 1863 uprising and reference to the battle against the Mongols of 1241 indirectly cast a shadow on Poland's eastern neighbor. With respect to Poland's Jewish minority, John Paul paid a visit to the monument to the Warsaw Ghetto Uprising. However, he did not meet with representatives of Poland's Jewish community separately but rather as part of an ecumenical meeting at the primate's residence with representatives of the eight churches on the Polish Ecumenical Council, with Jews and Muslims as seeming add-ons to what was primarily a Christian event and at which the pope said nothing to Jews in particular.

During the 1987 visit, John Paul continued with his periodic references to Poland's history of oppression by its two powerful neighbors, as well as to examples of cases of resistance to germanization and Nazi invasion. He also once again beatified a Pole who had suffered under Russian occupation, in this case a woman murdered during an attempted rape by a Russian soldier. As was his habit, he used generic terms such as "invaders" or non-national adjectives such as "tsarist" or "Hitlerite" rather than "Germans," "Russians," or "Soviets" when mentioning the perpetrators of these injustices. For the third pilgrimage in a row, the pope visited a site connected with the suffering of Poland's Jews during the war, in this case the former camp at Majdanek. He also met with representatives of Poland's Jewish community in Warsaw on the final day of his pilgrimage. However, both events were problematic in their own way. At Majdanek, in John Paul's brief address commemorating the victims and survivors, he did not mention Jews in particular, though they accounted for most of the camp's death toll. At the Warsaw meeting, John Paul had many kind words for his Jewish audience. He recalled his visit to Rome's synagogue, the first ever by a pope, and pointed to the joint regard for the patriarch Abraham shared by Christians and Jews. Most significantly, in referring to their "special calling [as] . . . heirs of that choice to which God is faithful," John Paul spoke to Jews in light of the "dual covenant" rather than "supersessionist" orientation—that is, he recognized that they remained in covenant with God as Jews, not being superseded by Christians in that respect. While this approach struck a chord presumably pleasant to Jewish ears, other aspects of the pope's address were dissonant. In speaking of the wartime horrors, John Paul told his Jewish partners that "your threat was also our threat," though not realized to such a degree for Christians; that the Church looked upon the extermination of the Jews "in a spirit of deep solidarity" with them; and that he himself had a special relationship to the Jews, having together with them survived these past events. Such words, true as far as they went and surely heartfelt and sincere, could sound to Jews like an equation of Polish and Jewish suffering that failed to appreciate fully the uniquely horrible situation that Jews faced in wartime Poland, as well as a neglect of Polish antisemitism and of those situations where Catholic Poles showed not sympathy and solidarity but rather hostility toward Jews. Moreover, the pope, in line with Catholic doctrine, emphasized the purifying power of suffering, an identification that sat much better with Poles, who regarded the Polish dead as compatriots martyred under the Nazi occupation in defense of faith and nation, than with Jews, many of whom were rounded up and killed simply because they fit a Nazi racial category.[4]

POLAND, CHRISTIANITY, AND EUROPE, EAST AND WEST

Another important dimension of the papal pilgrimages involved the pope's position on the place of Poland, and of Christianity, in the eastern and western halves of an ever-evolving Europe. For the pope, as for nearly all Poles, Poland was an integral part of Europe, and the pope used three of his featured saints to buttress that point. As noted above, Saint Stanisław's martyrdom illustrated that Poland faced the same kinds of conflict between ecclesial and secular authorities in the Middle Ages as did the English and Germans; Saint Hedwig's son gave his life protecting the western Christian lands from eastern invaders; and Saint Wojciech's tomb was the site of a momentous meeting that brought the German emperor and representatives of the pope to Poland. John Paul also emphasized that in his view Christianity was at the root of Europe's history, just as it was central to Poland's own history and culture and that it would be necessary for Europe's future spiritual unity. He also made it clear that he understood Christianity in Europe as consisting of both a western and an eastern tradition. For the pope, Poland, given its geographical location and historical connections with Eastern Christians, served as a bridge between the two traditions, as did the current fact of a Slavic pope from Poland.

During the 1983 visit, John Paul continued these themes—Poland's role as historically part of the West and defender of its welfare, now reinforced by his commemoration of Sobieski's triumph in breaking the 1683 siege of Vienna; the close link between Catholicism and Polish history; and Poland's special situation between East and West. To this point, whenever the pope spoke of the West, it was either to note that Poland was historically an integral part of the West, to highlight the contributions Poles made to defending the West, or to note Poland's special role in connecting the West to the East. By

1987, however, we see John Paul adding additional dimensions, chiefly negative, to his consideration of the West. He acknowledged that the West too had problems, noting twice during the visit that it was not just in Poland but also in the West that youth were unable to find employment commensurate with their talents and education. He treated the West as a temptation for Poles seeking better material conditions, chastising those who abandoned family to seek their fortune abroad and exhorting youth not to desert their fatherland via emigration. He spoke critically of those "completely secularized" places where people lived "as if God did not exist," of the "free countries" where God's laws on the sanctity of human life and marriage were violated in the name of freedom.

John Paul was particularly concerned about the potential misuse of freedom, warning Poles against it as early as 1983 and bringing it up several times during the 1987 visit. For the pope (and for Catholicism), freedom and truth went together—truth detached from freedom turned into license, which John Paul identified in the legalization of abortion and the undermining of traditional sexual and marital norms found in many secularized Western countries. Freedom was a result of choice, not its precondition, and genuine freedom would result only if one chose in accord with truth. These affirmations were increasingly prominent in the pope's speeches and homilies in 1987, as were his criticisms of what he saw as the tragic results of abuse of freedom manifested in abortion, addiction, and other societal ills. John Paul's growing emphasis on what he regarded as the negative aspects of the West became even more prevalent once the communist regime saw its demise in Poland and across the region in 1989.

THE 1991 VISIT TO POSTCOMMUNIST POLAND

John Paul's 1991 pilgrimage came in a quite different context and saw the pope combining past approaches and teachings with new emphases. Two aspects of the visit stand out. First, there was relatively little postcommunist triumphalism, as the pope focused on the present shortcomings of Poles and his vision for their future, structuring the visit along the lines of the Ten Commandments and pointing out places where his compatriots were falling short. Second, John Paul devoted considerable attention to outreach toward the Christian East, whether in terms of the Russian Orthodox Church, or Poland's own Eastern Orthodox, Eastern Rite Catholic, and Ukrainian minorities.

As with most of his previous pilgrimages, this one corresponded with an anniversary year—it was two hundred years since the Constitution of May 3, 1791—and John Paul used the occasion to celebrate that constitution and present it as a model for present-day Poland. He also drew heavily from Poland's history, citing further examples of Poles' struggle for freedom (the insurrection of 1830, the successful fight for independence during World War I and subsequent victory over Soviet Russia, the resistance against the Nazis, and the Solidarity movement), as well as times when they abused freedom, in particular the eighteenth century, when Polish nobles defended their "golden freedom" to the detriment of the common good. John Paul also beatified an eighteenth-century Polish Franciscan whose life of service to the poor stood out in a time known for its selfishness. The pope hoped that present-day Poles would not squander the new opportunity for freedom that the early 1990s presented to them, and he exhorted them not to misuse that freedom.

As in the pope's earlier visits, human rights occupied a crucial place in the papal vision for Poland's future, and they were embedded in a broader framework of Catholic social teaching. John Paul reiterated and expanded on some of his favorite themes during this visit—the primacy of culture over economics, the priority of persons over things and of "being" over "having," and the centrality of ethics to economics. He expressed the hope that Poland would not merely imitate the West in its socioeconomic transformation but rather forge its own way by combining the free market with social solidarity. He warned Poles against dismantling social support networks for the needy, succumbing to consumerist attitudes, and embracing the sexual libertinism and easy access to abortion prevalent in much of the West.

It was in his attitude toward the West that John Paul's visit made one of its strongest impressions. Although he had already begun noting some of the West's negatives to Poles in 1987, by 1991 this approach had become full blown. The pope repeatedly pointed out problems with Western societies during his visit—sexual libertinism, consumerist attitudes, and poverty amid great wealth.

It was a civilization that was departing from its Christian heritage, plagued by "practical atheism," and in spiritual crisis, itself in need of redemption. Its history included ethnic genocide and exaggerated class struggle. It was seeking freedom from Christ, not through Christ, and thus freedom was turning into license, which meant slavery to sin, not liberation. The pope was especially irate at suggestions that Poland needed to "earn" its entry into Europe, noting angrily all the sacrifices that Poles had made for Europe over the centuries, especially in recent times.

For John Paul, freedom and truth were connected, and the moral truths of the Ten Commandments were the guarantor that freedom would be used properly—for the moral improvement and flourishing of individual persons as well as for the common good of society.

In sociopolitical terms, a society where freedom was linked with truth meant one in which abortion would be illegal, religion would have a public role, traditional marriage would be supported, people would eschew consumerist values, and sufficient social safeguards would be available for those losing out during the economic transformation. It was also a society that avoids fanaticism and fundamentalism of both the religious and secular varieties, as well as xenophobia and an excessive and vulgar nationalism, and that treats with benevolence those who come to Poland seeking better lives.

John Paul's repeated stress on greater tolerance fit nicely with the second major aspect of his 1991 visit—his outreach to Poland's minorities and neighbors, especially those of the Eastern Christian tradition. The pope spent approximately half of his visit in eastern Poland, including a stop at Przemyśl, site of recent conflict between Catholic Poles and Eastern Rite Ukrainians. At various events he greeted crowds in the Ukrainian, Russian, Belarusian, or Church Slavonic languages. He spoke of Europe as stretching from the Atlantic to the Urals, thereby integrating the often-neglected East into

Europe conceptually. He spoke fondly of his hopes of visiting Russia someday. Through word and deed, John Paul encouraged better relations between Roman and Eastern Rite Catholics, Catholics and Eastern Orthodox, and Poles and Ukrainians. The Eastern Orthodox were "sister churches" that shared much in common with the Western Church and whose current revival was welcomed by Rome. The pope called for mutual forgiveness and continuing dialogue, and he expressed his sympathy for past and present sufferings of the Eastern Christians. He tried to finesse the tense relations between Eastern Rite Catholics and the Orthodox, welcoming the current revival of the former while warning against a triumphalism that would alienate the latter. The pope attended an ecumenical worship service at the Orthodox cathedral in Białystok and called for reconciliation between squabbling Poles and Ukrainians in Przemyśl, while speaking kindly about Eastern Rite Catholics. In tune with John Paul's standard practice of connecting current issues to past saints, John Paul beatified two figures known for their sympathy for Eastern Christians during his visit to eastern Poland.

The positive spirit that John Paul brought to his interactions with Eastern Christians also pervaded his relations with other minorities living in Poland. During a visit to northeastern Poland, the pope praised the local Lithuanian community and supported its efforts at preserving its language, identity, and culture. He also spoke to pilgrims from Lithuania very positively about their homeland and had a fruitful meeting with a delegation of visiting Lithuanian officials. In Warsaw, John Paul attended an ecumenical service at a Lutheran church, where he explicitly challenged the traditional association of Polishness with Catholicism by noting that Lutheran Poles too had suffered under the Nazi occupation, and he cited two Polish Lutheran churchmen who had distinguished themselves during the war in the Polish cause. Finally, John Paul held a meeting with representatives from Poland's Jewish community, speaking to them at greater length than he had in 1987. The pope reiterated the basic points he had made previously but went on to add something missing from the earlier meeting—a recognition that antisemitism in Christian Europe had played a role in the sufferings experienced by the Jews during the Holocaust. As John Paul put it, crimes against Jews were sometimes "inscribed into the structure of thought and custom," and he noted that the horrors of the Holocaust led "the nations of Christian civilization" to take up "the arduous work of uprooting from their mentality all unjust prejudices toward the Jews and other manifestations of anti-Semitism."[5]

FINAL WORDS

In summation, an examination of the first four of John Paul's papal pilgrimages to Poland leaves us with certain insights into this great personality of modern Polish, European, and Church history.

First, if there was an overriding principle at the foundation of John Paul's teaching to his fellow Poles, it was the connection between freedom and truth. Made most explicit during the 1991 visit, it was at least implied throughout all the pilgrimages. It was also the foundation for the heavy stress the pope placed on human rights, in particular the rights of workers, during the communist-era visits and for his far-reaching concerns about Poland's moral future during the 1991 visit. For the pope, issues such as peace, Church-state relations, and the solution to Poland's current and future problems were connected to respect for human rights and, more broadly, to the integration of freedom and truth.

Second, John Paul had an instinct for handling the communist regime. He knew when to push forward, when to step back, and when to step to the side. He could keep up the pressure on the regime without inciting the crowds to violence or undermining those in state leadership least hostile to the Church. Social peace for the pope was never disconnected from his other values, such as human rights or national sovereignty. He is an important reason why the fall of communism in Poland came with little violence.

Third, John Paul knew how to make the saints, heroes, events, and developments of Poland's past relevant in the present. Because he himself was immersed in Polish history and culture and had the Catholic concepts of sacred places and the liturgical calendar at his disposal, the past was always present during the papal pilgrimages. In the pope's hands, even medieval saints could become players in a modern political drama, and the triumphs and tragedies of Poland's history could be used to comfort, inspire, warn, and instruct Poles.

Fourth, John Paul was able to reach out to Poland's historic "others," be they domestic minorities such as Jews, Ukrainians, Lutherans, and Eastern Christians or foreign powers such as Germany or Russia, while maintaining his credibility as a patriotic Pole. Even when speaking critically of Poland's partitioners and occupiers, he avoided xenophobic comments and made sympathetic gestures. His outreach to Poland's ethnic and religious minorities stressed unity, healing of past wounds, and reconciliation. The pope was a role model for how one can be proud of one's own nation and its history and culture, while being benevolent toward those with whom that nation has had problematic relations in the past.

Fifth, the pope displayed a nuanced view of Europe, as well as Poland's position within it. He did not fit snugly into a Cold War paradigm of East versus West. He saw Poland as clearly a part of the West, integrated into Europe for more than a millennium and having contributed much to it, including much Polish blood. At the same time, he regarded Europe as stretching from the Atlantic to the Urals, and he viewed the Orthodox Church not as some eastern appendage but as Christianity's "second lung," brothers and sisters and equals. John Paul saw Poland, given its geographic situation, historical experience, Slavic language, and Christian faith, as a bridge between Western and Eastern Europe. Finally, though far more sympathetic to the West than to the Soviet Union during the Cold War, the pope was at the same time very suspicious of certain features found in Western societies—rampant consumerism, sexual libertinism, aggressive secularism, and practical atheism. His hope was that as Poland got reintegrated into Western institutions, it would not imitate the West but rather develop an alternative Polish way that could serve as a model for a better Europe.

Sixth, despite his immense popularity both in Poland and globally, John Paul was not seeking to win a popularity contest. We see this

most starkly in his 1991 visit, when he eschewed a triumphal celebration of the end of communism and instead showered Poles with
criticism of what they were doing wrong and liable to do wrong in the
future. This should not be read, however, as John Paul being shocked
and suddenly disillusioned that postcommunist Poland was not turning out how he had hoped. His uneasiness about Poland's future was
already evident during the 1987 visit. It is rather an indication that the
pope took a prophetic approach to his homeland, exhorting Poles to
connect freedom and truth and warning them about the consequences
should they fail to do so. Such concerns were paramount for a pope
who had helped bring his compatriots to the threshold of a hopeful
yet perilous new era and who would soon lead the Catholic Church
into its third millennium.

ACKNOWLEDGMENTS

I WOULD LIKE TO THANK ALL THOSE WHO ASSISTED ME DURING the course of this project and to apologize in advance to anyone I may have inadvertently left out. First, I would like to thank the Department of History at the University of Washington for its support, above all in the form of the Jon Bridgman Endowed Professorship in History, which funded my research travel and summertime research. I would also like to thank the archivists and librarians in Warsaw, at the Archiwum Akt Nowych, the Instytut Pamięci Narodowa, and the Biblioteka Narodowa, as well as Professor Andrzej Paczkowski, all of whom gave me valuable assistance during my research visits to Poland. I would also like to thank Molly Pucci for providing helpful advice to me while in Warsaw and connecting me with the IPN and its resources. In addition, I would like to thank the staff at the University of Washington Libraries, in particular Michael Biggins, for helping me to procure a number of crucial sources. I would also like to thank Maryla Klajn and Christina Manetti, for providing research assistance at key points in the process, and Eric Johnson, for his timely and much appreciated technical assistance.

I additionally want to express my gratitude to those scholars who read and commented on all or part of my manuscript or conference papers based on it or who provided other types of scholarly assistance related to this project. These scholars include Robert Alvis, Sean Brennan, David Curp, Father Grzegorz Dobroczyński, SJ, David Doellinger, Robert Goeckel, Jonathan Huener, Łukasz Kamiński, Krzysztof Łazarski, Andrzej Nowak, Steve Pfaff, James Wellman, and Jennifer Wynot. I would also like to thank those friends—some academics, some not—with whom I discussed the project and related issues over the years, including Elena Campbell, Michael Lounsbery, Steven Miner, Matthew Ouimet, and Andy Simons.

I would like to offer special thank-yous to Piotr Kosicki, who helped me to get oriented as I moved into the new field of Polish and Catholic studies from my earlier interests in the history of Slovakia; to Marty Manor Mullins, for encouraging me to incorporate into my study the resources from Poland's communist regime; and to James Mace Ward, for his suggestion that I take the book beyond the communist era into the early 1990s.

I would also like express my appreciation to those who hosted me for lectures based on my research, including the Newman Center at the University of Washington, Blessed Sacrament Parish in Seattle, and the Polish Studies Endowment at the University of Washington.

I am especially grateful to the University of Pittsburgh Press, in particular Peter Kracht and Jonathan Harris, for their helpful suggestions, editorial insights, and eagerness to see our project through to completion. Working with them, once again, has been a pleasure.

Finally, I would like to thank my wife, Cheryl, for her love, support, and companionship over the past forty years, including the years I spent working on this project.

NOTES

Introduction

1. Evelyn Waugh used this phrase to describe World War II in his 1947 novella *Scott-King's Modern Europe*.

2. This discussion of Poland under communism draws especially from Andrzej Paczkowski, *Revolution and Counterrevolution in Poland, 1980–1989: Solidarity, Martial Law, and the End of Communism in Europe* (Rochester, NY: University of Rochester Press, 2015), 3–10. See also Joseph Rothschild, *Return to Diversity: A Political History of East Central Europe since World War II* (New York: Oxford University Press, 1993), 150–53, 191–203.

3. For one of the best short surveys of the Catholic Church in communist Poland, see Robert Alvis, *White Eagle, Black Madonna: One Thousand Years of the Polish Catholic Tradition* (New York: Fordham University Press, 2016), 218–50. Alvis's work has informed this introduction, as has that of Jerzy Kloczowski, *A History of Polish Christianity* (Cambridge: Cambridge University Press, 2000), 308–36; and Maryjane Osa, *Solidarity and Contention: Networks of Polish Opposition* (Minneapolis: University of Minnesota Press, 2003), esp. 59–80.

4. For extended coverage of the Great Novena, see Osa, *Solidarity and Contention*, 59–80.

5. In the Catholic Church in Poland, one bishop was designated as primate and held the top position in the hierarchy. In November 1948, Pope Pius XII appointed Wyszyński to this position, which included serving as archbishop of Gniezno-Warsaw, administratively combining Poland's ancient capital with its modern one.

6. Quoted in Hanna Diskin, *The Seeds of Triumph: Church and State in Gomułka's Poland* (Budapest: Central European University Press, 2001), 117.

7. The Joint Commission was established in July 1949, ceased operation in 1967, and was reconstituted in September 1980. See Bohdan Szajkowski, "New Law for the Church in Poland," *Religion in Communist Lands* 17, no. 3 (1989): 198.

8. Kloczowski, *History of Polish Christianity*, 328.

9. Osa, *Solidarity and Contention*, 79.

10. For biographical material on Wojtyła, see especially George Weigel, *Witness to Hope: The Biography of Pope John II* (New York: HarperCollins, 2001).

11. See Brian Porter-Szűcs, *Faith and Fatherland: Catholicism, Modernity, and Poland* (Oxford: Oxford University Press, 2011), 45–46, 114, for Wojtyła's enthusiasm for the Second Vatican Council in the 1960s and 1970s. Weigel, *Witness to Hope*, 145–80, is an entire chapter devoted to Wojtyła in relation to Vatican II during this period.

12. As an indication of the relative weight given to the three visits, the four leading English-language biographies of John Paul II collectively devote fifty-six pages to John

Paul's 1979 visit, twenty-nine pages to the 1983 visit, and thirteen pages to the 1987 visit; see Weigel, *Witness to Hope*; Tad Szulc, *Pope John Paul II: The Biography* (New York: Scribner, 1995); Carl Bernstein and Marco Politi, *His Holiness: John Paul II and the Hidden History of Our Time* (New York: Doubleday, 1996); and Jonathan Kwitny, *Man of the Century: The Life and Times of Pope John Paul II* (New York: Henry Holt, 1997). Only Weigel seems to have grasped the significance of the 1987 visit, devoting twice as much attention to it as to the 1983 visit, though only one-fourth the attention he gave to the 1979 one.

13. World Youth Day was launched in the 1980s under John Paul's pontificate and consisted of a global gathering of Catholic youth for several days at a different venue every two or three years. The event also featured a visit by the pope.

14. The only major event the pope addressed in Częstochowa that was not geared toward youth was a meeting of theologians from Central and Eastern Europe at which he emphasized the Church's suffering under communism across the region and the new hopes and opportunities present since 1989. For John Paul's address to these theologians, see Jan Paweł II, *Pielgrzymki do Ojczyzny 1979–1983–1987–1991–1995–1997–1999–2002: Przemówienia, homilie* (Kraków: Znak, 2005), 820–26.

15. For the pope's addresses at WYD, see Jan Paweł II, *Pielgrzymki do Ojczyzny*, 793–817.

16. The discrepancy in numbering is because John Paul visited Poland twice in 1991, but that second visit is treated as part of the first.

17. Jan Paweł II, *Pielgrzymki do Ojczyzny*. The Vatican website has the official texts for nearly all of these speeches and sermons, but these are not transcripts and thus do not include any of John Paul's extemporizing or otherwise going off-text. Thus, using them can be misleading, as sometimes the most significant things John Paul said were alterations or additions to the official text (that is, the one given in advance to journalists, government officials, etc.).

18. Andrzej Paczkowski has pointed out the dual nature of Rakowski's "diaries," as both diary and memoir, in his article "Pułapki 'Dzienników' Rakowskiego," *Polityka*, April 9, 2013. Paczkowski notes that Rakowski toned down his language in places; removed or reworded passages that reflected unfavorably on certain individuals; supplemented daily entries with documentation not in the original; and disaggregated longer, summary-style entries in the diary into shorter accounts under the dates when said events occurred. As an example of the latter, the manuscript of Rakowski's diary covered the death of a Polish communist in one extensive entry dated December 31, 1961, whereas in the published book the matter was spread over five daily entries beginning on December 20, 1961. I am treating Rakowski's "diaries" as memoir rather than a real-time account of events, though they can also serve the latter purpose to a great degree if used with sufficient caution, as Paczkowski notes.

Chapter 1. Catalyst

1. Peter Raina, *Wizyty apostolskie Jana Pawła II w Polsce: Rozmowy przygotowawcze Watykan—PRL—Episkopat* (Warsaw: Książka Polska, 1997), 7.

2. George Weigel, *Witness to Hope: The Biography of Pope John Paul II* (New York: HarperCollins, 2001), 300–301.

3. Edward Gierek, *Smak życia: Pamiętniki* (Warsaw: BGW, 1993), 126.

4. Andrzej Friszke and Marcin Zaremba, eds., *Wizyta Jana Pawła w Polsce 1979: Dokumenty KC PZPR i MSW* (Warsaw: Biblioteka "Więzi," 2005), 140. Gromyko did note, however, that there was potential for cooperation between the Soviet bloc and the Vatican with respect to peace and disarmament.

5. Friszke and Zaremba, *Wizyta Jana Pawła*, 138–39.

6. The feast of Saint Stanisław falls on May 8 in Poland, but it is generally celebrated on the first Sunday thereafter, which in 1979 was May 13.

7. See James Ramon Felak, "Pope John Paul II, the Saints, and Communist Poland: The Papal Pilgrimages of 1979 and 1983," *Catholic Historical Review* 100, no. 3 (2014): 560–65, for a more detailed discussion of interpretations of Saint Stanisław and how the pope made use of the saint's story during his first two pilgrimages to Poland.

8. Jan Kubik, *The Power of Symbols against the Symbols of Power: The Rise of Solidarity and the Fall of State Socialism in Poland* (University Park: Pennsylvania State University Press, 1994), 132.

9. Kubik, *Power of Symbols*, 133.

10. Raina, *Wizyty apostolskie*, 12–14. In this collection, Raina presents a series of approximately two dozen documents pertaining to the Church-state negotiations from January to May 1979.

11. This emphasis on national reconciliation is seen in John Paul's apostolic letter *Rutilans agmen*, issued on May 8, 1979, Poland's official feast day of Saint Stanisław. In it, the pope speaks of Stanisław as "an instrument of reconciliation" between Poland's citizens, be they rulers or ruled, and God. However, John Paul also notes "the heritage of firmness and courage in professing the truth" that Stanisław bequeathed to Poles; see John Paul II, *Rutilans agmen* (Polish-language text), available at www.vatican.va. There are mistranslations in the English text provided on the Vatican website.

12. Although Pentecost has lost much of its popular significance in the United States, it remains a major church holy day in Poland. I was reminded of this when I recently went out one Sunday to visit the University of Warsaw library, only to find the notice "Closed for Pentecost."

13. Quoted in Jan Józef Lipski, *A History of the Workers' Defense Committee in Poland, 1976–1981*, trans. Olga Amsterdamska and Gene M. Moore (Berkeley: University of California Press, 1985), 333.

14. Lipski, *History of the Workers' Defense Committee*, 333–34.

15. Lipski, *History of the Workers' Defense Committee*, 338.

16. For John Paul's speech at the airport, see Jan Paweł II, *Pielgrzymki do Ojczyzny 1979–1983–1987–1991–1995–1997–1999–2002: Przemówienia, homilie* (Kraków: Znak, 2005), 9–11. Subsequent quotations in the text, in translation, are from this source. For the welcoming speeches by Jabłoński and Wyszyński, see *Trybuna Ludu*, June 4, 1979.

17. *New York Times*, June 3, 1979.

18. For Gierek's speech, see *Tygodnik Powszechny*, June 10, 1979.

19. Quotations, in translation, from John Paul II's speech at Belvedere in this paragraph and the next all come from Jan Paweł II, *Pielgrzymki do Ojczyzny*, 15–19.

20. Estimates varied. Polish police reports put the crowd size at 170,000; see Instytut Pamięci Narodowa, BU 0296/216/3, F. 153. The *Washington Post* on June 3, 1979, reported

250,000, the *New York Times* of June 3, 1979, estimated 290,000, and *Time*'s issue of June 11, 1979, suggested as many as a half million. Weigel places 300,000 at the event, with another 750,000 overflowing into the surrounding streets. Kubik, apparently counting the overflow in addition to those inside Victory Square, estimates a million. Weigel, *Witness to Hope*, 292; Kubik, *Power of Symbols*, 139.

21. For descriptions of the event, see Kubik, *Power of Symbols*, 139–40; and *New York Times*, June 3, 1979.

22. For John Paul's homily at Victory Square, see Jan Paweł II, *Pielgrzymki do Ojczyzny*, 20–25. Translated quotations in this and subsequent paragraphs, unless noted otherwise, are from this source.

23. A preliminary report on the papal pilgrimage drafted for the Communist Party's Central Committee made specific mention of the pope's words on Saint Stanisław, the Warsaw Uprising, and the centrality of the Christian faith for understanding Poland's history as problematic elements of John Paul's homily at Victory Square. Friszke and Zaremba, *Wizyta Jana Pawła*, 248.

24. This teaching is especially apparent in Vatican II's Pastoral Constitution on the Church in the Modern World, which states that Christ "fully reveals man to himself." *Gaudium et spes*, section 22, December 7, 1965, http://www.vatican.va/archive/hist_councils/ii_vatican_council/documents/vat-ii_cons_19651207_gaudium-et-spes_en.html.

25. With the "old oak" reference, John Paul was using a metaphor from Piotr Skarga, a great Jesuit preacher and writer from the Catholic Reformation in late sixteenth- and early seventeenth-century Poland.

26. In John 12:24 (Revised Standard Version, Catholic edition, used here and elsewhere, unless noted otherwise), the gospel writer has Jesus Christ saying, "Truly, truly, I say to you, unless a grain of wheat falls into the earth and dies, it remains alone; but if it dies, it bears much fruit."

27. Saint Wojciech was a tenth-century bishop who was martyred while on a mission to spread Christianity to pagans along the Baltic coast. He is also known as Saint Adalbert. He will be further discussed below. Saint Maximilian Kolbe was a Polish priest who gave his life at Auschwitz to save a fellow campmate. More will be said about him below.

28. With the phrase "for your freedom and ours," John Paul was quoting a slogan from the nineteenth century suggesting that Polish soldiers fought not only for the freedom and the independence of Poland but for other peoples as well.

29. The pope's words in Polish were "Niech zstąpi Duch Twój! / Niech zstąpi Duch Twój! / I odnowi oblicze ziemi. / Tej Ziemi! / Amen."

30. *Washington Post*, June 3, 1979; Mieczysław Rakowski, *Dzienniki polityczne 1979–1981* (Warsaw: Iskry, 2004), 70–72; Weigel, *Witness to Hope*, 293, 295.

31. References herein to the regime's observations and analyses of the papal visit are based on a series of reports produced by government, party, and security officials monitoring and analyzing the visit. These can be found in the collections of the Office of Confessional Affairs (Urząd do Spraw Wyznań, or USW) and the Central Committee of the Polish United Workers Party (Komitet Centralny Polskiej Zjednoczonej Partii Robotniczej, or KC PZPR), including its Administrative Department (Wydział Administracyjny, or WA) at the Archiwum Akt Nowych (AAN), and the collections

of the Ministry of the Interior (Ministerstwo Spraw Wewnętrznych, or MSW) at the Instytut Pamięci Narodowa (IPN) in Warsaw.

32. AAN, USW, 137/18, F. 62–68.

33. In his address upon arrival at Warsaw's airport, John Paul said, "I desire that the internal unity of my countrymen be a fruit of my visit." Jan Paweł II, *Pielgrzymki do Ojczyzny*, 9.

34. AAN, USW, 137/18, F. 9–18; AAN, USW, 137/11, F. 91–116. Porter-Szűcs devotes an entire chapter of his book to the Pole-Catholic equation; see Brian Porter-Szűcs, *Faith and Fatherland: Catholicism, Modernity, and Poland* (Oxford: Oxford University Press, 2011), 328–59.

35. AAN, USW, 137/11, F. 91–116.

36. "Informacja Sytuacyjna Nr. 4," MSW report, June 3, 1979, in IPN BU 0296/217/1, F. 151–57.

37. "Informacja Sytuacyjna Nr. 5," MSW report, June 4, 1979, in IPN BU 0296/217/1, F. 158–65.

38. For a more detailed discussion of Saint Wojciech and John Paul II's words about him during the 1979 pilgrimage, see Felak, "Pope John Paul II, the Saints," 558–60.

39. Robert Alvis, *White Eagle, Black Madonna: One Thousand Years of the Polish Catholic Tradition* (New York: Fordham University Press, 2016), 9.

40. For John Paul's homily in Gniezno, see Jan Paweł II, *Pielgrzymki do Ojczyzny*, 33–39. Subsequent quotes, in translation, from the homily are from this source.

41. By Eastern Christians, John Paul meant all those Christians in the Eastern liturgical tradition, both Orthodox and Eastern Rite Catholic, not those geographically in the eastern parts of the country, though most Christians of the Eastern liturgical tradition did in fact live in Poland's eastern regions.

42. For a discussion of the Ostpolitik of John XXIII and Paul VI, see Frank J. Coppa, *Politics and the Papacy in the Modern World* (Westport, CT: Praeger, 2008), 157–60; and Weigel, *Witness to Hope*, 227–31.

43. For a discussion of John Paul's Eastern policy and how it differed from that of his predecessors, see Weigel, *Witness to Hope*, 232–33, 295–300.

44. Jan Paweł II, *Pielgrzymki do Ojczyzny*, 30–32. Estimated numbers of attendees vary, from the regime's figure of 280,000 (IPN BUA, 0296/216/3, F. 154), to Weigel's one million (*Witness to Hope*, 308), with the *Washington Post* of June 3, 1979, reporting "up to half a million."

45. "Rota" (the word means "oath") was composed in the early twentieth century to commemorate the Polish victory over the Teutonic Knights at the Battle of Grunwald in 1410. The original lyrics had overtones of resistance to German oppression, but during the communist period Poles often altered the lyrics to imply resistance to Soviets and Russians.

46. The author of a police report of June 9, 1979, claims to have learned from unnamed clerical sources that Bishop Ignacy Tokarczuk of Przemyśl was upset with John Paul for "approving of the organs of State Security," as well as for not promoting him to the rank of cardinal, and thus absented himself from a meeting of clergy with the pope in Kraków. See "Meldunek Nr. 9," MSW report, June 9, 1979, in IPN BU, 0296/217/1, F. 234–36.

47. Jan Paweł II, *Pielgrzymki do Ojczyzny*, 40–42.

48. John Paul is quoting Adam Mickiewicz's 1832 work *Księgi narodu polskiego i pielgrzymstwa polskiego* (published in English as *The Books and the Pilgrimage of the Polish Nation*).

49. *New York Times*, June 3, 1979; and *Washington Post*, June 4, 1979, respectively.

50. "Informacja Sytuacyjna Nr. 5," MSW report, June 4, 1979, in IPN BU 0296/217/1, F. 158–165. See also AAN, PZPR KC 1354, XIA/1249, F. 16–28. (Note: the archivists at the AAN, when identifying a file of documents, sometimes wrote KC PZPR and sometimes wrote PZPR KC.)

51. AAN, USW, 137/18, F. 62–68; AAN, USW, 137/11, F. 91–116. See also Friszke and Zaremba, *Wizyta Jana Pawła*, 248–49.

52. AAN, USW, 137/18, F. 9–18.

53. For Kania's letter to Macharski, see Friszke and Zaremba, *Wizyta Jana Pawła*, 164–66.

54. For the notes of the conversation between Kąkol and Macharski, see AAN, PZPR KC 1354, XIA/1249, F. 81–84.

55. For Szablewski's notes on his meetings with Casaroli, see Friszke and Zaremba, *Wizyta Jana Pawła*, 167–70.

56. For an in-depth discussion of the place of Mary in Polish national and religious thinking and culture, see Porter-Szűcs, *Faith and Fatherland*, esp. 360–90.

57. The *New York Times* of June 5, 1979, and *Time*'s issue of June 18, 1979, put the crowd at half a million; the regime claimed 120,000 (IPN BU 0296/216/3, F. 155), which was also the figure given on Polish television; Weigel claims more than a million (*Witness to Hope*, 309). For the text of the Częstochowa homily, see Jan Paweł II, *Pielgrzymki do Ojczyzny*, 45–52; translated quotes in subsequent text are from this source.

58. *Time*, June 18, 1979.

59. Description of the event and quote from *New York Times*, June 5, 1979.

60. For John Paul's speech to the Conference of the Episcopate of Poland, see Jan Paweł II, *Pielgrzymki do Ojczyzny*, 82–95. Translated quotations from this speech are from this source.

61. Indeed, one headline on the conference hyperbolically stated, "Pope Tells Polish Bishops to Resist Communists." *Washington Post*, June 6, 1979.

62. For John Paul's homily to pilgrims from Lower Silesia (and the region around Opole), see Jan Paweł II, *Pielgrzymki do Ojczyzny*, 103–7. For a more detailed discussion of Saint Hedwig and the ends to which John Paul employed her, see Felak, "Pope John Paul II, the Saints," 565–66.

63. The traditional Polish understanding of the Battle of Legnica is that it provided enough of an obstacle to the Mongols to prevent their continued westward advance, thus sparing western Europe from invasion. John Paul took this interpretation when he gave his homily to the Lower Silesians, and he expressed it again when he spoke at Legnica in 1997. However, historians have identified a number of other reasons why the Mongols halted their advance at this time and withdrew to the East, which can be found in Peter Jackson, *The Mongols and the West, 1221–1410* (Harlow, UK: Pearson Longman, 2006), 71–74.

64. For a discussion of the concept that Poland historically served as a "bulwark of Christendom," absorbing and/or repelling attacks by infidels and schismatics from the East and thereby keeping western Europe safe from non-Catholic invaders, see Lonnie

R. Johnson, *Central Europe: Enemies, Neighbors, Friends*, 2nd ed. (New York: Oxford University Press, 2002), 64–65.

65. For documents showing how the issue of visiting Trzebnica came up during preparations for the papal visit, see Raina, *Wizyty apostolskie*, 66, 81, 111.

66. For John Paul's speech to the faculty and students from KUL, see Jan Paweł II, *Pielgrzymki do Ojczyzny*, 129–32. The phrases quoted in translation come from pages 131–32.

67. AAN, PZPR KC, 1354, XIA/1249, F. 86–105. See also Raina, *Wizyty apostolskie*, 111, 116.

68. AAN, PZPR KC, 1354, XIA/1249, F. 86–105; *Washington Post*, June 6, 1979. The regime also vetoed an attempt by the pope to plan a visit to the Millennium factory in Częstochowa; see Raina, *Wizyty apostolskie*, 116.

69. For the homily to pilgrims from Upper Silesia and the Dąbrowski Basin, see Jan Paweł II, *Pielgrzymki do Ojczyzny*, 133–38. Subsequent translated quotations are from this source.

70. Both of these comments obliquely referenced government economic policies that made it necessary for mothers with children at home to work outside the home as well.

71. See, for example, AAN, USW, 137/11, F. 91–116; and AAN, PZPR KC 1354, XIA/1249, F. 16–28.

72. AAN, USW, 137/21, F. 111–26. The same author warned that anticlericalism was a nineteenth-century bourgeois ideology that Marxists should not accept uncritically.

73. For Paul VI, see Jan Paweł II, *Pielgrzymki do Ojczyzny*, 45–52, 59–65; for Silesia, see 133–38.

74. Jan Paweł II, *Pielgrzymki do Ojczyzny*, 78–81.

75. *New York Times*, June 5, 6, 1979; *Washington Post*, June 5, 6, 1979.

76. For complaints about problems with domestic media coverage, see *New York Times*, June 3, 9, 10, 1979; *Washington Post*, June 7, 10, 1979; and Weigel, *Witness to Hope*, 302, 322.

77. Kubik, *Power of Symbols*, 148–49.

78. *Washington Post*, June 7, 1979; *New York Times*, June 7, 1979.

79. For coverage and descriptions of these papal events, see Jonathan Huener, *Auschwitz, Poland, and the Politics of Commemoration, 1945–1979* (Athens: Ohio University Press, 2003), 212–25; Weigel, *Witness to Hope*, 314–16; *New York Times*, June 8, 1979; and *Washington Post*, June 8, 1979.

80. Huener (*Auschwitz, Poland*, 288) cites *Der Spiegel*'s estimate of 300,000; the regime put the crowd at 450,000 (IPN, BU 0296/216/3, F. 151). *Tygodnik Powszechny*'s June 17, 1979, issue noted "hundreds of thousands"; the *Washington Post* of June 8, 1979, cited Church estimates of one million; and Weigel noted "more than one million" (*Witness to Hope*, 315). This was one of the rare instances of the government's figures not being on the low end of the estimates, surely a reflection of the fact that the Polish state authorities welcomed a visit of the pope to Auschwitz in hopes that it would draw attention to Polish suffering and heroism, (West) German imperialism, and the Soviet role in Poland's liberation; see Huener, *Auschwitz, Poland*, 218.

81. For John Paul's homily at Birkenau, see Jan Paweł II, *Pielgrzymki do Ojczyzny*, 154–58. Translated quotations in subsequent paragraphs are from this source.

82. Włodkowic (ca. 1370–1435) was a late medieval Kraków academician who argued against the Teutonic Knights' conquest of non-Christian peoples in the Baltic region,

most famously at the Church's Council of Constance in 1414. His commitment to peaceful international relations based on mutual respect has earned him consideration as a pioneer in modern human rights theory.

83. Huener, *Auschwitz, Poland,* 219.

84. Jan Paweł II, *Pielgrzymki do Ojczyzny,* 156.

85. "Address of the Holy Father Paul VI to the United Nations Organization," October 4, 1965, http://www.vatican.va/content/paul-vi/en/speeches/1965/documents /hf_p-vi_spe_19651004_united-nations.html.

86. Interestingly, in a homily that was interrupted more than twenty times by applause, these comments were among those that drew the most sustained applause.

87. Huener in *Auschwitz, Poland,* insightfully and thoroughly traces the twists and turns of the Polish communist regime's efforts to instrumentalize Auschwitz over the decades for its political, diplomatic, and ideological ends.

88. Contrary to common perceptions, most of the killing of Jews by Nazi Germany took place in death camps farther to the east or simply near the locales where victims resided. Timothy Snyder, *Bloodlands: Europe between Hitler and Stalin* (New York: Basic Books, 2010), viii. According to the United States Holocaust Memorial Museum, approximately 1,082,000 people were murdered at the Auschwitz-Birkenau complex, of whom Jews numbered approximately 960,000. "Auschwitz," entry in the Holocaust Encyclopedia, United States Holocaust Memorial Museum, www.ushmm.org. See also "Poland Agrees to Change Auschwitz Tablets," *New York Times,* June 17, 1992, on the agreement of the postcommunist Polish regime to change the memorial tablets at Auschwitz-Birkenau to reflect the fact that it was mainly Jews who were killed there.

89. Six million is the traditional number claimed by Poland and Poles with respect to overall wartime losses, with Poles and Jews supposedly each accounting for half that number. However, Timothy Snyder points out that the actual number seems to have been closer to 4.8 million, with the 6 million figure put forth after the war by one of Poland's communist leaders for the political objective of making it seem like Poles and Jews had lost equal numbers during the war. In fact, deaths of Jews from Poland made up the greater part of the number, perhaps around 2.7 million. Snyder, *Bloodlands,* 406.

90. These issues are discussed at length in Huener, *Auschwitz, Poland.*

91. Kolbe's canonization upset a number of Jewish leaders and organizations worldwide. Kolbe headed a publishing operation in the town of Niepokalanów that produced the most antisemitic Catholic periodical in interwar Poland. Kolbe also accepted the anti-Jewish propaganda of the *Protocols of the Elders of Zion* at face value. Kolbe's defenders note, however, that only 31 of Kolbe's 1,006 extant writings even mentioned Jews, that he admonished his colleagues on at least one occasion against stirring up animosity toward Jews, that he helped shelter hundreds of Jews at Niepokalanów when the war broke out, and that his criticism of Jews was never hateful or violent and was not aimed at traditional or religious Jews but rather at the modern, secularized ones whom Kolbe regarded as in league with, or even directing, Freemasons against the Catholic Church. For more on Kolbe and this controversy, see Ronald Modras, "Pope John Paul II, St. Maximilian Kolbe, and Antisemitism: Some Current Problems and Perceptions Affecting Catholic-Jewish Relations," *Journal of Ecumenical Studies* 20, no. 4 (1983): 630–39; and Porter-Szűcs, *Faith and Fatherland,* 307–9.

92. As Huener notes, the audience would have noticed the contrast between the restrained words of John Paul and the "hyperbolic praise traditionally lavished on the Red Army by representatives of the government." Huener, *Auschwitz, Poland*, 219.

93. Huener notes that this reference to the Soviets may have been in part a response to concerns of Poland's communist authorities that the Soviet Union's role in the liberation of Poland from Nazism was being neglected during the papal visit. Huener, *Auschwitz, Poland*, 219. Huener's supposition is surely correct, as Szablewski's notes show that the government placed enormous importance on the ceremonies at Auschwitz and expected the pope to accommodate their concerns there. See Friszke and Zaremba, *Wizyta Jana Pawła*, 168–69.

94. Huener points out that by raising the issue of human rights, as well as presenting Poland's wartime suffering in the context of the struggle for Polish national independence rather than simply the war or the fight against fascism, the pope implicitly drew a parallel with Poland's situation in 1979. Huener, *Auschwitz, Poland*, 219–21.

95. See *Trybuna Ludu*, June 11, 1979; AAN, USW, 137/11, F. 91–116; AAN, USW, 137/21, F. 111–26; and AAN, PZPR KC 1354, XI A/1249, F. 16–28.

96. For John Paul's homily at Nowy Targ, see Jan Paweł II, *Pielgrzymki do Ojczyzny*, 159–62; subsequent translated quotations are from this source. For the pope's expressed concern that some pilgrims hoping to attend the event in Nowy Targ were not present (an implicit implication of the policy of Poland and its Soviet bloc allies), see *Washington Post*, June 9, 1979.

97. For John Paul's speech to youth at Skałka, see Jan Paweł II, *Pielgrzymki do Ojczyzny*, 172–75; the translated quote is from this source.

98. For these comments, see Jan Paweł II, *Pielgrzymki do Ojczyzny*, 176–79. Translated quotes that follow are from this source.

99. Weigel, *Witness to Hope*, 317.

100. "Informacja Sytuacyjna Nr. 10," MSW report, June 9, 1979, in IPN BU 0296/217/1, F. 189–95.

101. For more on the Ark of the Lord Church and Wojtyła's role in getting it built, see Weigel, *Witness to Hope*, 189–90; and Stanisław Dziwisz, *A Life with Karol: My Forty-Year Friendship with the Man Who Became Pope* (New York: Doubleday, 2008), 33–36.

102. Katarzyna Zechenter, "Evolving Narratives in Post-War Polish Literature: The Case of Nowa Huta (1950–2005)," *Slavonic and East European Review* 85, no. 4 (2007): 674–76. Construction of the new church finally began in October 1967, and the church was consecrated in May 1977 by Cardinal Wojtyła himself.

103. This was no small procession. The police estimated five thousand participants (IPN BU, 0296/217/1, F. 189–95) and the *New York Times* of June 10, 1979, ten thousand.

104. For accounts of the papal Mass at Mogiła, see *New York Times*, June 10, 1979; *Washington Post*, June 10, 1979; and Weigel, *Witness to Hope*, 317–18.

105. For John Paul's homily at Mogiła, see Jan Paweł II, *Pielgrzymki do Ojczyzny*, 186–91. Translated quotes that follow are from this source.

106. Police reports put the attendance at eighty thousand. "Informacja Sytuacyjna Nr. 11," MSW report, June 10, 1979, in IPN BU 0296/217/1, F. 196–201. The *Washington Post* reported on June 10, 1979, that thousands "jammed the abbey's tiny courtyard, and hundreds of thousands of people lined the route to the abbey."

107. This courageous young priest, Józef Kurzeja, was hounded and harassed by the authorities until he died of a heart attack at the age of thirty-nine in 1976. See Weigel, *Witness to Hope*, 190–91, for more on Father Kurzeja.

108. For John Paul's address to the delegation of foreign bishops, see Jan Paweł II, *Pielgrzymki do Ojczyzny*, 196–97.

109. Police reports put the attendance at six hundred thousand. "Informacja Sytuacyjna Nr. 12," MSW report of June 11, 1979, in IPN 0296/217/1, F. 202–7. The *New York Times* of June 11, 1979, estimated the crowd at a million, while the *Washington Post* of June 11, 1979, put it at "perhaps two million." Weigel (*Witness to Hope*, 318) estimated two million to three million.

110. For John Paul's homily at the Kraków Commons, see Jan Paweł II, *Pielgrzymki do Ojczyzny*, 198–205. Subsequent translated quotations are from this source.

111. Typically in the Catholic tradition, a nation's "baptism" is regarded as the date when its ruler accepted Christianity. Thus, Kievan Rus' was baptized along with Prince Vladimir in 988, Hungary with King Stephen in 1000, and Poland with Prince Mieszko in 966. John Paul may be unique in adding a symbolic national confirmation to this discourse.

112. The scriptural verses he quoted were John 20:22, where Jesus breathes on his apostles and says, "Receive the Holy Spirit"; 1 Thessalonians 5:19, where Saint Paul writes, "Do not quench the Spirit"; and Ephesians 4:30, in which Saint Paul writes, "Do not grieve the Holy Spirit, in whom you were sealed for the day of redemption."

113. *New York Times*, June 11, 1979.

114. For John Paul's farewell address at the Kraków airport, see Jan Paweł II, *Pielgrzymki do Ojczyzny*, 207–9. The translated quote is from this source.

115. AAN, USW, 137/20, F. 213.

116. "Spotkanie," *Polityka*, June 23, 1979, in AAN, USW, 137/20, F. 230–32.

117. John Paul's appearances at Victory Square and at Auschwitz-Birkenau were televised nationwide; other major events were broadcast locally.

118. *Trybuna Ludu*, June 11, 1979.

119. AAN, USW, 137/11, F. 91–116; AAN, USW, 137/21, F. 111–26; AAN, PZPR KC 1354, XIA/1249, F. 16–28; "Informacja Sytuacyjna Nr. 3," MSW report, June 2, 1979, in IPN BU 0296/217/1, F. 143–50.

120. "Informacja Sytuacyjna Nr. 6," MSW report, June 5, 1979, in IPN BU 0296/217/1, F. 166–70.

121. AAN, USW, 137/21, F. 111–26.

122. AAN, USW, 137/11, F. 91–116; "Informacja Sytuacyjna Nr. 6," MSW report, June 5, 1979, in IPN BU 0296/217/1, F. 166–70; AAN, USW, 137/18, F. 9–18.

123. AAN, USW, 137/11, F. 91–116.

124. AAN, USW, 137/18, F. 9–18; "Informacja Sytuacyjna Nr. 6," MSW report, June 5, 1979, in IPN BU 0296/217/1, F. 166–70. The latter report refers to the claim that John Paul, during his homily at Warsaw's Victory Square, incited the crowd into singing "We want God." See also AAN, USW, 137/18, F. 62–68; and AAN, USW, 137/11, F. 91–116.

125. "Informacja Sytuacyjna Nr. 6," MSW report, June 5, 1979, in IPN BU 0296/217/1, F. 166–170; AAN, USW, 137/18, F. 9–18.

126. "Informacja Sytuacyjna Nr. 7," MSW report, June 6, 1979, in IPN, BU 0296/217/1, F. 171–76; AAN, USW, 137/18, F. 9–18; AAN USW, 137/18, F. 62–68.

127. "Informacja Sytuacyjna Nr. 7," MSW report, June 6, in IPN BU 0296/217/1, F. 171–76.

128. Weigel, *Witness to Hope*, 302–3.

129. AAN, 1354 KC PZPR, WA, L1/316; see also AAN, USW, 137/18, F. 9–18. In line with Weigel, Polish journalist Jan Szczepański, writing in *Polityka*, noted that through the crowd marshals, the Church demonstrated its capability of organizing the masses in a striking manner, mobilizing volunteers who worked effectively and with dedication because of their obedience toward the Church. AAN, PZPR KC 1354, XIA/1249, F. 11–15.

130. Adam Biela and Jerome J. Tobacyk, "Self-Transcendence in the Agoral Gathering: A Case Study of Pope John Paul II's 1979 Visit to Poland," *Journal of Humanistic Psychology* 27, no. 4 (1987): 390–405.

131. Józef Makselon, "Fascynacja i wezwanie: Papieskie odwiedziny w Ojczyźnie," in *Sympozjum naukowe z okazji 15-lecia pontyfikatu Jana Pawła II, Kraków, 11–12 X 1993* (Kraków: Wydawnictwo Naukowe Papieskiej Akademii Teolog, 1994), 207–23. Subsequent quotes, in translation, are from this source.

132. For Anna Kamieńska's contribution, see *Więź*, no. 7–8, July–August 1979, 228–30. Subsequent quotes, in translation, are from this source.

133. For Jan Józef Lipski's contribution, see *Więź*, no. 7–8, July–August 1979, 238–40.

134. For Stanisław Stomma's contribution, see *Więź*, no. 7–8, July–August 1979, 261–65.

135. For Jan Józef Szczepański's contribution, see *Więź*, no. 7–8, July–August 1979, 265–67.

136. Quoted in *Time*, June 11, 1979. The *New York Times* of June 2, 1979, quoted him as saying, "There will be a strengthening of the spiritual energy of society. . . . This is very important: society will gain knowledge of its strength en masse. It very rarely happens here that there are such masses of people gathered, and these people will be sort of united spiritually. This will give them a feeling and understanding of their own strength."

Chapter 2. Comforter

1. Andrzej Friszke and Marcin Zaremba, eds., *Wizyta Jana Pawła w Polsce 1979: Dokumenty KC PZPR i MSW* (Warsaw: Biblioteka "Więzi," 2005), 68–70. In public opinion surveys carried out on June 11 and 12, 1979, 87 percent of Poles said they had a "large interest" in the visit and 9 percent an "average" interest (69).

2. Friszke and Zaremba, *Wizyta Jana Pawła*, 69–71.

3. Friszke and Zaremba, *Wizyta Jana Pawła*, 69.

4. Friszke and Zaremba, *Wizyta Jana Pawła*, 71–72.

5. Friszke and Zaremba, *Wizyta Jana Pawła*, 72.

6. Robert Alvis, *White Eagle, Black Madonna: One Thousand Years of the Polish Catholic Tradition* (New York: Fordham University Press, 2016), 237.

7. Jan Józef Lipski, *A History of the Workers' Defense Committee in Poland, 1976–1981*, trans. Olga Amsterdamska and Gene M. Moore (Berkeley: University of California Press, 1985), 338.

8. Adam Michnik, *The Church and the Left* (Chicago: University of Chicago Press, 1993), 223.

9. Michnik, *Church and the Left*, 223, 225.

10. Lipski, *History of the Workers' Defense Committee*, 331.

11. See Andrzej Paczkowski, *Revolution and Counterrevolution in Poland, 1980–1989: Solidarity, Martial Law, and the End of Communism in Europe* (Rochester, NY: University of Rochester Press, 2015), 6, for a discussion of the impact of John Paul's 1979 visit.

12. Jan Kubik, *The Power of Symbols against the Symbols of Power: The Rise of Solidarity and the Fall of State Socialism in Poland* (University Park: Pennsylvania State University Press, 1994), 144. See chapter 5 (129–52) of Kubik's work for an in-depth analysis of John Paul's 1979 pilgrimage and its profound impact on Polish society.

13. Maryjane Osa, *Solidarity and Contention: Networks of Polish Opposition* (Minneapolis: University of Minnesota Press, 2003), esp. 168, 176, 181.

14. For an in-depth discussion of the development of independent publishing in communist Poland, see Siobhan Doucette, *Books Are Weapons: The Polish Opposition Press and the Overthrow of Communism* (Pittsburgh, PA: University of Pittsburgh Press, 2018), chapter 2 of which (33–68) covers the late 1970s.

15. Osa, *Solidarity and Contention*, 161–63.

16. Paczkowski, *Revolution and Counterrevolution*, 12.

17. Paczkowski, *Revolution and Counterrevolution*, 15.

18. Paczkowski, *Revolution and Counterrevolution*, 13–14.

19. Osa, *Solidarity and Contention*, 80, 149; Paczkowski, *Revolution and Counterrevolution*, 14.

20. For the text of the Gdańsk Accords, see Andrzej Paczkowski and Malcolm Byrne, eds., *From Solidarity to Martial Law: The Polish Crisis of 1980–1981; A Documentary History* (Budapest: Central European University Press, 2007), 70–81.

21. Joseph Rothschild, *Return to Diversity: A Political History of East Central Europe since World War II* (New York: Oxford University Press, 1993), 159–60.

22. Osa, *Solidarity and Contention*, 181.

23. Paczkowski, *Revolution and Counterrevolution*, 17–18.

24. Paczkowski, *Revolution and Counterrevolution*, 224.

25. Rothschild, *Return to Diversity*, 162.

26. Paczkowski, *Revolution and Counterrevolution*, x.

27. Paczkowski, *Revolution and Counterrevolution*, 70.

28. Aleksandra Mierzwińska and Jan Żaryn, "Episkopat Polski wobec wprowadzenia stanu wojennego," *Arcana: Kultura–Historia–Polityka*, no. 66 (November–December 2005): 151–52.

29. The communiqué was delivered to the government. It was supposed to be read out in Poland's churches as well, but in the wake of the massacre at the Wujek mine, Glemp canceled the reading. Nevertheless, it was read out in eleven of Poland's thirty dioceses. Mierzwińska and Żaryn, "Episkopat Polski," 150–52.

30. Mierzwińska and Żaryn, "Episkopat Polski," 151.

31. Mierzwińska and Żaryn, "Episkopat Polski," 151.

32. Biblioteka Narodowa (hereafter BN), Jerzy Turowicz Papers, uncataloged (in storage) (hereafter, Turowicz Papers), General audience of December 16, 1981, and Angelus address of January 31, 1982.

33. BN, Turowicz Papers, General audience of December 16 and Angelus address of December 20, 1981.

34. BN, Turowicz Papers, Angelus address of January 10, 1982.

35. BN, Turowicz Papers, Angelus addresses of December 13 and 20, 1981.

36. BN, Turowicz Papers, John Paul II to Jaruzelski, December 18, 1981. Jaruzelski refused to accept the letter, apparently because certain portions offended him, such as John Paul's comparison of the present situation with the wartime occupation. See Mierzwińska and Żaryn, "Episkopat Polski," 152–53; and Jan Żaryn, "Jan Paweł II a stan wojenny," in *Pielgrzymka nadziei: II wizyta Jana Pawła w ojczyźnie; Materiały pokonferencyjne* (Warsaw: Muzeum Jana Pawła II i Prymasa Wyszyńskiego and Instytut Pamięci Narodowej, 2014) (hereafter, *Pielgrzymka nadziei*), 107–8.

37. Żaryn, "Jan Paweł II a stan wojenny," in *Pielgrzymka nadziei*, 108; Mierzwińska and Żaryn, "Episkopat Polski," 152–53.

38. Paczkowski, *Revolution and Counterrevolution*, 224–25. As Paczkowski puts it, the regime-Solidarity-Church triangle was now the regime-Church axis.

39. Paczkowski, *Revolution and Counterrevolution*, 227–28.

40. Paczkowski, *Revolution and Counterrevolution*, 227.

41. See Jerzy Kloczowski, *A History of Polish Christianity* (Cambridge: Cambridge University Press, 2000), 334–35; Paczkowski, *Revolution and Counterrevolution*, 225, 227, 232–34; and Andrzej Ursynowski, "Kościół—bliżej wieczności niż solidarności," *Biuletyn Informacyjny, "Solidarność za granicą,"* no. 47–48 (December 13, 1982): 6–9, for a discussion of the assistance provided by the Church during martial law.

42. Peter Raina, *Wizyty apostolskie Jana Pawła II w Polsce: Rozmowy przygotowawcze Watykan—PRL—Episkopat* (Warsaw: Książka Polska, 1997), 123, 125.

43. Raina, *Wizyty apostolskie*, 126.

44. See Raina, *Wizyty apostolskie*, 127, 160; "Evaluation of the Second Visit of John Paul II to Poland," July 8, 1983, 26–27, in AAN, USW, 137/35, F. 31–59 (hereafter, USW report).

45. Raina, *Wizyty apostolskie*, 197.

46. Raina, *Wizyty apostolskie*, 127.

47. Raina, *Wizyty apostolskie*, 129–31.

48. Raina, *Wizyty apostolskie*, 131–34.

49. Raina, *Wizyty apostolskie*, 136–38.

50. Raina, *Wizyty apostolskie*, 135.

51. Raina, *Wizyty apostolskie*, 139–43.

52. Another possible date for a visit centered on October 10, when Blessed Maximilian Kolbe was to be canonized, but the state opposed this timetable on the grounds of insufficient time to prepare and the potential for poor weather. A further possibility was May 3–13, in connection with the anniversary of the 1981 assassination attempt on John Paul II and the feast of Our Lady of Fatima. Raina, *Wizyty apostolskie*, 135, 140–41.

53. "Tenets Regarding the Preparations" is described in "Appraisal of the Visit of the Pope," June 24, 1983, 1–2, in AAN, WA, Wydział Administracyjny, 1354 KC PZPR, LI/318, F. 59–90 (hereafter, KC report).

54. *Biuletyn Informacyjny*, no. 47/48, December 13, 1982, 8; Adam Dziurok, "Kościół w Polsce a II pielgrzymka w perspektywie stanu wojennego," in *Pielgrzymka nadziei*, 81–82; Żaryn, "Jan Paweł II a stan wojenny," in *Pielgrzymka nadziei*, 106.

55. Dziurok, "Kościół w Polsce," 84–85.

56. Dziurok, "Kościół w Polsce," 83.

57. Mieczysław Rakowski, *Dzienniki polityczne 1981–1983* (Warsaw: Iskry, 2004), 402.

58. *Biuletyn Informacyjny*, no. 63, June 1, 1983, 2.

59. Quoted in *Biuletyn Informacyjny*, no. 63, June 1, 1983, 3.

60. Żaryn, "Jan Paweł II a stan wojenny," in *Pielgrzymka nadziei*, 106.

61. Quoted in *Biuletyn Informacyjny*, no. 63, June 1, 1983, 4.

62. *Biuletyn Informacyjny*, no. 63, June 1, 1983, 5.

63. Quoted in *Biuletyn Informacyjny*, no. 63, June 1, 1983, 3.

64. Quoted in Dziurok, "Kościół w Polsce," 81.

65. For notes on and summaries of discussions between representatives of the government and of the Catholic episcopacy pertaining to these issues in the months leading up to the visit, see Raina, *Wizyty apostolskie*, esp. 151–78, 181–88, 200–207.

66. See Raina, *Wizyty apostolskie*, 171, 177, 183, 185–88, 199–200, 212.

67. Raina, *Wizyty apostolskie*, 190.

68. Raina, *Wizyty apostolskie*, 194–95.

69. Wałęsa was released from detention in November 1982, and the internment centers closed down and the internees were released on December 23. The regime made it clear, however, that martial law was only being "suspended" and thus could be restored at once should the situation warrant it. Moreover, some activists remained in state custody, awaiting prosecution for alleged "conspiratorial activities," or were already in prison. Prisoners had the option to apply for pardon but not for amnesty. Paczkowski, *Revolution and Counterrevolution*, 217–20.

70. See Raina, *Wizyty apostolskie*, 208–9, for the Church and state agreements in spring 1983 pertaining to John Paul's visit.

71. Raina, *Wizyty apostolskie*, 192–94.

72. Raina, *Wizyty apostolskie*, 210–14.

73. *Biuletyn Informacyjny*, no. 63, June 1, 1983, 2.

74. *Biuletyn Informacyjny*, no. 60, April 27, 1983, 2.

75. For the TKK statement of March 23, 1983, see *Biuletyn Informacyjny*, no. 59, April 13 1983, 3.

76. Grzegorz Majchrzak, "'Wyjdźmy mu na spotkanie . . . ' 'Solidarność' wobec II pielgrzymki Jana Pawła II do Polski," in *Pielgrzymka nadziei*, 93–94.

77. *Biuletyn Informacyjny*, no. 65, June 29, 1983, 3; Majchrzak, "Wyjdźmy mu na spotkanie," in *Pielgrzymka nadziei*, 92–95.

78. *Biuletyn Informacyjny*, no. 65, June 29, 1983, 5.

79. For Jabłoński's speech at the airport, see *Trybuna Ludu*, June 17, 1983, and *Tygodnik Powszechny*, June 26, 1983.

80. For John Paul's arrival speech at Warsaw's airport, see Jan Paweł II, *Pielgrzymki do Ojczyzny 1979–1983–1987–1991–1995–1997–1999–2002: Przemówienia, homilie* (Kraków: Znak, 2005), 213–14. Subsequent translated quotes from the speech are from this source.

81. *New York Times*, June 17, 1983.

82. *Washington Post*, June 17, 1983; *New York Times*, June 17, 1983.

83. For John Paul's homily at the memorial service for Cardinal Wyszyński, see Jan Paweł II, *Pielgrzymki do Ojczyzny*, 215–19. Subsequent translated quotes are from this source.

84. One observer noted a crowd of six thousand to eight thousand. Rakowski, *Dzienniki polityczne 1981–1983*, 562. Another writer puts the crowd at "tens of thousands." Timothy Garton Ash, *The Uses of Adversity* (New York: Vintage, 1990), 42.

85. *New York Times*, June 17, 1983.

86. *Washington Post*, June 18, 1983; *New York Times*, June 18, 1983.

87. For John Paul's speech at Belvedere, see Jan Paweł II, *Pielgrzymki do Ojczyzny*, 222–26. Translated quotes that follow are from this source.

88. These were among the "tenets" that representatives of the government and the episcopate had agreed to in advance of the visit. See KC report, June 24, 1983, 11.

89. KC report, June 24, 1983, 5.

90. "Evaluation of the Second Visit of John Paul II to Poland," July 8, 1983, 13, in AAN, USW, 137/35, F. 31–59 (hereafter, USW report).

91. *New York Times*, June 18, 1983. Rakowski, who was present, observed that Jaruzelski was "tremendously agitated" and that his leg shook until halfway through his speech. Rakowski, *Dzienniki polityczne 1981–1983*, 562.

92. Garton Ash, *Uses of Adversity*, 56.

93. For Jaruzelski's speech, see *Trybuna Ludu*, June 18–19, 1983; and *Tygodnik Powszechny*, June 26, 1983. Quotations, in translation, are from these sources.

94. Jaruzelski is alluding to the great Polish Romantic poet of the nineteenth century, Juliusz Słowacki, whose poem "My Testament" includes these words: "Lecz zaklinam—niech żywi nie tracą nadziei / I przed narodem niosą oświaty kaganiec; / A kiedy trzeba, na śmierć idą po kolei, / Jak kamienie przez Boga rzucane na szaniec!" (Yet I implore you—let the living not lose hope / And before the nation carry the lamp of learning / And when necessary, go to their death in turn / Like stones tossed by God on the rampart!)

95. *Washington Post*, June 18, 1983; *New York Times*, June 18, 1983.

96. USW report, July 8, 1983, 8, 20.

97. This information comes from the USW report, July 8, 1983, 20, and the KC report, June 24, 1983, 4. It is also found in Rakowski's diary-memoir, *Dzienniki polityczne 1981–1983*, 565.

98. *New York Times*, June 18, 1983.

99. The *Washington Post* on June 18, 1983, estimated the crowd at "more than a million" and the *New York Times* on June 18, 1983, gave a figure of "about a million." Communist sources put the crowd size at six hundred thousand. USW report, July 8, 1983, 5.

100. For John Paul's homily at Decennial Stadium, see Jan Paweł II, *Pielgrzymki do Ojczyzny*, 234–43. Quotations in this and subsequent paragraphs, in translation, are from this source.

101. Hebrews 13:8.

102. The regime did like, however, that John Paul made specific reference to the achievements of reconstruction in the northern and western parts of Poland. "After the Visit of John Paul II to Poland 1983 (II)," September 21, 1983, by the Department of Ideological Problems of Socialist Construction of the Institute of Fundamental Problems of Marxism-Leninism (hereafter, M-L report), 150, in AAN, PRPZ KC, XI/890.

103. *New York Times*, June 18, 1983; *Washington Post*, June 18, 1983.

104. *New York Times*, June 19, 1983.

105. *Washington Post*, June 18, 1983; USW report, July 8, 1983, 4.

106. *New York Times*, June 19, 1983.

107. The *New York Times* of June 19, 1983, estimated the crowd at 250,000; the government source, 150,000. USW report, July 8, 1983, 4.

108. For John Paul's homily at Niepokalanów, see Jan Paweł II, *Pielgrzymki do Ojczyzny*, 246–53. Subsequent quotations, in translation, are from this source.

109. Germany was the country responsible for Kolbe's death; Japan was the country where he was active during the 1930s at Mugenzai no Sono, a town inhabited by members of Catholic religious orders, akin to Niepokalanów.

110. In 1981, Poland's bishops had begun exploring the possibility of a sort of "new Marshall Plan" for Poland, whereby assistance from Western countries could be procured and allocated toward the improvement of Poland's private sector in agriculture. In June 1982, Glemp discussed this "Program of Assistance for Polish Agriculture" with Cardinal Joseph Hoeffner of the West German Conference of Bishops, who in turn in July discussed the matter with U.S. president Ronald Reagan and with Pope John Paul. See Józef Baran, "Fundacja Rolnicza Episkopatu Polski," in *Encyklopedia Solidarności*, http://www.encysol.pl/wiki/Fundacja_Rolnicza_Episkopatu_Polski.

111. USW report, July 8, 1983, 4.

112. *Washington Post*, June 19, 1983.

113. *New York Times*, June 19, 1983. The USW report, July 8, 1983, 2–3, noted that the pope would use "effective pauses" to encourage applause of a political character, as well as employ "intonation of voice, half a word, or even silence" to manipulate the crowd into his desired responses. The report made specific reference to the singing of "Boże coś Polskę" in this respect.

114. *Washington Post*, June 19, 1983.

115. For John Paul's speech to the pilgrims from the Diocese of Szczecin-Kamieńska, see Jan Paweł II, *Pielgrzymki do Ojczyzny*, 257–60. Subsequent quotes, in translation, are from this source.

116. The government put attendance at six hundred thousand (USW report, July 8, 1983, 5); Garton Ash at "half a million" (*Uses of Adversity*, 43); and the *Washington Post* of June 19, 1983, estimated "more than a million."

117. USW report, July 8, 1983, 6.

118. KC report, June 24, 1983, 14.

119. *New York Times*, June 19, 1983; *Washington Post*, June 19, 1983.

120. Garton Ash describes the event, which he attended, in *Uses of Adversity*, 47–48.

121. For John Paul's speech to youth at Częstochowa, see Jan Paweł II, *Pielgrzymki do Ojczyzny*, 261–66. Quotes, in translation, that follow are from this source.

122. The Jasna Góra Appeal, dating to the celebrations in 1966 of Poland's millennium of Christianity, is brief: "Maryjo, Królowo Polski, / Jestem przy Tobie, pamiętam, czuwam" (Mary, Queen of Poland / I am at your side, I remember, / I am vigilant).

123. John Paul was interrupted by applause more than twenty times during the last sixteen minutes of his speech.

124. This latter admonition could refer to the desire to emigrate or even to the flight into drug and alcohol abuse or sexual libertinism that John Paul on other occasions noted as particular pitfalls for the youth of Poland and elsewhere.

125. Rakowski reports having informed Jaruzelski about the homily that evening by phone, noting that the general "was clearly upset and furious." Rakowski, *Dzienniki polityczne 1981–1983*, 563.

126. USW report, July 8, 1983, 10–11.

127. AAN, 1354, KC PZPR, Wydział Administracyjny, LI/317, 60.

128. *New York Times*, June 20, 1983.

129. AAN, 1354, KC PZPR, Wydział Administracyjny, LI/317, 61.

130. The government source put the crowd at five hundred thousand (USW report, July 8, 1983, 5); the *New York Times* of June 20, 1983, put it at "about a million people"; and the *Washington Post* of June 20, 1983, claimed "up to a million people," noting that about half the crowd had their view of the pope obscured by forest but could listen to him over loudspeakers.

131. *New York Times*, June 20, 1983.

132. For John Paul's homily at the Jubilee mass at Jasna Góra, see Jan Paweł II, *Pielgrzymki do Ojczyzny*, 270–77. Subsequent quotes, in translation, are from this source.

133. This was also the only point at which the pope's homily was interrupted by applause, in contrast to the dozens of interruptions the night before. Unlike the previous evening, when he indulged interruptions, John Paul at once admonished the crowd not to interrupt him.

134. For John Paul's speech to the bishops' conference, see Jan Paweł II, *Pielgrzymki do Ojczyzny*, 285–93. Quotes, in translation, that follow are from this source.

135. John Paul then got a chuckle from his audience by adding that when he gave this speech at the ILO, the Polish delegation approached him afterward and told him they completely shared his position, perhaps an indication of how little faith Polish communists had in their own ideology by that time.

136. USW report, July 8, 1983, 5.

137. KC report, June 24, 1983, 11. Henry Kamm noted in his *New York Times* article on June 21, 1983, that journalists did not receive copies of John Paul's text until the afternoon of the next day, instead of the usual several hours beforehand, suggesting that John Paul had extensively rewritten his comments for the Jasna Góra Appeal.

138. USW report, July 8, 1983, 16.

139. For Jabłoński's speech at the Kraków airport, see *Trybuna Ludu*, June 24, 1983.

140. The *New York Times* on June 21, 1983, put the crowd at "hundreds of thousands"; the government put it at six hundred thousand. USW report, July 8, 1983, 5.

141. *New York Times*, June 21, 1983.

142. For the text of John Paul's homily at Poznań, see Jan Paweł II, *Pielgrzymki do Ojczyzny*, 299–306. Subsequent quotes, in translation, are from this source.

143. For the government's view on John Paul's patriotic statements, see USW report, July 8, 1983, 14.

144. *Washington Post*, June 21, 1983; *New York Times*, June 21, 1983.

145. The *New York Times* of June 21, 1983, estimated the crowd at "about a million people"; the Catholic Church's estimate was 1.5 million (according to the *Washington Post*, June 21, 1983). The government put it at nine hundred thousand. USW report, July 8, 1983, 5.

146. *Washington Post*, June 21, 1983.

147. For John Paul's homily at Katowice, see Jan Paweł II, *Pielgrzymki do Ojczyzny,* 308–15.

148. John Paul noted in his introductory comments that he had hoped to hold this event at the shrine in Piekary, but the crowds would not fit, hence the move to the airfield near Katowice.

149. "Szczęść Boże!" means "God bless!"

150. *Washington Post,* June 21, 1983.

151. USW report, July 8, 1983, 9.

152. USW report, July 8, 1983, 9–10.

153. USW report, July 8, 1983, 15.

154. KC report, June 24, 1983, 18.

155. *New York Times,* June 22, 1983.

156. *New York Times,* June 22, 1983.

157. For John Paul's homily at Wrocław, see Jan Paweł II, *Pielgrzymki do Ojczyzny,* 319–26. Subsequent quotes, in translation, are from this source.

158. The *New York Times* of June 22, 1983, put the attendance at "about one million," the *Washington Post* of June 22, 1983, estimated "nearly one million," and the government's report estimated seven hundred thousand. USW report, July 8, 1983, 5.

159. "Bulwark of Christendom," or *antemurale Christianitatis,* was the concept that a particular country historically absorbed attacks from Eastern invaders, thereby protecting western Europe and Western Christianity from particular enemies, such as the Muslim Tatars and Ottomans, the Orthodox Russians, and the atheistic Soviets. With respect to the Battle of Legnica, historians have challenged traditional Polish views on the significance of that event in halting the Mongol advance. Besides the Polish or Western resistance, they have argued that the Mongols' objectives were more limited, that their high command was deeply divided, that they lacked sufficient pasturage for their horses, and that they experienced a succession crisis on account of the death of the Great Khan at this time. See Peter Jackson, *The Mongols and the West, 1221–1410* (Harlow, UK: Pearson Longman, 2006), 71–74, for a discussion of these additional factors.

160. The geography is more symbolic than real here, as the Tumski Bridge crosses only a part of the Odra, connecting the city of Wrocław with a small island in the river. It is only farther north that the Odra forms the Polish-German border.

161. Although he does not mention it here, the pope, when he was still Archbishop Wojtyła, also participated in the (in)famous 1965 letter of the Catholic bishops of Poland to those of West Germany. Inspired by the Second Vatican Council, as well as by hopes that German bishops would take part in the Polish millennium of Christianity celebrations in 1966, it was drafted by Bishop Kominek, with edits by Wyszyński and Wojtyła. The letter called for reciprocal forgiveness and reconciliation between the two nations, including the appeal that "we forgive and we ask forgiveness." Poland's communist regime used the letter in a propaganda effort to brand Poland's bishops as unpatriotic, given the letter's recognition of German suffering and apology for wrongs committed by Poles against Germans in the war's aftermath. For an in-depth analysis of the letter and its implications, see Piotr H. Kosicki, "*Caritas* across the Iron Curtain? Polish-German Reconciliation and the Bishops' Letter of 1965," *East European Politics and Societies* 23, no. 2 (2009): 213–43.

162. USW report, July 8, 1983, 14; KC report, June 24, 1983, 25.

163. *New York Times*, June 22, 1983.

164. KC report, June 24, 1983, 3, 14; USW report, July 8, 1983, 14–15.

165. M-L report, September 21, 1983, 142–43.

166. *Washington Post*, June 22, 1983.

167. Estimates vary widely, from "tens of thousands" (*New York Times*, June 22, 1983), to "several hundred thousand" (*Washington Post*, June 22, 1983), to 750,000 (USW report, July 8, 1983, 5).

168. For John Paul's homily at St. Anne's Mountain, see Jan Paweł II, *Pielgrzymki do Ojczyzny*, 329–35.

169. Raina, *Wizyty apostolskie*, 163.

170. The *New York Times* on June 23, 1983, estimated the crowd at "two million people or more," and the *Washington Post* on that same date suggested numbers of "up to two million" or "approximately two million." Government estimates were much lower though still considerable, at nine hundred thousand. USW report, July 8, 1983, 5.

171. For the text of John Paul's homily at the beatification mass in Kraków, see Jan Paweł II, *Pielgrzymki do Ojczyzny*, 342–51. Quoted passages, in translation, are from this source.

172. *Washington Post*, June 23, 1983.

173. *Washington Post*, June 23, 1983.

174. The *Washington Post* of June 23, 1983 estimated a crowd of three hundred thousand, whereas the government put the figure at only one hundred thousand. USW report, July 8, 1983, 5.

175. For the text of John Paul's homily at Mistrzejowice, see Jan Paweł II, *Pielgrzymki do Ojczyzny*, 354–59.

176. *Washington Post*, June 23, 1983.

177. *Washington Post*, June 23, 1983. According to a government report, the demonstrators were from out of town, including from Gdańsk, and were easy to reroute given their lack of knowledge of the local geography. USW report, July 8, 1983, 16.

178. *Washington Post*, June 20, 1983.

179. Paczkowski, *Revolution and Counterrevolution*, 231.

180. The meeting was called "our important success" in the Central Committee's assessment of the visit. KC report, June 24, 1983, 4.

181. Rakowski, in his diary-memoir, celebrated the meeting as proof for the world that the pope "recognized the leader of a 'military junta' as a person who could be his co-negotiator and partner." Rakowski, *Dzienniki polityczne 1981–1983*, 567.

182. See, for example, *New York Times*, June 24, 1983.

183. Paczkowski notes that the visit came at the pope's request (*Revolution and Counterrevolution*, 231) as do the USW report, July 8, 1983, 18, and KC report, June 24, 1983, 4, 11, 24, the Polish media at the time (per *New York Times*, June 23, 24, 1983; and *Washington Post*, June 23, 1983), and papal biographers (Carl Bernstein and Marco Politi, *His Holiness: John Paul II and the Hidden History of Our Time* [New York: Doubleday, 1996], 383; Tad Szulc, *Pope John Paul II: The Biography* [New York: Scribner, 1995], 394). On the other hand, Jonathan Kwitny (*Man of the Century: The Life and Times of Pope John Paul II* [New York: Henry Holt, 1997, 480]) places the initiative for the meeting on Jaruzelski, as do some sources cited by Western media (e.g., *New York Times*, June 24, 1983).

184. Rakowski, *Dzienniki polityczne 1981–1983*, 571–72.

185. *New York Times*, June 26, 1983.

186. *Washington Post*, June 24, 1983; *New York Times*, June 27, 1983.

187. *Washington Post*, July 1, 1983. PRON was a pro–Communist Party movement set up by Jaruzelski in 1982 to mobilize his supporters. It included, among other members, several Catholic organizations sympathetic to the regime, along with party-affiliated representatives.

188. In some interviews after the fall of communism, Jaruzelski spoke warmly of John Paul II and characterized their conversation at Wawel as "cordial" and ending on "a very constructive note." Bernstein and Politi, *His Holiness*, 395; Szulc, *Pope John Paul II*, 394–95.

189. Rakowski, *Dzienniki polityczne 1981–1983*, 567.

190. Rakowski, *Dzienniki polityczne 1981–1983*, 571.

191. Rakowski, *Dzienniki polityczne 1981–1983*, 567.

192. See Bernstein and Politi, *His Holiness*, 385; and Paweł Zyzak, *Lech Wałęsa idea i historia: Biografia polityczna legendarnego przywodcy "Solidarności" do 1988 roku*, 2nd ed. (Warsaw: Arkana Historia, 2009), 478, for the conflicting accounts. See USW report, July 8, 1983, 20, for the regime's account; and Lech Wałęsa, *Droga do prawdy: Autobiografia* (Warsaw: Świat Książki, 2008), 204–10, for the Solidarity leader's rather inconsequential account.

193. On Wałęsa's evident disappointment after the meeting, Zyzak cites a comment by a Vatican official, Father Roberto Tucci, director general of Vatican Radio and the person responsible for helping plan papal trips abroad, who noted that "before the meeting with the pope[,] Wałęsa appeared very joyful and sure of himself, during the conversation he looked very tense, and after its conclusion he was clearly disappointed." Zyzak also cites Solidarity activist Jarosław Kaczyński, who noted that the meeting with John Paul left Wałęsa very much dejected and filled with pessimism. Zyzak, *Lech Wałęsa*, 479, 480. The comment by Tucci can be found in Rakowski, *Dzienniki polityczne 1981–1983*, 599.

194. *Washington Post*, June 23, 1983.

195. *New York Times*, June 28, 29, 1983, July 1, 1983. Father Tucci's account of the meeting supports this view and may even be the source of it. While in Kraków, John Paul had allegedly instructed Father Henryk Jankowski, the pro-Solidarity pastor of Saint Brigida's in Gdańsk and confidant of Wałęsa, to inform Wałęsa that he should withdraw from public life for a certain period, that is, "until the situation changes." Rakowski, *Dzienniki polityczne 1981–1983*, 600.

196. Quoted in *Washington Post*, June 25, 1983.

197. Quoted in *Washington Post*, June 26, 1983.

198. *New York Times*, June 27, 1983.

199. USW report, July 8, 1983, 21; *New York Times*, June 29, 1983; *Washington Post*, July 2, 1983.

200. Rakowski, *Dzienniki polityczne 1981–1983*, 573.

201. Zyzak, *Lech Wałęsa*, 481–82. Zyzak also notes here that it was the Western media and Western governments' interest in Wałęsa that had enhanced his influence.

202. This was the view of Zbigniew Brzezinski, the former U.S. national security advisor and career Soviet affairs expert. See *Washington Post*, June 26, 1983.

203. *Washington Post*, June 24, 1983. See also USW report, July 8, 1983, 18.

204. For the text of John Paul's speech at the Balice airport, see Jan Paweł II, *Pielgrzymki do Ojczyzny*, 366–68. Subsequent quotes, in translation, are from this source.

205. "Chatted amiably" quote from *Washington Post*, June 24, 1983. The original text of Jabłoński's speech at Kraków's airport is from *Trybuna Ludu*, June 24, 1983.

206. In fact, it is a basic tenet of Catholic social teaching that freedom can be used well or poorly, a point made frequently by John Paul throughout his career. In an analysis of the visit, the USW report indicated that this statement by John Paul was "useful from our point of view," and Jabłoński indeed used it at the farewell event at Kraków's airport. USW report, July 8, 1983, 16.

207. The KC report cited the pope's emphasis on the interdependence of rights and obligations favorably and regarded John Paul's farewell address as "beneficial for us." KC report, June 24, 1983, 4.

208. For the text of Łopatka's speech, see *Trybuna Ludu*, June 25–26, 1983. Subsequent quotes, in translation, are from this source.

209. Garton Ash notes, for example, that John Paul, in contrast to the 1979 visit, did not mention "the future of the churches elsewhere in Eastern Europe and the special mission of the Slav pope to reassert the unity of Christian Europe from the Atlantic to the Urals," a leitmotif of his pontificate. Garton Ash, *Uses of Adversity*, 44.

210. Jan Paweł II, *Pielgrzymki do Ojczyzny*, 223.

211. Some of Poland's bishops, for example, Ignacy Tokarczuk of Przemyśl or Henryk Gulbinowicz of Wrocław, were unequivocal supporters of Solidarity, in contrast to Primate Glemp.

212. *Biuletyn Informacyjny*, no. 68, July 27, 1983, 3.

213. For the interview with Bujak, see *Biuletyn Informacyjny*, no. 68, July 27, 1983, 4–5. Subsequent quotes, in translation, are from this source.

214. *KOS* quoted in *Biuletyn Informacyjny*, no. 68, July 27, 1983, 5–6.

215. Underground publications were mixed in their view of the pro-Solidarity demonstrations that broke out after a number of the papal events. While some publications seemed to take delight in them, others spoke more critically. One underground trade union publication criticized the demonstrators for acting against the expressed wishes of John Paul to disperse peacefully and for creating a distraction from the far greater show of support for Solidarity that had been going on around the altar during mass for gigantic crowds. See *Biuletyn Informacyjny*, no. 68, July 27, 1983, 7–8.

216. Quoted in Majchrzak, "Wyjdźmy mu na spotkanie," in *Pielgrzymka nadziei*, 95–96.

217. Quoted in Majchrzak, "Wyjdźmy mu na spotkanie," in *Pielgrzymka nadziei*, 102.

218. Majchrzak, "Wyjdźmy mu na spotkanie," in *Pielgrzymka nadziei*, 101

219. Majchrzak, "Wyjdźmy mu na spotkanie," in *Pielgrzymka nadziei*, 98.

220. Quoted in Majchrzak, "Wyjdźmy mu na spotkanie," in *Pielgrzymka nadziei*, 102

221. Quoted in Garton Ash, *Uses of Adversity*, 60.

222. Garton Ash, *Uses of Adversity*, 60.

Chapter 3. Critic

1. This summary of Poland's situation for the years after martial law draws especially from Joseph Rothschild, *Return to Diversity: A Political History of East Central Europe since World War II* (New York: Oxford University Press, 1993), 162, 181–87, 212–16; and

Andrzej Paczkowski, *Revolution and Counterrevolution in Poland, 1980–1989: Solidarity, Martial Law, and the End of Communism in Europe* (Rochester, NY: University of Rochester Press, 2015), 283–313.

2. Although upwards of four hundred Poles were arrested in 1985, most were freed in a subsequent amnesty in September 1986. Paczkowski, *Revolution and Counterrevolution*, 285, 288.

3. For Father Popiełuszko's activities, see Tadeusz Krawczak and Cyprian Wilanowski, eds., *Kościół w stanie wojennym: Wybór dokumentów z Archiwum Akt Nowych* (Warsaw: Instytut Wydawniczy Pax, 2008), 313; Robert Alvis, *White Eagle, Black Madonna: One Thousand Years of the Polish Catholic Tradition* (New York: Fordham University Press, 2016), 218; and Paczkowski, *Revolution and Counterrevolution*, 182.

4. For the operations against Father Popiełuszko, see Jan Żaryn's introduction to Jolanta Mysiakowska, ed., *Aparat represji wobec księdza Jerzego Popiełuszki 1982–1984*, vol. 1 (Warsaw: Instytut pamięci narodowej, 2009), 57–64.

5. The opposition claimed that only 66 percent of Poles participated, whereas the regime put the proportion at 79 percent. Paczkowski, *Revolution and Counterrevolution*, 288.

6. *Washington Post*, October 16, 1986. See also Gregory F. Domber, *Empowering Revolution: America, Poland, and the End of the Cold War* (Chapel Hill: University of North Carolina Press, 2014), 167.

7. Peter Raina, *Wizyty apostolskie Jana Pawła II w Polsce: Rozmowy przygotowawcze Watykan–PRL–Episkopat* (Warsaw: Książka Polska, 1997), 223.

8. Raina, *Wizyty apostolskie*, 226–28.

9. This issue was discussed at length in the meeting of the Joint Commission of September 23, 1986. See Raina, *Wizyty apostolskie*, 237–42.

10. Raina, *Wizyty apostolskie*, 253–54.

11. Raina, *Wizyty apostolskie*, 242, 262–63.

12. This issue regarding security forces came up a number of times in the negotiations; see Raina, *Wizyty apostolskie*, 253, 272, 277, 289.

13. Raina, *Wizyty apostolskie*, 241, 265.

14. Raina, *Wizyty apostolskie*, 245, 246. The problem of Father Jankowski came up a number of times during negotiations (239, 253, 254, 273).

15. Raina, *Wizyty apostolskie*, 251–53.

16. Raina, *Wizyty apostolskie*, 253–54.

17. Raina, *Wizyty apostolskie*, 241.

18. Raina, *Wizyty apostolskie*, 251–52.

19. Raina, *Wizyty apostolskie*, 223–24.

20. Raina, *Wizyty apostolskie*, 227, 261.

21. Raina, *Wizyty apostolskie*, 264.

22. Archbishop Dąbrowski presented these arguments for Gdańsk most fully at the meeting of the Joint Commission on September 23, 1986; see Raina, *Wizyty apostolskie*, 238–40. The case for Gdańsk was also made in a letter from Gdańsk's Bishop Tadeusz Gocłowski to John Paul II on February 22, 1986, and a letter from Gocłowski to Archbishop Dąbrowski (Secretary of the episcopate) on September 1, 1986 (229–30, 236–37, respectively).

23. Raina, *Wizyty apostolskie*, 258. Łopatka shared this information with Archbishop

Dąbrowski at their meeting in the wake of Jaruzelski's visit to Rome (Raina misdates the document as from January 1, though given its references to the January 13 meeting, the meeting took place later in January). Jaruzelski's meeting with John Paul, his first official visit to the West since he declared martial law in 1981, lasted seventy minutes, more than twice as long as is customary in papal meetings with world leaders. *New York Times,* January 14, 1987.

24. See Raina, *Wizyty apostolskie,* 237, 239, 240, 266.

25. Raina, *Wizyty apostolskie,* 262–63.

26. Raina, *Wizyty apostolskie,* 273.

27. For the text of the roundtable, see *Tygodnik Mazowsze,* no. 213, May 27, 1987.

28. John Paul would in fact both meet with Wałęsa and visit Popiełuszko's grave.

29. For example, an article in *Tygodnik Mazowsze,* no. 215, June 17, 1987, that assessed the pilgrimage noted the fear that John Paul would be coming to Poland to visit "the grave of Solidarity."

30. For the text of Solidarity's letter to the pope, see *Tygodnik Mazowsze,* no. 214, June 3, 1987. Subsequent quotes, in translation, come from this source.

31. For the text of the statement, see *Tygodnik Mazowsze,* no. 214, June 3, 1987. Subsequent quotations, in translation, are from this source.

32. For the welcoming speeches of Jaruzelski and Glemp, see *Trybuna Ludu,* June 9, 1987; and *Tygodnik Powszechny,* June 14, 1987.

33. For John Paul's speech at the airport upon arrival, see Jan Paweł II, *Pielgrzymki do Ojczyzny 1979–1983–1987–1991–1995–1997–1999–2002: Przemówienia homilie* (Kraków: Znak, 2005), 371–72.

34. For Jaruzelski's speech at the Royal Castle, see *Trybuna Ludu,* June 9, 1987; and *Tygodnik Powszechny,* June 14, 1987. Subsequent quotations, in translation, are from these sources.

35. *Washington Post,* June 9, 1987.

36. For John Paul's speech at the Royal Castle, see Jan Paweł II, *Pielgrzymki do Ojczyzny,* 382–86. Subsequent quotations, in translation, are from this source.

37. *New York Times,* June 9, 1987.

38. For example, the preamble to the Universal Declaration of Human Rights opens as follows: "Whereas recognition of the inherent dignity and of the equal and inalienable rights of all members of the human family is the foundation of freedom, justice and peace in the world . . . THE GENERAL ASSEMBLY proclaims THIS . . . as a common standard of achievement for all peoples and all nations." "Universal Declaration of Human Rights," United Nations, http://www.un.org/en/universal-declaration-human-rights/.

39. For John Paul's homily opening the Eucharistic Congress, see Jan Paweł II, *Pielgrzymki do Ojczyzny,* 387–91.

40. For John Paul's speech at KUL, see Jan Paweł II, *Pielgrzymki do Ojczyzny,* 394–402. Subsequent quotations in the main text, in translation, are from this source.

41. This recognition by John Paul that the West had problems too begins to emerge during the 1987 pilgrimage and becomes full blown during the 1991 visit.

42. "III. Pielgrzymka Jana Pawła II w Polsce—ocena wstępna," in IPN BU 0296/215/2, F. 290–310; *New York Times,* June 10, 1987. See also *Washington Post,* June 10, 1987, for a nearly identical estimate of crowd size.

43. *Washington Post*, June 10, 1987.

44. For the text of John Paul's homily at Lublin, see Jan Paweł II, *Pielgrzymki do Ojczyzny*, 410–16.

45. Although the *Washington Post* of June 10, 1987, noted that the mention of Popiełuszko elicited only "a ripple of restrained applause" among the crowd, the applause did last for a full seventeen seconds, on the long side in terms of applause during papal speeches.

46. Raina, *Wizyty apostolskie*, 283; *New York Times*, June 7, 1987.

47. *Washington Post*, June 11, 1987. Vatican estimates were as high as 2 million, according to the *New York Times* of June 11, 1987. Local police put the number at 650,000. "III. Pielgrzymka Jana Pawła w Polsce," in IPN, BU 0296/215/2, F. 290–310.

48. *New York Times*, June 11, 1987.

49. For John Paul's homily at Tarnów, see Jan Paweł II, *Pielgrzymki do Ojczyzny*, 420–28. Translated quotations in subsequent paragraphs are from this source.

50. The government dragged out negotiations with the Church over the foundation, demanding that some of the funds go to state-run industry ancillary to agriculture, that receipt of Western aid be tied to the lifting of Western sanctions against Poland, that the foundation's revenues be taxed, and that other conditions meant to prevent the successful realization of the program be satisfied. See Józef Baran, "Fundacja Rolnicza Episkopatu Polski," in *Encycklopedia Solidarnośći*, http://www.encysol.pl/wiki/Fundacja_Rolnicza_Episkopatu_Polski.

51. For John Paul's homily at the vespers service, see Jan Paweł II, *Pielgrzymki do Ojczyzny*, 429–33. The translated quote that follows is from this source.

52. "III. Pielgrzymka Jana Pawła II w Polsce," in IPN BU 0296/215/2, F. 290–310.

53. The police put the estimate at seven hundred thousand. "III. Pielgrzymka Jana Pawła II w Polsce," in IPN BU 0296/215/2, F. 290–310. The *Washington Post* of June 11, 1987, estimated less than a million, while the *New York Times* of June 11, 1987, offered the figure of a "million and a half." These estimates are a good example of the wide range found in estimating crowd size. Still, even the low estimate of seven hundred thousand is quite a crowd.

54. "III. Pielgrzymka Jana Pawła II w Polsce," in IPN, BU 0296/215/2, F. 290–310.

55. For descriptions of the event at the Commons by the security services and the Western media, see "III Pielgrzymka Jana Pawła w Polsce," in IPN BU 0296/215/2, F. 290–310, for the former, and *New York Times*, June 11, 1987, for the latter.

56. For John Paul's homily at Kraków's Commons, see Jan Paweł II, *Pielgrzymki do Ojczyzny*, 434–39. Subsequent quotes, in translation, are from this source.

57. In fact, the prayer was of more recent provenance, and it became especially popular across Poland during the time of Solidarity. See Jan Okoń, "'*Modlitwa za Ojczyznę* ks. Piotra Skargi'—w poszukiwaniu autora i gatunku," *Acta Universitatis Lodziensis, Folia Litteraria Polonica* 3, no. 21 (2013): 19–42, for an article-length study of this prayer and its ambiguous origins; see also Jan Okoń, "Piotr Skarga w nauczaniu Jana Pawła II w jego podróżach do ojczyzny," *Ruch literacki* 53, no. 6 [315] (2012): 711–30.

58. For John Paul's homily at Wawel Cathedral, see Jan Paweł II, *Pielgrzymki do Ojczyzny*, 440–43.

59. Ruthenian lands are the western parts of the medieval state of Kievan Rus', comprising much of present-day Ukraine and Belarus.

60. Saint Kazimierz (Kazimieras in Lithuanian) (ca. 1458–1484) was a member of the ruling Jagiellonian family and known for his piety and charity.

61. For John Paul's speech at the window of the archbishop's residence in Kraków, see Jan Paweł II, *Pielgrzymki do Ojczyzny*, 444–49. Quotes, in translation, in subsequent paragraphs are from this source.

62. "III. Pielgrzymka Jana Pawła II w Polsce," in IPN BU 0296/215/2, F. 290–310.

63. For the text of John Paul's homily at Szczecin, see Jan Paweł II, *Pielgrzymki do Ojczyzny*, 450–58. Subsequent quotes, in translation, are from this source.

64. *Washington Post*, June 12, 1987.

65. The police put the crowd at "around 200,000" and the Church, at 450,000. "III. Pielgrzymka Jana Pawła II w Polsce," in IPN BU 0296/215/2, F. 290–310. The *Washington Post* of June 12, 1987, estimated "hundreds of thousands."

66. *Washington Post*, June 12, 1987.

67. "III. Pielgrzymka Jana Pawła II w Polsce," in IPN BU 0296/215/2, F. 290–310; *Washington Post*, June 12, 1987.

68. For the text of John Paul's homily to the people of the sea at Gdynia, see Jan Paweł II, *Pielgrzymki do Ojczyzny*, 468–75. Subsequent quotes, in translation, are from this source.

69. *New York Times*, June 12, 13, 1987; *Washington Post*, June 12, 1987. For the Solidarity leader's account, see Lech Wałęsa, *Droga do prawdy: Autobiografia* (Warsaw: Świat Książki, 2008), 241–42.

70. *New York Times*, June 15, 1987.

71. Raina, *Wizyty apostolskie*, 281–82.

72. "III. Pielgrzymka Jana Pawła II w Polsce," in IPN BU 0296/215/2, F. 290–310.

73. For John Paul's homily at Westerplatte, see Jan Paweł II, *Pielgrzymki do Ojczyzny*, 476–84. Subsequent quotations, in translation, are from this source.

74. The Gospel according to Matthew tells the story of a rich young man who asked Jesus Christ what he needed to do in order to gain eternal life, and Jesus told him to obey the commandments. When the young man replied that he already did that, Jesus told him, "Go, sell what you possess and give to the poor, and you will have treasure in heaven; and come, follow me." Not wanting to part with his many possessions, the rich young man went away sorrowful (Matthew 19:16–22). This was one of John Paul's favorite Gospel accounts.

75. For John Paul's homily to the sick at the Marian Basilica, see Jan Paweł II, *Pielgrzymki do Ojczyzny*, 485–89.

76. *New York Times*, June 13, 1987. See also George Weigel, *Witness to Hope: The Biography of Pope John Paul II* (New York: HarperCollins, 2001), 547.

77. For the prominent police presence and preventative measures, see *New York Times*, June 13, 1987; and *Washington Post*, June 13, 1987.

78. *Washington Post*, June 13, 1987.

79. *Washington Post*, June 13, 1987.

80. George Weigel tells the story in his *Witness to Hope*, 544. The altar was designed by Marian Kołodziej, set designer at the Gdańsk Theatre and former prisoner at Auschwitz, and the operation involved hundreds of hours of volunteer labor.

81. The *New York Times* of June 13, 1987, estimated the crowd at "one million," while

the *Washington Post* of June 13, 1987, put it at 750,000, and the police reported it at 700,000. "III. Pielgrzymka Jana Pawła II w Polsce," in IPN BU 0296/215/2, F. 290–310.

82. For John Paul II's homily in Gdańsk, see Jan Paweł II, *Pielgrzymki do Ojczyzny*, 490–98. Subsequent quotations, in translation, are from this source.

83. *New York Times*, June 13, 14, 1987; *Washington Post*, June 13, 1987; "III. Pielgrzymka Jana Pawła II w Polsce," in IPN BU 0296/215/2, F. 290–310.

84. "III. Pielgrzymka Jana Pawła II w Polsce," in IPN, BU 0296/215/2, F. 290–310.

85. These words by John Paul could be taken not only as an admonition to the crowd to avoid violence but also to the state authorities and the police.

86. *Tygodnik Powszechny* noted on June 21, 1987, that eighty thousand had assembled at the venue to await the pope, with others who had been standing along the papal transit route expected to arrive a bit later. For John Paul's Jasna Góra Appeal, see Jan Paweł II, *Pielgrzymki do Ojczyzny*, 499–504, from which come the subsequent quotations, in translation, in the paragraph.

87. Mieczysław Rakowski, *Dzienniki polityczne 1987–1990* (Warsaw: Iskry, 2005), 90–92.

88. *New York Times*, June 14, 1987; *Washington Post*, June 14, 1987.

89. Barcikowski related this account to Rakowski, according to the latter's diary-memoir entry of June 18, 1987. Rakowski, *Dzienniki polityczne 1987–1990*, 91–92.

90. *Washington Post*, June 14, 1987; *New York Times*, June 14, 1987.

91. For John Paul's homily at the Chapel of the Miraculous Image, see Jan Paweł II, *Pielgrzymki do Ojczyzny*, 505–7. Subsequent quotations, in translation, in this paragraph are from this source.

92. For John Paul's farewell speech at Jasna Góra, see Jan Paweł II, *Pielgrzymki do Ojczyzny*, 508–10. Subsequent quotations, in translation, are from this source.

93. The police report claimed a crowd of four hundred thousand. "III. Pielgrzymka Jana Pawła II w Polsce," in IPN, BU 0296/215/2, F. 290–310. *Tygodnik Powszechny* on June 21, 1987, put it at five hundred thousand.

94. "III. Pielgrzymka Jana Pawła II w Polsce," in IPN, BU 0296/215/2, F. 290–310.

95. "III. Pielgrzymka Jana Pawła II w Polsce," in IPN, BU 0296/215/2, F. 290–310.

96. *Trybuna Ludu*, June 9, 1987.

97. For John Paul's speech at Uniontex in Łódź, see Jan Paweł II, *Pielgrzymki do Ojczyzny*, 520–28. Quotations, in translation, in subsequent paragraphs are from this source.

98. "III. Pielgrzymka Jana Pawła II w Polsce," in IPN, BU 0296/215/2, F. 290–310.

99. "III. Pielgrzymka Jana Pawła II w Polsce," in IPN, BU 0296/215/2, F. 290–310. The *Washington Post* on June 14, 1987, put the audience at "more than 1,000," one of the rare cases of a papal event in which the communist count seemed higher than that in the Western press.

100. For John Paul II's speech at Warsaw's Church of the Holy Cross, see Jan Paweł II, *Pielgrzymki do Ojczyzny*, 529–34. Subsequent quotations, in translation, are from this source.

101. This comment and a later one in which John Paul recognized "the special alliance that in recent years was achieved in Poland between the creators of culture and the people of labor" were the two statements in John Paul's speech that drew sustained applause from the audience.

102. This policy was not without controversy. Cardinal Glemp was reportedly not

always happy with the use of churches for lectures and theatrical performances, as well as the presence of nonbelievers in the churches for those events. See *New York Times*, June 15, 1987; and *Washington Post*, June 14, 1987. Paczkowski notes that lay culture with no direct connection to religion began moving into the churches on a rather large scale, with artists and performers having no other venues available to them after the declaration of martial law in December 1981. Paczkowski, *Revolution and Counterrevolution*, 234. Paczkowski provides an example of a difference of opinion between Glemp and the dissident Union of Polish Artists (239).

103. For police reporting and analysis of the event at the Church of the Holy Cross, see "Oceny, komentarze, i wydarzenia związane z wizytą Jana Pawła II w Polsce," in IPN, BU 0296/215/2, F. 255–67; "Wnioski, prognozy i rekomendacje," in IPN, BU 0296/215/2, F. 279–89; and "III. Pielgrzymka Jana Pawła II w Polsce," in IPN, BU 0296/215/2, F. 290–310.

104. "Oceny, komentarze, i wydarzenia," in IPN, BU 0296/215/2, F. 255–67; "III. Pielgrzymka Jana Pawła II w Polsce," in IPN, BU 0296/215/2, F. 290–310. Among the attendees were the novelist Tadeusz Konwicki, the film director Andrzej Wajda, and Catholic intellectual and editor Tadeusz Mazowiecki.

105. "III. Pielgrzymka Jana Pawła II w Polsce," in IPN, BU 0296/215/2, F. 290–310.

106. See the concluding chapter for more on the pope's meeting with Jewish community representatives.

107. "Oceny, komentarze, i wydarzenia," in IPN, BU 0296/215/2, F. 255–67.

108. The *New York Times* of June 16, 1987, put the crowd at five thousand, while the police put it at seven thousand. "III. Pielgrzymka Jana Pawła II w Polsce," in IPN, BU 0296/215/2, F. 290–310.

109. "III. Pielgrzymka Jana Pawła II w Polsce," in IPN, BU 0296/215/2, F. 290–310.

110. *Biuletyn Informacyjny*, no. 172, August 19, 1987; *Tygodnik Mazowsze*, no. 215, June 17, 1987.

111. See chapter 4 for discussion of John Paul's outreach to Eastern Rite Catholics and Ukrainians in 1991, as well as for a discussion of Eastern Rite Catholicism in general.

112. The police put the crowd size at "around 500,000." "III. Pielgrzymka Jana Pawła II w Polsce," in IPN, BU 0296/215/2, F. 290–310. However, given the pattern of low estimates by police, it was likely larger. *Tygodnik Mazowsze*, no. 215, June 17, 1989, gave an estimate of one million, while *Biuletyn Informacyjny*, no. 168, June 24, 1987, reported a crowd of eight hundred thousand.

113. For John Paul's homily on Defilad Plaza, see Jan Paweł II, *Pielgrzymki do Ojczyzny*, 541–46. Subsequent quotations, in translation, are from this source.

114. *Tygodnik Powszechny*, June 21, 1987; *New York Times*, June 15, 1987. The monstrance is the vessel into which the Eucharist, or more specifically the Body of Christ, is placed for special devotional acts and blessings.

115. IPN, BU 0296/215/2, F. 290–310; *New York Times*, June 15, 1987.

116. At issue here are not relations between Poland and Vatican City, which are interstate relations, but rather between Poland and the central leadership of the Catholic Church as a whole.

117. Jan Żaryn, *Kościół, naród, człowiek czyli opowieść optymistyczna o Polakoch w XX wieku* (Warsaw: Instytut Pamięci Narodowej, Wydawnictwo Neriton, 2012), 334–35, 338–39.

118. Żaryn, *Kościół, naród, człowiek*, 332–43, gives significant attention to the hopes and expectations of the various sides with respect to the papal visit.

119. For John Paul's speech to the bishops, see Jan Paweł II, *Pielgrzymki do Ojczyzny*, 547–51. Quotations, in translation, in the main text paragraph are from this source.

120. *Washington Post*, June 23, 1987.

121. *New York Times*, June 16, 1987.

122. For Jaruzelski's and Glemp's speeches, see *Trybuna Ludu*, June 15, 1987. Quotations, in translation, in the main text paragraph are from this source.

123. *New York Times*, June 15, 16, 1987; *Washington Post*, June 15, 1987.

124. For John Paul's farewell speech at Warsaw's airport, see Jan Paweł II, *Pielgrzymki do Ojczyzny*, 552–55. Quotations, in translation, in the main text paragraph are from this source.

125. "III. Pielgrzymka Jana Pawła II w Polsce," in IPN, BU 0296/215/2, F. 290–310,

126. Quoted in *Trybuna Ludu*, June 15, 1987.

127. See *New York Times*, June 15, 1987, for an analysis of the visit along these lines.

128. Rakowski, *Dzienniki polityczne 1987–1990*, 90.

129. Rakowski's diary-memoir entries from June 15 through 18 and from June 22 all note either his own assessment or that of other party members and groups, with the visit regarded as a clear victory for the pope over Jaruzelski. Rakowski, *Dzienniki polityczne 1987–1990*, 89–92.

130. *Tygodnik Mazowsze*, no. 215, June 17, 1987.

131. *Tygodnik Mazowsze*, no. 216, July 1, 1987.

132. *KOS*, no. 120–21, June 17, 1987, reprinted in *Biuletyn Informacyjny*, no. 173, September 2, 1987.

133. Warszawski sees this last teaching as an indictment of classical liberalism, an observation that would come up during John Paul's 1991 visit to a postcommunist Poland.

134. *Tygodnik Mazowsze*, no. 215, June 17, 1987.

135. Outreach to religious and ethnic minorities would be a major part of the next papal pilgrimage to Poland, in June 1991, as we shall see.

136. In their biography of John Paul II, Bernstein and Politi even give their chapter on John Paul after 1989 the title "The Angry Pope." Carl Bernstein and Marco Politi, *His Holiness: John Paul II and the Hidden History of Our Time* (New York: Doubleday, 1996).

137. "Fragmenty niektórych wystąpień Jana Pawła II," in IPN BU 0296/215/2, F. 312–15.

Chapter 4. Prophet

1. Coverage of this period is drawn especially from Joseph Rothschild, *Return to Diversity: A Political History of East Central Europe since World War II* (New York: Oxford University Press, 1993), 181–87, 212–16; and Andrzej Paczkowski, *Revolution and Counterrevolution in Poland, 1980–1989: Solidarity, Martial Law, and the End of Communism in Europe* (Rochester, NY: University of Rochester Press, 2015), 283–321.

2. The elections were semidemocratic in that 65 percent of the seats in the lower house were guaranteed to the Communist Party and its allies and only 35 percent were open to competition from Solidarity.

3. Robert Alvis, *White Eagle, Black Madonna: One Thousand Years of the Polish Catholic Tradition* (New York: Fordham University Press, 2016), 238. Indeed, two pro-Solidarity

priests were murdered by "unknown perpetrators" shortly before the Round Table Talks got under way; see Paczkowski, *Revolution and Counterrevolution*, 295.

4. Alvis, *White Eagle, Black Madonna*, 253.

5. For example, in a 1990 survey, 90 percent of Poles regarded the Catholic Church as the most respected institution in Polish public life; that proportion had slipped to 58 percent by 1992. Alvis, *White Eagle, Black Madonna*, 255.

6. Jan Paweł II, *Pielgrzymki do Ojczyzny 1979–1983–1987–1991–1995–1997–1999–2002: Przemówienia homilie* (Kraków: Znak, 2005), 600, 768–70.

7. Examples below are drawn from the pope's homilies and speeches during his 1991 visit; all of these are from Jan Paweł II, *Pielgrzymki do Ojczyzny*; the page number will be given in parentheses in the main text.

8. Jane L. Curry surveyed and analyzed polling data from Poland during the months leading up to the papal visit of 1991. A poll by the Center for Public Opinion Research from March 1991 reported that 58 percent of Poles thought the Catholic Church was acting in the public interest, placing the Church four points behind the Polish army and four points ahead of Polish television. (In November 1990, the Church had drawn a positive rating from 90 percent of Poles.) The same poll reported that 30 percent thought the Church was acting against the public interest, up from 10 percent a year earlier. The poll also reported divisions within Polish society over abortion, religious education, and the media. Other polls reported that 67 percent thought the Church had too much influence over the government. See Jane L. Curry, "Are the Church and Public Opinion at Variance?" *Report on Eastern Europe* 2, no. 28 (July 12, 1991): 14–18; and Jan B. de Weydenthal, "Catholic Bishops Call for Cooperation between Church and State," *Report on Eastern Europe* 2, no. 20 (May 17, 1991): 15–17.

9. *Report on Eastern Europe* 2, no. 20 (May 17, 1991), 34; 2, no. 21 (May 24, 1991): 40; Curry, "Are the Church and Public Opinion at Variance?," 17–18; *New York Times*, May 16, 1991.

10. For example, in April 1990 the Ministry of Health issued regulations that limited access to abortions, while the Ministry of Education decided that religious education would be a part of the school curriculum beginning with the 1990–1991 academic year. Hanna Jankowska, "Abortion, Church and Politics in Poland," *Feminist Review* 39, no. 1 (1991): 177; Curry, "Are the Church and Public Opinion at Variance?," 16.

11. For the homily at Płock, see Jan Paweł II, *Pielgrzymki do Ojczyzny*, 696–702.

12. George Weigel, *Witness to Hope: The Biography of Pope John Paul II* (New York: HarperCollins, 2001), 642, 643–44.

13. Jonathan Kwitny, *Man of the Century: The Life and Times of Pope John Paul II* (New York: Henry Holt, 1997), 626.

14. Quoted in Kwitny, *Man of the Century*, 627.

15. Carl Bernstein and Marco Politi, *His Holiness: John Paul II and the Hidden History of Our Time* (New York: Doubleday, 1996), 487, 493.

16. For the debate over abortion in Poland, see Curry, "Are the Church and Public Opinion at Variance?"; Mirella W. Eberts, "The Roman Catholic Church and Democracy in Poland," *Europe-Asia Studies* 50, no. 5 (July 1998): 817–42, esp. 823–26; Małgorzata Fuszara, "Legal Regulation of Abortion in Poland," *Signs* 17, no. 1 (1991): 117–28; Jankowska, "Abortion, Church and Politics in Poland"; Andrzej Kulczycki,

"Abortion Policy in Postcommunist Europe: The Conflict in Poland," *Population and Development Review* 21, no. 3 (1995): 471–505; and De Weydenthal, "Catholic Bishops Call for Cooperation," 15–17.

17. Marek Okolski, "Abortion and Contraception in Poland," *Studies in Family Planning* 14, no. 11 (1983): 266–73; Kulczycki, "Abortion Policy," 477–79.

18. Kulczycki, "Abortion Policy," 483.

19. Curry, "Are the Church and Public Opinion at Variance?," 15; *Report on Eastern Europe* 2, no. 22 (May 31, 1991): 41.

20. Curry, "Are the Church and Public Opinion at Variance?," 16; *New York Times*, May 9, 1991. For the bishops' appeal, see *Tygodnik Powszechny*, May 12, 1991.

21. *Report on Eastern Europe* 2, no. 21 (May 24, 1991): 41. For more on polling data, see Curry, "Are the Church and Public Opinion at Variance?," 15.

22. A note of caution about the use of such data in the abortion debate. Taking the results of the mid-May poll, groups favoring abortion rights typically present such results as "Only Nineteen Percent of the Population Supports a Ban on Abortion" or "Eighty Percent of Respondents Favor Legal Abortion"; antiabortion groups present it as "Sixty-Eight Percent of Respondents Want Restrictions on Access to Abortion" or "Overwhelming Majority of the Population Opposes Abortion on Demand." This approach also reflects the situation we find in debates over abortion in the United States, where the debate is driven by uncompromising idealists at the "prochoice" and "prolife" extremes, while a large proportion of the population is unwilling to embrace either an absolute ban on abortion or unfettered access. This middle group is extremely diverse; it could contain the person who would ban abortion for everything but rape and incest, as well as the person who would permit it for everything but sex selection. Activists on both extremes try to spin this middle group to serve their own purposes, so an accurate picture of social attitudes toward abortion needs data that differentiate the various currents within that middle group. Especially critical in this context is the wording of survey questions and how they are asked. As Kulczycki writes, "Opinion polls that probe public attitudes about abortion are notoriously sensitive to the phrasing of question and their field execution." Kulczycki, "Abortion Policy," 482.

23. *Tygodnik Powszechny*, October 14, 1990, quoted in Kulczycki, "Abortion Policy," 491.

24. Jankowska, "Abortion, Church and Politics in Poland," 178; *New York Times*, February 6, 1991.

25. The external pressure on Poland regarding the abortion issue was not only coming from the Vatican. In early May, deputies from the European Parliament appealed to the Polish Parliament to reject the antiabortion bill; see *New York Times*, May 9, 1991. A similar intervention had been made by European parliamentarians in 1990; see Kulczycki, "Abortion Policy," 489.

26. Kulczycki, "Abortion Policy," 484; Curry, "Are the Church and Public Opinion at Variance?," 15; *Report on Eastern Europe* 2, no. 21 (May 24, 1991): 41; and 2, no. 22 (May 31, 1991): 32.

27. Kulczycki, "Abortion Policy," 482. One poll taken on the eve of the Sejm debate found 76 percent of respondents favoring a national referendum. *Report on Eastern Europe* 2, no. 21 (May 24, 1991): 41.

28. For John Paul's homily at Kielce, see Jan Paweł II, *Pielgrzymki do Ojczyzny*, 613–19. Subsequent quotations, in translation, are from this source. The attendance figure is from the *Washington Post*, June 4, 1991.

29. For John Paul's homily at Radom, see Jan Paweł II, *Pielgrzymki do Ojczyzny*, 620–26. Subsequent quotations, in translation, are from this source.

30. The attendance figure of 250,000 is from the *Washington Post*, June 5, 1991.

31. This is likely a reference to the 1980 film *The Silent Scream*, which depicts graphically the abortion of an eleven-week-old fetus. It is available online at www.silentscream.org.

32. As archbishop of Kraków, the future pope was a leading supporter of such initiatives in his diocese and set up the first shelters for unmarried pregnant women in need in Poland in the 1970s. Kulczycki, "Abortion Policy," 479.

33. For John Paul's speech at the Royal Castle, see Jan Paweł II, *Pielgrzymki do Ojczyzny*, 713–16. The subsequent translated quotation is from this source.

34. For John Paul's speech to antiabortion parliamentarians, see Jan Paweł II, *Pielgrzymki do Ojczyzny*, 720–21.

35. Bobbio was "Italy's leading legal and political philosopher, and one of the most authoritative figures in his country's politics," according to his obituary in *The Guardian* on January 13, 2004. A liberal socialist committed to the twin ideals of civil liberties and social and economic justice, Bobbio, a professed agnostic, had spoken out against abortion. *Zenit*, January 14, 2004, http://www.zenit.org/article-9126?l=english.

36. John Paul quite prominently implicated men in the abortion question in a number of his official writings. See John Paul II, *Crossing the Threshold of Hope* (New York: Knopf, 1994), 206; his encyclical *Evangelium vitae* (March 25, 1995), 59; his apostolic letter *Mulieres dignitatem* (August 15, 1988) (14); and his "Letter to Women" (June 6, 1995), 5.

37. For John Paul's Angelus reflection, see Jan Paweł II, *Pielgrzymki do Ojczyzny*, 757–59. The subsequent translated quotation is from this source.

38. For John Paul's speech to the Conference of the Episcopate of Poland, see Jan Paweł II, *Pielgrzymki do Ojczyzny*, 760–67.

39. Saint Paul instructs Timothy to preach, correct, rebuke, and encourage "in season and out of season" (2 Timothy 4:2, NIV).

40. The term for "noble minded" that John Paul used was *szlachetny*.

41. For the question of religious instruction in public schools, see Curry, "Are the Church and Public Opinion at Variance?," 16; De Weydenthal, "Catholic Bishops," 16; and Eberts, "Roman Catholic Church and Democracy," 821–23. De Weydenthal cites a nationwide public opinion survey of May 1990 that showed approximately 60 percent of Poles favoring religious education in public schools, with 27 percent opposed to it; that proportion continued, as shown in a later poll of March 1991. Curry cites a March 1991 poll that showed 46 percent of Poles supporting optional religious education and an additional 28 percent favoring compulsory religious education.

42. For John Paul's speech in Włocławek, see Jan Paweł II, *Pielgrzymki do Ojczyzny*, 681–87. Subsequent quotations, in translation, are from this source.

43. For issues involving the media, see Curry, "Are the Church and Public Opinion at Variance?," 16; De Weydenthal, "Catholic Bishops," 17; and *Report on Eastern Europe* 2, no. 19 (May 10, 1991): 29.

44. *Report on Eastern Europe* 2, no. 19 (May 10, 1991): 29.

45. For John Paul's homilies in Olsztyn, see Jan Paweł II, *Pielgrzymki do Ojczyzny*, 665–80. Subsequent quotations, in translation, are from this source.

46. See De Weydenthal, "Catholic Bishops," 15–16; and *Report on Eastern Europe* 2, no. 19 (May 10, 1991): 29.

47. Eberts, "Roman Catholic Church and Democracy," 826.

48. For example, a poll cited in late February 1991 by the newspaper *Gazeta Wybórcza* reported that 67 percent of those polled thought the Church had too much influence over the government. De Weydenthal, "Catholic Bishops," 17.

49. For John Paul's homily in Lubaczów, see Jan Paweł II, *Pielgrzymki do Ojczyzny*, 595–603.

50. For John Paul's homily at Olsztyn, see Jan Paweł II, *Pielgrzymki do Ojczyzny*, 674–80. The final quotation in the main text paragraph is from this source.

51. See *Gaudium et spes*, available at http://www.vatican.va/archive/hist_councils/ii_vatican_council/documents/vat-ii_const_19651207_gaudium-et-spes_en.html.

52. Jan Paweł II, *Pielgrzymki do Ojczyzny*, 732.

53. For John Paul's homily at Kielce, see Jan Paweł II, *Pielgrzymki do Ojczyzny*, 613–19. Subsequent quotations, in translation, are from this source.

54. For John Paul's homily at Łomża, see Jan Paweł II, *Pielgrzymki do Ojczyzny*, 628–34.

55. For John Paul's homily at Włocławek, see Jan Paweł II, *Pielgrzymki do Ojczyzny*, 688–95.

56. From John Paul's homily at Kielce on June 3, Jan Paweł II, *Pielgrzymki do Ojczyzny*, 616.

57. From John Paul's homily at Łomża on June 4, Jan Paweł II, *Pielgrzymki do Ojczyzny*, 631.

58. For instance, John Paul's address to teachers and students on June 6 in Włocławek contained a beautiful discussion of the practice of mentoring young people: "Who among us has not had in their life and not recalled with gratitude some such person—a pastor, teacher, professor, or friend—who knew how to uncover for us a new world of value and arouse a lasting enthusiasm for it, and even give a whole direction to life?" Jan Paweł II, *Pielgrzymki do Ojczyzny*, 684.

59. For information on Poland's economy at this time, see Jan B. de Weydenthal, "The First Hundred Days of Walesa's Presidency," *Report on Eastern Europe* 2, no. 14 (April 5, 1991): 9–12; *The Economist*, May 25, June 15, 1991; and weekly news reports from *Report on Eastern Europe* 2, nos. 20–22 (May 17, May 24, and May 31, 1991).

60. After the end of mass in Białystok on June 5, the pope spoke of the increasing degradation of the natural environment and how it had reached "an alarming degree" in Poland. He called nature a common good of humanity that people ought to care for with a spirit of responsibility and respect. Jan Paweł II, *Pielgrzymki do Ojczyzny*, 649. On June 7, John Paul spoke at a prison in Płock and supported efforts to make prisons more humane; he said that incarceration was punishment enough and that prisoners should be spared assaults on their health, their family ties, and their feelings of personal dignity. For John Paul's speech to prisoners at Płock, see Jan Paweł II, *Pielgrzymki do Ojczyzny*, 703–6.

61. For John Paul's homily at Lubaczów, see Jan Paweł II, *Pielgrzymki do Ojczyzny*, 595–603. Subsequent quotations, in translation, are from this source.

62. For John Paul's speech at Łomża, see Jan Paweł II, *Pielgrzymki do Ojczyzny*, 639–41. The subsequent quotation, in translation, is from this source.

63. Except for the crowd at his concluding mass in Warsaw on June 9, the audience at the pope's meeting with representatives of the world of culture was the most boisterous of the entire visit. For John Paul's speech at the National Theatre, see Jan Paweł II, *Pielgrzymki do Ojczyzny*, 734–40. Subsequent translated quotations in the main text paragraph are from this source.

64. For John Paul's homily at Białystok, see Jan Paweł II, *Pielgrzymki do Ojczyzny*, 642–50. Subsequent quotes, in translation, are from this source. John Paul suggested that the woman he was beatifying at that day's mass, Mother Bolesława Lament, was a model of sensitivity toward those living in poverty and other forms of neglect and marginalization. Mother Lament was the founder of an order of sisters who set up custodial schools in eastern Poland and beyond and who herself experienced poverty and suffering, and the pope remarked on the special sensitivity she had shown toward human poverty. She was especially moved by the plight of "neglected people in society, people pushed to the so-called margins of life and even to the criminal world" (644).

65. For John Paul's homily at Płock, see Jan Paweł II, *Pielgrzymki do Ojczyzny*, 696–702. Subsequent quotations, in translation, are from this source.

66. For John Paul's speech at the Royal Castle, see Jan Paweł II, *Pielgrzymki do Ojczyzny*, 713–16. The subsequent translated quotation is from this source.

67. This example, as well as the terms "freedom of indifference" and "freedom for excellence" for these two understandings of freedom, are found in the work of the Belgian theologian Servais Pinckaers, O.P., especially *The Sources of Christian Ethics* (Washington, DC: Catholic University of America Press, 1995).

68. Among John Paul's most extensive discussions of freedom were his homily at mass in Płock on June 7 and his homily at the mass beatifying Blessed Father Rafał Chyliński in Warsaw on June 9. He also discussed the issue during two events connected with Poland's Constitution of May 3, 1791—a speech to government representatives on June 8 at the Royal Castle in Warsaw, as well as a thanksgiving service at the Cathedral of Saint John the Baptist in Warsaw that same day. See Jan Paweł II, *Pielgrzymki do Ojczyzny*, 696–702, 750–56, 713–16, 717–19, respectively.

69. Jan Paweł II, *Pielgrzymki do Ojczyzny*, 752–53. That gifts and tasks go together is a standard concept in Catholicism and one for which John Paul had a particular fondness.

70. In this connection, John Paul noted the infamous Confederation of Targowica of 1792, when a number of Polish noblemen allied with Russia in order to defend their traditional privileges against those Polish patriots who sought to save Poland from destruction through a program of constitutional reform. The episode ended up facilitating the ultimate destruction of Poland in 1795.

71. This mass had the distinction of having the liveliest audience of any of the papal masses or events of the 1991 visit. John Paul was interrupted nearly thirty times by applause, including a round lasting more than a minute when he renewed his 1979 call for the Holy Spirit to come down and renew the face of Poland.

72. For John Paul's homily at the beatification mass for Father Chyliński, see Jan Paweł II, *Pielgrzymki do Ojczyzny*, 750–56.

73. Norman Davies, *God's Playground: A History of Poland*, vol. 1, *The Origins to 1795* (New York: Columbia University Press, 1982), 535.

74. For John Paul's speech at the Royal Castle, see Jan Paweł II, *Pielgrzymki do Ojczyzny*, 713–16.

75. For John Paul's speech at the thanksgiving service at the cathedral, see Jan Paweł II, *Pielgrzymki do Ojczyzny*, 717–19.

76. While superficially it might seem that John Paul is doing with the Constitution of May 3, 1791, what many conservative Protestant American Christians do with America's foundational documents, that is, reading religion into them in anachronistic ways, the May 3 Constitution, unlike America's founding documents, did in fact refer to God as Trinity, that is Father, Son, and Holy Spirit, the Son being Jesus Christ. Jesus gets no official mention by America's founders.

77. Eastern Rite Catholics, also called Greek Catholics, Byzantine Catholics, and Uniates, constitute a hybrid between Eastern and Western Christianity. Essentially, they are Christians who, formerly Orthodox, joined the Catholic Church while retaining many of the features of Eastern Orthodox Christianity. For example, their liturgy follows Eastern rather than Roman procedures, hence the name Eastern Rite, as distinct from the Roman Rite, which is followed by the overwhelming majority of Catholics. They maintain from the Eastern tradition the centrality of icons in worship, the sacrament of Chrismation, parts of the Eastern Church calendar, and in many places a married clergy; in line with Western Christianity, they regard the pope as head of the Church and recite the Nicene Creed in its Western version. Eastern Rite Christians are commonly found in lands where Orthodox people had come under the rule of a Roman Catholic power, which presented them with the opportunity to join the Catholic Church while retaining much of the Eastern Christian tradition. Most Eastern Rite Catholics originated in areas taken over by the Polish-Lithuanian Commonwealth or the Austrian Empire during the early modern period.

78. For coverage of the relationship between the Roman Catholic Church and Eastern Christians in Poland and/or the Soviet Union during the pontificate of John Paul II, see Joseph Loya, "Interchurch Relations in Post-Perestroika Eastern Europe: A Short History of an Ecumenical Meltdown," *Religion in Eastern Europe* 14, no. 1 (1994): 1–17; Serge Keleher, "Out of the Catacombs: The Greek-Catholic Church in Ukraine," *Religion in Communist Lands* 19, no. 3–4 (1991): 251–63; and Weigel, *Witness to Hope*, 208, 298, 369–70, 399, 571–76, 603–4, 607–8, 638–41.

79. Loya, "Interchurch Relations," 2.

80. For a discussion of this problem, see Chris Hann, "Postsocialist Nationalism: Rediscovering the Past in Southeast Poland," *Slavic Review* 57, no. 4 (1998): 840–63; and Weigel, *Witness to Hope*, 643.

81. Jan B. de Weydenthal, "The Pope Appeals in Poland for a Christian Europe," *Report on Eastern Europe* 2, no. 25 (June 21, 1991): 20. Kievan Rus' was a medieval state that both Russians and Ukrainians viewed as a forerunner of their modern statehood.

82. One scholar cites estimates of between 60,000 to 90,000 Polish victims and between 15,000 and 30,000 Ukrainian victims in these massacres. Serhii Plokhy, *The Gates of Europe: A History of Ukraine* (New York: Basic Books, 2015), 281. Another notes that from 1943 to 1947, 50,000 to 100,000 Poles and Ukrainians were murdered and

1.5 million forced to leave their homes in these operations. See Timothy Snyder, "'To Resolve the Ukrainian Problem Once and for All': The Ethnic Cleansing of Ukrainians in Poland, 1943–1947," *Journal of Cold War Studies* 1, no. 2 (1999): 87.

83. Hahn, "Postsocialist Nationalism," 852.

84. *New York Times*, June 3, 1991.

85. For this term, see, for example, John Paul's encyclical letter of 1987, *Redemptoris mater*, 34, or his apostolic letter of 1988, *Euntes in mundum*, 12.

86. See, for example, see the pope's words at an Eastern Rite Ukrainian liturgy at Saint Peter's in Rome on July 10, 1988, quoted in Weigel, *Witness to Hope*, 576.

87. Plokhy, *Gates of Europe*, 287.

88. Although the term "Uniate" has traditionally been used by Roman Catholic, Eastern Rite, and Orthodox Christians to describe Eastern Rite Christianity, today it is generally regarded as derogatory by Eastern Rite Christians.

89. Weigel, *Witness to Hope*, 608.

90. The Soviet Union at this time was home to approximately ten million Roman Rite Catholics. De Weydenthal, "Pope Appeals," 19.

91. *New York Times*, June 3, 6, 1991.

92. For John Paul's homily at Rzeszów, see Jan Paweł II, *Pielgrzymki do Ojczyzny*, 576–79. Subsequent translated quotations in the paragraph are from this source.

93. For John Paul's speech to the Eastern Rite Catholics at Przemyśl, see Jan Paweł II, *Pielgrzymki do Ojczyzny*, 586–91; translated quotations that follow are from this source. The Church of the Sacred Heart of Jesus in Przemyśl had at one time belonged to the Jesuits.

94. Myroslav Lubachivsky (1914–2000), a Ukrainian Eastern Rite priest in interwar Poland who was studying abroad when World War II started, immigrated to the United States and served the Ukrainian community there as well as the Vatican for several decades as leader of Ukrainian Eastern Rite Catholics. Pope John Paul II made him archbishop in 1979 and cardinal in 1984. Lubachivsky returned to Ukraine in March 1991 after fifty-three years of exile. See Michael Bourdeaux's obituary for him in *The Guardian*, January 29, 2001.

95. The pope's reference was to the original plan to give the Carmelite church to the Greek Catholics for five years while a new cathedral was built for them, a plan thwarted by the protests of local Polish nationalists.

96. *New York Times*, June 3, 1991.

97. For John Paul's homily in Białystok, see Jan Paweł II, *Pielgrzymki do Ojczyzny*, 642–50.

98. For John Paul's address at the ecumenical service at the Cathedral of Saint Nicholas, see Jan Paweł II, *Pielgrzymki do Ojczyzny*, 654–58. Subsequent quotations, in translation, are from this source.

99. For John Paul's speech at the bishops' meeting in Warsaw, see Jan Paweł II, *Pielgrzymki do Ojczyzny*, 760–67. Subsequent quotations, in translation, are from this source.

100. What John Paul meant by "evangelization" in this context was the attempt to minister to people who were nominally Christian or who were members of nations or ethnic groups that were traditionally Christian but who had either lost touch with the Christian faith or had their ties to it radically diminished while living for decades under the atheistic Soviet regime.

101. Jan Paweł II, *Pielgrzymki do Ojczyzny*, 568.

102. Jan Paweł II, *Pielgrzymki do Ojczyzny*, 766. Because of John Paul's strong ecumenical sensitivities, the pope would not accept an invitation to visit the Soviet Union, or Russia, unless it was endorsed by the leadership of the Russian Orthodox Church. For this reason, he ultimately never was able to visit Russia, one of the pope's saddest regrets of his pontificate.

103. See De Weydenthal, "Pope Appeals," 19.

104. For John Paul's speech to pilgrims from Lithuania at Łomża, see Jan Paweł II, *Pielgrzymki do Ojczyzny*, 635–38. Subsequent quotations, in translation, are from this source.

105. *New York Times*, June 6, 1991.

106. For John Paul's speech at the ecumenical service, see Jan Paweł II, *Pielgrzymki do Ojczyzny*, 745–49. The subsequent translated quote is from this source.

107. Jan Paweł II, *Pielgrzymki do Ojczyzny*, 618–19. Subsequent quotations, in translation, are from this source.

108. For John Paul's homily at the beatification mass for Father Chyliński, see Jan Paweł II, *Pielgrzymki do Ojczyzny*, 750–56. Subsequent translated quotes are from this source.

109. For John Paul's speech to the diplomatic corps, see Jan Paweł II, *Pielgrzymki do Ojczyzny*, 728–33.

110. For John Paul's homily at Olsztyn, see Jan Paweł II, *Pielgrzymki do Ojczyzny*, 665–73.

111. This phenomenon is known as "practical atheism." Jan Paweł II, *Pielgrzymki do Ojczyzny*, 755–56.

112. For John Paul's homily at Włocławek, see Jan Paweł II, *Pielgrzymki do Ojczyzny*, 688–95. Subsequent quotations, in translation, are from this source.

113. John Paul, in his final two days in the country, reiterated the Polish contribution to Europe in recent times. In addressing the Polish government on June 8, he spoke of the Battle of Warsaw of August 1920, when Polish forces won a decisive victory against Soviet Russia, one that put the Red Army in retreat and spared Central Europe a greater communist incursion. He also spoke of the Polish struggle to defend society against the totalitarian communist system after World War II, culminating in the Solidarity movement of the 1980s. See Jan Paweł II, *Pielgrzymki do Ojczyzny*, 714–15. At his airport farewell on June 9, he noted that "Poles set their hand to liberating Europe from two cruel systems of inhuman totalitarianism." For John Paul's farewell speech at Warsaw's airport, see Jan Paweł II, *Pielgrzymki do Ojczyzny*, 768–70.

114. From the time of his election, John Paul had regarded the election of a Slavic pope as providential, part of God's plan for the liberation of Eastern Europe from communism and the reintegration of a Christianity and a Europe that had been divided into East and West.

115. Jan Paweł II, *Pielgrzymki do Ojczyzny*, 732.

116. Jan Paweł II, *Pielgrzymki do Ojczyzny*, 732.

117. Jan Paweł II, *Pielgrzymki do Ojczyzny*, 761. John Paul issued the call for a synod of Europe's bishops on April 22, while visiting Velehrad in the Czech region of Moravia. Velehrad was symbolically important to the pope's efforts to bring East and West together, as it was believed to be the former diocese of Saint Methodius, an Orthodox

bishop from the ninth century renowned in Eastern and Western Christianity as a great missionary to the Slavic peoples. In fact, John Paul had proclaimed Methodius, along with his fellow missionary and brother Saint Cyril, as co-patrons of Europe in 1980, together with Saint Benedict.

118. *Tygodnik Powszechny*, June 23, 1991.

119. Józef Makselon, "Recepcja Papieskiego przesłania dzisiaj," *Arka* 52, no. 4 (1994): 94–98.

120. *Tygodnik Powszechny*, June 1, 1997.

121. While the mass events from earlier pilgrimages sometimes drew more than a million people and often in the upper hundreds of thousands, this pilgrimage drew most often in the lower hundreds of thousands. For example, estimates were 150,000 for Koszalin (*Washington Post*, June 2, 1991); 150,000 for Kielce (*Washington Post*, June 4, 1991); 250,000 for Radom (*Washington Post*, June 5, 1991); 150,000 for Włocławek (*New York Times*, June 8, 1991); and "several hundred thousand" for Warsaw (*New York Times*, June 11, 1991). The event at Rzeszów drew half a million (*Washington Post*, June 3, 1991). (Of course, the August visit to Częstochowa for World Youth Day drew enormous crowds on a scale resembling those of John Paul's communist-era pilgrimages).

122. For examples of a nuanced approach to controversial issues in speeches by John Paul, see his discussion of religious education at Włocławek, the media at Olsztyn, and Church-state relations at Lubaczów and Olsztyn, all discussed earlier in this chapter.

123. Quoted in *Tygodnik Powszechny*, June 1, 1997.

124. See Ewa Ochman, *Post-Communist Poland: Contested Pasts and Future Identities* (New York: Routledge, 2013), 17–19, for a discussion of this issue in postcommunist Poland.

125. The verse is from the Gospel of Mark (6:4). The analogy is only partly apt, however, given that the pope had met a considerable degree of "dishonor" in places outside Poland, for example during his May 1985 visit to the Netherlands. Still, there is something especially poignant about a situation in which a beloved figure does not receive from his own people the enthusiastic support to which he was accustomed.

126. For the views of critics and defenders, see Bernstein and Politi, *His Holiness*, 491; and Weigel, *Witness to Hope*, 643–44.

127. Peter Hebblethwaite, "Let My People Go: The Exodus and Liberation Theology," *Religion, State and Society* 21, no. 1 (1993): 112.

128. Bernstein and Politi, *His Holiness*, 489.

129. Bernstein and Politi draw this analogy in *His Holiness*, 487–88. They also report that in a 1994 letter to an old friend, Juliusz Kydryński, the pope noted Moses's wisdom in keeping the people of Israel in the desert for forty years before they could enter the land of Canaan, because it meant that those who remembered being slaves would die off and thus a completely new generation would inhabit the promised land (496).

Conclusion

1. Jan Paweł II, *Pielgrzymki do Ojczyzny 1979–1983–1987–1991–1995–1997–1999–2002: Przemówienia homilie* (Kraków: Znak, 2005), 25.

2. Although Poles overwhelmingly identify as Roman Catholic, the country has small Orthodox, Lutheran, Reformed (Calvinist), Jewish, and Muslim minorities.

3. Jan Paweł II, *Pielgrzymki do Ojczyzny*, 204.

4. Huener discusses the paradigms of resistance and sacrificial martyrdom prevalent in Polish commemoration of the Auschwitz dead, along with the marginalization of Jewish suffering in such commemoration during the communist period; see Jonathan Huener, *Auschwitz, Poland, and the Politics of Commemoration, 1945–1979* (Athens: Ohio University Press, 2003), esp. 48, 155, 205, 243.

5. Jan Paweł II, *Pielgrzymki do Ojczyzny*, 743.

SELECTED BIBLIOGRAPHY

Archival Collections

Archiwum Akt Nowych (AAN), Warsaw
Urząd do Spraw Wyznań (USW)
Komitet Centralny Polskiej Zjednoczonej Partii Robotniczej (KC PZPR)
Komitet Centralny Polskiej Zjednoczonej Partii Robotniczej—Wydział
Administracyjny
Biblioteka Narodowa (BN), Warsaw
Jerzy Turowicz Papers, uncataloged (in storage)
Instytut Pamięci Narodowa (IPN), Warsaw
Ministerstwo Spraw Wewnętrznych

Periodicals

Biuletyn Informacyjny	*Trybuna Ludu*
Economist	*Tygodnik Powszechny*
New York Times	*Washington Post*
Polityka	*Więź*
Report on Eastern Europe	*Zenit*
Time	*Znak*

Memoirs

Dziwisz, Stanisław. *A Life with Karol: My Forty-Year Friendship with the Man Who Became Pope.* New York: Doubleday, 2008.

Gierek, Edward. *Smak życia: Pamiętniki.* Warsaw: BGW, 1993.

Rakowski, Mieczysław. *Dzienniki polityczne 1979–1981.* Warsaw: Iskry, 2004.

Rakowski, Mieczysław. *Dzienniki polityczne 1981–1983.* Warsaw: Iskry, 2004.

Rakowski, Mieczysław. *Dzienniki polityczne 1987–1990.* Warsaw: Iskry, 2005.

Wałęsa, Lech. *Droga do prawdy: Autobiografia.* Warsaw: Świat Książki, 2008.

Other Primary Sources

Friszke, Andrzej, and Marcin Zaremba, eds. *Wizyta Jana Pawła w Polsce 1979: Dokumenty KC PZPR i MSW.* Warsaw: Biblioteka "Więzi," 2005.

Jan Paweł II. *Pielgrzymki do Ojczyzny 1979–1983–1987–1991–1995–1997–1999–2002: Przemówienia, homilie.* Kraków: Znak, 2005.

John Paul II. *Centesimus annus.* Encyclical, May 1, 1991.

John Paul II. *Crossing the Threshold of Hope.* New York: Knopf, 1994.

John Paul II. *Dives in misericordia.* Encyclical, November 30, 1980.

John Paul II. *Dominum et vivificantem.* Encyclical, May 18, 1986.

John Paul II. *Ecclesia de Eucharistia*. Encyclical, April 17, 2003.

John Paul II. *Euntes in mundum*. Apostolic letter, January 25, 1988.

John Paul II. *Evangelium vitae*. Encyclical, March 25, 1995.

John Paul II. *Fides et ratio*. Encyclical, September 14, 1998.

John Paul II. *Laborem exercens*. Encyclical, September 14, 1981.

John Paul II. "Letter to Women." Pastoral letter, June 29, 1995.

John Paul II. *Mulieres dignitatem*. Apostolic letter, August 15, 1988.

John Paul II. *Redemptor hominis*. Encyclical, March 4, 1979.

John Paul II. *Redemptoris mater*. Encyclical, March 25, 1987.

John Paul II. *Redemptoris missio*. Encyclical, December 7, 1990.

John Paul II. *Rutilans agmen*. Apostolic letter, May 8, 1979.

John Paul II. *Slavorum apostoli*. Encyclical, June 2, 1985.

John Paul II. *Sollicitudo rei socialis*. Encyclical, December 30, 1987.

John Paul II. *Ut unum sint*. Encyclical, May 25, 1995.

John Paul II. *Veritatis splendor*. Encyclical, August 6, 1993.

Krawczak, Tadeusz, and Cyprian Wilanowski, eds. *Kościół w stanie wojennym: Wybór dokumentów z Archiwum Akt Nowych*. Warsaw: Instytut Wydawniczy Pax, 2008.

Michnik, Adam. *The Church and the Left*. Chicago: University of Chicago Press, 1993.

Mysiakowska, Jolanta, ed. *Aparat represji wobec księdza Jerzego Popiełuszki 1982–1984*. Volume 1. Introduction by Jan Żaryn. Warsaw: Instytut Pamięci Narodowej, 2009.

Paczkowski, Andrzej, and Malcolm Byrne, eds. *From Solidarity to Martial Law: The Polish Crisis of 1980–1981; A Documentary History*. Budapest: Central European University Press, 2007.

Raina, Peter. *Wizyty apostolskie Jana Pawła II w Polsce: Rozmowy przygotowawcze Watykan—PRL—Episkopat*. Warsaw: Książka Polska, 1997.

Selected Secondary Sources

Alvis, Robert. *White Eagle, Black Madonna: One Thousand Years of the Polish Catholic Tradition*. New York: Fordham University Press, 2016.

Baran, Józef. "Fundacja Rolnicza Episkopatu Polski." In *Encycklopedia Solidarności*. Last modified November 11, 2013. http://www.encysol.pl/wiki/Fundacja_Rolnicza_Episkopatu_Polski

Bernstein, Carl, and Marco Politi. *His Holiness: John Paul II and the Hidden History of Our Time*. New York: Doubleday, 1996.

Biela, Adam, and Jerome J. Tobacyk. "Self-Transcendence in the Agoral Gathering: A Case Study of Pope John Paul II's 1979 Visit to Poland." *Journal of Humanistic Psychology* 27, no. 4 (1987): 390–405.

Coppa, Frank J. *Politics and the Papacy in the Modern World*. Westport, CT: Praeger, 2008.

Curry, Jane L. "Are the Church and Public Opinion at Variance?" *Report on Eastern Europe* 2, no. 28 (July 12, 1991): 14–18.

Davies, Norman. *God's Playground: A History of Poland*. Volume 1, *The Origins to 1795*. New York: Columbia University Press, 1982.

de Weydenthal, Jan B. "Catholic Bishops Call for Cooperation between Church and State." *Report on Eastern Europe* 2, no. 20 (May 17, 1991): 15–17.

de Weydenthal, Jan B. "The First Hundred Days of Walesa's Presidency." *Report on Eastern Europe* 2, no. 14 (April 5, 1991): 9–12.

de Weydenthal, Jan B. "The Pope Appeals in Poland for a Christian Europe." *Report on Eastern Europe* 2, no. 25 (June 21, 1991): 18–21.

Diskin, Hanna. *The Seeds of Triumph: Church and State in Gomułka's Poland.* Budapest: Central European University Press, 2001.

Domber, Gregory F. *Empowering Revolution: America, Poland, and the End of the Cold War.* Chapel Hill: University of North Carolina Press, 2014.

Doucette, Siobhan. *Books Are Weapons: The Polish Opposition Press and the Overthrow of Communism.* Pittsburgh, PA: University of Pittsburgh Press, 2018.

Dziurok, Adam. "Kościół w Polsce a II pielgrzymka w perspektywie stanu wojennego." In *Pielgrzymka nadziei,* 79–90.

Eberts, Mirella W. "The Roman Catholic Church and Democracy in Poland." *Europe-Asia Studies* 50, no. 5 (July 1998): 817–42.

Felak, James Ramon. "Pope John Paul II, the Saints, and Communist Poland: The Papal Pilgrimages of 1979 and 1983." *Catholic Historical Review* 100, no. 3 (2014): 555–74.

Fuszara, Małgorzata. "Legal Regulation of Abortion in Poland." *Signs* 17, no. 1 (1991): 117–28.

Garton Ash, Timothy. *The Uses of Adversity: Essays on the Fate of Central Europe.* New York: Vintage, 1990.

Hann, Chris. "Postsocialist Nationalism: Rediscovering the Past in Southeast Poland." *Slavic Review* 57, no. 4 (1998): 840–63.

Hebblethwaite, Peter. "Let My People Go: The Exodus and Liberation Theology." *Religion, State and Society* 21, no. 1 (1993): 105–14.

Huener, Jonathan. *Auschwitz, Poland, and the Politics of Commemoration, 1945–1979.* Athens: Ohio University Press, 2003.

Jackson, Peter. *The Mongols and the West, 1221–1410.* Harlow, UK: Pearson Longman, 2006.

Jankowska, Hanna. "Abortion, Church and Politics in Poland." *Feminist Review* 39, no. 1 (1991): 174–181.

Johnson, Lonnie R. *Central Europe: Enemies, Neighbors, Friends.* 2nd ed. New York: Oxford University Press, 2002.

Keleher, Serge. "Out of the Catacombs: The Greek-Catholic Church in Ukraine." *Religion in Communist Lands* 19, no. 3–4 (1991): 251–63.

Kloczowski, Jerzy. *A History of Polish Christianity.* Cambridge: Cambridge University Press, 2000.

Kosicki, Piotr H. "*Caritas* across the Iron Curtain? Polish-German Reconciliation and the Bishops' Letter of 1965." *East European Politics and Societies* 23, no. 2 (2009): 213–43.

Kubik, Jan. *The Power of Symbols against the Symbols of Power: The Rise of Solidarity and the Fall of State Socialism in Poland.* University Park: Pennsylvania State University Press, 1994.

Kulczycki, Andrzej. "Abortion Policy in Postcommunist Europe: The Conflict in Poland." *Population and Development Review* 21, no. 3 (1995): 471–505.

Kwitny, Jonathan. *Man of the Century: The Life and Times of Pope John Paul II.* New York: Henry Holt, 1997.

Lipski, Jan Józef. *A History of the Workers' Defense Committee in Poland, 1976–1981.* Translated by Olga Amsterdamska and Gene M. Moore. Berkeley: University of California Press, 1985.

Loya, Joseph. "Interchurch Relations in Post-Perestroika Eastern Europe: A Short History of an Ecumenical Meltdown." *Religion in Eastern Europe* 14, no. 1 (1994): 1–17.

Majchrzak, Grzegorz. "'Wyjdźmy mu na spotkanie . . . ' 'Solidarność' wobec II pielgrzymki Jana Pawła II do Polski." In *Pielgrzymka nadziei*, 91–103.

Makselon, Józef. "Fascynacja i wezwanie: Papieskie odwiedziny w Ojczyźnie." In *Sympozjum naukowe z okazji 15-lecia pontyfikatu Jana Pawła II, Kraków, 11–12 X 1993*, 207–23. Kraków: Wydawnictwo Naukowe Papieskiej Akademii Teolog, 1994.

Makselon, Józef. "Recepcja Papieskiego przesłania dzisiaj." *Arka* 52, no. 4 (1994): 94–98.

Mierzwińska, Aleksandra, and Jan Żaryn. "Episkopat Polski wobec wprowadzenia stanu wojennego." *Arcana: Kultura—Historia—Polityka*, no. 66 (November–December 2005): 148–65.

Modras, Ronald. "Pope John Paul II, St. Maximilian Kolbe, and Antisemitism: Some Current Problems and Perceptions Affecting Catholic-Jewish Relations." *Journal of Ecumenical Studies* 20, no. 4 (1983): 630–39.

Ochman, Ewa. *Post-Communist Poland: Contested Pasts and Future Identities.* New York: Routledge, 2013.

Okolski, Marek. "Abortion and Contraception in Poland." *Studies in Family Planning* 14, no. 11 (1983): 266–73.

Okoń, Jan. "'Modlitwa za Ojczyznę' ks. Piotra Skargi'—w poszukiwaniu autora i gatunku." *Acta Universitatis Lodziensis, Folia Litteraria Polonica* 3, no. 21 (2013): 19–42.

Okoń, Jan. "Piotr Skarga w nauczaniu Jana Pawła II w jego podróżach do ojczyzny." *Ruch literacki* 53, no. 6 (2012): 711–30.

Osa, Maryjane. *Solidarity and Contention: Networks of Polish Opposition.* Minneapolis: University of Minnesota Press, 2003.

Paczkowski, Andrzej. "Pułapki 'Dzienników' Rakowskiego." *Polityka*, April 9, 2013.

Paczkowski, Andrzej. *Revolution and Counterrevolution in Poland, 1980–1989: Solidarity, Martial Law, and the End of Communism in Europe.* Translated by Christina Manetti. Rochester, NY: University of Rochester Press, 2015.

Pielgrzymka nadziei: II wizyta Jana Pawła II w ojczyźnie; Materiały pokonferencyjne. Warsaw: Muzeum Jana Pawła II i Prymasa Wyszyńskiego, Instytut Pamięci Narodowej, 2014.

Plokhy, Serhii. *The Gates of Europe: A History of Ukraine.* New York: Basic Books, 2015.

Pinckaers, Servais, O.P. *The Sources of Christian Ethics.* Washington, DC: Catholic University of America Press, 1995.

Porter-Szűcs, Brian. *Faith and Fatherland: Catholicism, Modernity, and Poland.* Oxford: Oxford University Press, 2011.

Rothschild, Joseph. *Return to Diversity: A Political History of East Central Europe since World War II.* New York: Oxford University Press, 1993.

Snyder, Timothy. *Bloodlands: Europe between Hitler and Stalin.* New York: Basic Books, 2010.

Snyder, Timothy. "'To Resolve the Ukrainian Problem Once and for All': The Ethnic Cleansing of Ukrainians in Poland, 1943–1947." *Journal of Cold War Studies* 1, no. 2 (1999): 86–120.

Szajkowski, Bohdan. "New Law for the Church in Poland." *Religion in Communist Lands* 17, no. 3 (1989): 196–208.

Szulc, Tad. *Pope John Paul II: The Biography.* New York: Scribner, 1995.

Ursynowski, Andrzej. "Kościół—bliżej wieczności niż solidarności." *Biuletyn Informacyjny, "Solidarność za granicą,"* no. 47–48 (December 13, 1982): 6–9.

Weigel, George. *Witness to Hope: The Biography of Pope John Paul II.* New York: HarperCollins, 2001.

Żaryn, Jan. "Jan Paweł II a stan wojenny." In *Pielgrzymka nadziei,* 105–12.

Żaryn, Jan. *Kościół, naród, człowiek czyli opowieść optymistyczna o Polakoch w XX wieku.* Warsaw: Instytut Pamięci Narodowej, Wydawnictwo Neriton, 2012.

Zechenter, Katarzyna. "Evolving Narratives in Post-War Polish Literature: The Case of Nowa Huta (1950–2005)." *Slavonic and East European Review* 85, no. 4 (2007): 658–83.

Zyzak, Paweł. *Lech Wałęsa, idea i historia: Biografia polityczna legendarnego przywodcy "Solidarności" do 1988 roku.* 2nd ed. Warsaw: Arkana Historia, 2009.

INDEX